MARY ELLEN BOAL

ARCHIBALD BOAL

MARY ELIZABETH HOPE

JOHN THOMAS HOPE

PIONEER FAMILIES
OF THE MIDWEST

By
BLANCHE L. WALDEN

Volumes I–III

CLEARFIELD

Volume I
Originally published
Ann Arbor, Michigan, 1939

Volume II
Originally published
Athens, Ohio, 1941

Volume III
Originally published
Athens, Ohio, 1941

Reprinted, three volumes in one, for
Clearfield Company, Inc. by
Genealogical Publishing Co., Inc.
Baltimore, Maryland
1998

International Standard Book Number: 0-8063-4791-0

Made in the United States of America

INTRODUCTION

It is not the aim of this publication to furnish complete genealogies of the families presented, but rather to bridge the earlier records in order that descendants may trace their own lines without great
difficulty. Each year time, fire and flood take their toll of our heritage of old Bible records, portraits, court records, etc., so it has
been thought best to preserve these left to us for future generations.

It is the desire of the compiler to be able to complete several
volumes of this series, (Volume II is now being prepared) each to con-
tain six families; the volumes being kept small in order that descendants
may secure copies without prohibitive cost. The index of Volumes I and
II to be found in Volume II.

Abbreviations used with meanings are:

b. - born	unm. - unmarried
d. - died	d. in inf. - died in infancy
d.y. - died young	m. - married

The compiler wishes to here express gratitude to all those who
have so graciously aided and made possible this publication by supplying
data from records in their possession and especially to Ethel Boal,
Eleanor Martin, C. W. Porter and Grace Davis for their invaluable contributions of manuscript data.

In each case the pioneer father is given the number 1, the eldest
child is number 2, etc., so each individual member of a family has a number given only to one member of that family. Thus it is a very simple
matter for a descendant to trace his line back to the pioneer by following
the numbering. His parent's number appears as the head of a family and
again as a child on an earlier page, his grandparent will head the family
in which his parent's name appears as a child, etc.

                                                    B. L. Walden

TABLE OF CONTENTS

William Harper was born at Belfast, Ireland in the year 1750. About 1770 he married Elizabeth whose surname is believed to have been Johnson. She was likewise born in the North of Ireland in 1750.

The exact date of their emigration to America is not known although it was after Feb. of 1786 and prior to 1796 as they were living near Carmichael Town, Pa. when tax lists were made for the latter date.

About 1797 they removed, with their younger children, to Marietta, Ohio and William Harper joined the little band of pioneers which left there in canoes to explore the Hock-Hocking valley in quest of a site for a new settlement in the Ohio country. They landed at a location where the town of Athens now stands and prepared a few log cabins in anticipation of removing their families there.

After looking over the field, William Harper decided to locate one mile west of the present site of Athens, on the opposite bank of the river and there establish a ferry.

Isaac Barker Sr. likewise built his cabin there, but on the north bank of the Hock-Hocking. As soon as the log cabins were ready for occupancy William Harper brought his family from Marietta. A few other cabins were soon erected and the settlement was named Elizabethtown, for Mrs. Harper who was the first white woman to establish a home in that immediate vicinity.

William Harper was a man much interested in local affairs. He was one of the first trustees of Athens township, also serving in that capacity in 1808, 1812, 1815 and 1816. He was the second treasurer of Athens county (1806) and served also in that capacity from 1809 to 1811. In 1811 he was elected a justice of the peace.

The early land entries of the county show that William Harper was an original land holder with 146 $\frac{6}{10}$ acres.

He owned and operated a ferry known as Harper's Ferry, one mile west of Athens on the Chillicothe road from the year 1797 until his death Dec. 24, 1830. His eldest son John Harper who came from Fayette county, Pa. in 1812 was associated with his father and continued to operate the ferry for some years following his father's death.

Elizabeth Harper preceded her husband in death, dying Sept. 9, 1825. They are buried in the old West State Street Cemetary at Athens, Ohio.

The last Will and Testament of William Harper is of record in Athens County Will Bk. 2 P. 126 as follows:

"I, William Harper of the township and county of Athens and State of Ohio, considering the uncertainty of this mortal life and being of sound and perfect mind blessed be Almighty God for the same do make and publish this my Last Will and Testament in manner and form following:

Item 1 - first it is my desire that my farm may be disposed of in the manner and way as my executors think best to suit my heirs.

Item 2 - I devise that all the moveable property that I am possessed of may be sold in the manner and way above mentioned.

Item 3 - I desire that whatever notes or accounts may be found belonging to me may be collected and when the full amount of all the debts that will be coming from my estate, that the same may be added together and then divided between my seven children equally that is John Harper, Charles Harper, William Harper, Elizabeth Harper Abbott, Isable Harper Barker, Christian Harper Barker and Alexander Harper.

I do also appoint and nominate Calvary Morris and Edmund Dorr executors of this my last Will and Testament revoking all others.

Given under my Hand and Seal this 29th day of May A.D. 1827
In presence of   William Harper   seal
Joseph Seaman
Wareham Gibbs Proved 11th day of Mar. A.D. 1833

Issue of William and Elizabeth Harper:
     2. John b. in 1771 in Ire.
     3. Charles b. Mar. 4, 1775 in Ire.
     4. William Jr. b. 1776 in Ire.
twins { 5. Elizabeth b. Apr. 16, 1780 in Ire.
        6. Isabel b. Apr. 16, 1780 in Ire.
     7. Christiana b. Sept. 19, 1783 in Ire.
     8. Alexander b. Feb. 5, 1786 in Ire.

2. JOHN JOHNSON HARPER[2] (WM.[1])

John Harper (1771-1853) was a weaver by trade. In tax records of the year 1800 he was listed as a single man living in Luzerne township of Fayette County, Pa.

He married Mrs. Fanny (Little) Norris and in the spring of 1812 they removed with their family to Athens County, Ohio, where Fanny Harper died Aug. 29, 1833 aged 60 years,

10 months and 23 days.

He passed away Dec. 1, 1953 aged 82 years, 5 months, 23 days. They rest in the old West State Street Cemetary at Athens.

Issue of John and Fanny Harper:
9. Theron b. 1809 in Fayette Co., Pa.
10. Derastus
11. Clarissa d. 1841 unm.
12. Albert b. 1812 in Pa.

3. CHARLES HARPER² (WM.¹)

Charles Harper (1775-1854) was living in Luzerne township of Fayette County, Pa. in 1796 and 1797 as given in tax records of that county. He married Ann Cook (1778-1849) and in March of 1799 they were living near Carmichael town, Green County, Pa.

In company with the family of Thomas Armstrong, Charles and Ann Harper with their infant son William embarked at the mouth of Muddy Creek on the Monongahela river and started for the Hock-hocking valley late in March 1799. They arrived at the mouth of the river in April and the women came overland on horseback with their babies while the men poled the boat laden with their household goods up the stream to Harper's Ferry.

In 1811 Charles Harper bought land in the vicinity of "The Plains" (then known as Pickets Plains) where they lived until death.

Ann Cook Harper died Sept. 21, 1849 aged 71 years while Charles Harper lived until Dec. 2, 1854. They were laid to rest in the pioneer cemetary located a short distance north of The Plains, Ohio. Their children were:

13. William b. 1798 in Pa.
14. Elizabeth
15. Robert b. Nov. 15, 1803 at Athens, Ohio
16. Frances
17. Christiana b. Mar. 31, 1811.
18. Isabella b. 1819.
19. Charles b. 1814.
20. Alexander.

4. WILLIAM HARPER JR.² (WM.¹)

William Harper (b. 1776 in Ire. was living in 1850 in Fairfield County, Ohio). He married Sarah---probably in Pa. She died in 1848/9. They lived in Athens county several years as he was listed in tax lists

1820 and 1826, served as constable in 1829 and on a jury in 1832. Probably moved to Fairfield county prior to 1842 at which date he bought a farm there in Richland township. They had several children but names for only two of them are available:

21. Elizabeth b. ca 1800.
22. James b. ca 1805.

5. ELIZABETH HARPER² (WM.¹)

Elizabeth Harper (1780-1845) married probably in Green County, Pa. Frederick Abbott (b. Oct. 22, 1774 and d. May 18, 1842). They removed to Athens County, Ohio and there Elizabeth Harper Abbott died May 31, 1845. They rest in the old West State Street Cemetary at Athens. They had the following children:

Children: Abbott

23. William b. 1801 in Pa., m. 1824 Asenath Harper who d. 1837 aged 33 yrs.
24. John F.
25. Mariah 1804-1884 unm.
26. Joseph
27. Benjamin
28. Elizabeth Ann b. Apr. 29, 1806.
29. Isabelle 1812-1827.
30. Christanna b. 1818, m. 1842 Samuel H. Mansfield (b. 1814 in Ohio).
31. Alexander b. 1822, m. 1841 Martha Stewart a daughter of Columbus B. Stewart.

6. ISABELLE HARPER² (WM.¹)

Isabelle Harper (1780-1854) married Apr. 1, 1801 Michael Barker (b. Nov. 4, 1775 and d. June 10, 1857), the eldest son of Captain Isaac Barker and his wife Rhoda (Cook) Barker. They lived many years opposite the present location of the West Union Street Cemetery. She died Feb. 22, 1854. Their issue:

Children: Barker

32. Joseph b. June 7, 1804.
twins { 33. Elizabeth b. Sept. 11, 1805.
{ 34. Isabelle b. Sept. 11, 1805, m. 1825, Hiram Kingsbury.
35. Jane M. b. Dec. 14, 1807.
36. Amy b. 1815.
37. Sarah b. 1817-1880 unm.
38. Rhoda
39. Ann m. George Hewitt (See Barker Genealogy for descendants.)

7. CHRISTIANA HARPER² (WM.¹)

Christiana Harper (1783-1837) married Apr. 10, 1804 Isaac Barker Jr. (son of Capt. Isaac and Rhoda Barker). He became a very prominent citizen serving as county sheriff, collector of rents for the Ohio University, councilman of Athens, treasurer of Athens County and common pleas judge. He was also one of the early innkeepers of the town of Athens.

Sorrow was a frequent guest in the Barker home as the long row of little graves in the West State Street Cemetary attests.

Christiana Harper Barker died Oct. 14, 1837 and is buried, as is many another pioneer mother, with her babies. Isaac Barker died Mar. 30, 1873 aged 94 years. Their children were:

Children: Barker

40. Maria d. in inf. 1806.
41. Isaac d. in inf. 1806.
42. William d. in inf. 1810.
43. Isaac No. 2. d. in inf. 1814.
44. Maria C. (No. 2)
45. Elizabeth
46. Alexander d. in inf. 1816.
47. Milton d. in inf. 1822.
48. Charles (?)
(See Barker Genealogy for descendants.)

8. HON. ALEXANDER HARPER² (WM.¹)

Alexander Harper (1786-1860) came as a child with his parents to Penn. from Ireland. His political career began with an appointment as deputy sheriff in Athens County. He studied law and served as prosecuting attorney in the aforesaid county 1812 to 1813. In 1815 he removed to Muskingum County where he was elected representative to the Ohio state legislature 1820 and 1821. He resigned to become president-judge of Muskingum County common pleas court 1822 to 1836. He ran for Congress and was elected, serving 1837 to 1839 defeated in 1838 but was elected again in 1842, and served for two terms. He retired to private practice after defeat in the 1846 election but was reelected in 1850 and served another term, 1851 to 1853. After his fourth term he again retired to private practice in Zanesville. He married Apr. 27, 1816 Rachel Reed. His death occurred Dec. 1, 1860 with interment in Greenwood Cemetary. Of his children only the names of two are available:

49. Elizabeth Harper, b. 1820.
50. James R. Harper b. 1823 - attorney at law

9. THERON HARPER³(JOHN, WM.¹)

Theron Harper (1809-1850?) was a cabinet maker by trade and pieces of his handcraft are still owned by descendants. He married Nov. 14, 1830, Katherine Allen (b. 1810 in Ohio). They removed to Allen County, Indiana, prior to 1836 but returned to Athens County before 1841. They had issue:

51. Amanda b. 1832 in Ohio.
52. Amelia b. 1836 in Ind.
53. Roderick b. 1841 in Ohio.
54. George b. 1844 in Ohio.
55. Eliza b. 1844 in Ohio.
56. John b. 1848 in Ohio.

10. DERASTUS HARPER³ (JOHN, WM.¹)

Derastus Harper m. Dec. 3, 1838 Mary H. Bierce in Athens County, Ohio. After the death of his uncle Abraham Little in Fayette County Pa., in 1836, he bought out the shares of the other heirs and is believed to have removed back to Pa. Nothing is known of his descendants.

12. ALBERT HARPER³ (JOHN,² WM.¹)

Albert Harper (b. 1813 and d. after 1860) m. May 21, 1840 Mrs. Eliza Polley (b. 1815 in N.Y.). He served as Athens township trustee from 1843 to 1849. Their issue:

57. Adaline b. 1844.
58. F.A. b. 1846.
59. Mary E. b. 1848.
60. Hester A. b. 1854.
61. James E. b. 1858.

13. WILLIAM HARPER³ (CHAS², WM.¹)

William Harper (b. about 1798) married Aug. 2, 1820 Persocia Manoir, a daughter of Pierre Manoir (from Paris, France) and his wife Elizabeth Picket. The latter was a daughter of James Picket, very early settler at The Plains, Ohio. The children of William and Persocia Harper were:

62. Mary Ann m. Mr. Timmons and removed to Ind.
63. Robert Cooke b. Sept. 16, 1824.
(probably other children).

- - - - -

14. ELIZABETH HARPER³ (CHAS.² WM.¹)

Elizabeth Harper (b. ca 1800) m. Aug. 30. 1820 Daniel Herrold (d. Apr. 1829) as his second wife and had issue:

64. Sophia Herrold
65. Franklin Herrold

15. ROBERT HARPER³ (CHAS.² WM.¹)

Robert Harper (1803-1851) m. Sept. 24, 1826 Eliza Owens (b. 1806 in Pa.) and resided in Athens county, O. They had:

66. Edmond Dorr b. 1828. He was a tin and copper-smith by trade. He m. Aug. 9, 1849 Diana Morris. They were divorced and Nov. 15, 1859 he m. Ann E. Sanderson.
67. Eliza Ann b. 1829, m. Apr. 6, 1851 Wm. Russell.
68. Eliphalet b. 1837.
69. Cyrus B. b. Sept. 30, 1838.
70. Amy b. 1845.
71. Martha b. 1848. teacher.

16. FRANCES HARPER³ (CHAS.² WM.¹)

Frances Harper married John C. White and had issue:

72. Hiram White)
73. Horace White) twins

17. CHRISTIANA HARPER³ (CHAS.² WM.¹)

Christiana Harper (1811-1873) m. in 1837 Isaac Matheny (b. Sept. 26, 1812 and d. Oct. 12, 1867 at Warrensburg, Mo.). Christiana Harper Mathenydied May 19, 1873. They had issue:

Children: Matheny

74. Mary Frances b. May 25, 1838.
75. Loring Glazier b. June 1, 1840.
76. Albert H. b. Sept. 13, 1842.
77. Carlos F. b. Nov. 5, 1844.
78. Anna Cook b. Feb. 12, 1847.
79. Leroy M. b. Sept. 3, 1849.
80. Luzerne C. b. Feb. 16, 1853.

19. CHARLES HARPER JR.³(CHAS.² WM.¹)

Charles Harper Jr. (1814-1868) m. ca 1840 Mary Welch (d. Apr. 26, 1856 aged 37 yr. 1 mo.). They are buried at The Plains,

Ohio. They had issue:

81. Christiana b. 1841.
82. Alexander b. 1843.
83. Emily b. 1846.
84. Mary E. b. 1848.
85. Hamilton b. 1850.
(and probably others).

21. ELIZABETH HARPER³(WM. JR.² WM. SR.¹)

Elizabeth Harper (b. 1800) m. Dec. 23, 1824 Charles Cunningham (b. 1796 in Del.) in Athens County, Ohio. They removed to Richland township of Fairfield County and were living there in 1850. They had issue:

86. Mary A. Cunningham b. 1828.
87. Charles Cunningham b. 1832.
88. Elmira Cunningham b. 1835.
(there may have been other children).

22. JAMES HARPER³ (WM. JR.² WM. SR.¹)

James Harper (b. 1805) m. Rebecca ------ (b. 1795 in Md.) and had issue:

89. William b. 1829.
90. Benjamin b. 1831) twins
91. Joseph b. 1831)
92. Elizabeth b. 1833.
93. Susan F. b. 1836

49. ELIZABETH HARPER³ (ALEXANDER,² WM.¹)

Elizabeth Harper (b. 1820) m. about 1838 Mr. Caldwell and had issue:

94. Alexander H. Caldwell b. 1839.
95. James Caldwell b. 1842.

51. AMANDA HARPER⁴ (THERON,³ JOHN,² WM.¹)

Amanda Harper (b. 1832) m. 26 Jan. 1854 William Young and had issue:

Children: Young

96. Orville M.D. of Columbus, O.
97. Theodore of Nelsonville, O.
98. Theron m. Mary Graham.
99. Moressa
100. Pearl unm.

- - - - -

52. AMELIA ANN HARPER[4](THERON,[3] JOHN,[2] WM.[1])

Amelia Harper (b. 1836) m. 9. Mar. 1854 Aaron Young (b. 1831) served as private in Co. C. 62nd Reg. O.V.I. in the Civil War. His discharge describes him as being "5 ft. 5 in. in height, light complexion, blue eyes and brown hair." They had ten children:

Children: Young

101. Theron, teacher of No. Dacoto, m. and had 7 children.
102. Mary d.y.
103. Catherine
104. Alonzo m. Elizabeth Ross
105. Rosencranz
106. Hattie m. Mr. Hanley
107. Sara Ida m. John Hunter
108. Almeda Augusta
109. James Roderick
110. Aaron Hastings deceased.

63. REV. ROBERT COOKE HARPER[4](Wm.[3], Chas.[2], Wm.[1])

Robert C. Harper (1824-1899) attended subscription school for about ten months as there were no public schools at that time. He was licensed to exhort Sept. 3, 1849 and permitted to preach funerals in private homes, school houses and in the woods at grove meetings. He was licensed to preach the Gospel Sept. 16, 1852 by Dr. Amos Wilson at Salem Chapel in the Athens circuit, Marietta District of the Ohio conference, ordained deacon Sept. 4, 1859 by Bishop Thos. A. Morris and an elder in 1864. He served as a circuit preacher in Ohio, Va., Ky., Ind., Ill. and Mo., traveling on an average of 43 miles per week for 42 years. He was a great reader of the Bible and in 1896 he had read it through 144 times or an average of twice each year for his entire life.

Politically he said that "he was first a Whig, next a 'Know-nothing' and now (July 24, 1896) and evermore a Republican!"

He married June 20th, 1844 Catherine Six (b. June 9, 1822 and d. June 3, 1866). She was a daughter of George and Catherine Six of Athens County, Ohio.

Rev. Robert Cooke Harper d. the 31st of March 1899. Their children were:

111. Leo 1845-1845.
112. Vinton 1848-1850.
113. Isadore F. b. Jan. 22, 1850.
114. Henderson 1852-1852.
115. Sarepta F. b. Mar. 21, 1854.
116. Mary E. b. Dec. 24, 1856.
117. William W. b. 1860, d. 1898 unm.

Robert Cooke Harper m. 2nd Apr. 4, 1867 Maria Amanda Caldwell and had

118. Robert
119. Amanda

68. ELIPHALET HARPER[4] (ROBT.[3], CHAS.[2] WM.[1])

Eliphalet W. Harper (b. 1837) m. Oct. 25, 1857 Sarah Russell (b. 1832) in Athens County, Ohio and had issue:

120. Vesta C. b. 1860.
121. Clarence S. b. 1861.
122. Eliza F. b. 1863.
123. Myron b. 1865.
124. David E. b. 1866.
125. Nettie A. b. 1869.
(and possibly others).

69. CYRUS B. HARPER[4] (ROBT.[3] CHAS.[2] WM.[1])

Cyrus B. Harper (b. 1838) teacher of Athens County, m. about 1858/9 Martha ----- (b. 1840) and had at least one child:

126. Lora A. b. 1860.

(It is thought there were other children.)

75. LORING GLAZIER MATHENY[4](CHRISTIANA,[3] CHAS.[2] WM.[1])

Loring G. Matheny (1840-1932) teacher of Athens County, Ohio, attended Albany Manual Training Institute and Ohio University. At the outbreak of the Civil War he was among those who enlisted in the 63rd Reg. O.V.I. He served until the close of the war, being mustered out with the commission of second lieutenant. He married Nov. 17, 1869 Hannah M. Martin (b. Aug. 12, 1844 and d. Apr. 9, 1914). She was a daughter of William and Mary Ann (Bodine) Martin who came to Athens County from Hunterdon County in New Jersey. Issue of Loring and Hannah Matheny were:

Children: Matheny

127. Edward S. 1870-1892.
128. Gertrude M. b. 1872 - No issue.
129. Charles M. b. 1874 - m. 1900 to Lola Wiley and had issue.
130. Luella b. 1876.
131. William M. - No issue
132. Mary E. b. 1880 - No issue
133. Harry R. b. 1884.

113. ISADORE HARPER⁵(ROBT.⁴ WM.³ CHAS.⁴ WM.¹)

Isadore Harper (1850-1891) m. Jan.
22, 1868 William Henry Martin (b. Aug. 18,
1845 and d. Mar. 13, 1923). He was a son of
William and Mary (Bodine) Martin who came
from Hunterdon County, N.J., to Athens County, Ohio. Isadore Harper Martin died Dec.
30, 1891. They had ten children:

Children: Martin

134. William Harper, M.D. b. Aug. 25, 1871.
m. 1895 Vira Hope (No. 42 Hope lineage)
resides at 301 Montana Ave., Detroit,
Mich.
135. Eleanor Morris b. Oct. 8, 1873 in
Athens County, Ohio. unm.
136. Mary Catherine b. Jan. 5, 1877, m. 1900
to J. W. Bull; she is a graduate nurse
and resides at Columbus, Ohio. - No
issue.
137. Adda Bertha 1879-1936. unm.
138. Frederick Peter b. Nov. 21, 1882, is
m. and has one son, resides near Lodi,
Ohio.
139. Maria Belle b. Apr. 16, 1887, she married Gordon Ensminger and had three
children.
140. Robert Henry b. June 28, 1889, he m.
Jane Lemon and had three children. They
reside at West Salem, Ohio.
(Three children died in infancy.)

115. SAREPTA F. HARPER⁶(ROBT.⁴ WM.³
CHAS.⁴ WM¹)

Sarepta Harper (b. 1854) m. Charles
W. Griswold farmer of near Athens, Ohio and
had issue:

Children: Griswold

141. Hoyt - deceased.
142. Charles b. Nov. 2, 1874.
143. Luzerne b. Nov. 11, 1876 - deceased
144. Carrie
145. Ellen b. Mar. 15, 1878.

116. MARY E. HARPER⁵ (ROBT.⁴ WM.³
CHAS.⁴ WM.¹)

Mary E. Harper (b. 1856) m. Maphet

Young and resided at Youngstown, Ohio. Their
issue:

Children: Young

146. Clinton of Youngstown, Ohio.
147. Frederick of Pittsburg, Pa.
148. Daisy - unm.
149. Cora b. Nov. 12, 1876, m. Thos. Woods.
150. Grace B. b. Nov. 9, 1878.
151. Hattie m. David Hunter and had issue.
152. Maphet Jr. b. June 12, 1890, he m.
Anita Young and resides at Youngstown,
O.

133. HARRY MATHENY⁵ (LORING⁴ CHRISTIANA³
CHAS.⁴ WM.¹)

Harry R. Matheny (b. 1884) attended
Ohio University at Athens, Ohio, taught school,
mining engineer seven years, now vice presi-
dent and plant manager of Chrysler Motor Parts
Co., at Highland Park, Mich. He married Edith
Hemenway in 1912. She is a descendant of
Ralph Hemenway of Roxbury, Mass. 1629. Mr.
Matheny is a charter member of the Palestine
Masonic lodge, Clinton Valley country club and
a member of the Chamber of Commerce. Their
children are:

Children: Matheny

153. Harry Richard b. Feb. 14, 1914. Grad. of
Univ. of Arizona and Michigan State
College. Now with Chrysler Motor Parts
Corp.
154. Jean Elizabeth b. Dec. 29, 1916. Grad.
of Univ. of Mich. and Detroit Business
College. She m. 1938 Dr. Wm. F. Northrup Jr.
155. Ann Christine b. May 3rd, 1924.
156. William Loring b. Aug. 15, 1925.

THE NAME

Harper originated as a surname when
used to designate one particularly skilled in
the art of playing the harp, as Charles le
harper (Charles the harper) and is of considerable antiquity. The Harper family has been
one of outstanding prominence in both England
and Ireland as well as in America.

1. ROBERT REANEY

Robert Reaney was born Aug. 1, 1766 near Belfast, Ireland. He married about 1788 Jennet McKee (b. Feb. 24, 1768). In the autumn of 1792 in company with his elder brothers James and William, he embarked with his wife and little son James on an old sailing schooner bound for America. They were six weeks at sea and the three-year-old James became quite ill so it was a disheartened little company that landed at Baltimore, Md. Oct. 1st 1792.

Eight days after their arrival a second son John was born in Baltimore and there Nov. 16th of the same year little James died a victim to the hardships which the voyage had entailed.

Robert Reaney followed the trade of shoemaker in Baltimore for a time but was living in Sheppensburg, Cumberland County, Pa. in 1793 at which time his brother James Reaney married Elizabeth Bromfield. They probably remained there only long enough to make money sufficient for the trip to Washington County as James was living there in 1799 and Robert was located across the border in the panhandle of Virginia (now W. Va.). William went to Beaver County (now Lawrence County, Pa.).

In 1809 Robert was living in Washington County, Pa. but removed from that locality to Guernsey County, Ohio prior to 1817.

In Guernsey County records is a notation of the apprenticeship of James Low to Robert Reainey dated Aug. 5, 1826.

"James Low aged nine years on Feb. 28th, son of Mary Fulk of the township of Westland, Guernsey County, Ohio----for ten years (from) Feb. last 1837----for food, drink and clothing----the said James to be taught----reading, writing, arithmetic and trade of shoemaker as well as the single rule of Three----(at the end of his apprenticeship)----James to be given a new Bible and two suits of wearing apparel.

	Mary Fulk
(signed)	
(Witness)	James his X Low
Isaac Reainey	Robert Reainey

In 1829 the Reaney family removed to Morgan County, Ohio where Robert "took up a claim" of eighty acres in Morgan township. This farm is still in the possession of a descendant and the original log cabin still stands.

The Reaneys were staunch Presbyterians and drove or rode horseback each Sunday to the Deerfield church, a distance of several miles.

Robert Reaney died Mar. 28, 1844 and Jennet his wife died Oct. 11th of the same year. Both are buried in the church yard adjoining the Deerfield Presbyterian church.

The last Will of Robert Reaney is of record in Morgan county, Ohio in Book O. P. 151 as follows:

"I, Robert Reaney of Morgan township and county of Morgan and state of Ohio taking into consideration my advanced age, being of sound and perfect memory do hereby make this my last Will and Testament.

First, I direct that my debts be paid. At this time they are very trifling. After that is done the balance of my property I divide as follows: to each of my sons viz., John, William and Robert I give ten cents as a token of remembrance, to each of my daughters viz., Mary, Anna, Maria and Jane I give the like sum of ten cents each.

Second, I hereby give to my wife Jane the use of my other property that I may be possessed of for and during her natural life and after her decease I give the same viz., all the property that is then unexpended for her support, real and personal and mixed to my son Isaac Reaney for his sole use. Should my son Isaac die without issue, not leaving a child I direct that the property that I leave him be divided in equal proportion between my male children that may survive him the said Isaac.--this 24th Jan. 1832.

Witnessed by   Robert Reaney
Wm. Dawes
Mary Dawes
(A codicil dated Nov. 8, 1836 leaves a horse, saddle and a new suit of clothes to his grandson William Tingle.)
Will proved May 7, 1844

As might be expected this Will was not received with approval by the other children, however they all accepted it with a fair amount of grace excepting Maria and Jane who insisted on having what they considered their share of their father's property.

To understand the reason for the terms of the Will, it is necessary to go back to the early childhood of Isaac the youngest son. Quite early in his youth he was stricken with a malady known as "White Swelling" in one leg which necessitated amputation, even a greater tragedy in those times than at present.

Robert Reaney in parental anxiety over this youngest son so afflicted and incapacitated for earning a livelihood, determined to compensate Isaac in some measure for the handicap which was his.

The other children were strong and established in homes of their own, he would leave Isaac as well prepared for life's viscissitudes as possible, and he did! However as previously stated Maria and Jane insisted that they be given a share and Isaac being peace-loving and likewise very fond of his sisters agreed to give them each one hundred dollars worth of merchandise from the store (where he sold his farm products) over a period of ten years.

Each autumn Jane and Maria made the journey to the old homestead to visit their brother and to collect their ten dollars worth of sugar, calico, flour or whatever they happened to need.

The family record of Robert and Jennet Reaney was copied by Isaac in his family Bible and the following births are of record therein:

2. James b. Sept. 25, 1789, d. 1792.
3. John b. Oct. 8, 1792.
4. William b. May 17, 1795.
5. Mary b. Nov. 20, 1796.
6. Robert M. b. Sept. 1, 1799.
7. Anna b. Jan. 3, 1801.
8. Maria b. June 14, 1802.
9. Matilda b. Dec. 10. 1805.
10. Jane b. Apr. 27, 1807.
11. Isaac b. Mar. 7, 1809.

3. JOHN RAINEY[2] (Rob't. Sr.[1])

John Rainey (1792-1882) followed the same migrations as his father and married in Guernsey County Ohio, Apr. 10, 1817 Rhoda Ann King (who was born in Conn.).

He was a shoemaker and followed that trade in his early life, later he became a mail carrier and served in that capacity for fifty years.

John and Rhoda (King) Rainey were the parents of nine children. She died ca 1839 in Morgan County, Ohio.

Issue
12. Martha Jane b. Apr. 29, 1819.
13. William b. Jan. 8, 1821.
14. Robert b. Nov. 20, 1822.
15. James b. Apr. 14, 1825.
16. Amos. b. ca 1828. d. in Civil War.
17. Rhoda Ann b. Nov. 15, 1831.
18. Charlotte b. Mar. 4, 1833.
19. Lydia b. Nov. 30, 1834.
20. Edward 1836-1858. unm.

John Rainey married in Morgan County, Ohio, June 23, 1840 Mary H. Ady. They had one son.

21. John Quincey d. in inf.

For his third wife he married Mrs. Catherine (Crawn) Delong who had several children, some of whom intermarried with the Rainey children. She died Sept. 2, 1863 and about 1872 he married a fourth wife, Mrs. Abigail Bigford.

He died Aug. 5, 1882 lacking but two months of being 90 years of age.

He dropped the "e" from the earlier spelling of "Reainey" and his descendants use the more usual spelling Rainey.

4. WILLIAM RAINEY[2] (ROBT.[1])

William Rainey (b. 1795) removed with his parents to Morgan County, Ohio. He married there July 4, 1830 Sarah Hughs. Nothing is known of his descendants.

6. ROBERT M. RAINEY JR.[2](ROBT. SR.[1])

Robert M. Rainey (1799-1864) was born in the panhandle of Virginia (now W. Va.). He removed with his parents to Guernsey county and later to Morgan County, Ohio.

He married Oct. 15, 1829 Nancy Ann Nelson and had by her three daughters. She died early in 1835.

Issue
22. Priscilla Rainey b. ca 1830.
23. Jane b. ca 1832, she m. Mr. Balliard of Galion, Ohio.
24. Martha (?) b. ca 1834, remained in Morgan County with an aunt.

Robert M. Rainey married Mar. 19, 1835 Sabra N. Piper (b. Mar. 8, 1811 in Mass. and d. at Fostoria, Ohio June 25, 1920). He died Aug. 29, 1864.

- - - - -

Issue
25. John 1836-1861. unm.
26. Sarah 1837-1920. unm.
27. Edwin b. Apr. 5, 1839.
28. Isaac b. Jan. 24, 1841.
29. Silvanus b. Nov. 1842. m. and had issue.
30. Robert 3rd b. Nov. 17, 1844.
31. Jackson b. May 18, 1846. no issue.
32. James b. Mar. 19, 1848.
33. Albert b. June 29, 1850.
34. Eunice b. Sept. 14, 1852.

7. ANNA REANEY[2] (ROBT.[1])

Anna Reaney (1801-1842) married Sept. 1819 John Boal (See No. 4 Boal Lineage).

8. MARIA REANEY[2](ROBT.[1])

Maria Reaney (b. 1802) m. Apr. 12, 1823 Archibald Boal Jr. and removed to Muskingum County, Ohio. (See No. 5 Boal lineage).

9. MATILDA REANEY[2](ROBT.[1])

Matilda Reaney (1805-1829) married Sept. 30, 1824 Benoni Tingle. She died Apr. 26, 1829 leaving two small sons who were reared by Robert and Jennet Reaney.

Issue
35. Robert T. Tingle b. Nov. 4, 1825.
36. William Tingle b. Mar. 30, 1827.

10. JANE REANEY[2] (ROBT.[1])

Jane Reaney (b. 1807) married John Nelson and had issue:

Children: Nelson

37. Isaac
38. Seth
39. Henry b. 1838.
40. Robert b. 1840.
41. John b. 1843.

11. ISAAC RANEY[2] (ROBT.[1])

Isaac Raney (1809-1862) the chief beneficiary of his father's Will remained on the home farm in Morgan County until his death Jan. 11, 1862.
He married Jan. 30, 1845 Sarah Smith a daughter of Eli Smith. She was born June

9, 1819 in Fayette County, Pa. and died Apr. 25, 1894. They had three children, namely:

42. Lovina b. Nov. 11, 1845.
43. Elizabeth M. (1848-1867) no issue.
44. Eli Asberry b. Dec. 25, 1853.

12. MARTHA JANE RAINEY[3] (JOHN,[2] ROBT.[1])

Martha J. Rainey (1819-1688) married Cyrus Kingsbury Hawes (b. Feb. 14, 1815) and resided at Oxford, Wisconsin. She died there Sept. 13, 1888 and he died the same place. Dec. 21, 1896.

Children: Hawes

Issue
45. Ursala b. Oct. 8, 1843.
46. Permelia b. Feb. 13, 1845.
47. Sarah b. Aug. 3, 1846.
48. Lydia b. Sept. 4, 1848.
49. Mary b. ca 1850.
50. Luther John b. Aug. 7. 1851.
51. Orpha b. Jan. 8, 1854.
52. Frances b. Apr. 30, 1856.

13. WILLIAM RAINEY[3] (JOHN,[2] ROBT.[1])

William Rainey (1821-1901) married Aug. 30, 1844 in Seneca County, Ohio Sarah Ann DeLong (b. Oct. 12, 1819--died Sept. 28, 1897). They lived in Seneca and Williams counties Ohio. He was a United Brethern preacher.

Issue
53. Mary b. Aug. 31, 1845.
54. John W. b. ca 1847. d. in Civil War. unm.
55. Julius A. b. Mar. 7, 1849.
56. Rhoda (1850-1851).
57. Martha J. (1851-1853).
58. Sarah Elizabeth (1855-1925). No issue.
59. Rosetta (1856-1856).
60. William Joseph b. May 30, 1859.

14. ROBERT RAINEY[3] (JOHN,[2] ROBT.[1])

Robert Rainey (1822-1905) farmer of Morgan County, Ohio married Mar. 7, 1844. Rebecca Walters (b. May 5, 1825 and d. July 14, 1849). He died Oct. 6, 1905.

Issue
61. Sarah Louisa b. Apr. 29, 1845.
62. Rhoda Ann b. Apr. 2, 1847.
63. William W. b. Jan. 26, 1849.

Robert Rainey married second ca 1850
Rebecca A. Carnes (b. 1830) and had:

64. John (1851-1890) m. and had issue.
65. James C. b. 1853.
66. Lewis b. 1856, went to Okla.
67. Eli b. 1858, went to Arizona. unm.
68. Emma A. b. 1860.
69. Charles 1863-1884. unm.
70. Joseph b. 1864, went to Central America. unm.
71. George b. 1869. No issue.

15. JAMES RAINEY³ (JOHN,² ROBT.¹)

James Rainey (1825-1882) of Norwalk,
Ohio, married ca 1846 Mary Brown. He died
at Norwalk, Ohio. Oct. 18, 1882.

Issue
72. Alice
73. Clara
74. Eva
75. James Vernon

17. RHODA ANN RAINEY³ (JOHN,² ROBT.¹)

Rhoda Ann Rainey (1831-1915) married
Dec. 2, 1849 Andrew Jackson DeLong (b. Sept.
18, 1824) d. Aug. 5, 1891) and had issue:

Children: DeLong

76. Catherine Elizabeth b. Jan. 25, 1851.
77. Sarah J. b. June 3, 1854.
78. Rhoda Ann b. Dec. 20, 1858
79. George W. b. Sept. 18, 1860.

18. CHARLOTTE RAINEY³ (JOHN,² ROBT.¹)

Charlotte Rainey (1833-1912) m. Apr.
13, 1854 Jesse Deweese (b. Nov. 20, 1830) d.
Aug. 15, 1892). He was a son of James Watson
Deweese and Sarah Ann Woods. They removed
from Morgan County to Williams County, Ohio.
She died Jan. 6, 1912 at Angola, Ind.

Children: Deweese

Issue
80. John Berick m. thrice and had issue.
81. Amos R. m. and had issue.
82. Anna Sarah m. and had issue.
83. James Watson
84. Mary Emily m. and had issue.
85. Jessie Evaline b. 1878. m. Mr. Seidenbecker and resides at 5839 Burns Ave., Detroit, Mich.

19. LYDIA MARIA RAINEY³ (JOHN,² ROBT.¹)

Lydia Rainey (1834-1921) married
Mar. 15, 1855 Josiah Boyer (1831-1911) and
had issue:

Children: Boyer

86. Emma b. July 17, 1856. m. Wm. Halloway of Camden, Mich. and had issue.
87. Charles Edward b. Feb. 15, 1858. d. 1929.
88. Josiah Newton b. Mar. 18, 1860. d. 1934.
89. William E. b. Mar. 15, 1863. d. 1923.
90. John G. b. June 12, 1866 of Montpelier, Ohio.

27. EDWIN RAINEY³ (ROBT. M.,² ROBT.¹)

Edwin Rainey (1839-1924) married Feb.
25, 1866 Mary M. Traver (b. Sept. 7, 1849.
d. May 24, 1882). He died Feb. 24, 1924.

Issue
91. Eli b. May 27, 1868.
92. Elizabeth b. Jan. 8, 1870. m. O.E. Dillon and had issue.
93. Frederick b. Aug. 9, 1875.

28. ISAAC RAINEY³ (ROBT. M.,² ROBT.¹)

Isaac Rainey (1841-1897) married in
1863 Susanna Fox (b. Mar. 10, 1840. d. June
17, 1914).

Issue
94. John b. Jan. 13, 1864.
95. Martha (1865-1936) m. Fred Craley and had issue.
96. Lucinda Jane (1867-1898) m. Albert Smith and had issue.
97. Mary E. b. Aug. 4, 1869 m. Mr. Jordan and had issue.
98. Robert William b. June 26, 1871. No issue.
99. Amos (1877-1833).
100. Nellie (1881-1930) m. Geo. Murray and had issue.

30. ROBERT RAINEY³ (ROBT. M.,² ROBT.¹)

Robert Rainey (1844-1897) was an
Evangelical Minister. He married Antha
Boughton (b. 1844 and d. Sept. 23, 1917). He
died June 10, 1897.

Issue
101. Jennie b. May 4, 1876.
102. Mary

103. Schyler Dill Rainey b. Mar. 3, 1884.
104. Atta May b. May 3, 1888.

32. JAMES RAINEY[3] (ROBT. M.[2] ROBT.[1])

James Rainey (b. 1848) married Libbie
Wininger (d. 1924). Their issue

105. Sarah m. F. A. Henry and had issue.
106. Nettie m. Geo. Carpenter and had issue.
107. Alma m. Seymour Babcock and had issue.
108. Delbert m. Elma Finch and had issue.
109. Roy m. Cora Heith and had issue.
110. Sylvanus
111. Lottie

33. ALBERT RAINEY[3] (ROBT. M.[2] ROBT.[1])

Albert Rainey (1850-1934) married
Oct. 27, 1878 Mary Lavina Ruse (b. 1855). He
died July 18, 1934 at Spencerville, Ohio.

Issue
112. Ora S. b. Aug. 20, 1879.
113. Armedia E. b. Nov. 16, 1882.
114. Bertha B. b. Apr. 11, 1887.
115. Milan Robert b. Feb. 25, 1891.

34. EUNICE RAINEY[3] (ROBT. M.[2] ROBT.[1])

Eunice Rainey (1853-1932) married
Feb. 19, 1874 Henry Wininger (b. Feb. 16,
1850 and d. Apr. 15, 1914).

Issue
116. Charles Henry Wininger b. Oct. 13, 1879.
117. Sabra Ellen b. Oct. 25, 1882.

35. ROBERT TINGLE[3] (MATILDA,[2] ROBT.[1])

Robert Tingle (b. 1825) married Jane
Kime and resided in Williams County, Ohio.
Their issue:

Children: Tingle

118. Elias m. Alice Myers and had issue.
119. Lewis m. and had issue.
120. James E. m. and had issue.
121. Ellen m. and had issue.
122. Libbie m. J. J. Blue of Montpelier, O.

36. WILLIAM TINGLE[3] (MATILDA,[2] ROBT.[1])

William Tingle (b. 1827) married
probably in Williams County Phoebe--and had

Children: Tingle

123. Hubert b. Oct. 6, 1848.
124. Hannah m. Jas. McCave and had one son.
125. Anna m. Mr. Miller and had issue.
126. Elnora m. Austin Gilbert and had 3 sons.

42. LAVINIA RANEY[3] (ISAAC,[2] ROBT.[1])

Lavinia Raney (1845-1882) m. ca 1866
James Earich (1839-1898) carpenter of near
Malta, Ohio. She died Jan. 4, 1882.

Children: Earich

Issue
127. Flora b. 1867. No issue.
128. U. Grant (1868-1920) m. Mary Wilson.
129. Elizabeth b. 1870. d.y.
130. Eli W. b. 1872, m. Elizabeth Rainey (#162)
131. Isaac J. 1874-1896. unm.
132. Albert b. 1875, m. Rebecca Wright and
      had issue.
133. George E. b. 1878. m. May Benjamin and
      had issue.

44. ELI ASBERRY RANEY (ISAAC, ROBT.)

Eli Raney (1853-1923) farmer and
teacher of near Malta, Ohio, married Jan. 1,
1880 Laura J. Thompson (1858-1906). He died
Feb. 5, 1923.

Issue
134. Sarah Abigail b. Oct. 17, 1880, m. Alfred
      Bush of Crooksville, O. and had issue.
135. Estell Coler b. Aug. 18, 1882.
136. Bessie Viola b. Dec. 16, 1884.
137. Flora Lela b. June 19, 1887, m. Mr. Moore
      and had issue.
138. John Kelly b. Apr. 25, 1890. Architect
      of Bowling Green, O.
139. Mary Jane b. Apr. 25, 1890. m. Paul
      Brunning of White House, O.
140. Lewis Earl (1893-1895).

53. MARY CATHERINE RAINEY[4] (WM.[3]
      JOHN,[2] ROBT.[1])

Mary C. Rainey (1845-1922) married
Aug. 31, 1866 Jason Maze (b. Jan. 4, 1835 in
Ohio and died Aug. 10, 1906 at Ellsworth, Kansas.) They removed from Williams County to
Kansas in Dec. 1875 where they took up a homestead. She died Apr. 15, 1922 at Poplar
Bluff, Mo. but burial was made in the family
lot at Ellsworth, Kas.
      Issue of Mary Rainey and Jason Maze
her husband were

Children: Maze

141. Walter W. b. Sept. 28, 1867 at Bryan, O.
142. Maurice E. b. Oct. 14, 1871 at Pioneer, O.
143. Howard J. 1875-1909, unm.
144. Robert N. b. Jan. 16, 1878 at Pioneer, O.
145. Julius D. b. Nov. 3, 1880 at Ellsworth,
      Kan.

55. JULIUS AUGUSTUS RAINEY⁴ (WM.³ JOHN,²
ROBT.¹)

Julius A. Rainey (1849-1933) married
Thera Ann Sweeney (b. Mar. 29, 1849 and d.
Jan. 15, 1916). Their issue

146. Della May (1873-1928) m. 1891 George B.
Howald and had issue.
147. Hattie Louella b. 1874. m. in 1894
Charles Foster Howald and had issue.
148. Emma Jane b. 1879. m. 1896 Albert F.
Gofourth and had issue.
149. Stella Blanche b. 1882. m. 1900 Claud
A. Sawyer and had issue.

60. WILLIAM JOSEPH RAINEY⁴ (WM.³ JOHN,²
ROBT.¹)

Wm. Joseph Rainey (1859-1914) married Dec. 29, 1881 Edna R. Crawford.

Issue
150. Charles Wesley b. Dec. 1, 1882.
151. Clyde Joseph b. Oct. 8, 1888.

61. SARAH LOUISA RAINEY⁴(ROBT.³ JOHN² ROBT.¹)

Sarah L. Rainey (b. 1845) married
June 1, 1865 Joseph Finley (b. Sept. 4, 1843)
son of James and Mary (Pennell) Finley and
resided at McConnellsville, Ohio.

Children: Finley

Issue
152. Martha b. June 15, 1866. No issue.
153. Mary R. b. Dec. 2, 1867. No issue.
154. Rhoda A. b. May 10, 1870.
155. Frank b. Jan. 3, 1873.
156. Ella b. May 19, 1875.
157. Walter b. May 30, 1878.
158. Sadie b. June 10, 1880.
159. Frederick b. Aug. 13, 1882.

62. RHODA ANN RAINEY⁴ (ROBT.³ JOHN² ROBT.¹)

Rhoda A. Rainey (1847-1870) married
Oct. 29, 1867. Isaac Griest of Morgan County,
Ohio and had issue:

160. Elizabeth R. Griest b. Aug. 1, 1868.
d. 1893 m. 1880 George DeLong.
161. Robert William b. Sept. 7, 1869.

63. WILLIAM W. RAINEY⁴ (ROBT.³ JOHN² ROBT.¹)

Wm. W. Rainey (1849-1931) of Morgan

County, Ohio. Married Jane Strahl and had
issue:

162. Elizabeth b. Apr. 10, 1876.
163. Anna b. Jan. 22, 1877.
164. Ella b. Oct. 28, 1879.
165. Frank Wm. b. Sept. 15, 1881.
166. Charles
167. Edward of Malta, Ohio.

65. JAMES C. RAINEY⁴ (ROBT.³ JOHN² ROBT.¹)

Jas. C. Rainey (1853-1935) of near
Malta, Ohio. Married Lucy Jane Williams
and had issue:

168. Effie m. Mr. Daniels of Nevada, O.
169. Flora m. Mr. Brewer of Harpster, O.
170. Albert of California.
171. Clarence of Lexington, O.
172. Carl of California.
Five other children (deceased) names unknown.

91. ELI RAINEY⁴ (EDWIN³ ROBT. JR.² ROBT. SR¹)

Eli Rainey (b. 1868) of Jackson, Michigan. Married Oct. 19, 1892 Carrie Belle
Angevine (b. July 28, 1869). Their children
were:

173. Cecil b. June 19, 1896.
174. Archie 1897-1898.
175. Leone Mary b. Aug. 16, 1899.

93. FREDERICK RAINEY⁴ (EDWIN³ ROBT. M.² ROBT.¹)

Frederick Rainey (b. 1875) of Fostoria, Ohio. Married Myrtle Jenny (b. 1882)
and had:

176. Cecil H. b. Aug. 22, 1906.
177. Mabel J. b. Sept. 27, 1908.
178. Harold E. b. Oct. 24, 1910.
179. Florence E. b. Feb. 11, 1913.
180. Hazel R. b. Mar. 6, 1915.
181. Clara M. b. Aug. 6, 1916.
182. Mary
183. Roy
184. Marguerite Ester

94. JOHN RAINEY⁴ (ISAAC³ ROBT. M.² ROBT.¹)

John Rainey (b. 1864) of Fostoria,
O. Married 1892 Mary DeWald and had issue:

185. Howard b. 1893.
186. Clarence 1896-1916. unm.

108. DFLBERT RAINEY⁴(JAS.³, ROBT. M.², ROBT.¹)

Delbert Rainey married Elma Finch and had issue:

187. Cleo m. DeLoy Berton.
188. Ruth m. Ervin Snyder.
189. John

109. ROY RAINEY⁴ (JAS.³ ROBT. M.² ROBT.¹)

Roy Rainey married Cora Heith and had

190. Hubert

135. ESTELL COLER RAINEY⁴ (ELI³ ISAAC² ROBT.¹)

Estell C. Rainey (b. 1882) graduate of Ohio University 1908 and of Ohio State University 1912. Organizer and general manager of "Ranco" the Automatic Reclosing Circuit Breaker Company of Columbus, Ohio. Resides at 2528 Coventry, Rd. He married Aug. 29, 1908 Myrtle Gallaher and they have four children:

Children: Raney

191. Eldon Dwight b. July 17, 1910.
192. Roy Eugene b. Nov. 18, 1912.
        Grad. of Univ. of Cincinnati 1937.
      . Patent attorney of Columbus, O.
193. Geraldine b. Sept. 27, 1914.
        Grad. of Univ. of Cincinnati--member of Chi Omega, Tau Pi Epsilon and Omicron Nu. M. Aug. 29, 1937 Paul Whisler Kohler of Boston, Mass.
194. Robert Glen b. Aug. 28, 1916. Kappa Phi Kappa--Ohio State University.

136. BESSIE VIOLA RANEY⁴ (ELI³ ISAAC² ROBT.¹)

Bessie Raney (b. 1884) married Spencer Tharp of Crooksville, Ohio and had issue:

Children: Tharp

195. Ronald
196. Ruth
197. Wallace
198. Owen

141. WALTER W. MAZE⁵(MARY C.⁴ WM.³,JOHN² ROBT.¹)

Walter W. Maze (b. 1867) served as teacher twelve years in the public schools of Ellsworth County, Kan., elected county Supt. of Schools for eight years, spent ten years in an abstract office, elected Secty-treas. of the Poplar Bluff Loan and Building Asso. and is a member of the Kiwanis Club and of the Westwood Hills Country Club. He married Aug. 31, 1897 Frances C. Corrigan at Holyrood, Kan. and had:

Children: Maze

199. Thelma G. b. July 8, 1898.
200. Jason C. b. Aug. 29, 1902.
201. Maxine M. b. July 28, 1904.
202. Walter W. Jr. 1907-1928. unm.
203. Katherine S. b. June 16, 1909.

142. MAURICE E. MAZE⁵ (MARY C.⁴ WM.³ JOHN² ROBT.¹)

Maurice Maze (b. 1871) married Feb. 2, 1898 Ada Bealby and resides in Ellsworth, Kan.

Children: Maze

Issue
204. Hazel m. Henry Armbrust of Chaflin, Kan.
205. Joseph m. Ruth Fishburn.
206. David of Ellsworth Co., Kan.
207. James of Lincoln Co., Kan.
208. Alice
209. Jesse of Ellsworth, Kan.

144. ROBERT N. MAZE⁵ (MARY C.⁴ WM.³ JOHN² ROBT.¹)

Robert N. Maze (1878-1918) married Dec. 18, 1904 at Hays City, Kan. to Mabelle Faulkner.

Children: Maze

Issue
210. Lucille of Kansas City, Mo.
211. Victor of Tulsa, Okla.
212. Donald of Kansas City, Mo.
213. Edwin of Kansas City, Mo.

145. JULIUS D. MAZE⁵ (MARY C.⁴ WM.³ JOHN² ROBT.¹)

Julius D. Maze (b. 1880) married July 11, 1907 Emma L. Allen and resides at Poplar Bluff, Mo.

Children: Maze
214. Allen d.y.

215. Faye m. Lee Powers of Poplar Bluff, Mo.
216. Mary Ann d.y.

150. CHARLES WESLEY RAINEY[5] (WM. J.[4] WM.[3]
     JOHN[2] ROBT.[1])

     Charles W. Rainey (1882-1913) mar-
ried Jan. 21, 1905.Edna J. Goshorn (b. 1883)
and had issue:

217. Ilah Fern (1907-1908).
218. Leland W. (b. 1910).

151. CLYDE JOSEPH RAINEY[5] (WM. J.[4] WM. J.[3],
     JOHN[2] ROBT.[1])

     Clyde Rainey (1888-1932) married
Apr. 10, 1909 Blanche B. Burlew and had

219. Elvin L. (1912-1912)
220. Kenneth
221. Eldon
222. Charles
223. Lowell
224. Doris Jean
225. Edna b. Apr. 1914.

162. ELIZABETH RAINEY[5] (WM.[4] ROBT.[3]
     JOHN[2] ROBT.[1])

     Elizabeth Rainey (b. 1876) married
Dec. 31, 1894 Eli Earich (see No. 130 this
lineage) of near Malta, O. and had

           Children: Earich

214. Clara d.y.
215. Alice m. Edison Blackburn.
216. Leonard m. Bonnie Davis.

165. FRANK WM. RAINEY[5] (WM.[4] ROBT.[3]
     JOHN[2] ROBT.[1])

     Frank Rainey (b. 1881) of Malta, O.
Married and had:

217. Carl of Galion, O.
218. Roy of McConnellsville, O.
219. Clyde of Crooksville, O.

166. CHARLES RAINEY[5] (WM.[4] ROBT.[3]
     JOHN[2] ROBT.[1])

     Charles Rainey farmer of near Leland,
Ill. Married and had issue:

220. Carroll
221. Arlene m. Mr. Johnson of Ottawa, Ill.

173. CECIL RAINEY[5] (ELI[4] EDWIN[3] ROBT. M.[2]
     ROBT.[1])

     Cecil Rainey (b. 1894) of Horton,
Mich. Married June 8, 1917 Essie Hart and had:

222. Ruth Elizabeth b. Mar. 25, 1918.
223. Gifford Edwin b. June 23, 1920.
224. Philip
225. Duane

185. HOWARD RAINEY[5] (JOHN[4] ISAAC[3] ROBT. M.[2]
     ROBT.[1])

     Howard Rainey (b. 1893) married Sept.
14, 1917 Nina Marie Henry (1898-1937) and had
issue:

226. Norma
227. Warren
228. John Jay

191. ELDON D. RANEY (ESTELL[4] ELI[3] ISAAC[2]
     ROBT.[1])

     Eldon D. Raney (b. 1910) Graduate of
Ohio State Univ. 1936--member of Tau Beta Pi,
engineer at Ranco Corp. at Columbus, Ohio.
Married July 25, 1933 Ruth Owen and had:

229. Carolyn Sue b. Dec. 24, 1934.
230. John David b. Oct. 27, 1937.

199. THELMA MAZE[6] (WALTER[5] MARY C.; WM.[3]
     JOHN[2] ROBT.[1])

     Thelma Maze (b. 1898) married Nov. 8,
1923 at Cape Girardeau, Mo. to E. W. Spradling and resides at Poplar Bluff, Mo.

Issue
231. Frances G. Spradling b. Dec. 22, 1936.

200. JASON C. MAZE[6] (WALTER[5] MARY C.[4]
     WM.[3] JOHN[2] ROBT.[1])

     Jason Maze (b. 1902) of Poplar Bluff,
Mo. Married Nov. 8, 1935 Minta Young and had:

232. James Walter b. July 5, 1937.

       - - - - -

1. ARCHIBALD BOAL

Archibald Boal was born Jan. 30, 1760 in County Down, Ireland of Scotch-Irish parentage. His youth was spent in the mountainous district of North Ireland and there in 1785 he married Jane Gordon also of Scotch descent.

On May 5, 1789 when their son James was but three days old they left their stone cottage on the mountain side and set sail from the shores of their native land for America. They were six weeks at sea, food and water were practically exhausted when land was sighted. Imagine the joy and excitement which prevailed among that anxious little band of Scotch-Irish!

But joy soon turned to consternation when it was discovered on landing that they had been sailing in a circle and had returned to the shores of old Erin. Nothing daunted they again stocked up with supplies and once more started across the Atlantic. This time they were successful in reaching their destination.

They settled in Milford township of Somerset County, Pa. where Archibald Boal worked at the trade of stone-masonry.

Shortly after the year 1800 they removed to the Northwest Territory locating temporarily in Jefferson County, Ohio, but glowing ideas of the beauties of the Muskingum Valley soon lured them on through the wilderness.

Along Meigs Creek they found a location suitable and there established a camp at the forks of the creek which still bears the name of Boal's Fork.

On March 26, 1806 Archibald Boal secured a patent for 320 acres of land in Meigs township for which he paid $339.86. Later he secured additional acreage in Morgan County which he subsequently divided among his four children.

About 1820 the Boals removed to Lemon Hill in Morgan County where they spent their remaining years.

Jane Gordon Boal was born in 1761 and died May 28, 1835.

Archibald Boal survived her almost a quarter of a century passing to a final rest at the grand old age of 98 years, 5 months, 20 days.

They were buried on the farm where they had lived so long but years later when a church was built in the vicinity their remains were disinterred and reburied in the little churchyard on the crest of Lemon Hill.

The Will of Archibald Boal was never offered for probate and is still in the possession of a descendant. It reads as follows

"In the name of the Benevolent Father of All, I, Archibald Boal of Bloom township, Morgan County, Ohio, do make and publish this my last Will and Testament.

Item 1. - I give and devise to my son James Boal all the stock, household goods, furniture possessions and other goods and chattels which may be at the time of my Decease during his natural life as aforesaid he however selling so much thereof as may be sufficient to pay my past debts at my decease. My real estate being divided between my three sons: James, John and Archibald previous to this which is to stand as it was divided.

Item II. - I devise and bequeath to my daughter Mary and her heirs one dollar more than she has all ready got and if there should be anything left at my decease except paying the funeral expenses I devise and bequeath the same to my son James and his heirs.

In testimony thereof I have hereunto set my hand and seal this 26th day of August in the year one thousand eight hundred and forty-seven."

his
Archibald   x   Boal

The children of Archie and Jane Gordon Boal were:

2. Mary b. ca 1786/7 in Ire.
3. James b. May 2, 1789 in Ire.
4. John b. 1792 in Pa.
5. Archibald Jr. b. 1799 in Somerset Co., Pa.

2. MARY BOAL[2] (ARCHIBALD[1])

When the Boal family moved from Meigs township into a section now incorporated in Morgan County, all the men within miles assembled for a "house-raisin!" Trees were cut down and sheared of their branches and the logs sawed into convenient lengths.

Among the little band of workers were four young men, all of whom were immediately captivated by the rare charm and

Gaelic beauty of Mary Boal. So intense was
the rivalry that one ingenious young man
suggested that they draw cuts for the privi-
lege of paying uncontested court to her.
This was agreed and John Briggs Jr. a young
"home-steader" in the vicinity drew the
lucky straw. He lost no time in taking full
advantage of the situation. They were married ca 1806 and lived the greater part of
their lives on Lemon Hill. In their later
years they went to Montgomery County, Illinois where they died.

Children: Briggs

Issue
6. John 3rd. b. Aug. 8, 1808.
7. James m. Oct. 21, 1830 Kiturah Pidcock.
8. Mary m. Sept. 3, 1833 Henry Smoot.
9. Eliza m. July 18, 1833 Andrew Foster.
10. Sarah Jane m. Apr. 16, 1839 Jonathan Fris-
by.
11. Archibald - Went to Texas.

3. JAMES BOAL[2] (ARCHIBALD[1])

James Boal remained with his parents,
caring for them in their later years and
therefore received a larger portion of their
estate. Among the personal belongings which
he inherited was a quaint little old leather
covered box, held together with miniature
hand-made nails and used to hold the valuable
papers of the family. It is lined with an
ancient newspaper bearing date of July 1763.
There is a pink trailing vine wandering over
the surface making it appear that the news
was printed on flowered wallpaper. A tiny
hand-made lock adds security.
James Boal married Jane McCarty
Apr. 10, 1833. She was born in Loudoun
County, Virginia in 1799 and died Apr. 10,
1847 in Morgan County, Ohio.
James Boal married secondly Mrs.
Sarah Morris. He died Mar. 21, 1867. Issue
of James and Jane McCarty Boal were:

12. Archibald b. Nov. 19, 1834.
13. Jane b. June 29, 1836.
14. Mary b. Jan. 29, 1838.
15. James b. Nov. 15, 1840.
16. John b. Jan. 4, 1842.

4. JOHN BOAL[2] (ARCHIBALD[1])

John Boal, farmer and carpenter by
trade was married Sept. 31, 1819 in Guernsey
County to Anna Reaney (See No. 7 Reaney
lineage). They removed to Perry County where

they resided in the vicinity of New Straitsville. Anna Reaney Boal died Nov. 5, 1842
and is buried in the old Hazleton cemetary
near Shawnee.

Issue
17. Archibald b. July 4, 1820.
18. Robert 1821-1822.
19. James b. Feb. 3, 1823.
20. William b. May 6, 1825.
21. Jane b. Oct. 4, 1827.
22. McKee b. Mar. 27, 1832.
23. Mariah 1835-1835.
24. John b. Dec. 1, 1836.
25. Isaac 1838-1918. No issue.
26. Nelson 1840-191?. No issue.
27. Mary d.y.

John Boal married second Nancy Baker
(b. 1826) Oct. 20, 1846. He died in 1874 aged
82 years with burial in the old Harbaugh Cemetary near New Straitsville, O.

Issue of second marriage:
28. Martha b. 1847.
29. Levi b. Jan. 23, 1849. Went South.
30. Jonathan b. Apr. 26, 1851.
31. Annis Esther b. Nov. 13, 1853.
32. Henry W. 1857-185?.
33. Sarah Margaret 1859-1861.
34. Samuel b. Nov. 23, 1861.
35. Keefer d. 1868.
36. Rachel Ann b. May 29, 1866.

5. ARCHIBALD BOAL JR.[2] (ARCH.[1])

There were only a few isolated settlements in the Muskingum valley when the
Boal family arrived there. Bears, deer, panthers and buffalo still roamed the forests.
Every man, of necessity, was a crack-
shot and even the young children were instruct-
ed in the use of firearms. Archie Boal Jr.
was, at the age of twelve years, one of the
best marksmen in that section.
One day while out with his father
searching for a cow which had strayed away
into the woods, they came upon a tree which
had fallen across the path. In one of the
higher branches a panther croutched ready to
spring,--in the twinkling of an eye, Archie
Jr. raised his gun and fired, killing the
panther instantly. He was in his early life,
always a great deer and wild game hunter and
many were the interesting stories he had to
tell his children and grandchildren.
He married Mariah Ruth Reaney (see No.
8 Reaney lineage) in Guernsey County, Apr. 12,
1823.
They removed to near Otsego in

Muskingum County where he followed the trades
of stone-mason and shoe-maker. He died in
1862.

Issue
37. Jane Melissa b. Sept. 12, 1824.
38. Robert R. b. June 8, 1826.
39. Mary E. b. June 28, 1828.
40. Mariah b. Sept. 21, 1830.
41. Eliza Ann b. June 21, 1832.
42. James b. 1834-1835.
43. Cyrus B. b. July 10, 1836.
44. Isaac W. b. Apr. 14, 1839. Was killed
    in the Civil War. No issue.
45. William F. b. June 24, 1841.
    Died 1865 in Civil War. No issue.
46. Francis M. b. May 11, 1844.

6. JOHN BRIGGS 3rd[3] (MARY[2] ARCH.[1])

John Briggs (1808-1897) was married
Apr. 21, 1831 to Susannah Miller (1810-1871)
and had:

Children: Briggs

47. Jackson b. Apr. 29, 1832 in Ohio.
48. Matilda b. Sept. 18, 1834.
49. John killed in Civil War. unm.
50. Archibald 1839-1917. unm.
51. Melissa b. Dec. 4, 1841.

12. ARCHIBALD BOAL[3] (JAS.[2] ARCH.[1])

Archibald Boal enlisted in 1864 in
company I of the 161st O.V.I. serving through
the remainder of the Civil War in the Shenan-
doah Valley and participating in the battle
of Maryland Heights. He was a member of the
Methodist church and of the Odd Fellows
lodge. He married Mar. 20, 1856 Martha
Strong (b. June 26, 1837 and d. Jan. 28,
1917). Archibald Boal d. Dec. 1, 1923.

52. Elizabeth Jean b. Mar. 24, 1857.
53. Sarah (1860-1900) No issue.
54. Cora d. 1932. No issue.
55. Myrta d.y.

13. JANE BOAL[3] (JAS.[2] ARCH.[1])

Jane Boal (1836-1901) married May 25,
1855 John Garret (son of Pennell Garret--see
Sharpless Genealogy by G. Cope) and removed
to Vernon County, Wisconsin where he died
in 1864.

Children: Garret

Issue
56. Emza b. Feb. 9, 1857.
57. James 1859-1859.
58. Anson b. Mar. 11, 1860.
59. Louise b. Aug. 1, 1862.
60. Georgia b. May 17, 1864.

Jane Boal Garret m. second about 1865
Duncan McHenry and to this union was born
one son:

61. Wilbert McHenry b. Dec. 31, 1866.

14. MARY BOAL[3] (JAS.[2] ARCH.[1])

Mary Boal (1838-1901) married Dec.
13, 1855 Isaac Warren (1834-1884) farmer of
Duncan Falls, Ohio. They had four children:

Children: Warren

62. John Ezra b. 1860
63. Lucy
64. Samuel J.
65. Cora b. Feb. 25, 1875.

15. JAMES BOAL[3] (JAS.[2] ARCH.[1])

James Boal (1840-1916) married June
14, 1877 Elizabeth McCann, James Boal, farmer
of Eaglesport, Ohio, died there May 13, 1916.

Issue
66. Hiram Edgar Boal (1878-1879).

16. JOHN BOAL[3] (JAS.[2] ARCH.[1])

John Boal (b. Jan. 4, 1842) teacher
for many years in the public schools of Morgan County, Ohio, married Mar. 23, 1879
Isabelle Strong (b. June 18, 1840 and d.
Oct. 24, 1930) and had two children:

67. Herbert Wellington b. Feb. 1, 1880.
68. Bertha Ethel b. Sept. 11, 1881. unm.

17. ARCHIBALD BOAL[3] (JOHN[2] ARCH.[1])

Archibald Boal (1820-1894) a farmer
of Hocking County, Ohio, lived near Logan.
He married Mar. 26, 1840 Mary Jane McClain
(1822-1903) and had:

69. Almira Eliazbeth
70. John Archibald b. Jan. 4, 1851.
71. Emeline b. Apr. 28, 1853.
72. Marshall H.

19. JAMES BOAL³(JOHN² ARCH.¹)

James Boal (1823-1909) was a farmer
of Morgan County, Ohio. He married Jan. 16,
1848 Rhoda Smith (1827-1912) a daughter of
Eli Smith. They were for many years, members
of the Wolf Creek, Christian church and are
buried in the old cematery near the church.
They had two children:

73. Mary Ellen b. Nov. 17, 1848 (m. John T.
    Hope see No. 9 Hope lineage).
74. Eli Smith b. Sept. 24, 1850.

20. WILLIAM BOAL³ (JOHN² ARCH.¹)

William Boal (1825-1897) was a farmer
of Perry County, Ohio near Snow Fork. He
married June 11, 1850 Sarah Jane Dugan (1831-
1866) and had:

75. Effie Jane
76. Archibald
77. James H. d.y.
78. William C. d.y.
79. Mary Ellen. No issue.
80. Rhoda Ann. No issue.
81. Annis d.y.
82. Emma
83. Alice
84. U. Grant

21. JANE BOAL³ (JOHN² ARCH.¹)

Jane Boal (b. 1827) was married
three times, first to James Knott by whom
she had five children (names not known).
By her second husband James Phillis
or Fillis, she had one child. Her third
husband was Nat Skinner. Nothing is known
of her descendants.

22. MCKEE BOAL³ (JOHN² ARCH.¹)

McKee Boal (1832-1910) was a farmer
of Vinton County, Ohio. He married Feb. 19,
1854 Agnes P. Dougan (b. Nov. 1830 in N.Y.).
She died in 1920.

Issue
85. Hugh Henry b. Dec. 17, 1854.

86. Lavina (1857-1873).
87. Jane b. 1859.
88. James Calvin d.y.
89. John Lyman b. Oct. 30, 1863.
90. Jemima Ellen b. 1867.
91. Archibald A. b. Jan. 23, 1872.
92. William Plyly M.D. b. 1875. No issue

24. JOHN BOAL³ (JOHN² ARCH.¹)

John Boal (1836-1896) farmer of
Macksville, Ohio. Married Sept. 2, 1858
Margaret Starritt (1842-1894) and had:

93. James Arthur
94. Annis Amanda (1865-1879).
95. John Robert (1861-1884).
96. Charles William (1869-1890).

30. JONATHAN BOAL³ (JOHN² ARCH.¹)

Jonathan Boal (b. 1851) married
Elizabeth Thisen and had:

97. John
98. Rose
99. Albert
100. Laura
101. Dora
102. Samuel

34. SAMUEL BOAL³ (JOHN² ARCH.¹)

Samuel Boal (1861-1918) was a railroad
employee for many years. He married Nov. 10,
1881 Ida B. Roberts (b. Aug. 16, 1865) and
had:

103. Martha Ann b. July 21, 1882. No issue.
104. Pearl b. Apr. 14, 1886.
105. Lillian b. May 30, 1888. No issue
106. Samuel Jr. b. Aug. 4, 1897. No issue.
107. Winifred b. Apr. 12, 1900.

36. RACHEL ANN BOAL³ (JOHN² ARCH.¹)

Rachel Ann Boal (b. 1866) married
Dec. 12, 1881 Robert Wharton and resides at
Thurston, Ohio. Issue:

Children: Wharton

108. John of Toledo, Ohio.
109. Minnie of Thornville, Ohio.
110. Ellsworth of Columbus, Ohio.
111. James of Columbus, Ohio.

112. Charles of Columbus, Ohio.
113. Anastasia of Newark, Ohio.
114. Fred of Columbus, Ohio.
115. Saul of Columbus, Ohio.
116. Paul of Columbus, Ohio.
117. Myrtle of Columbus, Ohio.
118. Mae of Columbus, Ohio.

37. JANE MELISSA BOAL³(ARCH. JR², ARCH.¹)

Jane Melissa Boal (1824-1904) married Nov. 15, 1848 David Bradford and removed to Isabel, Ill. They had at least one son and probably other children. She was killed by a car in 1904. Issue:

119. Chauncey Bradford.

38. ROBERT R. BOAL³ (ARCH.², ARCH.¹)

Robert R. Boal (1826-1881) stone mason, married Nov. 4, 1851 Lydia Ann Foster (a daughter of Charles Foster). They removed to Iowa where he died July 31, 1881.

Issue
120. William O. (1854-1860).
121. Cyrus Allen (1856-1924). No issue.
122. George Alva b. Oct. 11.
123. Nevada
124. Clara E.
125. Charles (1863-1881). No issue.

39. MARY E. BOAL³(ARCH. JR.², ARCH.¹)

Mary E. Boal (1828-1867) married May 19, 1850 George Wass and had:

Children: Wass

126. John
127. Munsel
128. Florence
129. Laura

40. MARIA BOAL³ (ARCH. JR.², ARCH.¹)

Maria Boal (1830-1868) married June 17, 1847 Israel H. Buker and had at least one child:

130. Melissa Buker

41. ELIZA ANN BOAL³(ARCH. JR.², ARCH.¹)

Eliza Ann Boal (b. 1832) married Mar.

10, 1853 William Vinsel. Their children were:

Children: Vinsel

131. Mary Jane
132. Emaline m. Mr. Trottman of Adamsville, O.
133. Corra m. Mr. Trottman of Coshocton, O.
134. John deceased
135. Otis
136. Hager of Arkansas

43. CYRUS B. BOAL³(ARCH. JR.², ARCH.¹)

Cyrus B. Boal (1836-1898) a stone mason by trade married Aug. 19, 1858 Catherine Elizabeth Melker (b. Mar. 24, 1837 and d. Mar. 14, 1904). He served about nine months in the Civil War. His discharge dated June 5, 1865 describes him as having dark hair and complexion and hazel eyes and being five feet, five and 1/2 inches in height. He died in Muskingum County, Ohio, Oct. 21, 1898. Their children were:

137. Seth b. Oct. 5, 1859.
138. Newton 1860-1892. No issue.
139. Victor 1861-1886. No issue.
140. Anderson 1863-1918. No issue.
141. George b. Oct. 5, 1864.
142. Marion b. Apr. 20, 1868.
143. Nathan 1869-1881. No issue.
144. Judson b. Apr. 7, 1871 - resides at Adamsville, Ohio.
145. Anna M. b. Jan. 31, 1873.
146. Alonzo b. Sept. 2, 1874 - resides at Adamsville, Ohio

46. FRANCIS M. BOAL³(ARCH. JR.², ARCH.¹)

Francis Boal (1844-1912) a stone mason and farmer of Muskingum, Ohio. Married Mar. 8, 1868 Anna Eliza Jordan (b. Oct. 28, 1845). He served as school director at Adamsville, Ohio and was a member of the Baptist church. Their children were:

147. Rosamond Arabel (1869-1879).
148. John W. b. Dec. 8, 1870).
149. Estella Francis b. Sept. 30, 1872. Married F. C. Spragg of Norwich, Ohio.
150. Charles L. b. Sept. 2, 1874. No issue.
151. Myrtle Olive b. Oct. 4, 1877.
152. Ann Eliza b. Jan. 5, 1881.
153. Alice A. b. Apr. 18, 1885.

- - - - -

47. JACKSON BRIGGS⁴(JOHN BRIGGS 3rd,
MARY² ARCH.¹)

Jackson Briggs (1832-1894) farmer of
Morgan County, Ohio. Married Dec. 26, 1852
Susannah Marshall (1833-1915) a daughter of
Wm. and Eliza Marshall. They removed to
Lawrence County, Mo. where he died May 26,
1894. They had issue:

Children: Briggs

154. John Sylvester (1854-1857).
155. Elizabeth Achsah b. Oct. 30, 1855.
156. Mary E. 1858-1867.
157. Laura Jane b. 1860. No issue.
158. Clara Belle 1862-1928. No issue.
159. Ida Florence b. Sept. 17, 1864.
160. Charles Elmer b. Mar. 20, 1868.
161. Myrtle Melissa b. Mar. 8, 1877. No is-
     sue.

51. MELISSA BRIGGS⁴(JOHN BRIGGS 3rd,³
MARY² ARCH.¹)

Melissa Briggs (1841-1876) married
Feb. 2, 1854 John Foreaker and had:

Children: Foreaker

162. Reece m. and had issue.
163. Wesley m. and had issue.
164. George m. and had issue.
165. Charles (1865-1887).

52. ELIZABETH JEAN BOAL⁴(ARCH.³
JAS.² ARCH.¹)

Elizabeth Jean Boal (b. 1857) married July 26, 1879 Ransom L. Renshaw (1856-
1924) fruit grower of near Lancaster, Ohio.
Their children were:

Children: Renshaw

166. Mabel b. Oct. 30, 1880. No issue.
167. Alberta b. Apr. 4, 1883.
168. Joyce b. Dec. 26, 1889. No issue.
169. George b. May 3, 1896. World War.

56. EMZA GARRET⁴(JANE³ JAS.² ARCH.¹)

Emza Garret (b. 1857) married Mar. 1,
1874 Albertus Wood of LaFarge, Wis. Issue:

Children: Wood

170. Edward b. 1874. No issue.

171. Lester b. 1876. No issue.
172. Cora b. 1879.
173. Benia b. 1881.
174. Bessie b. 1884.
175. Branson

58. ANSON GARRET⁴(JANE³ JAS.² ARCH.¹)

Anson Garret (1860-1904) married Jan.
1, 1895 Augusta Woodward and resided near
Malta, Ohio. He died Mar. 3, 1904 of heart
attack and is buried on Lemon Hill. Their
children were:

Children: Garret

176. William H. b. July 31, 1896.
177. Louise
178. Sydnor
179. Luther
180. Mary

59. LOUISE GARRET⁴(JANE³ JAS.² ARCH.¹)

Louise Garret (b. 1862) married Genos
Evans and resided in Wisconsin. Their children are:

181. Charles Evans of Wis.
182. Otto Evans had issue: Margaret & Robert.
183. Jack Evans had issue: Georgia, Maxine &
     Vernon.

60. GEORGIA GARRET⁴(JANE³ JAS.² ARCH.¹)

Georgia Garret (b. 1864) married first
Julian Allen and second F. W. Smith. She resides at Waterloo, Wis. Issue:

184. Loretta Allen d.y.
185. Maud Allen b. 1883.
186. Nellie Allen b. 1885. No issue.

61. WILBERT McHENRY⁴(JANE³ JAS.² ARCH.¹)

Wilbert McHenry (b. 1866) a salesman
of Cambridge, Ohio, married Sept. 7, 1890
Helen Thomas (d. 1933) and had issue:

187. Mabel McHenry
188. Hazel McHenry - teacher of Parkersburg,
     W. Va.
189. Fred McHenry

- - - - -

62. JOHN EZRA WARREN[4] (MARY[3] JAS.[2] ARCH.[1])

John E. Warren (b. 1860) proprietor of a feed store in Murray, Iowa, married Oct. 19, 1881 Emma Jane Nelson and had

Children: Warren

190. Carrie M.
191. Mary E. unm.
192. Rachel Belle
193. Harry James of Murray, Ia.
194. Guy E.
195. Herbert Ezra
196. Gladys Emma
197. Florence R.
198. John E. of Osceola, Ia.

63. LUCY WARREN[4] (MARY; JAS.[2] ARCH.[1])

Lucy Warren married first Dec. 1880 Frank Hivnor. She died at Zanesville, Ohio, Mar. 8, 1933. Their children were:

Children: Hivnor

199. Ella May b. June 7, 1881
200. Ona b. Jan. 26, 1884.
201. Sidney James
202. Edward d.y.
203. Harry

64. SAMUEL J. WARREN[4] (MARY[3] JAS.[2] ARCH.[1])

Samuel J. Warren farmer of Winterset, Ia. Married Sept. 4, 1892 Mary Thurman and had issue:

204. Lester E. Warren
205. Orvie Warren
206. Ona Glee Warren

65. CORA WARREN[4] (MARY[3] JAS.[2] ARCH.[1])

Cora Warren (b. 1875) married May 2, 1894 Grant I. Weter of Lorimer, Ia. and had

Children: Weter

207. Lucy Marie b. Sept. 27, 1899.
208. Carl Edward b. Jan. 10, 1905.
209. Ruth Darline b. Aug. 13, 1910.
210. Frank J. b. Apr. 14, 1913.

67. HERBERT WELLINGTON BOAL[4] (JOHN[3] JAS.[2] ARCH.[1])

Herbert W. Boal (b. 1880) comptroller of the Newport (Ky.) Rolling Mills, married Oct. 5, 1904 Lucie Waller Williams (b. July 5, 1882) a daughter of Jeremiah Williams (1844-1909) of Muskingum County, Ohio and his wife Margaret Francis (1846-1929). They had one daughter:

211. Margaret Isabelle b. Sept. 26, 1905. Graduated at Christ's Hospital, Cincinnati, Ohio.

69. ALMIRA ELIZABETH BOAL[4] (ARCH.[3] JOHN[2] ARCH.[1])

Almira Boal married May 28, 1872 John P. Dalton of Nelsonville, Ohio and had:

Children: Dalton

212. Charles of Nelsonville, Ohio.
213. Ruth Ethel b. Aug. 25, 1884 m. Mr. Blosser of Columbus, Ohio.
214. Mary E. Dalton b. Mar. 9, 1876. m. Mr. Elswick of Steubenville, Ohio.
215. Mahala Gertrude b. Sept. 5, 1879. m. Mr. Barnes of Nelsonville, Ohio.
216. Anna m. Mr. Decola of Harrisburg, Pa.
217. Lulu Ellen b. June 23, 1892.
218. Mabel b. Mar. 10, 1894 m. Mr. Barnes of Nelsonville, Ohio.
219. Cora B. b. June 19, 1889 in York township m. Mr. Arkley of Steubenville, Ohio.

70. JOHN ARCHIBALD BOAL[4] (ARCH[3] JOHN[2] ARCH.[1])

John A. Boal)1851-1908) married Oct. 30, 1879 J. Harriet Stitz (b. 1854) Issue:

220. Bertha
221. Bessie

71. EMELINE BOAL[4] (ARCH.[3] JOHN[2] ARCH.[1])

Emeline Boal (1853-1935) married Oct. 27, 1871 James B. Barnes of Logan, Ohio. She died Apr. 3, 1935. Their children were:

Children: Barnes
222. Pearl of Columbus, O. (now deceased).

223. Archibald of Logan, Ohio.
224. Charles W. of Logan, Ohio.
225. Mary m. V. J. Welde of Baltimore, Ohio.
226. Blanche (1880-1898). No issue.
227. Ethel m. Frank Nicley of Columbus, Ohio.
228. George (1885-1910). No issue.
229. Mabel b. Oct. 9, 1891.

72. MARSHALL H. BOAL⁴(ARCH.³ JOHN²,ARCH.¹)

Marshall Boal married 1877 to Sarah
H. Landis and lived in Zanesville, Ohio. He
had two children:

230. Anna m. Mr. Maddox of Zanesville, Ohio.
231. Orrin of Zanesville, Ohio.

73. MARY ELLEN BOAL⁴(JAS.³ JOHN² ARCH.¹)

Mary Ellen Boal (1848-1935) married
Nov. 28, 1869 John Thomas Hope (1847-1929)
son of Payton Hope. (See No. 9 Hope lineage.)

74. ELI SMITH BOAL⁴(JAS.³ JOHN², ARCH.¹)

Eli S. Boal (1850-1931) farmer of
Morgan County, Ohio. Married Aug. 18, 1872
Emeline Sanders, daughter of Benjamin Sanders.
She died July 31, 1888. Their children were:

232. Alva Walter b. June 27, 1874.
233. Almeda b. July 3, 1876.
234. Ethel b. Jan. 16, 1881.

Eli Smith Boal married second Feb. 14,
1889 Clara Eyman and they had one child:

235. Carrie Melinda b. Nov. 6, 1897.

75. EFFIE JANE BOAL⁴(WM.³ JOHN² ARCH.¹)

Effie Jane Boal married first Jan. 12,
1871 David Cummins and had issue

236. Fred Cummins of Newark, Ohio.
237. Minnie Cummins
238. Addie Cummins

Effie Jane Boal Cummins married second Adam Cummins (brother of David) and lived
at Barberton, Ohio. Issue (2nd marriage).

239. William Cummins

76. ARCHIBALD BOAL⁴ (WM.³ JOHN³ ARCH.¹)

Archibald Boal married May 12, 1872
Jane Smallwood (d. 1931) and resides at
Beaverton, Mich. Their children were

240. Walter
241. Charles
242. Clara
243. Sarah

82. EMMA BOAL⁴ (WM.³ JOHN² ARCH.¹)

Emma Boal married Rolland C. Hardgrove and resided at Beaverton, Mich. They
had

Children: Hardgrove

244. Charles
245. Shelby
246. Walter
247. George
248. Fred
249. Stella M.

85. HUGH HENRY BOAL⁴(MCKEE³ JOHN² ARCH.¹)

Hugh Henry Boal (b. 1854) married
Sarah E. Nickols and removed to Indiana where
he engaged in farming near Danville. They
had

250. Ernest (1881-1916). No issue.
251. Daisy L. - Nurse at Danville, Ind. unm.
252. Della b. Mar. 16, 1885.
253. Forest d.y.
254. Earl b. June 1, 1895.

87. JANE P. BOAL⁴(MCKEE³ JOHN² ARCH.¹)

Jane Boal (b. 1859) married Plyly
Teeters and resided in Vinton County, Ohio.
She died in May, 1933. Their issue:

255. Guy V. Teeters.

88. JOHN LYMAN BOAL⁴(MCKEE³ JOHN² ARCH.¹)

John L. Boal (b 1863 in Perry Co.,
O.) attended Central Normal College at Danville, Ind., graduating in 1894., studied
law at the University of Texas and admitted
to the bar in 1900. He taught school in
Ohio, Ind., and Texas, a total of twenty

years, from which he resigned to practice law. He served several years as city attorney of Yorktown, Texas from which office he resigned to accept the office of judge of Dewitt County, Texas. Judge Boal served in that office continuously to Jan. 1, 1923.

He is a master mason, 32° Scottish Rite Mason, a member of Alzafar Temple of the order of the Mystic Shrine at San Antonio, a charter member of Yorktown Lodge Knights of Pythas and charter member of the Kiwanis Club of Cuero, Texas.

He married Aug. 28, 1900 Emma H. Eckhardt (d. Mar. 21, 1918). They had one daughter:

256. Enid Agnes Boal b. Aug. 1, 1908. A
  graduate of Texas State University 1929.

  90. JEMIMA ELLEN BOAL (MCKEE[3], JOHN[2],
   ARCH.[1])

Jemima Ellen Boal (b. 1867) married first, Apr. 1, 1888 Robert Lyle and had issue:

257. Dessie Lyle

She married second Mahlon Arganbright of Londonderry, Ohio and had a son.

258. Orvan Arganbright

  91. ARCHIBALD A. BOAL[4] M.D. (MCKEE[3]
   JOHN[2] ARCH.[1])

Archibald A. Boal (b. 1872) graduated from the Kentucky School of Medicine and practiced for some years at Zaleski, Ohio, before removing to Columbus, Ohio where he now lives. He is a member of the Masonic lodge as well as a number of other lodges and politically is a staunch Democrat. He married Dec. 27, 1896 Rosa Sheer, daughter of Charles Sheer late of Zaleski, Ohio. They have one daughter:

259. Ruth Eleanor b. Mar. 31, 1905.

  93. JAMES ARTHUR BOAL[4] (JOHN[3]
   JOHN[2] ARCH.[1])

James Arthur Boal married Sept. 18, 1884 Emma J. Allen and they had

260. Lesley
261. A daughter who married Mr. Lanning.

104. PEARL BOAL[4] (SAM'L[3], JOHN[2], ARCH.[1])

Pearl Boals (b. 1886) operates a confectionary in Columbus, Ohio. He married June 22, 1905 Ida Gale (b. Dec. 15, 1884) and had issue:

262. Kenneth b. Mar. 3, 1906.
263. Francis O. (1910-1929)
264. Richard b. Aug. 8, 1913.

107. WINIFRED BOAL(S)[4] (SAM'L[3], JOHN[2], ARCH.[1])

Winifred Boals married Nov. 3, 1920 William Halley and had

265. Martha Jane Halley b. Sept. 12, 1921.

  122. GEORGE ALVA BOAL[4] (ROBT.[3], ARCH, JR.[2],
   ARCH.[1])

George A. Boal, farmer of Mt. Pleasant, Iowa married Feb. 13, 1889 Elizabeth Lucretia Wertenberger and had issue:

266. Orrell Delbert of Mt. Pleasant, Ia.
267. Charles Freeman of Lockridge, Ia.

  123. NEVADA BOAL (ROBT.[3], ARCH. JR.[2],
   ARCH.[1])

Nevada Boal married William Lyons and resided at Santa Barbara, Calif. She died there in May, 1934. They had one son.

268. Richard Lyons

  124. CLARA E. BOAL (ROBT.[3], ARCH. JR.[2],
   ARCH.[1])

Clara E. Boal married John Seay and is living at Long Beach, Calif. A daughter:

269. Winefred Seay married Harold Morse of
  Long Beach, California

130. MELISSA BUKER[4] (MARIA[3], ARCH. JR.[2], ARCH.[1])

Melissa Buker married Mr. Lane of New Concord, Ohio and had

Children: Lane

270. Alice m. Mr. Vesey
271. Flora m. Mr. Bowman
272. Elizabeth
273. Whitaker of New Concord, Ohio

131. MARY JANE VINSEL (ELIZA ANN,[3]
ARCH. JR.,[2] ARCH.[1])

Mary Jane Vinsel married Mr. Bell of
Adamsville, Ohio and had

274. Olive Bell m. Mr. Boice of Zanesville,
Ohio.
275. Maude Bell m. Mr. Thompson of Zanesville,
Ohio.

137. SETH BOAL[4] (CYRUS B.,[3] ARCH. JR.,[2] ARCH.[1])

Seth Boal (1859-1927) was a stone
mason and cement worker, a member of the
Moose lodge. He died Nov. 5, 1927 of heart
trouble. On Jan. 29, 1890 he married Anna
Spragg (b. Nov. 26, 1867) and had

276. George C. b. Dec. 17, 1890.
277. Hazel b. July 19, 1896.
278. Harry E. b. May 28, 1902.

141. GEORGE BOAL (CYRUS B.,[3] ARCH. JR.,[2]
ARCH.[1])

George Boal (1864-1930) barber by
trade and member of the Presbyterian church,
married Anna Simonton and had

279. Earl of Dallas, Tex.
280. Lawrence of Fort Worth, Tex.

142. MARION BOAL[4] (CYRUS B.,[3] ARCH. JR.,[2]
ARCH.[1])

Marion Boal (b. 1868) is a stone mason
and contractor of Canton, Ohio. He is a violinist and drummer, much interested in
music and is a Methodist. On Aug. 20, 1891
he married Anna Mary Jones (d. Dec. 10, 1923),
a daughter of John and Catherine Jones. They
had issue:

281. Mamie Vada b. May 30, 1892.
282. Clarence Jan
283. Grace L. grad. of Chicago Univ. and
teacher.
284. Nellie R. grad. of Miami Univ. and
teacher.
285. Robert J. (1904-1932). No issue.

145. ANNA M. BOAL[4] (CYRUS B.,[3] ARCH. JR.,[2]
ARCH.[1])

Anna M. Boal (b. 1873) married Edward
Kreider of Coshocton, Ohio and had

286. Emma Kreider m. Mr. Bailey of Coshocton,
Ohio.
287. Russell Kreider of Kalamazoo, Mich.

148. JOHN W. BOAL[4] (FRANCIS,[3] ARCH. JR.,[2]
ARCH.[1])

John W. Boal (b. 1870) farmer of near
Dresden, Ohio. Married Dec. 23, 1915 Lena A.
Eckelberry (b. July 22, 1887) and had issue:

288. Thelma b. Sept. 21, 1916.
289. Lawrence Martin b. Oct. 4, 1918.

151. MYRTLE OLIVE BOAL[4] (FRANCIS,[3]
ARCH. JR.,[2] ARCH.[1])

Myrtle Olive Boal (born 1877) married
Dec. 30, 1896 Henry A. Homrold of Sonora,
Ohio and had

290. Harold F. Homrold of Zanesville, Ohio.

152. ANN ELIZA BOAL[4] (FRANCIS,[3]
ARCH. JR.,[2] ARCH.[1])

Ann Eliza Boal married Aug. 19, 1903
Haamen Vernon of Adamsville, Ohio. They have
one son:

291. Clyde E. Vernon b. May 28, 1907.

153. ALICE A. BOAL[4] (FRANCIS,[3]
ARCH. JR.,[2] ARCH.[1])

Alice Boal (b. 1885) m. Jan. 19, 1916
Guy C. Lapp of Coshocton, Ohio and had

292. Welcome W. Lapp b. May 26, 1917.

155. ELIZABETH ACHSAH BRIGGS[5]
(JACKSON,[4] JOHN,[3] MARY,[2] ARCH.[1])

Elizabeth A. Briggs (1855-1881) married Mar. 25, 1875 Stephen Tom of Kingsville,
Mo. She died July 23, 1881. They had a
daughter:

293. Mary Belle Tom b. Nov. 30, 1880.

159. IDA FLORENCE BRIGGS (JACKSON,
JOHN, MARY, ARCH.)

Ida Briggs married Sept. 17, 1889
Geo. W. Adams of Nevsho, Mo. and had

294. Lloyd Adams

295. Winnie Mae Adams.

160. CHARLES ELMER BRIGGS (JACKSON,*
JOHN,³ MARY,² ARCH.¹)

Charles Briggs contractor of Murtaugh, Idaho. Married Nov. 24, 1891 Margaret
B. Pe:~is (1867-1932) and had issue.

Children: Briggs

296. Glen A. b. 1892 of Murtaugh, Idaho.
297. Fergus b. 1894 of Gooding, Idaho.
298. Susanna b. 1900) twins
299. Esther b. 1900)
300. Velma
301. William M. dairyman of Murtaugh, Idaho.

167. ALBERTA RENSHAW⁵ (ELIZ. J.,*
ARCH.³ JAS.² ARCH.¹)

Alberta Renshaw (1883-1926) married
Jan. 1908 Ralph B. Jacobs and had

302. Miriam Jacobs - actress of N.Y.C.
303. Jeanne Jacobs - actress of N.Y.C.
304. Renshaw Jacobs

176. WILLIAM H. GARRET⁵(ANSON,*
JANE,* JAS²., ARCH.¹)

Wm. H. Garrett (b. 1896) farmer of
Eagleport, Ohio. Married July 15, 1925
Erma Estella Rhinebarger and have on daughter.

305. Ermina Elaine Garret b. Aug. 11, 1932.

187. MABEL MCHENRY⁵(WILBERT,* JANE,³
JAS.² ARCH.¹)

Mabel McHenry (1891-1931) Graduate of
Ohio Northern Univ. Married William Crane
and had

306. Virginia Crane - Grad. of Ohio Univ. -
Member of Chi Omega.
307. William Crane of Parkersburg, W. Va.

189. FRED MCHENRY⁵(WILBERT,* JANE,³
JAS.² ARCH.¹)

Fred McHenry of Cambridge, Ohio,
graduated at Western Reserve Univ. He married Fern Stuart and had

308. Wilbert McHenry 2nd.
309. Theodore McHenry

190. CARRIE M. WARREN⁵(JOHN EZRA,* MARY,³
JAS.,² ARCH.¹)

Carrie M. Warren married Leroy S.
Myers farmer of Minnesota and had

Children: Myers

310. Lyle
311. Harold
312. Boyd
313. Emma
314. Thelma
315. Hazel

192. RACHEL BELLE WARREN⁵ (JOHN
EZRA,* MARY,³ JAS.,² ARCH.¹)

Belle Warren married Norman Zimmerman
and resides in Minnesota. Their children are

316. Cecil Zimmerman
317. Mae Zimmerman
318. Earl Zimmerman

194. GUY ELMER WARREN⁵ (JOHN EZRA,*
MARY,³ JAS.,² ARCH.¹)

Guy Warren farmer of Osceola, Ia.
Married Bertha Halterman and had

Children: Warren

319. Clarence
320. Paul
321. Julian
322. Andrea

195. HERBERT EZRA WARREN⁵ (JOHN EZRA,*
MARY,³ JAS.,² ARCH.¹)

Herbert Warren farmer of Lorimer, Ia.
Married Maude Brown and had

Children: Warren

323. Carl
324. Donald
325. Opal
326. Oma
327. Dale
328. Herbert E. Jr.
329. Agnes
330. Robert

196. GLADYS EMMA WARREN⁵ (JOHN EZRA,*
MARY,³ JAS.,² ARCH.¹)

Gladys E. Warren married E. Glenn

Johnson farmer of Murray, Ia. and had issue

331. Juanita Johnson d.y.
332. Warren Johnson

197. FLORENCE RUTH WARREN[5] (JOHN EZRA[4], MARY[3], JAS.[2], ARCH.[1])

Florence Warren married Sept. 1930 C. Earl Farr farmer of Murray, Ia and had

333. Doris Farr

199. ELLA MAY HIVNOR[5] (LUCY[4], MARY[3], JAS.[2], ARCH.[1])

Ella M. Hivnor (b. 1881) married June 9, 1901 Lemuel B. Spung of So. Zanesville, Ohio and had

334. Mabel Edith Spung b. July 21, 1903.
335. Verna Evelyn Spung b. Sept. 21, 1906.
336. Margaret Eleanor Spung b. Nov. 29, 1914.

200. ONA HIVNOR[5] (LUCY[4], MARY[3], JAS.[2], ARCH.[1])

Ona Hivnor (b. 1884) married Oct. 25, 1905 Henry Clawson of Zanesville, Ohio and had

337. Ruth Evelyn Clawson (1908-1927).

201. SIDNEY JAMES HIVNOR[5] (LUCY[4], MARY[3], JAS.[2], ARCH.[1])

Sidney James Hivnor farmer of near McConnellsville, Ohio, married Ruth Staker and had

Children: Hivnor

338. Clarence
339. Albert
340. Charles of McConnellsville, Ohio.
341. Walter
342. Archibald
343. Forrest
344. Martha Grace
345. Raymond

203. HARRY HIVNOR[5] (LUCY[4], MARY[3], JAS.[2], ARCH.[1])

Harry Hivnor of Akron, Ohio. Married Glovenia Jones and had

346. Robert Hivnor

204. LESTER EVERETT WARREN[5] (SAM'L[4], MARY[3], JAS.[2], ARCH.[1])

Lester Warren farmer of Winterset, Ia. Married Belva Gardner and had

347. Donald Warren

205. ORVIE WARREN (SAM'L[4], MARY[3], JAS.[2], ARCH.[1])

Orvie Warren farmer of Winterset, Ia. Married Eunice Beem and had

348. Helen Warren

206. ONA GLEE WARREN[5] (SAM'L[4], MARY[3], JAS.[2], ARCH.[1])

Ona G. Warren married Ray Hercock of Winterset, Ia. and had

Children: Hercock

349. Ethel
350. Norma
351. Delbert
352. Robert
353. Billy
354. Beverly Jean

207. LUCY MARIE WETER[5] (CORA[4], MARY[3], JAS.[2], ARCH.[1])

Lucy M. Weter (b. 1899) married May 11, 1921 Arley J. Lewis, teacher of Lorimer, Ia.

229. MABEL BARNES[5] (EMELINE[4], ARCH.[3], JOHN[2], ARCH.[1])

Mabel Barnes married William L. White and resides in Logan, Ohio. They have five daughters

Children: White

355. Marguerite
356. Lillian
357. Lucille
358. Marian
359. Betty

- - - - -

232. ALVA WALTER BOAL[5] (ELI[4] JAS.[3] JOHN[2] ARCH.[1])

Alva Boal, carpenter of Council Bluffs, Ia. Married Apr. 16, 1901 Claudia Hamilton (b. Dec. 18, 1880) and had issue:

360. Harry Walter b. Nov. 27, 1903.
361. Alva Clifford b. Oct. 9, 1908.

233. ALMEDA BOAL[5] (ELI[4] JAS.[3] JOHN[2] ARCH.[1])

Almeda Boal married Eldon Parsons farmer of Morgan County, Ohio and had

362. Mark Emmet Parsons b. Mar. 24, 1895.
363. Luke Parsons b. Mar. 24, 1895.

234. ETHEL BOAL[5] (ELI[4] JAS.[3] JOHN[2] ARCH.[1])

Ethel Boal married Daniel Parsons and had

364. Emeline Parsons
365. Alva Parsons
366. Viola Parsons

235. CARRIE MELINDA BOAL[5] (ELI[4] JAS.[3] JOHN[2] ARCH.[1])

Carrie Boal married Apr. 7, 1915 Walter S. Greathouse and resides Thornville, Ohio. They have four children:

Children: Greathouse

367. Leora F.
368. Wilford
369. Helen M.
370. Mary Louise

237. MINNIE CUMMINS[5] (EFFIE JANE[4] WM.[3] JOHN[2] ARCH.[1])

Minnie Cummins married first Dolph Nelson of Nelsonville, Ohio and had

371. John Nelson, graduate of Hiram College
372. Mildred Nelson
373. Charles Edward Nelson

238. ADDIE CUMMINS[5] (EFFIE JANE[4] WM.[3] JOHN[2] ARCH.[1])

Addie Cummins married Dr. Charles

Richards of Glouster, Ohio and had

374. Dean Richards d.y.
375. Mildred Richards, graduate of Ohio State University.
(Two others names not known.)

252. DELLA M. BOAL[5] (HUGH HENRY[4] MCKEE[3] JOHN[2] ARCH.[1])

Della Boal married Jan. 10, 1906 Otis Lane of Bruceville, Ind. and had

376. Harold Maurice Lane
377. Ernest Murle Lane

254. EARL BOAL[5] (C.H. HENRY[4] MCKEE[3] JOHN[2] ARCH.[1])

Earl Boal of Whiting, Ind. married Gladys Burkhart and had

378. Rexford E. b. Sept. 23, 1915.

255. GUY V. TEETERS[5] (JANE[4] MCKEE[3] JOHN[2] ARCH.[1])

Guy Teeters of Columbus, Ohio married Carrie Waxler, a daughter of Fenton E. Waxler of McArthur, Ohio and had

Children: Teeters

379. Vernon
380. Virgil
381. Gladys
382. Edson

257. DESSIE LYLE[5] (JEMIMA[4] MCKEE[3] JOHN[2] ARCH.[1])

Dessie Lyle married Claude Wyatt of Allensville, Ohio and had

383. Charles Wyatt

258. ORVAN ARGANBRIGHT[5] (JEMIMA[4] MCKEE[3] JOHN[2] ARCH.[1])

Orvan Arganbright of Londonderry, O. married Emma Fouts and had

384. Maxine Arganbright
385. Ernest Earl Arganbright

- - - - -

259. RUTH ELEANOR BOAL[6] (ARCH[4] MCKEE[3] JOHN[2] ARCH.[1])

Eleanor Boal graduate of Ohio State Univ. 1926 and 1927 (M.A.) psychologist married Oct. 1, 1927 Seward D. Legge, architect of Cuyahoga Falls, Ohio. Issue:

386. Roseanne Legge b. Feb. 8, 1929.
387. John Boal Legge b. Apr. 12, 1935.

262. KENNETH BOAL[5] (PEARL[4] SAM'L[3] JOHN[2] ARCH.[1])

Kenneth Boals of Columbus, Ohio married Nov. 3, 1926 Sara Agnes Melley and had

388. Molly Anne Boals
389. Bonnie Kay Boals

276. GEORGE C. BOAL[5] (SETH[4] CYRUS B.[3] ARCH.[2] ARCH.[1])

George C. Boal of Coshocton, O. married Jan. 17, 1912 Bernice Elsie Powelson (b. June 7, 1891). He is a member of the Masonic lodge and of the Methodist Church. Issue:

390. Anna Katherine b. Dec. 24, 1912.
Married Thos. Maitland of Urichsville, Ohio.
391. George Jr. b. June 14, 1916.

277. HAZEL BOAL[5] (SETH[4] CYRUS B.[3] ARCH. JR.[2] ARCH.[1])

Hazel Boal married June 26, 1916 Ray Livingston of Conesville, Ohio and had

392. Seth W. Livingston
393. Anna M. Livingston

278. HARRY E. BOAL[5] (SETH[4] CYRUS B.[3] ARCH. JR.[2] ARCH.[1])

Harry E. Boal, electrician of Coshocton, Ohio. Married Apr. 22, 1927 Lavada Haxton and had

394. Beverly Ann

282. CLARENCE JAN BOAL[5] (MARION[4] CYRUS[3] ARCH. JR.[2] ARCH.[1])

Clarence Jan Boal, instructor in Violin of Massillon, Ohio, married Sept. 1926 Mary Ann List, pianist. He served in the World War and is a member of the Baptist Church. They have one son:

395. Jan List Boal

360. HARRY WALTER BOAL[6] (ALVA[5] ELI[4] JAS.[3] JOHN[2] ARCH.[1])

Harry Boal of Council Bluffs, Ia. Married Apr. 3, 1926 Ruth Marie Carter (b. 1904) and had issue:

396. Richard Harry b. May 31, 1929.

361. ALVA CLIFFORD BOAL[6] (ALVA[5] ELI[4] JAS.[3] JOHN[2] ARCH.[1])

Clifford Boal, office manager of the "Omaha World Herald, married June 15, 1927 at Tekalmah, Neb. Katherine Hall Petty (b. May 12, 1908) and had

397. Lilah Ione b. June 27, 1928.
398. Jack Eugene b. Oct. 17, 1929.

THE NAME

Boal as a surname is said to be derived from the ancient Irish word "Buachall" and signifying "he who plows the fields to produce food." This is a particularly apt meaning as the Boal family has largely remained on the farm or ranch through the generations. Even to the present day more than 80% of the descendants are still engaged in some form of agriculture.

Arms: Ar. out of a Mount vert an oak tree
         ppr on a chief az. A crescent betw.
         two mullets ar.

Crest: An oak tree ppr.

Ref. O'Hart's Irish Pedegrees

1. PEYTON BURWELL HOPE

Peyton Hope was born in Prince William County, Virginia Mar. 11, 1803. He was a farmer and mail carrier. On Feb. 14, 1830 he married Mary Elizabeth Hope, his cousin, in Loudown County, Va. In October of 1837 they, with their three small children, Mrs. Elizabeth Hope (the mother of Peyton) Miss Jane Hope and Mrs. Sally Wilson (sisters of Mary Elizabeth Hope), Mr. Wilson and their children, John and James Hope (brothers of Peyton) and their families started in two large covered wagons for Ohio.

While crossing the mountains a cow belonging to one of the brothers became lost and the one wagon turned back to find it and they were never heard of again. After waiting for some time Peyton likewise went back in search but although they returned to the camp where the brothers had gone. No trace of them was found. It was thought that they had been captured by Indians. However the names of John and James Hope were found in early census records of Prince William County and it seems probable that becoming discouraged with the rough country they were crossing, they preferred to return to Virginia.

The Peyton Hope family, the Wilsons and the mother of Peyton and Miss Jane Hope continued on their way and settled in Saltlick township of Perry County Ohio where they purchased farms.

Peyton Burwell Hope died there Feb. 28, 1885 aged 82 years and is buried in Sulphur Springs Cemetery. A copy of an editorial which appeared in a New Lexington, Ohio newspaper at the time is as follows:

"We learn by a sketch published in another place that Peyton Hope is dead. Every year as regular as June taxes, he called at the Tribune office to pay for his paper. He lived on Sunday Creek when it was no joke to sojourn there. If he did not actually fight wild cats, catamounts and panthers, they were his near neighbors. He fought the stones, rocks and roots of the rugged hills and made them yield a subsistence.

Small in stature, he was uncommonly active. He carried with him an inward cheery hope, more potent than the name he bore.

When he bade us a cheery "Good Morning" last June, we thought he might live yet many years, but the old gentleman was nearing the eternal shore and now rests from his long and arduous labors."

Mary Elizabeth Hope was born in Prince William County, Virginia Apr. 6, 1812. She had an excellent literary taste and enjoyed writing bits of verse as a pastime. She was very religious, being a member of the Christian Church at Sulphur Springs near Shawnee, Ohio.

She had very little opportunity for early education and learned to write during the Civil War in order that she might correspond with her sons George and John Thomas who were in the Union Army. None of her letters to them have been preserved but two which she wrote to a grandaughter at a later date are in the possession of grandchildren. The first bearing date of 15, Dec. 1881, Shawnee, Perry Co., Ohio.

Dear Grandaughter,

I seat myself to answer your very welcome letter I received last mail. It made me twice glad, I was glad to hear from you and glad to see the picture of your baby brother. He was quite large at that age. I think he looks like Johnny.

Well we are as well as common. My health is better than it was all last winter and summer till July, I began to get better.

I got so weak I could not go down the steps. I tried patent medicine, I hit on the right kind at last. I got Hops Bitters and took two bottles and I can do all my work. I just finished washing. I would not have a doctor.

You wanted to know how burnet (Bernard) was getting. He is on the mend. He aint done one days work since last March. His boys have tended all the crops and put in the wheat this fall. It was good he had boys that could do his work. He doctored with Doc Priest all summer till four weeks past, he went to Uniontown to old Doctor Watkins.

He is better, he can carry a little stove wood and bucket of water—He is coming to Russell's next Sunday. I have some hopes of his getting well.—Grandpa has never been as well as he was before he had the mumps last spring. He never goes any place only on business.

Russell and myself would of come to see you summer after harvest but he went (to) work on the railroad and we had but one horse that works to the buggy, the old sorrel mare could not go so far. Father has bought another one but the weather has been cold now.

I would like you all to come up at Christmas meeting at our school house Christmas day. I have a big old roster I can make a big roast of--come All everyone.

Well Anna you said you had a new instrument of music. I would like to see it. I would rather see it than hear it!--How do Lizzie and Viry get along at school? I want Johnny's picture. I hear he is wearing pants and waist by this time.--Did you go to the yearly meeting last fall?

We did not go. Grandpa is not able. He has like sunstroke, was very bad since. I got a towel and wet it in cold water and shedd it on his head, after a while he got better.--Lewis is talking of coming soon if he can get some one to do the feeding while he is gone. Your Uncle Eli (Boal) has moved in his new house.

Milton Hope has been going to school. He learns very fast. Harley is as fat as he can be. I would (like to) see you all. It seems so long, it is over a year since any of you were here.

Dan Grim from Kansas was (here) last fall. He stayed four weeks. I will close now.--

Goodby Anny Hope from

Grandma

I am going to send you a piece of my new dress.---We all send our love to you all. Kiss the baby for me. Tell him that is from Grandma.

Mary Hope

She died July 3, 1888 and is buried in Sulphur Springs Cemetery.

Her obituary from the New Lexington, Ohio Tribune of July 6, 1888 and written by her son Bernard Hope says in part:

"From her sick bed Mother called to me to read to her from the New Testament, the book she dearly loved. She requested me to read the 103rd Psalm, the 15th Chapter of First Corinthians and the 17th Chapter of St. John. She said she was ready to depart but must wait until the Lord pleased to take her. She died as she lived relying on the promise of God."

Issue of Peyton and Mary Elizabeth Hope:

2. Amanda b. Jan. 9, 1831 in Va.
3. George Wm. b. Oct. 30, 1833 in Va.

4. Eliza Jane 1836-1850.
5. Margretta b. May 10, 1838.
6. Bernard b. Sept. 10, 1840.
7. Albert b. Oct. 8, 1842. d. 1848
8. Maria E. 1844-1847.
9. John Thomas ⎫
⎬ twins b. Apr. 5, 1847.
10. Alexander Campbell ⎭ - d. Apr. 6, 1847.
11. Peyton Lewis 1849-1914. unm.
12. Mary Ellen 1852-1856.
13. Russell b. Aug. 23, 1854.

2. AMANDA HOPE² (PEYTON¹)

Amanda Hope (b. 1831) married Sept. 23, 1855 Daniel Drake (son of Ralph and Catherine Drake) and removed to Adair County, Mo. where Daniel Drake followed the trade of carpenter at Wilmouthville. Their children were:

Children: Drake

14. John b. 1857.
15. Keturah b. 1859--lived in Calif.
16. Joseph b. 1861.
17. Ulyssis b. 1864.
18. William b. 1869.

3. GEORGE WILLIAM HOPE² (PEYTON¹)

George Hope (1833-1863) married Mar. 22, 1855 Emeline Williams (b. Feb. 8, 1835) and removed to Vernon County, Wisconsin.

When the Civil War broke out he was called to the Colors serving in Co. A. of the 25th Wisconsin infantry. He became ill and died at Memphis, Tenn., Sept. 21, 1863 and is buried there. His wife survived him many years, dying Mar. 6, 1920 at Vale, Ore. Their issue:

19. J. Albert 1856-1915. unm.
20. Charles F. 1857-1863.
21. Milton G. Hope b. Aug. 31, 1859.
22. Isaiah W. b. Sept. 28, 1861.

5. MARGRETTA HOPE (PEYTON)

Margretta Hope (b. 1838) married Nov. 29, 1855 Amos Grim (b. 1835) and they lived variously in Perry County, Ohio, Ill. Kansas, Kentucky, Iowa, Warrenton, Va., Dayton, O. (1902) and California where she died. Their family consisted of:

Children: Grim

23. William d. young (in Ill.)
24. George (1858-1861).
25. John (1859-1860).
26. Daniel b. 1863 in Perry Co., Ohio
27. Mary Elizabeth b. ca 1876.

6. BERNARD HARRISON HOPE (PEYTON)

Bernard Hope (1840-1912) farmer of
Perry County, Ohio was married Dec. 25,
1862 to Rachel Isabel Rogers (daughter of
Wm. Rogers). She was born Mar. 21, 1842 and
died Sept. 24, 1911. She was blessed with a
delightful sense of humor which endeared her
to all who knew her. Bernard Hope died Nov.
7, 1912 and is buried at Sulphur Springs.
Issue:

28. Clarinda Isabel b. Dec. 30, 1863.
29. George William b. Apr. 21, 1865.
30. John Franklin b. Feb. 8, 1868.
31. Burwell Granville b. Feb. 6, 1870.
32. Riley Walter b. Apr. 9, 1872.
33. Worley Alvadore b. Sept. 27, 1874.
34. Charles Seymore b. July 13, 1876.
35. Bertha May b. Oct. 31, 1878.
36. Addie Grace b. Sept. 19, 1880.
37. Nellie Blanche b. Oct. 6, 1882.
38. Dora Lodema b. 1884-1890.
39. Noah Elijah b. June 24, 1887.

9. JOHN THOMAS HOPE (PEYTON)

John Thomas Hope (1847-1929) farmer
of Perry County, Ohio married Nov. 28, 1869
Mary Ellen Boal (see 73 Boal lineage).
He served in the Civil War in the
131st. Ohio Inf., was a member of the Colum-
bus Golden Post, the Masonic lodge and the
Christian Church. In the spring of 1890
they removed to near Athens, Ohio. He died
July 31, 1929 and Mary Ellen Boal Hope died
Jan. 2, 1935. Both are buried in West
Union St. Cemetery at Athens. They had eight
children:

40. Rhoda Ann 1870-1891--m. 1890 J. H. Allen.
41. Mary Elizabeth b. Feb. 11, 1873--m.
    W. L. Walden (See 109. Dewees).
42. Alvira R. b. Mar. 17, 1876--m. W. H.
    Martin (See 134 Harper).
43. John Thomas b. Aug. 30, 1878.
44. James Garfield b. Jan. 28, 1881.
45. Clara L. Hope 1883-1887.
46. Ella E. 1885-1908--unm.
47. Albert 1887-1887.

13. RUSSELL SMITH HOPE (PEYTON)

Russell S. Hope (1854-1907) Merchant
resided in Perry County, Ohio, W. Va., Oregon,
and Clinton, Ind. He married first, Margaret
Ann Springer (b. Jan. 18, 1856 and died Aug.
11, 1891). She is buried at Sulphur Springs
near Hemlock, Ohio. They had three sons:

48. Milton 1876-1923. unm.
49. Harley Franklin b. Oct. 19, 1879.
50. Russell Cassius 1881-1881.

21. MILTON G. HOPE[3] (GEO.[2], PEYTON[1])

Milton Hope (1859-1927) graduated from
business college and became a banker at Vale,
Ore. He was a member of the Odd Fellows and
Knights of Pythias lodges.
He married Emma High (b. Sept. 28,
1862 and d. 1903) and had issue:

51. Lesley b. 1888.
52. Elizabeth b. 1895.
53. George M. b. 1900.

Milton Hope married second Feb. 5,
1907 Ora Smith (b. 1881) and had

54. Paul b. 1911.
55. William b. 1912.
56. Jean b. 1914.

22. ISAIAH W. HOPE[3] (GEO.[2], PEYTON[1])

Isaiah W. Hope (b. 1861) secretary of
Vale, Ore., received a business college education. He is a member of the A. F. and A. M.,
Odd Fellows and is a Republican. He married
in 1890 Lillie B. Gellerman (b. Mar. 17, 1870
and d. 1935) and had issue:

57. Norma E. b. 1892--teacher.
58. Erma D. b. 1896--teacher.
59. Mazie b. 1900--teacher.
60. Bernice b. 1903--teacher.
61. Hazel b. 1908--teacher.

26. DANIEL GRIM[3] (MARGRETTA[2], PEYTON[1])

Daniel Grim (b. 1863) married Oct. 17,
1894 Annie S. Woodzell (a daughter of Simon
and Martha Woodzell of Warrenton, Va.)
Names of issue unknown.

27. MARY ELIZABETH GRIM[3] (MARGRETTA[2], PEYTON[1])

Mary Grim (b. 1876) married in Dayton,

Ohio, Oct. 7, 1902 George Stephen Woodzell
son of Simon and Martha Woodzell of Warrenton,
Va. (Names of issue unknown).

28. CLARINDA HOPE³ (BERNARD², PEYTON¹)

Clarinda Hope (1863-1933) married
Jan. 14, 1894 Edmund L. Vest of Moxahala,
Ohio. She died Apr. 19, 1933. They had
issue:

Children: Vest

62. Alta married Chas. Shepherd and had issue.
63. Virgie (1900-1923) no issue.
64. Eldon married Loraine Smathers and had
    issue.
65. Lloyd

29. GEORGE WILLIAM HOPE³ (BERNARD², PEYTON¹)

William Hope (b. 1865) merchant,
married Aug. 17, 1893 Mary Hays of Vinton
County, Ohio. They lived in W. Va., Kansas,
Shade, Ohio., and now reside in Columbus,
Ohio. They had two daughters:

66. Elizabeth b. Oct. 19, 1898.
67. Marie b. Dec. 9, 1900

30. JOHN FRANKLIN HOPE³
(BERNARD², PEYTON¹)

John Hope (1868-1927) of Hemlock,
Ohio, married July 3, 1887 Lida Sullivan
(1867-1937) and had issue:

68. Pearl Ethel b. July 28, 1888.
69. Frank C. 1890-1891.
70. Howard b. Feb. 20, 1892.
71. Harry b. Jan. 6, 1894.
72. Dora b. Feb. 20, 1898.
73. Earl b. Aug. 20, 1904.
74. Mabel b. Mar. 30, 1906.
75. Lau Dell b. May 2, 1909.

31. BURWELL GRANVILLE HOPE
(BERNARD, PEYTON)

Burwell Hope (b. 1870) of near
Hemlock, Ohio, married Jeannette Hoy and had
issue:

76. Rita m. Mr. Schaer of Winchester, Ohio.
77. Dulcia
78. Burwell
79. Nobel d. young.

80. Elmer
81. Jeannette
82. Leona m. Aaron Carter.
83. Nellie
84. Kermit
85. Hazel
86. Ronda

33. WORLEY ALVADORE HOPE
(BERNARD², PEYTON¹)

Alvadore Hope (b. 1874) merchant of
Shawnee, Ohic, married Mary Eing (b. in
Germany) and had:

87. Elmer of Long Beach, Calif.
88. Ida m. Howard Johnston of Columbus, Ohio.
89. Maurice
90. Margaret
91. Richard
92. Vincent
93. Helen
94. Paul

37. NELLIE BLANCHE HOPE³
(BERNARD², PEYTON¹)

Nellie Hope (1882-1937) married
Mar. 19, 1903, Howard Joseph (b. Mar. 13,
1883 at Pomeroy, Ohio) and had issue:

Children: Joseph

95. Ruth Elaine m. Mr. Kime.
96. Harold m. Nina Yohe.
97. Ralph m. 1933 Helen King.
98. Mabel b. Feb. 4, 1912--Graduate of Ohio
    State Univ.

43. JOHN THOMAS HOPE³
(J. THOS², PEYTON¹)

John T. Hope (b. 1878) dairyman of
Athens, Ohio, Past Master of Pomona Grange,
married Nov. 27, 1901 Celia Coe (See 80
Francis lineage) and had issue:

99. Geraldine Coe, Assistant Alumni Secretary
            Ohio Univ., Member of
            Sigma, Sigma, Sigma. Stat
            Treas. (Ohio) Business and
            Professional Women's Club
            1936-1938.

100. Alton Russell b. July 9, 1904.
101. Harry Allen b. Dec. 28, 1911.
102. Carol Francis m. Mr. Heston of Amesville,
     Ohio.

103. Warren Harding b. July 9, 1920.

44. JAMES GARFIELD HOPE[3]
(J. THOS?, PEYTON[1])

Garfield Hope (b. 1881) dairyman of
Athens, Ohio. A member of the Elks lodge
and the Isaac Walton League. He married first
Miss Davis and second Lydia Harper. Issue:

104. Helen d. young.

49. HARLEY FRANKLIN HOPE[3]
(RUSSELL[2], PEYTON[1])

Harley Hope (b. 1879) Contractor and
Merchant of Matewan, W. Va., married Aug. 24,
1903 Dixie Harris.(b. Sept. 12, 1887 and had
seven sons:

105. Raymond L..b. June 20, 1904.
106. Harold S. b. Jan. 2, 1906.
107. Terrence W. b. Aug. 22, 1907.
108. Oswald P. b. Mar. 24, 1909.
109. Edward H. b. July 30, 1910.
110. Bernard F. b. Nov. 2, 1915.
111. Harley Franklin b. Jan. 5, 1930.

51. LESLEY HOPE[4] (MILTON[3], GEO[2], PEYTON)

Lesley Hope (b. 1888) attended
Pacific Univ., and is engaged in the real
estate business in Butte, Mont. He married
1913 Ruth Gaylord (b. 1890) and had:

112. Betty b. 1916.
113. Doris b. 1922.

52. ELIZABETH HOPE[4]
(MILTON[3], GEO[2]., PEYTON[1])

Elizabeth Hope (b. 1895) attended
business college and married in 1918 George
Marks of Rawlins, Wyo. and had

Children: Marks

114. Hope b. 1919.
115. Merle b. 1921.
116. Thomas b. 1926.

57. NORMA E. HOPE[4]
(ISAIAH[3], GEO[2]., PEYTON[1])

Norma Hope (b. 1892) married 1918
R. James Rasmusent, salesman of Portland,

Ore. He served in the World War as Ensign
in the Navy. They have two children:

117. James Rasmusent b. 1919.
118. Janet Rasmusent b. 1926.

58. ERMA D. HOPE[4]
(ISAIAH[3], GEO[2]., PEYTON[1])

Erma Hope (b. 1896) graduate of
Whitman Univ. 1920, married 1924 Gwy Lowny
of Cambridge, Md. He served with the Marines
in the World War. They have two children:

Children: Lowny

119. Joan b. 1927.
120. Richard b. 1930.

59. MAZIE HOPE[4] (ISAIAH[3], GEO[2]., PEYTON[1])

Mazie Hope (b. 1900) graduate of
Normal College 1922. She married 1923
Albert Cook (b. 1892) of Cheyenne, Wyo. and
had 121. Maxine Cook b. 1925.

66. ELIZABETH HOPE[4]
(WM[3]., BERNARD[2], PEYTON[1])

Elizabeth Hope (b. 1898) a graduate
of Ohio State Univ., she married June 9, 1923
Joseph Newland Basom (1899-1930) and had
issue:

Children: Basom

122. Eloise Hope b. Sept. 1924.
123. Marjorie Jane b. Apr. 1926.
124. William Joseph b. Jan. 21, 1930.

They now reside in Lawrence, Kansas.

67. MARIE HOPE[4] (WM[3]., BERNARD[2], PEYTON[1])

Marie Hope graduated at Ohio Univ.,
1922, married Aug. 19, 1927 Charles Dickson
of Sandusky, Ohio and had issue:

125. Thomas Hope Dickson b. Jan. 10, 1929.

68. PEARL ETHEL HOPE[4]
(JOHN[3], BERNARD[2], PEYTON[1])

Pearl Hope (1888-1926) married Mar.
21, 1909 Oliver Thompson of Columbus, Ohio

Children: Thompson

126. Carol Hope (1912-1912).
127. Madeleine M. b. Sept. 8, 1914.
128. Edna Eileen b. Jan. 13, 1918.

70. HOWARD HOPE[4]
(JOHN[3], BERNARD[2], PEYTON[1])

Howard Hope (b. 1892) of Clinton,
Ind., married Dec. 26, 1913 Helen VanHorn
(b. Oct. 25, 1893) and had:

129. Harold M. b. Sept. 24, 1914.
130. John W. b. July 10, 1916.
131. Virginia E. b. Dec. 26, 1918.
132. Betty J. b. Mar. 22, 1920.
133. Robert F. b. Mar. 5, 1922.
134. Helen L. b. Nov. 10, 1927.

71. HARRY HOPE[4] (JOHN[3],
BERNARD[2], PEYTON[1])

Harry Hope (b. 1894) of Pimento,
Ind., married July 27, 1914 Cora M. Ward
(b. Jan. 4, 1895) and had issue:

135. Marvin b. Sept. 9, 1917.
136. Ralph b. Sept. 12, 1919.
137. Juanita b. Sept. 6, 1920.
138. Harry Jr., b. Sept. 25, 1922.
139. Philip b. Jan. 17, 1924.
140. Ruth b. Nov. 7, 1926.
141. Joyce b. Dec. 21, 1929.

72. DORA HOPE[4] (JOHN[3],
BERNARD[2], PEYTON[1])

Dora Hope (b. 1898) married Nov. 28,
1914 Mr. Whitmer (b. 1895) of Columbus, Ohio
and had:

Children: Whitmer

142. Rolland b. Mar. 29, 1916.
143. Richard b. Nov. 23, 1918.

73. EARL HOPE[4] (JOHN[3],
BERNARD[2], PEYTON[1])

Earl Hope (b. 1904) of Columbus
Ohio married Aug. 17, 1928 Annabelle Wilson
and had:

144. William E. b. Sept. 2, 1930.
145. Earl Jr., b. 1938.

74. MABEL HOPE (JOHN,
BERNARD, PEYTON)

Mabel Hope (b. 1906) married Oct. 2,
1926 Charles Hoodlet of Columbus, Ohio and
had:

Children: Hoodlet

146. Constance Jean Hoodlet b. Feb. 13, 1928.

75. LAU DELL HOPE[4] (JOHN[3],
BERNARD[2], PEYTON[1])

Lau Dell Hope (b. 1909) married
Dec. 11, 1926 Wendell Love, teacher of
Corning, Ohio and had:

Children: Love

147. Patricia Lee Love b. Nov. 7, 1929.

100. ALTON RUSSELL HOPE[4]
(JOHN[3], BERNARD[2], PEYTON[1])

Alton Hope (b. 1904) dairyman of
Athens, Ohio, married Mary Elizabeth Woodburn
(daughter of Henry and Elizabeth of near
Marietta, Ohio) and had:

148. Barbara Ann b. Aug. 29, 1931.
149. Elizabeth Celia b. Nov. 12, 1937.

105. RAYMOND L. HOPE[4]
(HARLEY[3], RUSSELL[2], PEYTON[1])

Raymond Hope (b. 1904) bank teller
of Charleston, W. Va., married Margaret
Shonk and had:

150. Raymond L. Jr., b. Aug. 28, 1929.

THE NAME

Hope is a local or place name meaning a low valley between two hills. The
earliest mention found was Roger de la Hope
(Roger of the hope) in 1273 (Herifordshire)

HOPE LINEAGE NOTES

Due to a wholesale destruction of
Court record books by the Union Army during
the Civil War, many of the Northern Counties
of Virginia have only fragmentary records.

For this reason it has been impossible to trace completely the family lines of Peyton Hope and his wife Mary Elizabeth Hope, who was also his cousin. They were both grandchildren of Henry and Mary (Burwell) Hope of Prince William County, Va., who had sons: John, James, and William, daughters: Margaret and Elizabeth and probably several other children.

Henry Hope was a member of a prominent and well-to-do English family. Because of a disagreement with his father he ran away from home when just a youth, was seized by sailors and impressed into service on a sailing vessel from which he escaped, Many months later, while in port at Norfolk. He married Mary Burwell of Prince William County. She was, undoubtedly, a descendant of Major Lewis Burwell from Bedfordshire, England to Virginia in 1643.

Although urged to do so many times, by his wife, Henry Hope never wrote to his family and that contact was completely broken.

The lineages of many Hope families have been studied to no avail. The Hope name is one of much prominence in England, being the surname of the Earl of Lincoln (Henry P. C. Hope), the Duke of Newcastle, the Earl of Hopetown, the Marquess of Linlithgow and many of the lesser nobility.

OWEN DEWEES

Owen Dewees was born in Berks County, Pa., about 1754 and served with Berks County Militia in the Revolutionary War (See Pa. Archives--5th Series Vol. IV, P. 257 and 287, also the 6th Series Vol. III, P. 938 and 939). Following the war he served in the Northumberland County Militia as late as 1790.

He married in November, 1782 Mary Lee (b. 10, 7, 1755). She was a birthright Quakeress and on her marriage with Owen Dewees, a non-member, she was disowned and read "out of meeting."

They removed to Northumberland County but some years later she returned on a visit and "made acknowledgement" of her transgression and was received back into membership with her husband and small children.

They resided upon a farm in Northumberland County which was owned by Samuel Lee (father of Mary). At his death in 1802 he bequeathed the farm to Mary. Shortly thereafter they sold the home and removed to Belmont County, Ohio where they resided in Peas township until 1837 when they removed to Morgan township of Morgan County, Ohio, where all their children excepting Esther had preceded them.

Owen Dewees died in 1839 and his Will is of record in Bk. O., P. 100 as follows:

"Be it remembered that on the 18th day of the seventh month in the year of our Lord 1837 I, Owen Dewees of the County of Morgan and township of Morgan and state of Ohio, being of sound and disposing mind and memory do make and ordain this my last Will and Testament which is as follows, viz. First all my just debts and funeral expenses to be fully paid by my hereafter named executors. Second--to my beloved wife Mary Dewees, all the proceeds arising from this place whereon I now live, during her natural life—then to her daughters Margaret Dewees and Joanna Dewees--to have and to hold forever---Third--To my elder son Samuel Dewees, I will the sum of four hundred and fifty dollars, to my daughter Esther Purviance—four hundred and fifty dollars, to my son Thomas Dewees—four hundred and fifty dollars—to my daughter Hannah Grimes—four hundred and fifty dollars and to my youngest daughter Mary Wilson--four hundred and fifty dollars--the legacy coming from my cousin Joseph Ball's estate of Philadelphia to be equally divided among all my children--

to my grandson Owen Dewees--I appoint as executors James Cope and my daughter Margaret Dewees--

Owen Dewees

Will proved July 13, 1839.

At his request he was buried in the old "Hicksite" Friends burying grounds between Malta and Pennsville.

Mary Lee Dewees died Nov. 13, 1843, aged 89 years and was buried beside her husband. Their children were:

2. Samuel b. Nov. 1, 1783 in Pa.
3. Margaret b. 1786 in Pa.--unm.
4. Esther Dewees b. 12/5/1789 in Pa.
5. Thomas Dewees b. ca 1790 in Pa.
6. Hannah Dewees b. 6/24/1791 in Pa.
7. Mary Dewees b. 1799 in Pa.

2. SAMUEL DEWEES[2](OWEN[1])

Samuel Dewees (1783-1850) removed from Northumberland County, Pa. with his parents to Belmont County, Ohio. He married there about 1805 Hannah Berry (born 1785 in Va.) They removed to Morgan County, Ohio ca 1837 and he died there Feb. 8, 1850. Their children were:

8. Owen b. ca 1806.
9. David Berry
10. Julia Elma m. Jas. Lincoln
11. Emily m. 1. Jonathan Harris
             2. John Calahan
12. Ellis Lee b. 1815--m. 9/28/1848--
    Mary McGirr and removed to Indiana.
13. Thomas m. 4/16/1840 Leah Metcalf.
14. Anna m. 5/6/1844 Joshua S. Lincoln.
15. Hannah Maria m. 1/23/1845 Josiah Ward
16. Mary

4. ESTHER DEWEES[2](OWEN[1])

Esther Dewees (1789-1862) came as a young girl with her parents to Belmont County, Ohio. She married 5/28/1817 George Purviance (b. 2/24/1783 in Fayette County, Pa.) and resided near Smithfield, Ohio. She died there 5/10/1862 and George Purviance died 12/9/1863 and both are buried in the Friends Burying ground at Smithfield. They were the parents of ten children:

Children: Purviance

17. Samuel D. b. 6/28/1818.
18. Isaac b. 9/8/1819.
19. Mary D. b. 10/28/1820.
20. Martha b. 6/6/1822.
21. Richard B. b. 8/25/1823--d. 1850.
22. George W. b. 11/1/1824.
23. Owen D. b. 2/5/1827.
24. Elizabeth b. 11/4/1828.
25. Esther b. 2/26/1830.
26. Nathan b. 3/25/1834.

5. THOMAS DEWEES[2] (OWEN[1])

Thomas Dewees (b. 1790) removed from Belmont to Morgan County, Ohio about 1835. Due to the fact that three men of the name of Thomas Dewees, all with wives named Mary emigrated to Morgan County about the same time, it has been impossible to find definite proof of the descendants of this line.

6. HANNAH DEWEES[2] (OWEN[1])

Hannah Dewees (1791-1883) married Benjamin Grimes (1789-1848). This was a "Maud Muller" Romance! Hannah was in the field raking hay, along rode a handsome young man on horse-back who stopped and asked for a cup of water, which she ran to give him. Thanking her, he rode away, but to return another day for another drink of water!

After their marriage they removed to Morgan County, Ohio and later to Washington County where he died.

The Quaker disownment which followed her "marrying out" hurt Hannah keenly. One evening she dressed in the plain garments worn by the "Friends" of that day and went to Meeting. The coldness with which her arrival was received hurt her inexpressibly. The Spirit moved her to speak and she arose and with intense finality declared: "Thee can keep me out of Church but thee cannot keep me out of Heaven!" and turning she hastily left the astounded congregation, never to return.

Benjamin Grimes served in the War of 1812. He died Apr. 21, 1848 and Hannah Grimes died Dec. 24, 1883. They rest in Old Tabor Cemetery. Their issue:

Children: Grimes

27. George 1825-1839.
28. Owen b. June 3, 1826.

29. John 1827-1852--no issue.
30. Samuel 1831-1914--no issue.
31. Esther b. Apr. 10, 1833.
32. Hannah b. Nov. 18, 1835.
33. Joanna m. 1842 Abner Lewis.
34. Catherine m. 1841 Valentine Lewis.
35. Margaret m. 1842 George Jarvis.

7. MARY DEWEES[2] (OWEN[1])

Mary Dewees (b. 1799) married about 1823 Daniel Wilson (b. 1786). They removed in 1831 from Belmont to Morgan County, Ohio. They had at least five children, viz.

Children: Wilson

36. Daniel Jr. b. 1824.
37. Owen b. 1831.
38. Thomas b. 1836.
39. Margaret D. b. 1840.
40. Rachel b. 1849.

8. OWEN DEWEES[3] (SAMUEL,[2] OWEN[1])

Owen Dewees (b. 1806 in Belmont County, Ohio) married about 1832 Sarah Green (b. 1802) and resided in Roxbury township of Washington County, Ohio until about 1849 when he removed to Morgan County. Some years later he is said to have gone to Illinois where he died. They had three children:

41. Samuel b. 1833.
42. Elizabeth b. 1836.
43. William H. b. 1843.

9. DAVID BERRY DEWEES[3], (SAMUEL[2], OWEN[1])

David B. Dewees (b. 1808) of Morgan County married ca 1828 Rachel Kirby and removed to Indiana. They had issue:

44. Thomas Kirby b. 1829 (July 1)
45. Hannah b. 1831 (Oct. 28)
46. Isaac b. 1834 (Jan. 3)
47. Leander
48. Clinton
49. Robert

17. SAMUEL PURVIANCE[3] (ESTHER[2], OWEN[1])

Samuel D. Purviance (1818-1906) of near Smithfield, Ohio, married Mar. 26, 1840 Amelia Scott (b. May 6, 1824 and died Apr. 22, 1897) and had nine children, viz.

Children· Purviance

50. Rachel Ann b. 5/20/1841.
51. Mary Elizabeth b. 10/3/1843.
52. Esther Mariah b. 7/16/1845.
53. George Rossiter b. 5/31/1847.
54. Eleanor Adaline b. ca 1849.
55. Amanda b. 12/17/1851.
56. Emily b. 12/17/1851.
57. John Albert b. 10/31/1853.
58. Plummer b. 8/14/1858.

18. ISAAC PURVIANCE[3] (ESTHER[2], OWEN[1])

Isaac Purviance (1819-1898) married
Mar. 16, 1845 in Morgan County, Ohio, Hannah
Morgaridge and resided near Stockport, Ohio.
They had at least four children:

59. Mary E. b. 1847.
60. George H. b. 1853.
61. John A. b. 1859.
62. S. Ellsworth b. 1866.

20. MARTHA PURVIANCE[3] (ESTHER[2], OWEN[1])

Martha Purviance (1822-1904) married
in Jefferson County, Ohio Sept. 12, 1839
Amos M. Scott and removed to Morgan County,
Ohio. They had seven children:

Children: Scott

63. Isaac P. of Stockport, Ohio.
64. Esther E. m. Mr. Fox of Stockport, Ohio.
65. Anna Eliza m. Mr. Beach.
66. Martha J. m. Mr. Ellis of Pennsville, Ohio.
67. Amos M., Jr. of Roxbury, Ohio.
68. George B. of Stockport, Ohio.
69. Levi B. of Stockport, Ohio.

22. GEORGE W. PURVIANCE[3] (ESTHER[2], OWEN[1])

George W. Purviance (b. 1824) married
June 4, 1847 in Jefferson County, Ohio.
Dorcas Hopkins and had:

70. James C. b. 1848. (Probably others but
    names unknown.)

23. OWEN DEWEES PURVIANCE[3] (ESTHER[2], OWEN[1])

Owen D. Purviance (b. 1827) married
Eleanor_____(b. 1827) and had:

71. Richard b. 1851.
72. Harriet A. b. 1853.

73. Esther E. b. 1855.
74. Mary J. b. 1858.

26. NATHAN PURVIANCE[3] (ESTHER[2], OWEN[1])

Nathan Purviance (1834-1870) married
May 13, 1858 Henrietta Scott (b. 1841). She
was a daughter of William Scott. They had
issue:

75. William B. b. 1859.
76. Sarah E. b. 1861.
77. Cora J. b. 1865.
78. Anna B. b. 1867.
79. Lewis C. b. 1870.

28. OWEN· GRIMES[3] (HANNAH[2], OWEN[1])

Owen Grimes (1826-1916) married
Mar. 5, 1846 Delilah Rowland and had:

80. Benjamin (1847-1918) of Roxbury, Ohio.

Owen Grimes married second Alice Winn
(d. 1871) and had issue:

81. Charles
82. Mary Ella married Granville Plummer.
83. Anna married Thomas Hale.
84. George A.

Owen Grimes married third, Jan. 1, 1873
Sally Ann Petty (d. 1903) and had

85. Bertha b. May 30, 1874.
86. Samuel W.

31. ESTHER GRIMES[3] (HANNAH[2] OWEN[1])

Esther Grimes (1833-1870) married
Jan. 31, 1853 Alfred Burr (b. July 31, 1829).
He served in company C, 122 Ohio Infantry,
was wounded in the Battle of the Wilderness
May 6th and died June 1, 1864 and is buried
at Arlington Cemetery in grave 803. He was
a son of Wm. and Elizabeth (Moffett) Burr.
Esther Burr had great difficulty in
rearing her family but like many another
brave mother she met her trials with forti-
tude and succeeded in a fine way. Their
children were:

Children: Burr

87. Alcinda b. Mar. 11, 1854.
88. Emma S. b. 1856.
89. Warren 1858-1878 unm.
90. Clarence E. b. 1859 unm.

91. George Alfred b. Sept. 8, 1863.

36. DANIEL WILSON, JR.[3] (MARY[2], OWEN[1])

Daniel Wilson, Jr. (b. 1825) married Sept. 25, 1851 Martha Gregg daughter of Caleb and Millicent Gregg of Morgan County, Ohio. They removed to Pleasant Plain, Iowa in Apr. of 1853. They had

92. Caleb b. 1852.
(Names of other children unknown.)

41. SAMUEL DEWEES[4] (OWEN[3] SAM'L[2] OWEN[1])

Samuel Dewees (b. 1833) married May 15, 1853 in Athens County, Ohio Matilda Johnson (b. 1832) and had

93. Sarah A. b. 1854.
94. John F. b. 1857.
95. George W.

50. RACHEL ANN PURVIANCE (SAM'L[3], ESTHER[2], OWEN[1])

Rachel Purviance (1841-1918) married in Jefferson County, Ohio Aug. 25, 1859 Andrew McCain (1834-1874) and resided at Torch, Ohio. They had seven children:

Children: McCain

96. Addie 1861-1878.
97. Clara Belle - no issue.
98. Sarah Amelia m. Elmer Kemp.
99. John O. d. young.
100. Henrietta Elizabeth
101. Mary Melvina
102. Eliza Louella m. R. C. Sawyer, Vice Pres. of the Sinclair Oil Company and resides New York City.

51. MARY ELIZABETH PURVIANCE[4] (SAM'L[3], ESTHER[2], OWEN[1])

Mary Elizabeth Purviance (1843-1892) married Nov. 25, 1862 Lewis Ekey (1837-1915) and resided near Smithfield, Ohio. They had issue:

Children: Ekey

103. George McClelland Ekey b. 1864 unm.
104. Frank b. 1866.
105. Sarah Amelia b. 1869 unm.
106. Margaret b. 1872 unm.

52. ESTHER PURVIANCE[4] (SAM'L[3], ESTHER[2], OWEN[1])

Esther Purviance (1845-1906) married Nov. 25, 1862 William Milphard Walden (b. Dec. 6, 1838 and died May 13, 1918) in Jefferson County, Ohio. They removed to Athens County where they lived the rest of their lives. Although named "Esther" for her grandmother, Esther (DeWees) Purviance, she was called "Hester" and her name appears on the records as Hester Walden. She died Feb. 8, 1906 at Parkersburg, W. Va., with burial at Coolville, Ohio where they had resided many years. Their issue:

Children: Walden

107. John Samuel b. Mar. 31, 1864, married 1891 Hope Plumly and had issue.
108. Flora b. Jan. 26, 1867, married George Doan and had issue.
109. William Leroy b. Feb. 5, 1869, married 1891 Elizabeth Hope (41 Hope lineage).
110. Clara M. b. Feb. 2, 1871, and married Almond B. White - no issue.
111. Rachel E. 1874-1878.
112. George H. b. July 14, 1876 married 1900 Elizabeth Bentz and had issue.
113. Harry M. b. Aug. 11, 1885 married 1906 Emily Creesy and had issue.

54. ELEANOR A. PURVIANCE[4] (SAM'L[3], ESTHER[2], OWEN[1])

Eleanor Purviance (1849-1929) married Apr. 20, 1865 Nickolas Merryman (b. 1843) of near Smithfield, Ohio. She died Nov. 13, 1929. They had three children:

Children: Merryman

114. William O. b. 1871 in Nebraska.
115. George P. b. 1879 in Ohio.
116. Earl b. 1879 in Ohio.

55. AMANDA PURVIANCE[4] (SAM'L[3], ESTHER[2], OWEN[1])

Amanda Purviance (b. 1851) married Nathan Robers (b. 1844) and had issue:

Children: Roberts

117. Clarence b. 1870.
118. Lenna b. 1875.
119. Ella b. 1879.
120. Wylie

56. EMILY PURVIANCE[4] (SAM'L[3],
ESTHER[2], OWEN[1])

Emily Purviance (1851-1935) married
Mar. 30, 1875 in Jefferson County, Ohio
Albert Bargar (b. Mar. 5, 1852 and died
Mar. 12, 1927). They had three children:

Children: Bargar

121. Roscoe C. Bargar b. Jan. 27, 1876.
122. Cora Belle b. Dec. 13, 1877.
123. Mary Viola b. Jan. 3, 1880.

57. JOHN A. PURVIANCE[4]
(SAM'L[3], ESTHER[2], OWEN[1])

John Purviance (1853-1909) married in
Jefferson County, Ohio, Sept. 23, 1877 Anna
Brown. He died Apr. 5, 1909. Their issue:

124. Mabel (b. 1879) m. Mr. Deitrick.
125. Edward m. and had issue.
126. Ernest of Akron, Ohio.
127. Helen m. Mr. Beslsof Meredon, Conn.

58. PLUMMER PURVIANCE[4] (SAM'L[3],
ESTHER[2], OWEN[1])

Plummer Purviance (1858-1931) of
Smithfield, Ohio m. Mary Ong and had:

128. Orville of near Smithfield, Ohio.

87. ALCINDA BURR[4] (ESTHER[3],
HANNAH[2], OWEN[1])

Alcinda Burr (b. 1854) married
Sept. 12, 1875 Albert Allard and had issue:

Children: Allard

129. Ralph
130. Stella m. Geo. T. Capell of Columbus,
Ohio
131. Pearl d. young.

91. GEORGE ALFRED BURR[4],
(ESTHER[3], HANNAH[2], OWEN[1])

George Alfred Burr (b. 1863) married
Jan. 1, 1890 Virginia Hamlin (d. 1912) and
had issue:

132. Alfred H. b. Nov. 22, 1890.
Vanderbilt Univ. 1914. Lawyer and Sec.
Treas. of Wilson Stove Co., N. Little
Rock, Ark.

133. Laura m. Allen D. Stewart.
134. Edward E.--Artist-Musician--unm.

95. GEORGE W. DEWEES[5] (SAM'L[4],
OWEN[3], SAM'L[2], OWEN[1])

George Dewees, Merchant of Torch,
Ohio m. Ida M. Posey and had

135. Howard Arden b. Dec. 6, 1892.
136. Mabel m. Carl Kincade of Frost, Ohio.

98. SARAH AMELIA McCAIN[5] (RACHEL[4],
SAM'L[3], ESTHER[2], OWEN[1])

Sarah Amelia McCain married Elmer
Kemp and had

Children: Kemp

137. Ada Lenore m. Guy Morgan and had one son.

100. H. ELIZABETH McCAIN[5] (RACHEL[4],
SAM'L[3], ESTHER[2], OWEN[1])

Elizabeth McCain married August
Smith and resided in Beaumont, Tex. They had
one daughter:

138. Olive Augusta Smith--m. Ivar M. Bowles
of Houston, Tex. and had 4 children.

101. MARY M. McCAIN[5] (RACHEL[4],
SAM'L[3], ESTHER[2], OWEN[1])

Mary McCain married Henry Brewster
son of Sherman and Nancy (McLaughlin)
Brewster and resided variously at Torch, Ohio,
Weston, W. Va., and in Lakeland, Florida.
She died Feb. 29, 1936 in the South. Their
children were:

Children: Brewster

139. Frank McCain b. 1892.
140. Pauline m. Robert Pritchard of Weston,
W. Va., and had 3 children.
141. Virginia m. Ira Workman of Akron, Ohio.
142. John M. M.D., married Eleanor Fairfax
Clarke and resides in Washington, D.C.
143. Ruth m. Paul Given and had two children.
They reside in Washington, D.C.

135. HOWARD ARDEN DEWEES[6]
(GEORGE[5], SAM'L[4], OWEN[3],
SAM'L[2], OWEN[1])

Howard Dewees of Washington, D.C.

married and had issue

144. George Dewees.
145. Lyal Dewees.
146. Robert Dewees.

139. FRANK McCAIN BREWSTER⁶ (MARY⁵, RACHEL⁴, SAM'L³, ESTHER², OWEN¹)

Frank Brewster graduate of W. Va., Univ., 1917, served in World War--overseas July 1917 to June 1919 attaining the rank of 1st Lieut. of Ca. A., 15th U. S. Engineers. Pres. and General Manager of the Belmont Quadrangle Drilling Corp. and Pres. of the Otis Eastern Service Company of Bradford, Pa., 32nd degree Mason and Shriner, Beta Theta Pi, Scabbard and Blade, American Legion, Forty and Eight, Bradford Board of Commerce, Valley Hunt Club and Pennhills Golf Club. He married Apr. 5, 1921 Guinevere Chidester a daughter of John C. and Ida Chidester of Weston, W. Va. They have two children:

147. Frank, Jr., born July 24, 1922.
148. Ann b. Feb. 10, 1933.

DEWEES LINEAGE NOTES

Owen Dewees was a son of Cornelius Dewees (Jr.,) and his wife Margaret Richards and a grandson of Cornlius Dewees, Sr., and his wife Margaret Loftes (or Koster) and a great grandson of Garret Hendriks Dewees who came from Holland to Germantown, Pa., prior to Mar. 1, 1690. His mother Margaret Richards was a daughter of William and Elizabeth Richards of Berks County, Pa., and a grandaughter of Owen Richards who came from Merionethshire in Wales to Weaverstown, Berks County, Pa., in 1718.

THE NAME

Dewees is said to have originated as a surname in Holland about the twelfth century, meaning "the orphan" as Jan de wees (Jan the orphan).

LEE LINEAGE NOTES

Mary Lee Dewees was a daughter of Samuel Lee (1723-1802) and his wife Margaret Hughs (1726-1810) and a grandaughter of Anthony Lee (1679-1763) who came from Mansfield in Nottinghamshire in England 1701 and his wife Mary Whitacre (1694-1764) who was a daughter of Charles Whitacre of Berks County, Pa., and his first wife Sarah Baker. The latter came from England in 1684.

Margaret Hughs Lee (mother of Mary Lee Dewees) was a daughter of Ellis Hugh (1687-1764) and his wife Jane Foulke (1684-1766) and a grandaughter of John Hugh (1652-1736) who came from Merionethshire, Wales in 1698.

Jane Foulke Hugh was a daughter of Edward Foulke and his wife Eleanor Hugh (sister of John) who also came from Wales in 1698.

The lineage of Mary Lee Dewees through her great grandfather (John Hugh) and also her great grandmother (Eleanor Hugh Foulke) traces through seventeen generations to Meredith the last Prince of Powys, through twenty generations to John, King of England (1199 to 1216) and Isabella his queen, through twenty-six generations to Henry II Emperor of Germany (972-1024), through twenty-five generations to Duncan I of Scotland (see Shakespeare's Macbeth) and through twenty-six generations to William the Conqueror. Through early English royal lines, thirty-one generations to King Alfred the Great and thirty-three generations to Egbert, first king of all England, through Scottish royal lines of thirty-two generations to Kenneth MacAlpine first king of all Scotland.

The Foulke lineage is just as impressive tracing through sixteen generations to Rhivid Flaidd, Lord of Penllyn, twenty-four generations to Gryffyth ap Cynan, King of North Wales, other notable personages to whom descent can be traced are Maximus Magnus (Roman Emperor), Malcolm III of Scotland, Ferdinand III (king of Castile), Edward I, king of England, Rhodric Mawr, king of Wales and Charlemagne, emperor of France, Italy and Germany.

References on lineages:
  Dupuy Family -- Dupuy
  Merion in the Welsh Tract -- Glenn
  History of Gwynedd -- Jenkins
  Welsh Settlements of Pa. -- Browning
  Welsh Founders of Pa. -- Glenn
  In quisitions of Gloucestershire
  Compendium of American Genealogy -- Virkus
  Old Richland Families -- Roberts
  Families of Royal Descent -- Burke
  History of Wales -- Edwards
  Foulke Genealogical Tables -- Booth
  Quaker Memorials of Pa. and N. J.

1. DANIEL FRANCIS

Daniel Francis, a Frenchman native of the Isle of Guernsey, but a subject of Great Brittain, left a diary giving in brief the story of his journey from his native land and his wanderings after arriving in America. It is written quite legibly in French and is (in a somewhat free translation) as follows:

"We departed from Guernsey, the 21st of April 1806, for Jersey enroute to America. We arrived at Norfolk the 3rd of June after forty-three days passage. There we rested three days and then departed for Baltimore where we remained eleven days. We left for New York and arrived there the 24th of June.

We rested there eight days and then went to East Chester (now The Bronx, N.Y.) where we stayed until the 3rd of November 1809. Then we departed for Sempro for Sempronius in Cayuga Co., N.Y.), where we arrived after seventeen days (journey) and remained there until the 24th April 1813 when we departed for Niagara where we arrived after seven days' journey. We stayed there until the 18th of the month of May 1816, on which day we started for Hockhocking (valley) Ohio. We arrived there the 8th of June after seventeen days' passage.

(The next entry is six years' later), March 12, 1822.)

"We have quit our old farm in Canaan (township of Athens County, Ohio) to go about two miles above Athens."---"We have arrived the 21st of May 1826 at Stroud's Run in Canaan (township of Athens County, Ohio) where we stayed until the 27 April 1831.--- We departed for Homer (township of Morgan County, Ohio) where we remained until the 22 March 1832. Then we left there to go two miles above Athens where we remained until 23 June 1832 with William Six.---I came here the 12th April 1841 and remained until the first of October to go with Nicolas where I stayed until the 23rd April 1842." Here the chronicle ends! About forty pages of the diary have been cut out for some reason and lost to posterity.

The wife of Daniel Francis was Rachel whose surname has not come down to us. She died June 23rd, 1840 and is buried in Carbon Hill Cemetery. Another stone believed to be that of Daniel Francis has sunken into the ground with only the curved top of the slab showing above the surface. He was living Oct. 15, 1850 with his granddaughter Charlotte Francis Boyles of near Kimberly, Ohio and was then aged 92 years.

He left no will and no administration papers were filed in the County courts.

The family record written by Daniel Francis in his diary gives births as follows:

"I Daniel Francis was born the 23 June, 1759.

Rachel your mother was born 14 December 1756.

2. Rachel b. 30 Dec. 1782.
3. Suzanne b. 7 Nov. 1784.
4. Nicolas b. 10 Mar. 1787.
5. Elizabeth b. 19 July 1789.
6. Jean b. 24 Oct. 1790.
7. Judith b. 26 Oct. 1793.
8. Daniel b. 7 Sept. 1796.
9. Thomas b. 10 Dec. 1797.
10. Pierre b. 15 Sept. 1799.

Of Rachel and Suzanne nothing is known. They were probably married before their parents left Guernsey.

Likewise nothing is now known of Judith. She possibly married in New York state.

4. NICOLAS FRANCIS[2] (DANIEL[1])

Nicolas Francis (1787-1863) came with his parents to America in 1806 and to Ohio in 1816. He married 23 August 1817. Thankful Philips of Amesville, Ohio., she died prior to 1831 in Homer township of Morgan County.

Issue
11. Rachel Francis b. 1821.
12. Desire Francis b. 1825.
13. Dorsey - d. young.

Nicolas Francis remarried 16 Jan. 1831 in Washington County, Ohio Mercy Rathbun (1802-1891), a daughter of Gideon Rathbun.

They removed to what is now Carbon Hill in Ward township of Hocking County, Ohio where they resided until 1854 when they pushed westward into Jay County, Indiana. They lived there only a short time then went on into Iowa, stopping in Harrison County near Woodbine about 1856.

He died 28 May 1863 and is buried in Whitesborough Cemetery. Mercy Rathbun Francis died 19 March 1891 aged 89 years.

Issue
14. Thankful Francis b. April 26, 1832.
15. Laura Francis d. young.
16. Gideon Francis b. 1835.
17. Augusta Francis d. young.
18. Lucy Francis b. 1840.
19. Louisa Lucina Francis b. 1841.
20. Foster Francis b. 1845.

5. ELIZABETH FRANCIS[2] (DANIEL[1])

Elizabeth Francis (1789-1854) came with her parents to America. She married probably in New York state Mr. Brickley. Since there are no records of any Brickley administration or will in Athens County, it is assumed that he died in New York. She married second March 29, 1822 Ethan Beebe in Athens County Ohio where he died a few months later.

She removed with her parents about two miles Northwest of Athens in 1823, and there met a young widower by the name of William Six whom she married Sept. 2, 1824.

Record of any children is entirely lacking and it is believed that she had no issue by either marriage. Her neice Charlotte Francis lived with her for several years and was married from her home.

Elizabeth Francis Brickley Beebe Six died Jan. 4, 1854 and is buried near Kimberly, Ohio in what is now called the Boyles Cemetery.

6. JEAN FRANCIS[2] (DANIEL[1])

Jean Francis (1790-1870) never came to Ohio but remained in Cayuga County, New York. He married Jan. 25, 1820 in Owasco, Nancy Van Houten. In the census of 1860 his wife's given name is listed as Lydia so he was undoubtedly twice married.

He died March 4, 1870 and left a will naming his wife Lydia Francis and the following children:

21. Rachel Ann b. Apr. 26, 1826.
22. Nancy (married Mr. Marshall of Locke, N. Y.)
23. John of Chicago, Ill.
24. Hiram S. whose son was Judson F. Francis of New York, N. Y.

8. DANIEL FRANCIS[2] JR. (DANIEL SR[1].)

Daniel Francis Jr. (born 1796) was only twelve years of age when he came to this country with his parents. He married in Athens County Ohio Nov. 12, 1818 Martha Phillips a daughter of Daniel Phillips of near Amesville, Ohio. He was a farmer and owned two large tracts of land in the Northwest corner of Canaan township which he sold in 1832 and moved "west" ! Nothing further is known of him.

9. THOMAS FRANCIS[2] (DANIEL[1])

Thomas Francis (1797-1856) was the twenty-fourth alien to apply for Naturalization in Athens County, his first application being filed Oct. 9, 1823 and citizenship conferred Oct. 29, 1823.

He served as Marshall of Athens in 1832 and as councilman in 1834 to 1837.
He married Dec. 31, 1819 Polly Fulton who died about 1825.

Issue
25. Alexander b. ca 1820.
26. Daniel b. ca 1822.
27. Charles b. ca 1824.

He married second Dec. 2, 1826 Mrs. Elizabeth (Baker) Gray (b. 1801 in Mass.) the widow of Combs Gray and a daughter of Isaiah Baker.
Thomas Francis was killed Oct. 21, 1856 by falling off the first railroad bridge built in Athens County, having been employed on the project. Elizabeth Baker Gray Francis died June 11, 1886.
They are both buried in West State Street Cemetery at Athens, Ohio.

Issue (2nd marriage)

28. Charlotte b. 1827.
29. Minerva b. 1831.
30. Robert B. b. 1833 - d. young.
31. Thomas J. b. 1835.
32. Eben F. b. 1837.
33. Edward N. b. Aug. 2, 1838.
34. Mary A. b. June 23, 1840!
35. John Q. b. July 20, 1842.
36. William B. b. Mar. 20, 1844.

10. PIERRE FRANCIS[2] (DANIEL[1])

Pierre Francis (b. 1799) married in Athens County Feb. 10, 1823 Edith Cambe (or Camby). He purchased land in 1830, sold it in 1832 and is said to have moved "west." Nothing is known of his descendants.

11. RACHEL FRANCIS[3] (NICOLAS[2], DANIEL[1])

Rachel Francis (b. 1821) received a license to wed George Washington Pugsley son of James Pugsley June 10, 1841 and they were married shortly thereafter in Ward township of Athens County (now Hocking County, Ohio)
They removed to Harrison County Iowa in 1855 and kept a hotel at Woodbine. They had issue:

Children: Pugsley

37. Marcellus Pugsley b. 1842/3 in Ohio.
38. Georgiana b. 1846 in Ohio.
39. Francis C. b. 1848 in Ohio.

40. George b. 1850 in Ohio.
41. Charles b. 1852 in Ohio.
42. Laura b. 1856 in Iowa.
43. James R. b. 1859 in Iowa.

12. DESIRE FRANCIS[3] (NICOLAS[2], DAN'L[1])

Desire Francis (b. 1824) married July 30, 1843 Thomas Wilds (b. 1820 in Eng.) About 1855 they removed to Harrison County Iowa where they resided several years before moving to Kansas.

Children: Wilds

44. James b. 1845 in Ohio.
45. Maria F. b. 1851 in Ohio.
46. Mary b. 1856 in Iowa.
47. George W. b. 1860 in Iowa.
48. Rachel b. 1860 in Iowa.

14. THANKFUL FRANCIS (NICOLAS[2], DAN'L[1])

Thankful Francis (1832-1858) daughter of Nicolas Francis and his second wife Mercy Rathbun Francis, married June 24, 1852 Johnson Coe, (son of James Coe and descendant in the 8th generation from Robert Coe from England in 1634). He was born Nov. 5, 1826 and died Feb. 8, 1890.
Thankful Francis Coe died Aug. 19, 1858 leaving two small sons:

49. Gaston b. Sept. 2, 1853.
50. George b. 1857.

16. GIDEON FRANCIS[3] (NICHOLAS[2], DAN'L[1])

Gideon Francis (b. 1835) married Sarah Watson Tyndall. He removed to Oklahoma and died at McAlester. He had issue but only one name is known.

51. Ben

18. LUCY FRANCIS[3] (NICOLAS[2], DAN'L[1])

Lucy Francis (b. 1840) married ca 1859 Frank J. Porter (b. 1837 in Canada) and resided at Woodbine, Iowa.

Issue

Children: Porter

52. Emma b. 1860

53. Frances b. 1862.
54. Joseph b. 1863.
55. William b. 1865.
56. Edgar b. 1867.
57. Georgia b. 1870.

19. LOUISA LUCINA FRANCIS[3]
(NICOLAS[2], DAN'L[1])

Louisa Lucina Francis (b. 1841) married Amos Lawson and lived at Red Oak, Iowa. They are said to have had fifteen children but no names are available.

20. FOSTER FRANCIS[3]
(NICOLAS[2], DAN'L[1])

Foster Francis (b. 1845) married Emma Stevens and resided at Woodbine, Iowa. They had five children but only one name is available:

58. Joseph

21. RACHEL ANN FRANCIS[3]
(JEAN[2], DAN'L[1])

Rachel A. Francis (b. 1826 in N. Y.) married Daniel N. Curtis and lived at Moravia in Cayuga County, N. Y. She had one son

Children: Curtis

59. Frank S., (1855-1936) unm.

25. ALEXANDER FRANCIS[3]
(THOS[2], DAN'L[1])

Alexander Francis served in the Mexican war in the 2nd Ohio Infantry under Capt. Robert McLean and in Capt. Earharts' Company for which he received land warrant 5988. He married ca 1839.
Nancy _____(b. 1818 in Md.)
He died ca 1850 and his widow and children removed to Iowa in 1856.

Issue
60. Lucy b. 1840.
61. Julia b. 1842.
62. Charles b. 1844.
63. Melissa b. 1846.
64. Mary Ann b. 1848.

26. DANIEL FRANCIS[3] (THOS[2], DAN'L[1])

Daniel Francis (b. ca 1822) married Jan. 13, 1842 Eliza B. Conner and in 1860 was living in Summit County, Ohio. Names of issue unknown.

27. CHARLES FRANCIS[3] (THOS[2], DAN'L[1])

Charles Francis (b. ca 1824) was living in Fairfield County, Ohio in 1860. Nothing further is known of him.

28. CHARLOTTE FRANCIS[3] (THOS[2], DAN'L[1])

Charlotte Francis (b. 1827) married first May 14, 1843 Martin Boyles and lived near Nelsonville, Ohio. They removed to Illinois soon after their marriage, stayed there only a short time and returned to Ohio. In 1849 they went back to Illinois where he died about 1850.

She returned with her children to Ohio and July 19, 1855 married Elisha Benjamin (b. 1817).

Children: Boyles

Issue
65. Mary Elizabeth b. July 25, 1844 in Ill.
66. Minerva Boyles 1846-1861.
67. Charles A. b. 1848 in Ohio.
68. Martin b. 1850 in Ill.

69. Charlotte Benjamin b. 1856 in Ohio.
70. Jessie Florence Benjamin b. 1858 in Ohio.

29. MINERVA FRANCIS[3] (THOS.[2] DAN'L[1])

Minerva Francis (1831-1909) married 16 Oct. 1849 in Athens County, Ohio Joseph B. Eckley (1828-1902) and resided near Athens, Ohio.

Children: Eckley

Issue
71. Elizabeth b. 1852 - married Mr. Garnett and lived in Kansas.
72. Robert W. b. 1853 - married Miss Hawk.
73. Joseph Hadley (b. 1856) of Council Grove, Kansas.
74. Nettie Eckley b. 1861 - No issue.
75. Elma - went to Kansas.

33. EDWARD FRANCIS³ (THOS², DAN'L¹)

Edward Francis (b. 1838) blacksmith. Married 27 Feb. 1861 Sarah A. Walker (b. 1839) at Athens, Ohio.

Issue
76. Forrester (b. 1863) married Eliza Vore--no surviving issue.
77. Ethel married Harry Campbell--no issue.

36. WILLIAM B. FRANCIS³ (THOS²., DAN'L¹)

William B. (b. 1844) served in the Civil War and was for fifty years an engineer on the Hocking Valley railroad. He married Isabel_____ and resided at Athens, Ohio.

Issue
78. Warren married and had one daughter: Isabelle
79. Milly married L. Brown - no issue.

49. J. GASTON COE⁴ (THANKFUL³, NICOLAS², DAN'L¹)

Gaston Coe (1853-1915) farmer of near Nelsonville, Ohio., married April 13,

1877 Isabella Martin b. 1853 (daughter of Peter F. Martin) and had issue:

80. Celia married John T. Hope, Jr. See 43 - Hope lineage.
81. Letty married Mr. Hintz--no issue.

50. GEORGE COE⁴ (THANKFUL³, NICOLAS², DAN'L¹)

George Coe (b. ca 1857) resides near Chauncey, Ohio. He married Della Shaffer and had issue:

82. Olive Gertrude married Charles Daughterty and had issue.

THE NAME

The name Francis is a very common one signifying: the Frenchman as Daniel le Fraunceys (Daniel the Frenchman)

PIONEER FAMILIES
OF THE MIDWEST

By
BLANCHE L. WALDEN

2

FOREWORD

It is not the aim of this publication to furnish complete genealogies of the families presented, but rather to bridge the earlier records in order that descendants may trace their own lines without great difficulty. Each year time, fire and flood take their toll of our heritage of old Bible records, portraits, court records, etc., so it has been thought best to preserve these, left to us, for future generations.

In each of the family histories included in this series, the pioneer father is given the number 1, the eldest child is number 2, the second child is number 3, etc., so each individual member of a family has a number given only to one member of that family. Thus it is a very simple matter for a descendant to trace his line back to the pioneer by following the numbering. His parent's number appears as the head of a family and again as a child on an earlier page, his grandparent will head the family in which his parent's name appears as a child, etc.

Abbreviations used with meanings are:

b. - born	m. married
d. - died	unm. - unmarried
d.y. - died young	ca - about
d. in inf. - died in infancy	

The compiler wishes to here express gratitude to all those who have so graciously aided and made possible this publication by supplying data from records in their possession and especially to Hattie May Rice, Grace E. Jenison, Jennie Coe Jordan, Letty Coe Hintz, Augusta True, Mary Gardner Jones and Eva Davis Appelquist for their invaluable contributions of family records and portraits.

B. L. Walden

TABLE OF CONTENTS

23. Aaron Smith   22. Lavinia Smith   25. Sarah Smith

24. Eli Smith, Jr.   6. Eli Smith   28. Solomon Smith

29. Rhoda Smith   30. William R. Smith   26. Elizabeth Smith

1. THADDEUS SMITH

Thaddeus Smith was born May 6, 1742 (O.S.) in Amwell, Hunterdon County, New Jersey.

While the British were on Staten Island he was drafted to serve a term of one month in Capt. John Phillips' company, Col. Chambers' regiment in the War of the American Revolution.

He joined the forces at a place called Blazing Star and served one month, at the end of which term he reenlisted at Ringold's Tavern in Hunterdon county and was one of those designated to commandeer all boats on the river, in which to ferry General Washington's army across the Delaware. This expedition was in command of General Putnam.

Thaddeus Smith served, in all, more than a year and was in the battle of Princeton during which engagement, his middle finger was shot away. He stated in his application for a pension that he "well remembered seeing General Washington, General Putnam and Lord Sterling."

He likewise asserted that his birth was recorded in his family Bible which had been his father's bible, at whose home he resided when called into service and until May of 1803 when he removed to Shamokin on the Susquehanna River.

On May 7, 1804 he purchased a home there in Northumberland County where he resided for several years.

He next removed to the Cheat River valley and located in Springhill township of Fayette County, Penn, where he was residing when the 1810 census was taken.

Another change in residence came prior to 1820 with his removal to Mill Creek in Virginia (probably across the Ohio river from the Marietta settlement). While living in the latter location, two of the younger children are said to have died during an epidemic.

In the spring of 1829 he went to Rutland in Meigs County, Ohio where he was living Oct. 2, 1832 when granted a pension for his war service.

About 1834 he removed to Franklin County, Ind. where he died Apr. 12, 1839 with burial in Cedar Grove, an old burial ground eight miles south of Brookville.

Thaddeus Smith married in 1782 Ann Hise, a daughter of George Cosper Hise (d. 1801) of Amwell, Hunterdon County, N. J.

In her application for a soldier's widow's pension she stated that they were married by William Abbot, Esq., that there were several guests present and that they danced after the wedding.

She was born about 1752 and died in 1845 aged 93 years.

The children of Thaddeus and Anne (Hise) Smith were:

2. Nancy Smith b. July 20, 1783.
3. Benjamin Smith b. Jan. 1, 1787.

4. Zophar Smith b. Oct. 12, 1789.
5. Samuel Smith b. May 16, 1792.
6. Eli Smith b. Oct. 20, 1794.
7. Elizabeth Smith b. Dec. 20, 1800.
8. Ora Smith b. Dec. 10, 1802.
9. Jonathan Waters Smith b. Oct. 21, 1804.

2. NANCY SMITH[2] (THADDEUS[1])

Nancy Smith (1783-1835) married probably
in Northumberland County, Penn. about 1805
Peter Updike (b. 16 June 1786 near Reading,
Penn. and d. Mar. 25, 1861 in Franklin County,
Ind.).

They removed from Pennsylvania to
Franklin County, Ind. where she died June 4,
1835 and they are both buried in Big Cedar
cemetery eight miles east of Brookville, Ind.
Their children were:
10. Isaac Updike b. May 10, 1807.
11. Samuel Smith Updike b. June 5, 1810.
12. John S. Updike b. Mar. 12, 1813.
13. Delilah Updike b. Jan. 15, 1815.
14. Anne Updike b. Nov. 6, 1816.
15. Elijah Updike b. Aug. 4, 1818.
16. Harrison Updike b. Oct. 3, 1820.
17. Virgil McCracken Updike b. Aug. 31, 1822.
18. Aaron F. Updike b. July 8, 1824.
19. Ruth Updike 1830 - 1836.

3. BENJAMIN SMITH[2] (THADDEUS[1])

Benjamin Smith (b. 1787) married in
Pennsylvania ca 1810 Elizabeth _____.
They removed to Belmont County, Ohio where
they resided many years. They are said to
have later gone to Indiana but exact place
and date of emigration are unknown.

Several children were born to this union
but the name of only one is available;
20. Mary Ann Smith b. 28 Oct. 1815.

5. SAMUEL SMITH[2] (THADDEUS[1])

Samuel Smith (b. 1792) wheelwright by
trade, married ca 1814 Lutitia Updike a
daughter of Isaac Updike, in Fayette County,
Penn. They removed, by flatboat, down the
Ohio River to Franklin County, Ind. about
1817 and settled in Springfield township.
They had a large family but the names of only
three are available:
21. William Smith b. ca 1817 in Penn.
21A. Samuel Smith b. ca 1819 in Ind.
21B. Benjamin Smith b. 2 May 1825 in Ind.

6. ELI SMITH[2] (THADDEUS[1])

Eli Smith (1794 - 1885) married in 1812
Elizabeth Rouanzoin (1793-1833) in Fayette

County, Penn. They removed to Morgan County,
Ohio in the year of 1821 settling in Penn
township.

Elizabeth Rouanzoin Smith never liked the
new location and expressed a desire to return
to the old home in Pennsylvania many times.
Her husband finally promised her that he would
agree to go back if she would try to like the
Ohio country and stay just one year longer,
then if she still desired to return he would
go.

She died however before the year was up
and was buried in a field near the house.
Later others were buried there and it became
a cemetery which is now called Westland
cemetery. The stones and fence surrounding
their burial place have disintegrated and the
exact location is not now known. According to
the obituary of Eli Smith, his first wife died
in 1833. Very little is known about her, but
of one thing we are certain, she loved pretty
clothes and bright colors. Her dresses were
made up, by her daughters, into woolen com-
forts and one of them is still in possession
of a great grandaughter. There is a great
variety of colors and weaves which presumably
she carded, spun, dyed and wove the yarn from
which they were made herself.

In 1834 Eli C. Smith married second
Mrs. Ellen Corner Quigley Warner (d. Mar. 8,
1872). She was born and reared in England
and came to America with her first husband
soon after their marriage. A graphic story
is related in the History of Morgan County
(Ohio) of how she with her husband and a large
dog succeeded in treeing a huge bear. They
had no gun so she and the dog stood guard and
kept the bear in the tree while Mr. Quigley
walked three miles to their nearest neighbor
and borrowed a gun with which to shoot the
bear and then walked back.

The tree, an immense walnut, was later
felled and some enterprising citizens made
furniture to sell. There seems to be no
record of the size of it but such quantities
of furniture were said to have been made
from the wood that it must have been a very
large tree indeed!

Eli C. Smith died Nov. 23, 1885 aged 93
years, one month and eight days according to
his death record and also to the grave stone
inscription.

That is open to question however since
the record from his father's family Bible
gives his date of birth as Oct. 20, 1794,
which would make him aged 91 years, 1 month
and 13 days. Eli C. Smith made his mark on
legal documents and evidently could not write,
if he ever had a family record written down,
it was lost in one of the three fires which

destroyed his dwelling places at various times.

From his obituary we learn that he was a member of the Disciple Church for seventy years. "He never became discouraged concerning the work in the church; he always had a word of encouragement for all his brethren. No matter how inclement the weather would seem to be, he was always in his seat at Lord's day meeting.

We believe he was the most untiring Disciple we ever knew. He has frequently traveled 40 or 50 miles to meeting in our reformatory movement."

One of the Ministers of the Wolf Creek Church said of him:

"I knew Father Smith well. I became acquainted with him while holding meetings for the Wolf Creek Church in recent years. I scarcely ever missed him from the meetings. His presence, his heroic faith and his ever-cheerful spirit were an inspiration to me.

He loved everybody and everybody seemed to love him and to esteem him very highly. Seventy years a member of the church and during all this time never faltered, never grew weary in well-doing, never framed an excuse in order to shirk personal responsibilities.

What a grand record - what a noble Christian race he run. Four generations rise up to call him "blessed"! He was a tower of religious and moral strength in the community where he spent the greater part of his life, and when he fell, it was like the falling of a tall and majestic pine in the forest. He has been gathered to his fathers and his works follow him.

He told me that he never experienced a day of sickness in all his lifetime. He did not rust out, he wore out. The last time I saw him some twenty-seven months ago, he walked with the rest of the company with the quick movements of a boy. A grand old man was Eli Smith!

In appearance he was tall and powerfully built and in his later years at least wore a high silk hat, frock or Prince Albert coat and when the roads were good, he drove four horses to his carriage.

Much of his traveling however was done by horseback due to the poor roads in the county.

He died of a stroke of apoplexy from which he never rallied although he lived almost four days.

He is buried in the Wolf Creek Church yard.

The children of Eli C. Smith and his first wife Elizabeth Rouanzoin were:

22. Lavinia Smith b. 19 March 1913 in Penn.
23. Aaron Smith b. 1 Jan. 1815 in Penn.
24. George Washington Smith b. 1817 in Penn.
25. Sarah Smith b. 9 June 1819 in Penn.
26. Elizabeth Ann Smith b.   1821 in Penn.
27. Eli Smith Jr. b. ca 1823 in Ohio.
28. Solomon Smith b. ca 1825 in Ohio.
29. Rhoda Smith b. 15 Sept. 1827 in Ohio.
30. William R. Smith b. 17 Mar. 1829 in Ohio.
31. Samuel Smith b. and d. ca 1831 in Ohio.

Eli Smith had one son by his second wife Ellen (Corner) Smith:
32. Arthur F. Smith b. 1837 - married 1857 Susan Barrel but had no issue.

10. ISAAC UPDIKE[3] (NANCY[2], THADDEUS[1])

Isaac Updike (b. 1807) married Jan. 1, 1826 Jerusha Tharp by whom he had at least two children:
33. Wesley Updike
34. Joseph Updike

11. SAMUEL UPDIKE[3] (NANCY[2], THADDEUS[1])

Samuel Updike (1810-1834) married Mary Bright by whom he had at least one son. Samuel Updike died Mar. 2, 1834.
35. Levi Updike - lived in Texas

12. JOHN S. UPDIKE[3] (NANCY[2], THADDEUS[1])

John S. Updike (1813-1845) married Jan. 27, 1836 Amy Smith (d. 1837) and resided at Hamilton, Ohio. There was one daughter by this marriage:
36. Martha J. Updike b. 28 Dec. 1836.
John Updike married second ca 1838 Mary Ann _____ (d. 1845) and had three children:
37. Nancy Updike b ca 1839.
38. Henry Updike b. ca 1841.
39. Peter F. Updike b. 25 Sept. 1843.

13. DELILAH UPDIKE[3] (NANCY[2], THADDEUS[1])

Delilah Updike (1815-1842) married Jan. 28, 1836 Joel Tucker and had at least one son:
40. William Wesley Tucker 1842-1859.
There were probably other children.

14. ANN UPDIKE[3] (NANCY[2], THADDEUS[1])

Ann Updike (b. 1816) married Dec. 28, 1837 William Alexander and had seven children:
41. Kate Alexander
42. Nancy Alexander m. George Proctor and had twin sons.
43. Peter Alexander b. 18 Feb. 1840 - in Butler County, Ohio

45. George Alexander.
46. Thomas J. Alexander m. Ann George and
had one daughter.
47. William J. Alexander m. twice and had
issue.
48. Sarah Alexander m. B. F. Armstrong.

15. ELIJAH UPDIKE³ (NANCY², THADDEUS¹)

Elijah Updike (1818-1893) married in
1842 Ruth Wallace but there was no issue by
this marriage. He married second Mrs.
Matilda (Gilbreath) Luce and had three
children:
49. William Gilbreath Updike d. 1930.
50. Mollie Updike m. Mr. Shera and had one
son.
51. Frank M. Updike m. and had one son.

16. HARRISON UPDIKE³ (NANCY², THADDEUS¹)

Harrison Updike (b. 1820) married Dec.
10, 1842 Catherine Thurston and had eight
children:
52. Peter Updike.
53. Aaron Updike.
54. Emeline Updike m. Mr. Carson.
55. William Updike.
56. John W. Updike.
57. Sarah A. Updike.
58. Albert Updike.
59. Mary J. Updike.

17. VIRGIL M. UPDIKE³ (NANCY², THADDEUS¹)

Virgil McCracken Updike (1822-1859)
married Oct. 16, 1844 at Brookville, Ind.
Ruth Ann Sithen (b. Aug. 20, 1821 in N. J.
and d. Aug. 18, 1879 near Castana, Monona
County, Iowa.
They had eight children all born near
Brookville, Ind.
60. Emily Updike b. July 9, 1845.
61. Margaret Updike b. Nov. 13, 1846.
62. Monroe Updike (1848-1935) married Julia
Scott and had five children. Resided at
Halfway, Oreg.
63. Isaac W. Updike b. 12 Aug. 1849.
64. Semuel M. Updike b. 17 Feb. 1851.
65. John M. Updike b. 29 Aug. 1853.
66. Clarissa Elizabeth Updike b. 25 Feb. 1856.
67. Aaron Updike 1857-1892 unm.

18. AARON F. UPDIKE³ (NANCY², THADDEUS¹)

Aaron F. Updike (1824-1899) married
Sarah Stewart in 1847 and had seven children:
68. Elijah Updike.
69. Nancy Updike.
70. Mary Updike.
71. Martha Updike.

72. Victoria Updike.
73. Florence Updike.
74. Alice Updike.

20. MARY ANN SMITH³ (Benj.², THADDEUS¹)

Mary Ann Smith (1815-1905) married Dec.
31, 1835 Joseph Carter (b. Feb. 14, 1814) and
resided near Boston, Belmont County, Ohio.
They had ten children:
75. Thomas B. Carter b. 3 Mar. 1837.
76. James H. Carter b. 4 Dec. 1838.
77. Sarah A. Carter b. 20 Dec. 1840.
78. Fenton M. Carter b. 10 Apr. 1843, killed
in the Civil War 1864.
79. Samuel Carter 1845-1846.
80. Charlotte Carter 1847-1857.
81. John M. Carter b. 8 June 1849.
82. William B. Carter b. 4 Mar. 1852.
83. Ruth H. Carter b. 16 Apr. 1854.
84. Francis N. Carter b. 22 Oct. 1858.

21. WILLIAM SMITH³ (SAMUEL², THADDEUS¹)

William Smith (b. 1816) married
Delilah_____ and resided near Westport,
Ind. They had nine children:
85. Sarah Ellen Smith b. 23 Mar. 1835.
86. Samuel Oliver Smith b. 26 Feb. 1837.
87. David Milton Smith b. 26 June 1839.
88. Margaret Samantha Smith b. 18 Sept. 1841.
89. William Harrison Smith b. 19 May 1844.
90. John Wesley Smith b. 3 Apr. 1846.
91. Druzilla Angeline Smith b. 18 Aug. 1848.
92. Amanda Lutitia Smith b. 23 Sept. 1850.
93. Catherine Mary Smith b. 17 May 1853.

22. LAVINIA SMITH³ (ELI², THADDEUS¹)

Lavinia Smith (1813-1875) married first
Sept. 15, 1830 James Hummel (b. May 7, 1809
and d. Sept. 2, 1851) shoemaker and farmer of
near Malta, Ohio.
They had eleven children:
94. Isaac Hummel b. 22 Nov. 1831.
95. Julia Ann Hummel b. 22 Feb. 1833.
96. Elizabeth Hummel b. 15 Mar. 1834.
97. Sarah Hummel b. 23 Mar. 1836.
98. Ellen Hummel b. 10 July 1838.
99. Mary Hummel b. 20 Mar. 1840.
100. William Hummel b. 6 June 1841.
101. Martha Jane Hummel b. 30 Jan. 1844.
102. Solomon Hummel b. 11 Aug. 1845.
103. Alfred Hummel b. 16 May 1847.
104. Lewis T. Hummel b. 2 July 1849.
Lavinia Smith Hummel married second 1862
John F. Moody (1830-1915) a widower with four
small boys whom she reared to manhood.
She died Jan. 26, 1875 and is buried in
Wolf Creek cemetery.

23. AARON SMITH[3] (Eli[2], THADDEUS[1])

Aaron Smith (1815-1895) married Aug. 13, 1835 Eliza Newhouse (b. 10 Mar. 1817 in Westmoreland County, Penn. and d. Apr. 6, 1887 in Montgomery County, Iowa).

They resided in Morgan County, Ohio where their ten oldest children were born. He owned a farm but likewise operated a traveling community store business. He would drive a buggy or wagon and team of horses to Zanesville and buy a supply of drygoods and other staple articles and sell to the people through the country who were without transportation facilities.

He worked at salt wells and cut timber at the meager wages of thirty-seven cents a day. In the spring of 1853 he decided to go west where he could obtain cheap land. A large covered wagon was secured for the trip to which he hitched his team of horses. The furniture and personal possessions were all loaded and the family packed into the crevices, the whip cracked and the Smith family started on their journey westward. As the wagon rolled out of the yard, someone looked back and saw little Bartlett aged five eyars sitting on the otherwise deserted porch. They called for him to "come on" but he sat still, "I don't want to go way out west and live on corn bread" he wailed.

They traveled by land to Cincinnati where they loaded everything on a boat (the Silas Wright) and floated down the Ohio to the Mississippi river. The day before they reached the latter river the boat sprung a leak and all aboard had to help bail water all night. In the morning they transferred to the "Franklin Pierce" which succeeded in landing them safely at Davenport, Iowa, May 5, 1853.

From there they proceeded overland to what is now Olive township in Clinton County, Iowa where Aaron Smith purchased a farm of 160 acres. There was no house on the land so he bought a hewn log house some three miles distant and moved it by hitching 26 yoke of oxen to it. The house was very heavy and the great chains broke again and again but at length it was moved, and ready for occupancy. Later he added to the structure and had a nice seven room house.

There were no schools so he hired a teacher and had a school in an upstairs room for his own large family and some neighbor children. Five years later (1858) a stone school house was built near by and still stands. Only recently it was abandoned at which time the district was consolidated with the Calamus schools. It was long used for community singing and writing schools, for church and Sunday school.

In due course of time five more little Smiths were added to the family circle. When the baby was nine months old and the youngest boy aged four, they contracted Scarlet fever from the effects of which the boy died seven years later and the baby left deaf.

In 1858 Aaron Smith turned over his farm to his son James and daughter Sarah and removed to Dewitt, Iowa where he operated a hotel called the Pacific House and likewise conducted a mercantile business.

In 1872 they with their children: Purley, James, Hiram and Sarah and their families removed to Cherokee County, Iowa where John and Bartlett were already located. About 1875 Aaron and Eliza Smith went to Montgomery County where they remained until her death in 1887. He then returned to Cherokee County and made his home with his son Purley until his death which occurred May 7, 1895.

On their fiftieth wedding anniversary the citizens of their home town, Elliott, Iowa gave a picnic at Baxter Hall and sent the band to escort them and their relatives to the hall. Among the many gifts presented was $101.00 in gold.

They were devoted to their church and reared their children to revere it. A daughter Sarah had an excellent voice and always led the singing. One winter evening while the others were awaiting their arrival they heard sleighbells and said: "here come the Smiths" but the Smiths didn't come right then, they went on by the church for a long ride - the team was running away!

Aaron and Eliza Smith were of that vast multitude who formed the backbone of our nation. They not only built roads and houses, cleared the land and started schools and churches in the great midwest, they likewise reared up their children to be worthy citizens of the nation which they helped build. Their issue:

105. John McLain Smith b. 14 Feb. 1837.
106. Elizabeth Smith b. 26 Mar. 1838.
107. Sarah Emily Smith b. 6 May 1840.
108. Margaret Smith b. 22 Aug. 1842.
109. Eli Henry Smith b. 28 Jan. 1844.
110. James K. Polk Smith b. 2 Dec. 1845.
111. Purley Winfield Smith b. 5 Mar. 1847.
112. Bartlett Sargent Smith b. 19 Mar. 1848.
113. Georjane (Jennie) Smith b. 14 Jan. 1850.
114. George A. Smith b. 9 July 1851.
115. Hiram Smith b. 1 Sept. 1853.
116. Eliza Ellen Smith b. 16 Aug. 1855.
117. Annis Janette Smith b. 25 Aug. 1858.
118. Harvey Simeon Smith 1860-1871.

119. Rhoda Anna Smith b. 16 Nov. 1863.

24. G. WASHINGTON SMITH³ (ELI², THADDEUS¹)

George Washington Smith (b. 1817 in Penn.) married about 1840 Sarah Tanner (b. 1822 in Ohio) and resided in Morgan County, until about 1863 when they removed to Davis County, Iowa and settled in Bloomfield township.

He was a large man and resembled his brother Aaron in appearance.

The children of Washington and Sarah (Tanner) Smith were:

120. Margaret Smith b. 1841 in Ohio.
121. Ellen Smith b. 1843 in Ohio.
122. David Smith b. 1845 in Ohio.
123. Eli Smith b. 1847 in Ohio.
124. Henry Smith b. 1849 in Ohio.
125. John W. Smith b. 1851 in Ohio.
126. Elizabeth A. Smith b. 1853 in Ohio.
127. Noah Smith b. 1856 - drowned 1860.
128. Lavinia Smith b. 1858 in Ohio.
129. Amanda Smith b. 1860 in Ohio.
130. Maria E. Smith b. 1864 in Ohio.

25. SARAH SMITH³ (Eli², THADDEUS¹)

Sarah (Sally) Smith (1819-1894) married Jan. 30, 1845 Isaac Raney (1809-1862) and had by him three children:

131. Lavinia Raney 1845-1882, m. James Earich.
132. Elizabeth Raney 1848-1867 - no issue.
133. Eli Asberry Raney 1853-1923 - m. Laura Thompson. See Vol. 1 p. 9 for Raney descendants.

Sarah Smith Raney married second John Kelly but had no issue.

26. ELIZABETH A. SMITH³ (ELI², THADDEUS¹)

Elizabeth (Betty) Ann Smith (b. 1821) married Mar. 8, 1842 in Morgan County, Ohio, Josiah Bartlett Sargent (b. 1818 in Ohio) and resided there several years. In the late eighteen-fifties they removed to Greeley, Iowa where they were living when the 1860 census was taken. At that time the mother of Bartlett Sargent resided with them, her name was Lucretia Sargent aged then 76 years and her place of birth the state of Maine.

Bartlett and Betty (Smith) Sargent had five children all of whom were born in Ohio:

134. Lucretia Sargent b. 1843, m. Mr. Lull - no issue.
135. Marcellus Sargent b. 1846.
136. John Sargent b. 1849 } twins
137. Serena Sargent b. 1849 } twins
138. Newton Rathbun Sargent b. 1853 - unm.

27. ELI SMITH³ (ELI², THADDEUS¹)

Eli Smith (b. ca 1823) married May 22, 1845 Margaret Smith and is said to have removed to Iowa.

A letter from him to his sister Rhoda revealed that he later lived in the "Black Hills" country, presumably South Dakota. Later in life he went to California where the picture of him, included in this volume, was taken at Santa Monica with his brother Solomon.

Eli Smith had a number of children but their names are unknown.

28. SOLOMON SMITH³ (ELI², THADDEUS¹)

Solomon Smith (b. ca 1825) married in Morgan County, Ohio July 3, 1845 Lethinda Newman (b. 1827) a daughter of George Newman who came to Ohio from Maryland.

About 1853 Solomon Smith went to Iowa but his family remained in Ohio until they were grown and resided with Mr. Newman. Solomon Smith went from Iowa to Emporia, Kan. and late in life to California where he died. His children were:

139. Alexander Smith 1847-1931 of Montequma, Ia.
140. Harrison Smith b. June 1849 in Ohio.
141. Asbury Smith b. 2 Nov. 1850 - no issue.
142. James Bartlett Smith b. 1852.
143. Susannah Smith b. 1854.

29. RHODA SMITH³ (ELI², THADDEUS¹)

Rhoda Smith (1827-1912) married Jan. 16, 1848 James R. Boal (b. 3 Feb. 1823 and d. Oct. 28, 1909) a son of John and Anna (Rainey) Boal of Perry County, Ohio.

They resided on a farm near Malta, Ohio and were faithful members of the Wolf Creek Christian church which he served as elder for many years. He was a man of great faith and unusually tolerant of the shortcomings of his fellowman. He never failed to "return thanks" before each meal in such a reverent and impressive voice that all who sat with him had a feeling of reverence and of actual presence.

James and Rhoda Boal lived their religion. While they had only two children of their own they took and reared a number of orphans. Their children were:

144. Mary Ellen Boal b. 17 Nov. 1848.
145. Eli Smith Boal, b. 24 Sept. 1850.
    m. 1872 Emeline Sanders and had Alva, Almeda and Ethel Boal. He married second in 1889 Clara Eyman and had Carried M. Boal. (See Vol. 1 p. 22 and 27 for their descendants.

30. WILLIAM R. SMITH³ (ELI², THADDEUS¹)

William R. Smith (1829-1917) farmer of near Malta, O. married Oct. 30, 1851 Jane Newman (b. 27 Oct. 1829 and died Jan. 28, 1924).

In 1901 William and Jane Smith celebrated their Golden Wedding anniversary in traditional fashion. Over two hundred guests, a band and several speakers assembled that golden autumn day upon the large lawn surrounding the commodious old farmhouse renewing acquaintances and drinking from the old windlass well which had once belonged to their grandsire, Eli Smith.

Death came for Uncle Billy (as he was known to hundreds) on Dec. 30, 1917. Aunt Jane survived him six years. They had nine children:
146. Florence A. Smith 1853-1854.
147. Seth A. Smith b. 10 Dec. 1855.
148. Mary M. Smith b. 8 July 1857.
149. Solomon F. Smith b. 14 Apr. 1859.
150. Eli W. Smith b. 30 Nov. 1861.
151. Charles Edward Smith b. ca 1868.
152. Clarence E. Smith } b ca 1872
153. Clara E. Smith
154. Sarah Smith b. 1875, m. Harrison Parker. No issue.

41. KATE ALEXANDER⁴ (ANN³, NANCY², THADDEUS¹)

Kate Alexander married Rev. Jan Patrick and had at least two daughters:
155. Nancy Ann Patrick.
156. Sarah Jane Patrick.

43. PETER ALEXANDER⁴(ANN³, NANCY², THADDEUS¹)

Peter Alexander (1840-1925) married Nov. 24, 1864 Jane Proctor and had four children:
157. Anna Alexander m. Mr. Armstrong.
158. Mary Alexander m. Mr. Graybill.
159. Ida B. Alexander m. Mr. Earlewine.
160. Albert Alexander, was a shoe dealer.

45. GEORGE ALEXANDER⁴(ANN³, NANCY², THADDEUS¹)

George Alexander married Jane Pedigrew and had at least two daughters:
161. Molly Alexander m. Mr. Ketcham.
162. Lovella Alexander m. Mr. Armstrong.

49. WM. GILBREATH UPDIKE⁴ (ELIJAH³, NANCY², THADDEUS¹)

William Gilbreath Updike (d. Jan. 31, 1930) of near Westport, Ind. married and had two children:

163. Charles C. Updike of Indianapolis, Ind.
164. Mabel Updike m. Mr. Rehm of St. Paul, Ind.

60. EMILY UPDIKE⁴ (VIRGIL³, NANCY², THADDEUS¹)

Emily Updike (1845-1925) married Jasper Pattisson of Indiana and had six children but only one name is available. She died Oct. 27, 1925 at Modesto, Calif.
165. Frank Pattisson.

61. MARGARET UPDIKE⁴(Virgil³, NANCY², THADDEUS¹)

Margaret Updike (1846-1906) married William Patrick and had eight children, but one name available. She died Dec. 8, 1906 in Ute, Iowa.
166. Carrie Patrick.

63. ISAAC W. UPDIKE⁴ (VIRGIL³, NANCY², THADDEUS¹)

Isaac W. Updike (1849 - living 1940) farmer married Nov. 3, 1878 Jennie Crispin of Modesto, Calif., and had three children:
167. Estella Updike b. 7 Aug. 1879.
168. Virgil C. Updike b. 4 Nov. 1884 m. and had issue.
169. Grace A. Updike b. 5 Oct. 1890.

64. SAMUEL M. UPDIKE⁴ (VIRGIL³, NANCY², THADDEUS¹)

Samuel M. Updike (1851-1936) of Modesto, Calif., married Feb. 19, 1897 Christine Patron and had a son:
170. Joseph Updike.

65. JOHN M. UPDIKE⁴(VIRGIL³, NANCY², THADDEUS¹)

John M. Updike (1853-1934) married Mrs. Scott and resided at Modesto, Calif. They had one daughter:
171. Alice Updike.

66. CLARISSA E. UPDIKE⁴ (VIRGIL³, NANCY², THADDEUS¹)

Clarissa Elizabeth Updike (1856-1933) married in Iowa, Charles D. Butler and removed to Modesto, Calif. They had two children, names not given.

75. THOMAS B. CARTER⁴ (MARY A.³, BENJ²., THAD¹)

Thomas B. Carter (1837-1917) married Mar. 11, 1858 Nancy Finley and resided at Newark, Ohio, where he died Aug. 2, 1917. They had several children among whom were:
172. Elmer C. Carter.
173. Alice Carter m. Mr. Golden of Hemlock, O.

174. Clara Carter m. Mr. Beck of Los Angeles, Calif.

76. JAMES H. CARTER⁴ (Mary A.³, BENJ²., THAD¹.)

James H. Carter (1838-1912) of McConnellsville, Ohio, married Oct. 11, 1867 Harriet Lyne and had two sons:
175. Harry F. Carter of near Malta, Ohio.
176. John W. Carter of McConnellsville, Ohio

77. SARAH A. CARTER⁴ (MARY A.³, BENJ²., THAD¹.)

Sarah A. Carter (1840-1923) married Oct. 22, 1863 William Erwin of McConnelsville, Ohio and had issue:
177. John D. Erwin, b. 1864.
178. Minnie Erwin - d. y.
179. Joseph C. Erwin of Columbus, Ohio.

81. JOHN M. CARTER⁴ (MARY A.³, BENJ²., Thad¹.)

John M. Carter (b. 1849) married Jan. 21, 1872 Josephine Barnes who died Dec. 3, 1872. He later married Linda Bennett who died May 10, 1935. They resided at Cambridge, Ohio where he died Mar. 28, 1932.

82. WILLIAM B. CARTER⁴ (MARY A.³, BENJ²., THAD¹.)

William B. Carter (1852-1905) of Newark, Ohio. He married Martha Bishop and had three sons:
180. Ray Carter.
181. Lloyd Carter.
182. Truman Carter.

83. RUTH H. CARTER⁴ (MARY A.³, BENJ²., THAD¹.)

Ruth H. Carter (1854-1911) married Nov. 23, 1874 R. L. Burcher of near Malta, Ohio. She died there Jan. 20, 1911. They had four children:
183. Albert Burcher b. 6 Apr. 1876.
184. Ethel Burcher m. Mr. Glass and 2nd- Mr. Head.
185. Mary Burcher m. Mr. Slaughter of Chicago.
186. Montford Burcher, deceased.

84. FRANCIS N. CARTER⁴ (Mary A.³, BENJ²., THAD¹.)

Frank N. Carter (b. 1858) lived in Milwaukee and Cedar Rapids, Iowa. He married May 10, 1881 Stella Ryan and had at least two children:
187. Emmett Carter.
188. Ruth Carter.

86. SAMUEL O. SMITH⁴ (WM.³, SAM'L², THADDEUS¹)

Samuel Oliver Smith (b. 1837) married and had at least two children:
189. Corintha Smith unm. of Westport, Ind.
190. John Smith.

94. ISAAC HUMMEL⁴ (LAVINIA³, ELI², THAD¹.)

Isaac Hummel (1831-1908) married Oct. 4, 1855 Hannah Bingman (1837-1887) daughter of Joseph and Rachel (Thompson) Bingman. They had ten children:
191. Joseph B. Hummel b. 1856, m. Belle Hotchkiss and had issue.
192. Lavinia Hummel 1858-1913 m. Chas. Martin and had issue.
193. Alice Ann Hummel b. 1860 - m. Lorenzo Lovell and had issue.
194. Olive Jane Hummel b. 1863 m. Sanford L. Aldermann and had issue.
195. Charles F. Hummel b. 1865 m. Effie Bolan and had one son.
196. Julia E. Hummel b. 1867 m. T. Glen Denny of Zanesville, Ohio.
197. Laura Ellen Hummel b. 1871 m. Fred Alderman of Kansas.
198. Cora Alta Hummel b. 1874 m. John C. Gregg.
199. Isaac Franklin Hummel b. 1876 m. Margaret Lynn.
200. Effie H. Hummel b. 1881 m. Thurman Ellis and 2nd Dell Green.

95. JULIA A. HUMMEL⁴ (LAVINIA³, ELI², THADDEUS¹)

Julia Ann Hummel (1833-1912) married May 22, 1853 John A. Thompson and resided near Pennsville, Ohio. He was born Jan. 22, 1822 and died July 23, 1896. They had five children:
201. Lavinia Thompson b. 1855 m. A. B. Van Fossen.
202. Mary Jane Thompson b. 1856 m. John S. Pidgeon.
203. Rosella Thompson b. 1859 m. Manley Thompson.
204. Prudence Thompson b. 1863 m. Edmund Parker.
205. Solomon E. Thompson b. 1866 m. 1st Eva Ellis and 2nd Cora Marsh.

96. ELIZABETH HUMMEL⁴ (LAVINIA³, ELI², THAD.¹)

Elizabeth Hummel (1834-1869) married Dec. 23, 1852 William Balding (1832-1903). Their children were:
206. John M. Balding b. 1853 m. Kate M. Hamm.
207. Lewis Balding b. 1855 m. Ella B. Ligon and had issue.
208. Thomas Balding b. 1857 m. Dora Minor and had issue.
209. Lucy Balding b. 1859 m. Val Bergman and had issue.
210. Julia Balding b. 1861 m. Louis Bissantz and had issue.
211. Eli Balding b. 1863 m. Caroline Beier and had issue.
212. Frank Balding b. 1865 m. Mattie Gordon and had issue.
213. Thurman Balding b. 1867.
214. Seneca Balding b. and d. 1869.

97. SARAH HUMMEL⁴ (LAVINIA³, ELI², THADDEUS¹)

Sarah Hummel (1836-1911) married Oct. 29, 1855 William Miller (1832-1889) and had issue:
215. George Miller b. 1856 m. Mary Ralston and had issue.
216. Jennie Miller b. 1859 m. Charles Miller and had issue.
217. Mary Miller b. 1866 m. Ray Railey - no issue.
218. Carrie L. Miller 1868-1876.
219. Iva Miller b. 1869.
220. Maggie Miller b. 1872 m. Dan Wood and had issue.

98. ELLEN HUMMEL⁴ (LAVINIA³, ELI², THAD.¹)

Ellen Hummel (1838-1920) married Nov. 4, 1855 Joseph Parsons (1828-1898) of Pennsville, Ohio. They had three daughters:
221. Mary Parsons b. 29 Oct. 1856.
222. Oceanna Parsons b. 3 Mar. 1859.
223. Lavinia Parsons b. 6. Apr. 1862.

99. MARY HUMMEL⁴ (LAVINIA³, ELI², THAD.¹)

Mary Hummel (1840-1901) married Dec. 27, 1857 Adam McInturf (b. Jan. 27, 1832 and d. Jan. 3, 1888) a son of Daniel McInturf (b. 1794 in Penn.) and his wife Katherine Rouanzoin (b. Sept. 5, 1805 in Fayette County, Penn) a sister of Elizabeth Rouanzoin wife of Eli Smith.
The children of Adam McInturf and Mary Hummel were:
224. William McInturf b. and d. 1858.
225. Morgan McInturf 1860-1888 unm.
226. Olevia Jane McInturf b. 18 Jan. 1862.
227. Cydnor B. McInturf b. 12 June 1868.
228. Emma McInturf b. 25 May 1871.
229. Everett McInturf b. 7 Aug. 1873.
Mary Hummel McInturf married in 1900 Andrew M. Shuster (1843-1913). She died Aug. 9, 1901.

100. WILLIAM HUMMEL⁴ (LAVINIA³, ELI², THAD.¹)

William Hummel (b. 1841) married Feb. 7, 1861 Cynthia Bernhard (b. 1842) and had issue:
230. James Franklin Hummel (b. 1862).
231. George A. Hummel b. 1865 m. Cora B. Mellott.

101. MARTHA J. HUMMEL⁴ (LAVINIA³, ELI², THAD.¹)

Martha Jane Hummel (1844-1914) married Dec. 23, 1860 Isaac G. Naylor (1839-1917) of Stockport, Ohio. They had three children:
232. Frankie Naylor 1864-1865.
233. Mary L. Naylor b. and d. 1867.
234. Archie Naylor b. 1879 m. Bertha m. Niedrick.

102. SOLOMON HUMMEL⁴ (LAVINIA³, ELI², THAD.¹)

Solomon Hummel (b. 1845) married Sept. 20, 1866 Rachel Bernhard (b. 1846).

103. ALFRED HUMMEL⁴ (LAVINIA³, ELI², THAD.¹)

Alfred Hummel (1847-19) married Sept. 17, 1868 Carrie L. Pugh (b. Sept. 24, 1847). In their later years they resided at Athens, Ohio. They are both now deceased with burial at Hibbardsville. Their children were:
235. Clarence W. Hummel b. 4 Mar. 1870.
236. Ethel Jane Hummel b. 13 Sept. 1873.
237. Cecil Geno Hummel b. 21 June 1876.

104. LEWIS HUMMEL⁴ (LAVINIA³, ELI², THAD.¹)

Lewis T. Hummel (1849-1922) married Oct. 20, 1870 Sarah Ann Bingman (b. 17 Mar. 1854) and resided in Morgan County, Ohio. They had three children:
238. Lida Amanda Hummel b. 1872 m. E. Strode.
239. Archie M. Hummel b. 1881 m. Hattie Brooks.
240. John Earl Hummel b. 1884 m. Edna D. Wooly.

105. JOHN M. SMITH[4] (AARON[3], ELI[2], THAD.[1])

John McLain Smith (1837-1902) married in 1858 Christine Johnson (1832-1878) a daughter of John Johnson of Calamus, Iowa. He died June 23, 1902 and is buried at Villisca, Ia. Their children were:
241. Burgess Jefferson Smith b. 5 Aug. 1860.
242. Elizabeth Anna Smith b. July 1862.
243. Eliza Ellen Smith b. 27 Aug. 1864.
244. William Hall Smith b. 20 May 1866.
245. Caroline Christine Smith b. 27 Mar. 1868.
246. Eldora Smith b. 21 May 1872.
247. John Hayes Smith b. 1875.
248. Sophronia M. Smith b. and d. 1878.

106. ELIZABETH SMITH[4] (Aaron[3], ELI[2], THAD.[1])

Elizabeth (Libbie) Smith (1838-1914) married Oct. 19, 1854 Daniel B. McCully (b. 28 Mar. 1832 and d. Oct. 4, 1884) of Jefferson, Iowa. They had five children:
249. Harriet Elma McCully b. 16 Jan. 1856.
250. Eliza May McCully b. 19 Dec. 1857.
251. George Barton McCully b. 9 Jan. 1859.
252. Eli Monroe McCully b. 1864 d. 1865.
253. William Smith McCully b. 29 Sept. 1866.

107. SARAH E. SMITH[4] (AARON[3], ELI[2], THAD.[1])

Sarah Emily Smith (1840-1923) married first June 16, 1861 Wm. Nathan Hall (b. 16 June 1861 and d. Jan. 21, 1863).
She married second Fred A. Schaeffer on June 26, 1869 and resided at Dewitt, Iowa. He died Nov. 12, 1884 and she died Dec. 1, 1923. Their children were:
254. Hattie May Schaeffer b. 14 Sept. 1870.
255. Grace Elma Schaeffer b. 4 Oct. 1874.

108. MARGARET SMITH[4] (AARON[3], ELI[2], THAD.[1])

Margaret Smith (1842-1919) married 1858 Alonzo Coit (b. 27 Feb. 1836 and d. 18 Feb. 1920) and resided in Massachusetts for five years. In 1879 they removed to Breckenridge, Mo. She died Feb. 18, 1919. Their children were:
256. Ella Coit b. 8 Sept. 1859.
257. John Lincoln Coit b. 26 Mar. 1861 twins
258. George Hamlin Coit b. 26 Mar. 1861
259. Fred Coit b. 1 Oct. 1863.
260. May Coit b. 13 Jan.
261. Harry H. Coit - deceased
262. Earl Coit b. 25 Mar. 1865 - d. Mar. 30, 1940.

109. ELI H. SMITH[4] (AARON[3], ELI[2], THAD.[1])

Eli Henry Smith (1844-1911) married Sept. 11, 1864 Sarah Rebecca Owens of Davenport, Ia. She was born May 26, 1845 and died in 1936. He served in the Civil War three years in Co. H. 26th Inf. of Iowa. He died May 9, 1911 at Dennison, Iowa. Their children were:
263. Emma Frances Smith b. 26 Apr. 1866.
264. Belle Smith b. 22 Dec. 1867 - d. 1904.
265. Mary Elizabeth Smith b. 12 Sept. 1869.
266. William Wesley Smith b. 9 May 1880.

110. JAMES K. P. SMITH[4] (AARON[3], ELI[2], THAD.[1])

James Knox Polk Smith (1845-1934) married Oct. 24, 1874 Sarah Ann Radle (b. 13 July 1855 and d. Aug. 18, 1910 at Ewan, Wash.). He served in the Civil War with the 17th Iowa Cavalry and also in the Custer-Indian warfare. He was a member of General Custer Post number 25. He died at Ewan, Wash. Sept. 19, 1934. Their children were:

267. Purley Smith 1875-1876.
268. Myrtle Smith b. 26 Feb. 1877.
269. Leemoy Lucien Smith b. 16 Dec. 1878.
270. Nellie Frances Smith b. 5 Aug. 1880.
271. O. K. Smith b. 22 Mar. 1882.
272. Arwilda Smith b. 4 May 1883.
273. Harry Smith b. 10 June 1887 - d. 1888.
274. Ulah Tena Smith b. 14 Mar. 1889.
275. Daphne Marean Smith 1892-1893.
276. Aaron James Smith b. 11 July 1894.
277. Lady Faye Smith b. 24 Jan. 1900.

111. PURLEY W. SMITH[4] (AARON[3], ELI[2], THAD.[1])

Purley Winfield Smith (1847-1932) married Nov. 25, 1870 Lovisa Davisson of Wheatland, Ia. She was b. Feb. 16, 1846 and died Nov. 19, 1915 at Cherokee, Ia. He died Jan. 9, 1932. Their children were:
278. Earl Nathan Smith b. 26 Dec. 1874.
279. Arthur Smith b. 1 Aug. 1882.
280. Carrie May Smith b. 5 May 1890.

112. BARTLETT S. SMITH[4] (AARON[3], ELI[2], THAD.[1])

Bartlett Sargeant Smith (1848-1930) married first in 1872 Flora Dubes and had issue:
281. Ernest Smith - deceased.
282. Ervin Smith - deceased.
Bartlett S. Smith married second in 1880 Cordelia Hoyt (d. 1925) and had five children:

283. Thurman Smith.
284. Aaron Smith.
285. May Smith - deceased.
286. William Smith.
287. Bernice Smith m. Ed. Anderson.

113. GEORJANE SMITH[4] (AARON[3], ELI[2], THAD.[1])

Georjane (Jennie) Smith (b. 1850) married James Langfitt in 1867 at Dewitt, Ia. They had issue:
288. Sadie Langfitt b. 1868 - m. Mr. Bodecker (d. 1922).
289. Flora Langfitt b. 1870 - d. 1936, m. John W. Davis.
290. Rhoda Langfitt.
291. Hattie May Langfitt.
Jennie Smith married 2nd C. H. Day. He died 1922.

114. GEORGE A. SMITH[4] (AARON[3], ELI[2], THAD.[1])

George A. Smith (1851-1932) married first Aug. 13, 1871 Louise Albertina Leasure of Dewitt, Ia. She was born in Scotland June 9, 1852 and died Nov. 14, 1896. They had five children:
292. Clara Elizabeth Smith b. 15 July 1872.
293. Newton Smith b. 21 Mar. 1875 - d. 1930 at Radcliffe, Ia.
294. Purley Marcellus Smith b. 1879 - m. and had issue.
295. Grace L. Smith b. 1882, m. Mr. Rhinehart.
296. Elva Ella Smith b. Aug. 30, 1889 - d. 1924.
George A. Smith m. Sept. 1897 Mrs. Sophie Petersen and had one son:
297. Harold Smith b. 26 Apr. 1899.
George A. Smith died Jan. 4, 1932 at Big Rock, Iowa.

115. HIRAM SMITH[4] (AARON[3], ELI[2], THAD.[1])

Hiram Smith (1853-1896) of Breckenridge, Mo. married in 1880 Emma Horton but had no issue. They adopted one son: Purley Smith.

116. ELIZA E. SMITH[4] (AARON[3], ELI[2], THAD.[1])

Eliza Ellen Smith (1855-1896) married in 1878 Harry Harmon of Creston, Iowa. He was killed by a train Oct. 4, 1896. She died May 31, 1896 at Creston, Ia. They had thre children:
297. Maud Harmon b. 1879.
298. Roxie Harmon b. 1886.
299. Ruth Harmon b. 1892.

117. ANNIS J. SMITH[4] (AARON[3], ELI[2], THAD.[1])

Annis Janette Smith (b. 1858) married first July 3, 1876 Adam Friend and had three children:
300. Callie May Friend 1877-1878.
301. Charles Monroe Friend b. 3 Mar. 1880.
302. Rosa Friend 1882-1887.
Annis J. Friend married second 1896 Daniel Mara (d. 28 Oct. 1937) of Little Rock, Ark.

They had an adopted son Daniel Mara Jr.

119. RHODA A. SMITH[4] (AARON[3], ELI[2], THAD.[1])

Rhoda Ann Smith (b. 1863) married Nov. 27, 1880 William Morehead (d. Jan. 27, 1928). They had no issue.

120. MARGARET SMITH[4] (WASH[3], ELI[2], THAD.[1])

Margaret Smith (b. 1841) married first Isaac Boal (b. 1839). He was killed in the Civil War. They had no issue.
Margaret Smith Boal married second about 1866 Mr. Washington and had at least one child:
303. Laura J. Washington.
They removed to Davis County, Iowa with her parents about 1868/.9.

122. DAVID SMITH[4] (WASH[3], ELI[2], THAD.[1])

David Smith (b. 1845 in Ohio) married about 1868 Ruth_____ (b. 1849 in Ohio) and had at least one child:
304. Martha Smith b. 1870 in Iowa.
They removed to Davis County, Iowa with his parents.

135. MARCELLUS SARGENT[4] (ELIZABETH[3], ELI[2], THAD.[1])

Marcellus Sargent (b. 1846) married but date and wife's name are not available. They had four children:
305. Jessie Sargent m. Mr. Ray.
306. Lee Sargent.
307. Bartlett Sargent.
308. John Sargent.

136. JOHN SARGENT[4] (ELIZABETH[3], ELI[2], THAD.[1])

John Sargent (b. 1849) married and had three children:

309. May Sargent m. Mr. Varney of Calif.
310. Arlie Sargent m. Mr. Moore of Calif.
311. Florence Sargent - deceased.

137. SERENA SARGENT[4] (ELIZABETH[3], ELI[2], THAD.[1])

Serena Sargent (b. 1849) married Mr. Vaughn and had two children:
312. Mary Vaughn m. Ralph Barger, two sons.
313. Arthur Vaughn of Marion, Iowa.

140. HARRISON SMITH[4] (SOLOMON[3], ELI[2], THAD.[1])

Harrison Smith (1849-1929) married first Mary Herrod and had two children both of whom died young.
He married a second time and resided in Des Moines, Iowa. By his second wife he had at least two children:
314. Harrison Smith, Jr.
315. Frank Smith.

142. JAMES B. SMITH[4] (SOLOMON[3], ELI[2], THAD.[1])

James Bartlett Smith (b. 1852) married Ollie Head and had three children:
316 Bonnie Smith.
317. Ollie Smith.
318. Tad Smith.

143. SUSANNAH SMITH[4] (SOLOMON[3], ELI[2], THAD[1])

Susannah Smith (b. 1854) married Frank Cunningham and had at least seven children:
319. Mary Cunningham.
320. Jessie Cunningham.
321. Ottie Cunningham.
322. Fred Cunningham.
323. Clarence Cunningham.
324. Edward Cunningham.
325. Asbury Cunningham.
There was probably another child.

144. MARY ELLEN BOAL[4] (RHODA[3], ELI[2], THAD.[1])

Mary Ellen Boal (1848-1935) married Nov. 28, 1869 John Thomas Hope (1847-1929) a son of Peyton and Mary Elizabeth Hope of Perry County, Ohio. They removed to Athens County, Ohio and resided at Athens. Their children were:
326. Rhoda Ann Hope 1870-1891 (See Vol. 1. p. 31.)
327. Mary Elizabeth Hope b. 11 Feb. 1873.
328. Vira Rosella Hope b. 17 Mar. 1876

329. John Thomas Hope b. 30 Aug. 1878 (See #260 Coe lineage)
330. James Garfield Hope b. 28 Jan. 1881 (See Vol. 1. p. 31)
331. Clara L. Hope 1883-1887.
332. Ella E. Hope 1885-1908.
333. Albert Hope b. and d. 1887.

147. SETH SMITH[4] (WILLIAM[3], ELI[2], THAD.[1])

Seth Smith (1855-1934) of near Pennsville, Ohio married June 3, 1877 Amanda Risen. He died Apr. 22, 1934. Their children were:
334. Florence Smith b. ca 1878.
335. Blanche Smith m. Mr. Simpson of McConnelsville, Ohio.
336. Howard Smith of Chesterhill, Ohio.
337. Mable Smith m. Mr. Williams of Pennsville, Ohio.
338. Edith Smith m. Mr. Wood of Stockport, Ohio.
339. Kitty Smith m. Mr. Stokes of Frazysburg, Ohio.
340. Amy Smith m. Mr. Dougan of Stockport, Ohio.
341. Iva Smith m. Mr. Gifford of Malta, Ohio.

148. MARY M. SMITH[4] (WILLIAM[3], ELI[2], THAD.[1])

Mary M. Smith (b. 1857) married Oct. 30, 1888 Samuel Thisselle (d. 5 Nov. 1920) farmer of near Malta, Ohio. They had two children:
342. Benjamin Thisselle.
343. Laura Thisselle m. Arthur Eppley of Roseville, Ohio. She died without issue 1938.

149. SOLOMON F. SMITH[4] (WILLIAM[3], ELI[2], THAD.[1])

Solomon F. Smith (1859-1927) married July 19, 1886 Easter Newman (b. Apr. 18, 1867) and resided on a farm near Malta, Ohio.
He died Oct. 2, 1927. Their children were:
344. Nellie Smith b. Oct. 16, 1886 m. Edward Milligan.
345. John Rouanzoin Smith b. Nov. 1888.
346. Forest Smith b. Dec. 1, 1890.
347. Albert William Smith b. 1892.
348. Hazel Smith b. 1894, m. Newell Kane
349. Lee Smith b. 1897.
350. Bertha Smith b. 1899.
351. Fred C. Smith b. 1902, surveyor of Malta, Ohio.
352. Dale F. Smith b. 1904.

150. ELI W. SMITH[4] (WILLIAM[3], ELI[2], THAD.[1])

1884 Emily J. Barkhurst (now deceased) and had three children:
353. Bernice Smith.
354. Leonard Smith.
355. William Smith.

151. C. EDWARD SMITH⁴ (WILLIAM³, ELI², THAD.¹)

Charles Edward Smith (1868-1924) married Sept. 22, 1899 Florence Matson (deceased) and resided at Malta, Ohio. They had three children, two of whom died in infancy. Edward Smith died Jan. 18, 1924.
356. Freda Smith.

152. CLARENCE SMITH⁴ (WILLIAM³, ELI², THAD.¹)

Clarence Smith (b. 1872) farmer of near Malta, Ohio, married 1895 Mary A. Harrison but had no issue. He died as a result of a broken neck suffered in a fall on stair steps in 1932.

153. CLARA SMITH⁴ (WILLIAM³, ELI², THAD.¹)

Clara Smith (b. 1872) married Feb. 27, 1896 Theodore D. Barkhurst and resides at Casey, Ill. Their children were:
357. Beatrice Barkhurst m. Mr. Baird of Indianapolis, Ind.
358. Olive Barkhurst m. Mr. Plummer of Mattoon, Ill.
359. Mark Barkhurst of Ponca City, Okla.
360. Berk Barkhurst of Casey, Ill.
361. Ted Barkhurst of Great Falls, Mont.

167. ESTELLA UPDIKE⁵ (ISAAC⁴, VIRGIL³, NANCY², THAD.¹)

Estella Updike (b. 1879) married Oct. 21, 1900 W. Roscoe Service, farmer of Ceres, Calif. and had three children:
362. Newell Service b. 15 Nov. 1904 of San Francisco, Calif.
363. Vivian Service b. 16 Sept. 1906.
364. Evelyn Service b. 26 Nov. 1907 m. 1929 L. V. Etnyre of Turlock, Calif.

169. GRACE A UPDIKE⁵ (ISAAC⁴, VIRGIL³, NANCY², THAD.¹)

Grace A. Updike (b. 1890) married Dec. 25, 1922 Egbert R. Jones of Mississippi, and had a daughter:
365. Virginia Jones.

177. JOHN D. ERWIN⁵ (SARAH⁴, MARY A³, BENJ², THAD.¹)

John D. Erwin (1864-1928) banker of McConnelsville, Ohio married Etha_____ and had at least one child:
366. A daughter who m. C. Edgar Northrup.

183. W. ALBERT BURCHER⁵ (RUTH⁴, MARY³, BENJ², THAD.¹)

W. Albert Burcher (b. 1867) married May 30, 1901 Viola E. Pidgeon (b. 1879) daughter of John S. Pidgeon and Mary Jane Thompson (see #202 this lineage) and had issue:
367. Fonda Eleanor Burcher b. 20 Sept. 1908.
368. Paul Howard Burcher b. 10 May 1910.
369. Ronald Earl Burcher b. 22 July 1912.

221. MARY PARSONS⁵ (ELLEN⁴, LAVINIA³, ELI², THAD.¹)

Mary Parsons (1856-1940) married Oct. 26, 1873 Dr. T. J. Bingman of McConnelsville, Ohio. They had one daughter:
370. Lulu Bingman (1877-1912) m. Dr. Baxter.

222. OCEANNA PARSONS⁵ (ELLEN⁴, LAVINIA³, ELI², THAD.¹)

Oceanna Parsons (b. 1859) married Apr. 26, 1877 Samuel Parker Moody of McConnelsville, Ohio. They had three children:
371. Clyde L. Moody b. 1878 m. Emma Garret..
372. Chester J. Moody b. 1887 m. Matilda Shafer.
373. Leonard Moody b. 1890 m. 1st Ruth Pelton m. 2nd and had two children.

223. LAVINIA PARSONS⁵ (ELLEN⁴, LAVINIA³, ELI², THAD.¹)

Lavinia Parsons (1862-1934) married Sept. 11, 1886 Charles G. Coulson (1855-1932). She died in Akron, Ohio Oct. 15, 1934. Their children were:
374. Bernice Ellen Coulson b. 18 Sept. 1890 m. 1914 Martin K. Moore.
375. Leah Iris Coulson b. 12 May 1895.

226. OLEVIA J. McINTURF⁵ (MARY⁴, LAVINIA³, ELI², THAD.¹)

Olevia Jane McInturf (b. 1862) married Nov. 25, 1880 George B. Dougan (b. 1857) and had five children:
376. Carrie E. Dougan b. 13 Mar. 1882.
377. Ella Dougan b. 1 Oct. 1883.

378. Lawrence Dougan b. 3 Mar. 1891 d. 1891.
379. Arthur Riley Dougan b. 25 Jan. 1886.
380. Ernest Dougan b. 28 Mar. 1893.

227. CYDNOR B. MCINTURF[5] (MARY[4], LAVINIA[3], ELI[2], THAD.[1])

Cydnor B. McInturf (b. 1868) married June 27, 1897 Sadie Allen (b. 1871) and had issue:
381. LAWRENCE McIntruf b. 1898.
382. Edith McInturf b. 1900.
383. Ella McInturf b. 1902.
384. Clara McInturf b. 1910.

228. EMMA MCINTURF[5] (MARY[4], LAVINIA[3], ELI[2], THAD.[1])

Emma McInturf (b. 1871) married Mar. 10, 1891 Benjamin Marshall (b. 1863) and had issue:
385. Galen G. Marshall b. 1892 m. Mildred Penrod.
386. Anson A. Marshall b. 1894 d. 1918 m. Jessie Newton.
387. Larmer L. Marshall b. 1896 - World War Service.
388. Clyde C. Marshall b. 1900 - World War Service.
389. Otis F. Marshall b. 1902.
390. Jennie May Marshall b. 1904.

229. EVERETT McINTURF[5] (MARY[4], LAVINIA[3], ELI[2], THAD.[1])

Everett McInturf (b. 1873) married Sept. 9, 1896 Elizabeth Llewellyn (b. 1871) and had at least one child:
391. Anna E. McInturf b. 2 Sept. 1897.

235. CLARENCE HUMMEL[5] (ALFRED[4], LAVINIA[3], ELI[2], THAD.[1])

Clarence William Hummel (b. 1870) married Sept. 7, 1892 Effie Blanche Alderman (b. 1873 and d. June 15, 1910) a daughter of Warren Alderman. Their children were:
392. Mildred A. Hummel b. 1895 m. 1916 Melvin C. Wise.
393. Audrey I. Hummel b. 1897.
394. Errol Alderman Hummel b. July 5, 1899.
395. Fay E. Hummel b. 10 Dec. 1901.

236. ETHEL J. HUMMEL[5] (ALFRED[4], LAVINIA[3], ELI[2], THAD.[1])

Ethel Jane Hummel (b. 1873) married Aug. 25, 1900 Thomas S. Spurrier (b. 1868) and resides at Cuyahoga Falls, Ohio.

396. Forest Belle Spurrier b. 1902.
397. Mae Irene Spurrier b. 1903.
398. Ernest B. Spurrier 1905-1908.
399. Ernestine L. Spurrier b. 1908.
400. Alice C. Spurrier b. 1909-1910.
401. Mary M. Spurrier b. 1910.
402. Omar Cecil Spurrier b. 1912.
403. Ross Spurrier 1913-1914.
404. Woodrow W. Spurrier b. 1915.
405. Gertrude A. Spurrier b. 1917.

237. CECIL G. HUMMEL[5] (ALFRED[4], LAVINIA[3], ELI[2], THAD.[1])

Cecil G. Hummel (b. 1876) married Sept. 17, 1904 Alice Crosby (b. 1885) and had one son:
406. Alfred Thomas Hummel b. 1913.
Cecil Hummel married second in 1923 Mrs. Dorothy Haning Snowden and resides at Columbus, Ohio

241. BURGESS J. SMITH[5] (JOHN[4], AARON[3], ELI[2], THAD.[1])

Burgess Jefferson Smith (b. 1860) married Mar. 11, 1894 Ida May McDonald (b. 4 Nov. 1871) and had four children:
407. Homer Lorenzo Smith b. 20 May 1895 m. 1917 Theresa Wood.
408. Ellis Perry Smith b. 1 Feb. 1901 - d. 1903.
409. Valeria Delvine Smith b. 15 Sept. 1906 m. 1931 Wright Baylor.
410. Margaret Elizabeth Smith b. 12 Aug. 1909 - d. 1933.

242. ELIZABETH A. SMITH[5] (JOHN[4], AARON[3], ELI[2], THAD.[1])

Elizabeth Anna Smith (b. 1862) married Sept. 1885 Charles D. Snyder at Dixon, Iowa. They had issue:
411. Ernest Calvin Snyder b. July 1886.
412. Christina Snyder b. 11 Feb. 1888 - d. y.
413. John Franklin Snyder b. 3 May 1890 - no issue.
414. Carver B. Snyder 1891-1923 - no issue.

243. ELIZA E. SMITH[5] (JOHN[4], AARON[3], ELI[2], THAD.[1])

Eliza Ellen Smith (b. 1864) married first Nov. 2, 1884 James Miller and had one son:
415. George Miller b. 4 Sept. 1885.
Eliza Smith Miller married second Oct. 15, 1888 Henry Van Sickle and had issue:
416. Belle Van Sickle b. 25 Aug. 1891.
417. Frank Van Sickle b. 1 Jan. 1890. Was

from Cherokee County, Iowa. He was on the transport ship "Lincoln" when it was torpedoed and sunk and was afloat on a raft for eighteen hourse before he was rescued. He died June 9, 1928.

418. Maizie Van Sickle (1893-1921) m. F. M. Coats.

244. WILLIAM H. SMITH[5] (JOHN[4], AARON[3], ELI[2], THAD.[1])

William Hall Smith (b. 1866) married Mar. 12, 1890 Louie Leonard (d. 29 Nov. 1939) and resides at Quimby, Iowa. Their children were:
419. Bert Ransom Smith b. 29 Mar. 1892.
420. Russell Ray Smith b. 12 Sept. 1894.
421. Nelson Victor Smith b. 25 June 1896 - d. y.
422. Harold Hawley Smith b. 21 Nov. 1897.
423. Thelma Clare Smith b. 21 Oct. 1903.
424. William Stanhope Smith b. 12 June 1906.
425. Lela Celeste Smith b. 30 Nov. 1908.
426. Lewis Leland Smith b. 12 Oct. 1912.
William Hall Smith served as Representative in the 45th General Assembly of the state of Iowa in 1933 and in the special session of 1934.

245. CAROLINE C. SMITH[5] (JOHN[4], AARON[3], ELI[2], THAD.[1])

Caroline Christine Smith (b. 1868) married Mar. 17, 1893 Samuel Walter Spear and had four children:
427. Byron Glenn Spear b. 26 Jan. 1894.
428. Bertha Grace Spear b. and d. 1895.
429. Edna Bernice Spear 1896 - 1917.
430. Iowa Leona Spear b. 2 Aug. 1898. m. 22 June 1920 Delbert Earl Wilson at Des Moines, Ia. He died Dec. 11, 1939. She is hostess at the Albilene, Tex. Ladies Club.
Caroline C. Spear married second Marion Marsh on Jan. 27, 1905. He died in 1932 at Cherokee, Iowa. They had two children:
431. Nile H. Marsh b. 10 Dec. 1907.
432. Elma Sara Marsh b. 28 Dec. 1908 - d. 1922.

246. ELDORA SMITH[5] (JOHN[4], AARON[3], ELI[2], THAD.[1])

Eldora Smith (b. 1872) married Nov. 3, 1890 A. E. Crawford at Emerson, Iowa. Their children were:
433. Arthur E. Crawford b. 28 July 1891, he died in service with the 146th Field Artillery Supply Company Oct. 21, 1918.

434. Clyde William Crawford 1893 - 1907.
435. Mable Evelyn Crawford b. 16 Nov. 1895.
436. Vira Lucille Crawford b. 18 June 1897.
437. Lyle Crawford b. 1900 - d. 1907 at Sprague, Wash.
438. Edna May Crawford b. 26 Aug. 1906
Eldora Smith Crawford married second May 4, 1923 at Spokane, Wash., Anery Eichner Howard (b. 5 Dec. 1887 at Copenhagen, Denmark) son of Hans Christian Madsen former minister of War under the reign of H. M. S. King Christian the XI of Denmark.

247. JOHN H. SMITH[5] (JOHN M., AARON[3], ELI[2], THAD.[1])

John Hayes Smith (b. 1875) married Edith Snyder and had five children:
439. Edna Smith
440. Edith Smith
441. Beatrice Smith
442. Carver Smith
443. Ephraim Smith

249. HARRIET E. McCULLY[5] (ELIZABETH[4], AARON[3], ELI[2], THAD.[1])

Harriet Elma McCully (1856-1935) married Dr. Fay L. Warner (b. 15 Sept. 1849 and died Dec. 30, 1935) in 1874 and had five children:
444. Fred Warner b. 10 Aug. 1875.
445. Charles Warner b. 25 Mar. 1877 - d. 1 Dec. 1926 m. Florence Small.
446. Birdie Warner 1879-1880.
447. William Warner b. 1 Nov. 1892.
448. Florence Warner b. 8 Feb. 1895 m. J. S. Voreck of Davenport, Iowa.

250. E. MAY McCULLY[5] (Eliz., AARON[3], ELI[2], THAD.[1])

Eliza May McCully (1857-1938) married May 4, 1881 Judge Zala A. Church and had issue:
449. Iza L. Church.
450. Bessie Church m. D. E. Lyon of Jefferson, Iowa.
451. Theo Church m. Mr. Huston of Elk Rapids, Mich.

251. GEORGE B. McCULLY[5] (ELIZ., AARON[3], ELI[2], THAD.[1])

George Barton McCully (1859-1933) married Apr. 25, 1883 Ida V. Cozad and had issue:
452. Don C. McCully (1884-1922) no issue.
453. Bess M. McCully m. Paul B. Osgood, no issue.

253. WILLIAM S. McCully[5] (ELIZ[4]., AARON[3], ELI[2]., THAD.[1])

William Smith McCully (b. 1866) married Gertrude Head but had no issue. They adopted a daughter: Verna Guiser McCully. William S. and Gertrude Smith are now deceased.

254. HATTIE M. SCHAEFFER[5] (SARAH[4], AARON[3], ELI[2], THAD.[1])

Hattie May Schaeffer (b. 1870) married Jan. 22, 1893 Charles N. Rice (d. 3 Sept. 1937) and resides at Calamus, Iowa. They had nine children:
454. Grace Lillian Rice b. 29 Sept. 1894.
455. Thomas S. Rice b. 29 Aug. 1897 - unm.
456. Elsie Ione Rice b. 22 Aug. 1899.
457. Fred Aaron Rice b. 8 Aug. 1901 - unm.
458. Louis Z. Rice b. 17 Aug. 1903 - unm.
459. Sarah Christine Rice b. 4 June 1905.
460. Elizabeth Pearl Rice b. 20 Feb. 1907.
461. William Leonard Rice b. 19 May 1909 - d. 1929.
462. Ruth Marie Rice b. 15 May 1911.

255. GRACE E. SCHAEFFER[5] (SARAH[4], AARON[3], ELI[2], THAD.[1])

Grace Elma Schaeffer (b. 1874) married Apr. 14, 1898 Harry Isaac Jenison and resides at Grand Junction, Iowa. They have two children:
463. Clella Viola Jenison b. 28 Nov. 1900.
464. Helen Mabel Jenison b. 6 May 1909.

256. ELLA COIT[5] (MARGARET[4], AARON[3], ELI[2], THAD.[1])

Ella Coit (1859-1887) married June 27, 1883 Rev. Thomas Humphrey and resided at Breckenridge, Mo.

260. MAY COIT[5] (MARGARET[4], AARON[3], ELI[2], THAD.[1])

May Coit married L. Z. Wills and had at least one daughter:
465. Joy Wills.

263. EMMA F. SMITH[5] (ELI[4]., AARON[3], ELI[2], THAD.[1])

Emma Frances Smith (b. 1866) married Apr. 29, 1884 Clifton Thew at Denison, Ia. He was born Oct. 29, 1857 at Peru, N. Y., and died Feb. 14, 1937 at Spokane, Wash. Their children were:
466. Stephen Corkins Thew b. 6 May 1885.
467. Frank Addison Thew b. 1 Aug. 1887.

468. Eunice Thew b. 21 June 1889.
469. Lula Thew b. 17 May 1892.
470. Edith Vivian Thew b. 6 May 1895.
471. Violet A. Thew b. 6 Oct. 1903.
472. Oliver Morton Thew b. 18 Nov. 1906.

264. BELLE SMITH[5] (ELI[4]., AARON[3], ELI[2], THAD.[1])

Belle Smith (1867-1904) married Mr. Hapgood and had issue:
473. May Hapgood b. 26 Apr. 1889.
474. Loretta Hapgood b. 26 Jan. 1896.

265. MARY E. SMITH[5] (ELI[4]., AARON[3], ELI[2], THAD.[1])

Mary Elizabeth Smith (b. 1869) married Oliver M. Campbell July 5, 1887 and had issue:
475. Nettie Smith Campbell b. 8 Feb. 1902.

266. WILLIAM W. SMITH[5] (ELI[4]., AARON[3], ELI[2] THAD[1])

William Wesley Smith (b. 1880) married in 1904 Dell Marshall and had one child:
476. Grace Smith b. 30 July 1906.

268. MYRTLE SMITH[5] (JAS. K. P[4]., AARON[3], ALI[2], THAD.[1])

Myrtle Smith (1877-1933) married Dec. 1, 1902 Edward O. McNall of Ewan, Wash. and had issue:
477. Theo Clyde McNall b. 11 Apr. 1904.
478. Lura June McNall b. 1916-1917.
479. Athol Zoe McNall b. 21 Feb. 1920.

269. LEEMOY L. SMITH[5] (JAS. K. P[4]., AARON[3] ELI[2] THAD.[1])

Leemoy Lucian Smith (1878-1930) married Dec. 23, 1903 Mary McNall and had issue:
480. Eugenia Mary Smith b. 18 June 1905, m. G. M. Bell.
481. Irene Alexandria Smith b. 19 Dec. 1906.
482. Alice Lee Smith b. 3 Feb. 1910, m. H. Beauchene.
483. Vivian Smith b. 8 Jan. 1913, m. D. Beauchene.

270. NELLIE F. SMITH[5] (JAS. K. P[4]., AARON[3], ELI[2] THAD.[1])

Nellie Frances Smith (b. 1880) married Feb. 4, 1903 Mace Augustus Lynch (b. 4 Feb. 1903 and d. 2 Mar. 1917) and had issue:
484. Dwarda Isabel Lynch b. 17 June 1904.
485. Zoe Retha Lynch b. 5 Feb. 1906.
486. Aubrey James Lynch b. 10 June 1907.
487. Ercelle Sarah Lynch b. 3 Apr. 1909.

488. Beryl Mace Lynch b. 19, Mar. 1911.
489. Darrel Dale Lynch b. 23 June 1912.
  Nellie F. Lynch married second Elmer
Harper Sims of Spokane, Wash.

  271. O. K. SMITH[5] (JAS. K. P[4], AARON[3],
      ELI[2], THAD.[1])

  O. K. Smith (b. 1882) married June 15,
1915 Agnes Ruek d. 30 Apr. 1925) and had one
son:
490. Kenneth O. K. Smith b. 13 July 1918.
  O. K. Smith married second 1926 Olga
Ruek and had a son:
491. Warren Raymond Smith b. 11 Feb. 1937.

  272. ARWILDA SMITH[5] (JAS. K. P[4],
      AARON,[3] ELI[2], THAD.[1])

  Arwilda Smith (b. 1883) married Feb. 22,
1909 J. M. McNall and had issue:
492. Reah McNall b. 12 Feb. 1910.
493. Murray McNall b. 27 July 1912.

  274. ULAH T. SMITH[5] (JAS. K. P[4],
      AARON[3], ELI[2] THAD.[1])

  Alah Tena Smith (1889-1930) married
Mar. 14, 1915 J. M. Wood but had no issue.

  276. AARON J. SMITH[5] (JAS. K. P[4],
      AARON[3], ELI[2], THAD.[1])

  Aaron James Smith (b. 1894) married
July 3, 1919 Cleona Shelton and had issue:
494. Floyd James Smith b. 10 Jan. 1923.
495. Ruth Eileen Smith b. 20 Aug. 1934.

  277. LADY F. SMITH[5] (JAS. K. P[4],
      AARON[3], ELI[2], THAD.[1])

  Lady Faye Smith (b. 1900) married in
1918 Hollis E. Dickinson and had issue:
496. Virginia Myrtle Dickinson b. 20 Jan.
  1919.
497. June Jeneva Dickinson b. 1920.
498. Retha Lenore Dickinson b. 21 Mar. 1921.
499. Homer Allan Dickinson b. 26 Sept. 1926.
500. Joyce Dickinson b. 29, MAY 1931.
501. Yvonne Dickinson b. 12 Jan. 1933.
502. Larry Lee Dickinson b. 9 June 1936.

  278. EARL N. SMITH[5] (PURLEY[4],
      AARON[3], ELI[2], THAD.[1])

  Earl Nathan Smith (b. 1874) married May
31, 1915 at Cheroke, Iowa. Beulah Graham
and had two children:

503. Louise Earleen Smith b. 25 Jan. 1916.
504. Delbert Max Smith b. 24 May 1918.

  279. ARTHUR SMITH[5] (PURLEY[4], AARON[3],
      ELI[2], THAD.[1])

  Arthur Smith (b. 1882) married Dec. 13,
1911 Emma Kent Wheatley and had issue:
505. Raymond Dale Smith b. 7 Mar. 1913.

  280. CARRIE M. SMITH[5] (PURLEY[4],
      AARON[3], ELI[2], THAD.[1])

  Carrie May Smith (b. 1890) married Nov.
16, 1915 Delbert S. Ferrin of Cherokee, Iowa,
and had two children:
506. Kenneth Smith Ferrin b. 4 Apr. 1918.
507. Betty Kathleen Ferrin b. 9 Sept. 1920.

  292. CLARA E. SMITH[5] (GEO. A[4], AARON[3],
      ELI[2], THAD.[1])

  Clara Elizabeth Smith (b. 1872) married
June 1892 Abraham M. Hall and had issue:
508. Newton Hall b. and d. 1893.
509. Myrtle Hall d. y.
510. Purley Hall b. Mar. 1897.
511. Melba Hall b. 1899, m. Herbert Schneider.
512. Leona Hall b. 1901.
513. Audrey Hall b. 1903.
514. Ina Hall b. 1905, m. Ralph Paul.
515. Maud Hall b. 7 May 1907
516. Grace Hall b. 7 May 1907   twins
517. Fern Hall b. 25 Dec. 1910.

  296. ELVA E. SMITH[5] (GEO. A[4], AARON[3],
      ELI[2], THAD.[1])

  Elva Ella Smith (1889-1924) married ca
1910 Rudolph Schadt and had one daughter:
518. Lois Schadt b. 1911.

  297. HAROLD A. SMITH[5] (GEO. A[4], AARON[3],
      ELI[2], THAD.[1])

  Harold Anthony Smith (b. 1899) married
June 30, 1920 Edna Siebel and had issue:
519. Jeanette G. Smith b. 27 Dec. 1920.
520. Evelyn E. Smith b. 11 Sept. 1922.
521. Marjorie Ann Smith b. 30 Apr. 1929.
522. Harold H. Smith b. 10 Mar. 1935.

  301. CHARLES M. FRIEND[5] (ANNIS[4],
      AARON[3], ELI[2], THAD.[1])

  Charles M. Friend (b. 1880) married
Pauline_____and had a daughter:
523. Bernice Friend.

327. MARY E. HOPE⁵ (MARY ELLEN⁴, RHODA³, ELI², THAD.¹)

Mary Elizabeth Hope (b. 1873) married Dec. 24, 1891 William L. Walden (born 5 Feb. 1869 and died Oct. 8, 1902) a son of William and Hester (Purviance) Walden of Coolville, Ohio. Their children were:
524. Blanche L. Walden b. 12 Oct. 1892 at Coolville, Ohio
525. Marion A. Walden b. 2 Nov. 1897 at Pomeroy, Ohio
526. John Thomas Walden b. 3 Oct. 1901 - d. 1903.
527. Mary Walden b. and d. 1901   twins

334. FLORENCE SMITH⁵ (SETH⁴, WM³, ELI², THAD.¹)

Florence Smith (b. 1878) married Nov. 6, 1898 Howard White a son of Thomas and Rhoda (Henry) White. They had five children:
528. Melvin Leroy White b. 1 Aug. 1899.
529. Elsie Marie White b. 27 June 1901.
530. Carie Gladys White b. 5 Oct. 1904.
531. Frances Evalyn White b. 22 Sept. 1909.
532. Bernice Louise White b. 28 Aug. 1920.

345. JOHN R. SMITH⁵ (SOLOMON⁴, WM³, ELI², THAD.¹)

John Rouanzoin Smith (b. 1888) married in Sept. of 1910 Mildred Pennell (b. Oct. 1892) and resides near Malta, Ohio. They have two children:
533. Raymond Smith b. 5 May 1912.
534. Janice Smith b. 13 Jan. 1915.

346. FORREST SMITH⁵ (SOLOMON⁴, WM³, ELI², THAD.¹)

Forest Smith (b. 1890) married in 1916 Delbert Salzer (b. 1888) of Akron, Ohio and had at least three children:
535. Delbert Salzer, Jr. b. 1917.
536. Richard Salzer b. 1919.
537. Betty Jane Salzer b. 1922.

347. ALBERT W. SMITH⁵ (SOLOMON⁴, WM³, ELI², THAD.¹)

Albert William Smith (b. 1892) married 1921 Stella Walker (b. 1901) and resides at Athens, Ohio. He served in the World War in the Argonne. Their children were:
538. Bonnie Jean Smith b. 1922.
539. Martha Eileen Smith b. 1925.
539A. Donna June Smith b. 1931.

349. LEE SMITH⁵ (SOLOMON⁴, WM³, ELI², THAD.¹)

Lee Smith (b. 1897) married in May 1918 Ota Lynn (b. 1897) and resides at Malta, Ohio. He served in the World War. They had at least four children:
540. Marjorie Smith b. Dec. 1920.
541. Robert Smith b. Jan. L923.
542. Don Edward Smith b. July 1925.
543. Ruth Ann Smith b. Oct. 1927.

356. FREDA SMITH⁵ (EDWARD⁴, WM³, ELI², THAD.¹)

Freda Mae Smith married 29 May 1936 Attorney Robert Louis Drury a son of Clarence Drury of McConnelsville, Ohio. She is a graduate of Ohio University and a former teacher in the Malta public schools. They have one daughter:
544. Sarah Jean Drury b. 9 May 1937.

363. VIVIAN SERVICE⁶ (ESTELLA⁵, ISAAC⁴, VIRGIL³, NANCY², THAD.¹)

Vivian Service (b. 1906) married June 16, 1930 Walter M. Stewart of Modesto, Calif., and had one daughter:
545 Marilyn Stewart.

375. LEAH I. COULSON⁶ (LAVINIA⁵, ELLEN⁴, LAV³, ELI², THAD.¹)

Leah Iris Coulson (b. 1895) married Feb. 24, 1917 Dr. Fred V. Gammage and resides at Chattahooche, Fla. They have one daughter:
546. Gloria Gammage b. 29 June 1920, student at Florida State College for Women and a member of Pi Beta Phi sorority.

376. CARRIE E. DOUGAN⁶ (OLEVIA⁵, MARY⁴, LAV³, ELI², THAD.¹)

Carrie E. Dougan (b. 1882) married July 27, 1902 Daniel M. Abel and had one son:
547. Myron Dougan Abel b. 13 Dec. 1903.

377. ELLA DOUGAN⁶ (OLEVIA⁵, MARY⁴, LAV³, ELI², THAD.¹)

Ella Dougan (b. 1883) married 31 May 1905 E. D. Humphrey (b. 1876) and had issue:
548. Don D. Humphrey b. 4 Sept. 1908.
549. Nellie Humphrey b. 6 Apr. 1912.
550. Joe David Humphrey b. 23 Oct. 1919.

394. ERROL A. HUMMEL⁶ (CLARENCE⁵, ALF⁴, LAV³, Eli², THAD.¹)

Errol Alderman Hummel (b. 1899) served in the World War 1918. He married 30 Oct. 1922 Elizabeth A. Mulligan, a daughter of Hugh and Gertrude (Reeder) Mulligan of near Athens, Ohio.
Errol and Elizabeth Hummel have two daughters:
551. Martha Ann Hummel.
552. Nancy Ellen Hummel.

416. BELLE VAN SICKEL⁶ (ELIZA⁵' JOHN⁴, AARON³, ELI², THAD.¹)

Belle Van Sickle (b. 1891) married Feb. 26, 1913 Arthur E. Jones and had issue:
553. Agnes Esther Jones 1919-1927.
554. Velda Jones b. 2 Sept. 1929.

419. BERT R. SMITH⁶ (WM.⁵, JOHN⁴, AARON³, ELI², THAD.¹)

Bert Ransom Smith (b. 1892) married July 18, 1915 Elsie I. Brownmiller (d. 1921) and had issue:
555. Clifford B. Smith b. 13 July 1917.
556. Forrest P. Smith b. 14 Oct. 1918.
557. Opal E. Smith b. 1920 - m. Arthur Barton.
Bert R. Smith married second 28 Dec. 1922 Leona Meier and had issue:
558. Emmett Aaron Smith b. 18 Apr. 1924.
559. Doris Marie Smith b. 7 Sept. 1928.
560. Charlotte Jean Smith b. 8 Aug. 1930.

420. RUSSEL R. SMITH⁶ (WM.⁵, JOHN⁴, AARON³, ELI², THAD.¹)

Russell Ray Smith (b. 1894) entered service in the World War Feb. 24, 1918 and served with the 118th Co. Reg. Hdqtrs, 105th Signal Corps, 30th Division. He was in the Ypres Sector two months, later in the Somme Sector between Cambri and St. Quentin. As Motorcycle dispatch carrier he was wounded the night of Sept. 26th, 1918 while deliver-ing dispatches during the Hindenburg drive, which necessitated the amputation of his left leg above the knee. He was evacuated to a hospital in Rouen, France, then to a hospital in England and later sailed on the Mauretania and sent to Walter Reed Hospital in Washing-ton, D. C., where he spent five months, re-ceiving his honorable discharge Mar. 5, 1919.
Russell R. Smith married Aug. 3, 1924 Lillian Marie Eland and had issue:
561. Margaret Louise Smith b. 8 May 1926.
562. Betty Elaine Smith b. 28 June 1927.

563. Paul Wendell Smith b. 23 July 1932.
564. David Ray Smith b. 21 Mar. 1935.

422. HAROLD H. SMITH⁶ (WM.⁵, JOHN⁴, AARON³, ELI², THAD.¹)

Harold Hawley Smith (b. 1897) married Sept. 28, 1922 Carrie M. Nelson and had issue:
565. Helen Maxine Smith b. 18 Nov. 1923.
566. Leland Hawley Smith b. 18 Aug. 1926.

423. THELMA C. SMITH⁶ (WM.⁵, JOHN⁴, AARON³, ELI², THAD.¹)

Thelma Clare Smith (b. 1903) married Dec. 1, 1921 Walter E. Chase and had issue:
567. Fern Marie Chase b. 26 Jan. 1924.
568. Faith Elaine Chase b. 26 Mar. 1927.
569. Walter Leroy Chase b. 13 July 1931.

425. LELA CELESTE SMITH⁶ (WM.⁵, JOHN⁴, AARON³, ELI², THAD.¹)

Lela Celeste Smith (b. 1908) married June 15, 1938 Raymond E. Nonneman of Rockwell City, Iowa. They have a daughter:
570. Barbara Ann Nonneman b. 30 Aug. 1939.

426. LEWIS L. SMITH⁶ (WM., H⁵, JOHN⁴, AARON³, ELI², THAD.¹)

Lewis Leland Smith (b. 1912) married Aug. 27, 1932 Avonell Conley and had issue:
571. James Lewis Smith b. 19 Feb. 1936.
572. Jerry Donald Smith b. 11 Dec. 1938.
573. Judith Ann Smith b. 24 June 1940.

427. BYRON G. SPEAR⁶ (CAROLINE⁵, JOHN⁴, AARON³, ELI², THAD.¹)

Byron Glenn Spear (b. 1894) married June 29, 1920 Nina Victoria Berg of Storm Lake, Ia. She was born Sept. 24, 1899 and is a daughter of Gustafe Berg of Larrabee, Iowa. They had six children:
574. James Ardmore Spear b. 13 July 1922.
575. Byron G. Spear Jr. b. 13 Jan. 1924.
576. Norma Leona Spear b. 29 Dec. 1924.
577. Donna Darlene Spear b. 19 Feb. 1927.
578. Margaret Eileen Spear b. 3 Jan. 1930.
579. Caroline Natalie Spear b. 20 Dec. 1931.
Byron G. Spear served in the World War with the 13th Engineers R. R. regiment in France for more than twenty-one months under Col. Wm. C. Langfitt, Col. N. L. Howard, Col. C. W. Kutz and Col. C. L. Whiting.

431. NILE H. MARSH (CAROLINE[5] JOHN[4],
AARON[3], ELI[2], THAD.[1])

Nile H. Marsh (b. 1907) married Aug. 8,
1930 Edna Johnson of George, Iowa and had
issue:
580. Virgil M. Marsh b. 15 May 1931.
581. Barbara Jean Marsh b. 26 June 1932.
They now reside at Sioux City, Ia.

435. MABEL E. CRAWFORD[6] (ELDORA[5],
JOHN[4], AARON[3], ELI[2], THAD.[1])

Mable Evalyn Crawford (b. 1895) married
Nov. 6, 1912 Edward Baskett and had issue:
582. Florence Elma Baskett 1913-1933.
583. Eva Belle Baskett b. 21 Mar. 1915.
584. Evalyn May Baskett b. 10 June 1917.
585. Vivian Baskett b. 12 Sept. 1922.
586. Edna Eldora Baskett b. 20 Sept. 1929.

436. VIRA L. CRAWFORD[6] (ELDORA[5],
JOHN[4], AARON[3],, ELI[2], THAD.[1])

Vira Lucille Crawford (b. 1897) married
June 23, 1914 Frank Judson Harper and had
issue:
587. Willard Hudson Harper 1915-1916.
588. Helen Lucille Harper b. 11 June 1918,
m. Forest Blaine.
589. Edwin Arthur Harper b. 26 July 1920.
590. Elsie Eldora Harper 1922-1924.

438. EDNA M. CRAWFORD[6] (ELDORA[5],
JOHN[4], AARON[3], ELI[2], THAD.[1])

Edna May Crawford (b. 1906) married
29 Aug. 1931 Ferman J. Pasold at Spokane,
Wash. They had issue:
591. Ferman Joseph Pasold b. 7 Nov. 1932.
592. David Eugene Pasold b. 27 Dec. 1935.

454. GRACE LILLIAN RICE[6] (HATTIE M[5],
SARAH[4], AARON[3], ELI[2], THAD.[1])

Grace Lillian Rice (b. 1894) married
July 31, 1915 Clyde E. Warren and had issue:
593. Lois Lucille Warren b. 1917 d. 1918.
594. Doris Evelyn Warren b. 9 Jan. 1919.
595. Donna Arlene Warren b. 12 July 1923.

456. ELSIE I. RICE[6] (HATTIE M[5],
SARAH[4], AARON[3], ELI[2], THAD.[1])

Elsie Ione Rice (b. 1899) married 17
Sept. 1923 Guirney U. Sergeant and had one
child:
596. Marie Ione Sergeant b. 22 Feb. 1937.

459. SARAH C. RICE[6] (HATTIE M[5],
SARAH[4], AARON[3], ELI[2], THAD.[1])

Sarah Christine Rice (b. 1905) married
first June 26, 1922 Paul L. Tate and had
issue:
597. Verna M. Tate d. 1937.
Sarah C. Rice Tate married second May 23,
1927 William Stolte and had issue:
598. Helen Ann Stolte b. 19 Sept. 1933.

460. ELIZABETH P. RICE[6] (HATTIE M[5],
SARAH[4], AARON[3], ELI[2], THAD.[1])

Elizabeth Pearl Rice (b. 1907) married
Dec. 2, 1926 Donald L. Rodgers and had issue:
599. Donald Paul Rodgers b. 21 Aug. 1929.
600. Doloris May Rodgers b. 18 Sept. 1932.

462. RUTH M. RICE[6] (HATTIE M[5],
SARAH[4], AARON[3], ELI[2] THAD.[1])

Ruth Marie Rice (b. 1911) married Oct. 7,
1932 Carl F. Marolf and had issue:
601. Darlene Ellen Marolf b. 13 Sept. 1935.
602. Joan Louise Marolf b. 23 Jan. 1937.

463. CLELLA V. JENISON[6] (GRACE E[5],
SARAH[4], AARON[3], ELI[2], THAD.[1])

Clella Viola Jenison (b. 1900) married
Oct. 20, 1926 Leo Roscoe Wright of Jefferson,
Ia., and had issue:
603. Barbara Jane Wright b. 1927.
603A. Gerald Lee Wright b. 23 Nov. 1940.

464. HELEN M. JENISON[6] (GRACE[5],
SARAH[4], AARON[3], ELI[2], THAD.[1])

Helen Mabel Jenison (b. 1909) married
Nov. 17, 1925 Harold Edward Wright and had
issue:
604. Dale Eugene Wright b. 1926.
605. Phyllis Elaine Wright b. 1927.

466. STEPHEN C. THEW[6] (EMMA[5], ELI[4],
AARON[3], ELI[2], THAD.[1])

Stephen Corkins Thew (b. 1885) married
Dec. 4, 1907 Mary Alice Silletts (b. 23 Apr.
1888) and had issue:
606. Stephen John Thew b. 6 Oct. 1908.
607. Alice Marian Thew b. 11 Dec. 1910.
608. Robert Clifton Thew b. 29 Dec. 1912.
609. Stewart Charles Thew b. 26 Apr. 1915.
610. Harold Edmond Thew b. 5 Aug. 1919.
611. Katherine Thew b. 27 Jan. 1921.
612. Ruth Violet Thew b. 24 Nov. 1922.

613. Erma June Thew b. 6 June 1924.
614. Amy Marguerite Thew b. 23 Mar. 1927.
615. Lois Thew b. 11 Feb. 1930.
They reside at Bredenburg, Sask.

467. FRANK A. THEW⁶ (EMMA⁵, ELI⁴, AARON³, ELI², THAD.¹)

Frank Addison Thew (b. 1887) married Dec. 24, 1908 Amy Greenwood (b. July 21, 1890 at Plate, Ill.) and had issue:
616. Harold Addison Thew b. 24 Sept. 1909 at Creston, Wash.
617. Gladys Pauline Thew b. 29 May 1911.
618. Chester Frederick Thew b. 12 Sept. 1912 m. Lucile Squires.

468. EUNICE THEW⁶ (EMMA⁵, ELI⁴, AARON³, ELI², THAD.¹)

Eunice Thew (b. 1889) married July 14, 1913 Frank C. Schultz (b. May 18, 1884 at Grand Island, Neb.) and had issue:
619. Genevieve June Schultz b. 10 June 1915 in Wash.
620. Phyllis Marie Schultz b. 14 Dec. 1917.

469. LULA THEW⁶ (EMMA⁵, ELI⁴ʹ AARON³, ELI², THAD.¹)

Lula Thew (b. 1892) married Nov. 16, 1911 L. M. Benham and had issue:
621. Clifton Benham 1912-1926.
622. Jewell Benham b. 29 Apr. 1914 m. Lester Garber.

470. EDITH V. THEW (EMMA, ELI, AARON, ELI, THAD.)

Edith Vivian Thew (b. 1895) married Sept. 25, 1913 John Irvine Sterett at Davenport, Ia. They had six children:
623. Robert T. Sterett 1916-1934.
624. Verla V. Sterett b. 8 Nov. 1920.
625. John M. Sterett b. 9 Nov. 1926,
626. Ethel B. Sterett b. 17 June 1929.
627. William I. Sterett b. 6 Oct. 1932.
628. Erva F. Sterett b. and d. 1937.

471. VIOLET A. THEW⁶ (EMMA⁵, ELI⁴, AARON³, ELI², THAD.¹)

Violet A. Thew (b. 1903) married Apr. 11, 1924 at Drumheller, Canada Harold Schang. (b. 13 Nov. 1896) and had issue:
629. Lyle Schang b. 22 Sept. 1926 in Canada.
630. Clifton E. Schang b. 12 Nov. 1928 in Ind.

472. OLIVER M. THEW⁶ (EMMA⁵, ELI⁴, AARON³, ELI²̣,¹)

Oliver Morton Thew (b. 1906) married

Dec. 1, 1936 at Coeur de Alene, Ida. Charlotte Flottman (b. 26 Sept. 1919) and had issue:
631. Patricia Jean Thew b. 20 Oct. 1939 in Wash.

473. MAY HAPGOOD⁶ (BELLE⁵, ELI⁴, AARON³, ELI², THAD.¹)

May Hapgood (b. 1889) married May 12, 1907 William Stribly and had issue:
632. Louise Stribley b. 14 Mar. 1908.
633. Evaline Stribley b. 26 June 1911.

474. LORETTA HAPGOOD⁶ (BELLE⁵, ELI⁴, AARON³, ELI², THAD.¹)

Loretta Hapgood (b. 1896) married Sept. 21, 1921 James Earl Vesey and had issue:
634. James Addison Vesey b. 22 June 1925.

475. NETTIE S. CAMPBELL⁶ (MARY⁵, ELI⁴, AARON³, ELI², THAD.¹)

Nettie Smith Campbell (b. 1902) married July 15, 1936 Forrest Henry Bahruth and had one son:
635. Forrest William Bahruth b. 29 Apr. 1938.

477. THEO C. McNALL⁶ (MYRTLE⁵, JAS⁴, AARON³, ELI², THAD.¹)

Theo Clyde McNall (b. 1904) married first Charlotte Pickett and second Alice Stewart (dates not given) and resides at Ewan, Wash. He has two children:

636. Donna McNall b. 3 Aug. 1936.
637. Theo Clyde McNall b. 1938.

485. ZOE R. LYNCH⁶ (NELLIE⁵, JAS⁴, AARON³, ELI², THAD.¹)

Zoe Retha Lynch (b. 1906) married July 3, 1931 Holley Denton and had issue.
638. Donna D. Denton b. 21 Oct. 1938.

486. AUBREY J. LYNCH⁶ (NELLIE⁵, JAS⁴, AARON³, ELI², THAD.¹)

Aubrey James Lynch (b. 1907) married Oct. 23, 1926 Iva Bean and had issue:
639. LLoyd Aubrey Lynch b. 22 Sept. 1927.
640. Ronald Lynch b. Sept. 1929.

487. ERCELLE S. LYNCH⁶ (NELLIE⁵, JAS⁴, AARON³, ELI², THAD.¹)

Ercelle Sarah Lynch (b. 1909) married June 27, 1928 Rex Thomason and had issue:
641. Dale Dean Thomason b. 27 May 1930.
642. Gary Alan Thomason b. 9 Aug. 1936.

488. BERYL M. LYNCH⁶ (NELLIE⁵, JAS⁴,
AARON³, ELI², THAD.¹)

Beryl Mace Lynch (b. 1911) married Oct.
28, 1928 Maybelle Deitman and had issue:
643. Deloris Rae Lynch b. 9 May 1930.
644. Bonnie Lou Lynch b. 31 Oct. 1932.
645. Gladys Marie Lynch b. 21 Feb. 1934.
646. Boyd Mace Lynch b. 25 Nov. 1936.
647. Royce Melvin Lynch b. 28 July 1938.
648. Carolyn Lynch b. 11 Feb. 1940.

489. DARREL D. LYNCH⁶(NELLIE⁵, JAS⁴,
AARON³, ELI², THAD.¹)

Darrel Dale Lynch (b. 1912) married Jan.
7, 1938 Ina Leifer and had issue:
649. Darlene Ann Lynch b. 20 May 1939.

496. VIRGINIA M. DICKINSON⁶(LADY F⁵,
JAS⁴, AARON³, ELI², THAD.¹)

Virginia Myrtle Dickinson (b. 1919) married June 3, 1937 Herman Clarno and had issue:
650. Keith Kern Clarno b. 20 May 1938.

497. JUNE J. DICKINSON⁶ (LADY F⁵,
JAS⁴, AARON³, ELI², THAD.¹)

June Jeneva Dickinson (b. 1920) married
Aug. 18, 1937 James Hendrick and had issue:
651. James Hendrick, Jr., b. 3 Dec. 1938.

510. PURLEY HALL⁶ (CLARA⁵, GEO⁴, AARON³, ELI²,
THAD.¹)

Purley Hall (b. 1897) married May
Kellher and had issue:
652. Macelline b. 1922.

519. JEANETTE G. SMITH⁶ (HAROLD⁵, GEO⁴,
AARON³, ELI², THAD.¹)

Jeanette G. Smith (b. 1920) married June
14, 1939 Arnold Von Essen and had issue:
653. Joan E. Von Essen.

528. MELVIN L. WHITE⁶ (FLORENCE⁵, SETH⁴,
WM³, ELI², THAD.¹)

Melvin Leroy White (b. 1899) married
May 28, 1924 Mae Daugherty daughter of R. P.
and Minnie (Simons) Daugherty and had issue:
654. Melvin White, Jr., b. 1 Mar. 1925.
655. Ralph Glenn White b. 15 Oct. 1926.
656. Iola Mae White b. 6 Jan. 1929.
657. Ilah Faye White b. 3 July 1933 d. y.
658. Galen Duane White b. 5 Jan. 1935.

529. ELSIE M. WHITE (FLORENCE, SETH,
WM., ELI, THAD.)

Elsie Marie White (1901-1925) married
May 26, 1923 William Bowles a son of Howard
S. and Della (Hicks) Bowles, and had one
daughter:
659. Della Kathleen Bowles b. 25 June 1925.

530. CARRIE G. WHITE⁶ (FLORENCE⁵,
SETH⁴, WM³, ELI², THAD.¹)

Carrie Gladys White (b. 1904) married
Sept. 3, 1924 Walter Daugherty a son of R. P.
and Minnie (Simons) Daugherty and had issue:
660. Clarence Dean Daugherty b. 3 Feb. 1927.
661. Dora Belle Daugherty b. 28 Jan. 1929.
662. Rose Aleen Daugherty b. 20 July 1932.

531. F. Evalyn WHITE⁶ (FLORENCE⁵,
SETH⁴, WM³, ELI², THAD.¹)

Frances Evalyn White (b. 1909) married
Dec. 11, 1936 Stuart McFarland son of J. C.
and Sadie (Wilson) McFarland and resides at
Stockport, Ohio.

532. BERNICE L. WHITE⁶ (FLORENCE⁵,
SETH⁴, WM³, ELI², THAD.¹)

Bernice Louise White (b. 1920) married
Jan. 22, 1938 Henry Porter son of James and
Ethel (Jenkins) Porter and had issue:
663. Dorothy Deane Porter b. 9 Nov. 1938.

583. EVA B. BASKETT⁷ (MABLE⁶, ELDORA⁵,
JOHN⁴, AARON³, ELI², THAD.¹)

Eva Belle Baskett (b. 1915) married
Arnold Stone of Kellogg, Ia., and had issue:
664. George Arnold Stone b. 30 Oct. 1934 at
Kellogg, Ia.
665. Florence Margie Stone b. 4 Aug. 1936.

584. EVELYN M. BASKETT⁷ (MABLE⁶,
ELDORA⁵, JOHN⁴, AARON³, ELI²,
THAD.¹)

Evelyn May Baskett (b. 1917) married
Aug. 25, 1936 Lewis Shields of Wallace, Ida.
and had issue:
666. Thomas Mulford Shields b. 18 Apr. 1938.
667. Frank Joseph Shield b. 18 Feb. 1940.

594. DORIS E. WARREN⁷ (GRACE⁶, HATTIE⁵,
SARAH⁴, AARON³, ELI², THAD.¹)

Doris Evelyn Warren (b. 1919) married

3 Aug. 1938 Wayne D. Barber and had issue:
668. Douglas Wayne Barber b. 18 May 1939.

606. STEPHEN J. THEW[7] (STEPHEN[6],
EMMA[5], ELI[4], AARON[3] ELI[2],
THAD.[1])

Stephen John Thew (b. 1908) married
Aug. 13, 1936 Blanche Margaret Shillam (b.
3 Aug. 1916 in London, Eng.) and had issue:
669. Margaret Ruth Thew b. 22 Mar. 1940 in
Calgary, Alb.

607. ALICE M. THEW[7] (STEPHEN[6], EMMA[5],
ELI[4], AARON[3], ELI[2], THAD.[1])

Alice M. Thew (b. 1910) married Oct.
1933 Erwin Gardiner of Bassano, Alb., Canada
and had issue:
670. Duane Erwin Seeley b. 18 Mar. 1935.
671. Robert Douglas Seeley b. 26 Oct. 1936.

609. STEWART C. THEW[7] (STEPHEN[6],
EMMA[5], ELI[4], AARON[3], ELI[2],
THAD.[1])

Stewart Charles Thew (b. 1915) married
Sept. 25, 1937 Dorothy May Sparks (b. 3 May
1919) and had issue:
672. Robert Ross Thew b. 19 Feb. 1939 at
Calgary, Alb.

616. HAROLD A. THEW[7] (FRANK[6], EMMA[5],
ELI[4], AARON[3], ELI[2], THAD.[1])

Harold Addison Thew (b. 1909) married
Nov. 23, 1932 Mary Alise (b. 30 May 1909 in
Manitoba) and had issue:
673. Elaine Shirley Thew b. 12 June 1935.
674. Melvin Arthur Thew b. 25 July 1937.
They reside at Bassano, Alberta, Canada.

617. GLADYS P. THEW[7] (FRANK[6], EMMA[5],
ELI[4], AARON[3], ELI[2], THAD.[1])

Gladys Pauline Thew (b. 1911) married
Sept. 24, 1935 Robert Harold Nickle (b. 26
Nov. L908 Weyburn, Sask.) and had issue:
675. Ronald Keith Nickle b. 16 Nov. 1938 at
Calgary.

624. VERLA V. STERETT[7] (EDITH[6], EMMA[5],
ELI[4], AARON[3], ELI[2], THAD.[1])

Verla Verna Sterett (b. 1920) married
Nov. 12, 1938 Lawrence Lawson and had issue:
676. Beverly Carol Lawson b. 7 Sept. 1939.

The Name

Smith is the most common of all surnames.
It was applied to those engaged as artificers
in metal and wood. The particular family in
New Jersey to which Thaddeus Smith belonged
is believed to have come from Scotland.
There among the highlanders the "Smith"
ranked third in dignity to the chief. The
name originated when with the growing com-
plexity of civilization, it became necessary
to be able to designate a particular John or
James and so John who worked as a "Smith"
frequently became John the Smith and later
abbreviated to John Smith. Likewise the
children of John the Smith gradually assumed
"the Smith" as a patronym.

Smith Lineage Notes

Thaddeus Smith was the youngest son of
Eliphalet and Ann(_____) Smith of Amwell,
Hunterdon County, N. J. Eliphalet Smith died
in the aforesaid County and state about 1797
in which year his will was filed for probate.
The Will names his "wife Anna----his eldest
son Samuel, son Michael, a daughter Temperance
and his three youngest sons: Israel, David
and Thaddeus. Proof of his parentage has not
been found but he is not believed to have been
the immigrant ancestor.

Hise Lineage Notes

Ann Hise Smith, the wife of Thaddeus
Smith was the daughter of George Cosper Hise
who died in Amwell, Hunterdon County, N. J.
about 1801. In the settlement of his estate
which was administered by Nathaniel Wilson,
his widow: Charity Hise and the following
children signed renunciations of their re-
spective rights to administer the estate:
Jacob Hise, Andrew Hise, Ann Smith and
Elizabeth Barrel. There is an allusion to
other heirs whose names and whereabouts were
not known.
According to tradition in the family
the Hise family lived at one time on the ex-
treme frontier. One version states that
George Hise was a miller and another that he
was a blacksmith but according to both he was
a man of powerful physique and great strength.
A band of marauding Indians swooped down upon
his outpost home taking his wife and children
prisoners and burning the house. They killed
the baby by dashing its little head against a
tree trunk and then attempted to gain entrance

to the mill (or blacksmith shop). George
Hise saw them coming and secured one door
and stationed himself at the other with a
sledge hammer and as each Indian attempted
to force his way through the narrow opening,
Mr. Hise with a mighty blow, felled him.
After three or four had thus been killed
the remaining Indians gave up the attempt and
set fire to the building and made off with
their captives.

George Hise is said to have swam the
river or creek and escaped. He at once
started to try to rescue his family and one
by one he ransomed them over a period of
years. However one daughter remained so long
with the Indians that she would run off and
go back to them. After securing her release several times by ransom, he finally
gave up and she remained with them. Her
children were probably the "heirs whose
names and whereabouts are unknown referred
to in the estate settlement of George Cosper
Hise.

The daughter Elizabeth was one of the
last to be ransomed. She incurred the dis-
pleasure of the chief of the tribe by refus-
ing to do his bidding. He threw a tomahawk
at her and she ran into the forest. An Indian
squaw ran after her and together they succeeded in getting to another tribe which they
joined.

It is said that no member of the family
ever went back to the family home site.
Embittered by the treatment his family had
endured, Mr. Hise spent a great deal of time
hunting Indians, releasing their white
prisoners and assisting their escape.

Rouanzoin Lineage Notes

The parentage of Elizabeth Rouanzoin has
not been definitely established. She is be-
lieved to have been a sister of Solomon
Rouanzoin (or Routzahn) of Frederick County,
Maryland, who sold land in Morgan County,
Ohio to Eli Smith in 1822.

The Rauenzahn, Routzong, Rouanzoin family
sprung from an old patrician family of the
city of Mayence on the Rhine and at least
three members of the family came to America
from 1727 to 1750 and established themselves
in Pennsylvania German settlements, later
going down into Frederick County, Maryland.

Elizabeth Rouanzoin and her sister
Catherine (b. 1805) were both born in
Pennsylvania, probably in York County just
north of the border of Frederick in Maryland.

Their parents resided in Fayette County
Penn. in 1812 and where they moved from there
is not known.

1. CAPTAIN MATTHEW DORR

Matthew Dorr was born June 14, 1724 (O.S.) at Lyme, Conn. He served in the War of the American Revolution as captain of the sixth company in Col. Jonathan Latimer's regiment of Connecticut troops and took part in the battle of Saratoga. (See also "Conn. Men in War of Am. Rev." p. 505 and "Official Roster of Soldiers of the Am. Rev. buried in Ohio," p. 116, 117 compiled by Jane Dowd Dailey.)

He married first on the 4th of Nov. 1747 Elizabeth Palmer (d. 1775) and had by her ten children viz: Phebe, Edward, Helena, Matthew, Jr., Samuel G., Jonathan, Joseph, Elisha, Elizabeth and Russell, all of whom remained in the east and therefore do not belong in a study of midwestern pioneers.

It is however of interest to note that three, Matthew, Joseph and Elisha became prominent judges, that Jonathan was a physician and surgeon of some note and Samuel an inventor of a steam-power process for shearing broadcloth.

Captain Dorr married second in 1776 the widow Lydia (Wood) McLean of Silltown in North Lyme, Conn. He was a clothier and miller. In 1794 he with his wife and five younger children set out for the Ohio country but on reaching western Pennsylvania, news of the Indian warfare against the frontier settlements west of the Ohio river made it expedient to delay their journey some months so they did not arrive at the Marietta stockade until in 1795 where they lived for about two years because of Indian raids.

On the 18th of April 1797 Capt. Dorr purchased one hundred acres of "land situated in Adams township of Washington County in the territory northwest of the river Ohio" of the proprietors: Rufus Putnam, Manasseh Cutler, Griffin Green and Robert Oliver. In June of the same year he made a second purchase of one hundred acres at Waterford on the Muskingum.

About that time several Marietta settlers decided to remove up the Hock-hocking river to establish a new settlement in the wilderness forty miles west of the Marietta stockade.

There were a number of older men (veterans of the Revolution) and they took along several stout and hearty young men to do the rigorous work of paddling the canoes and scouting about. Among those who went in that capacity were Edmund, Baruch and William Dorr, sons of Capt. Dorr.

They were so pleased with the country at "Picket's Plains" (later called "Wolf's Plains") now known as "The Plains," that they pursuaded their father to remove to that locality which he did about 1798. A substantial log home was built and he resided there until his death on the 18th of Sept. 1801. He is said to have been buried in the old pioneer cemetery near the Plains. However any stone marking his final resting place has long since disintegrated.

Lydia (Wood) McLean Dorr survived him until Dec. 8, 1813 and is likewise said to be buried in that cemetery. Their children were:

2. Edmund Dorr b. 30 June 1777 in Conn.
3. Baruch Dorr b. 29 Aug. 1778 in Conn.
4. Lydia Dorr b. 30 July 1780 in Conn.
5. William Dorr b. 13 Dec. 1782 in Conn.
6. Rhoda Dorr b. 15 July 1784 in Conn.

2. JUDGE EDMUND DORR[2] (MATTHEW[1])

Edmund Dorr (1777-1852) removed with his parents from Connecticut to Ohio in 1794/5. Two years later he came with the first party of Athens County pioneers and located first at Middletown (now Athens) and later in Ames township (now Dover) near The Plains, O.

He married Feb. 7, 1799 Anna Farmer (1780-1844) but had no issue.

At the time of the War of 1812 he called out the militia as commanding colonel, without having first been appointed by government officials. It was whispered around that he lacked authority and many failed to appear when summoned. This called for a large number of court martials. Those tried on such charges were undoubtedly acquitted as he never received such a commission from the War department and there is no record of his service in that war.

Edmund Dorr served on grand juries many times from 1806 to 1833. He was appointed road viewer in 1808, elected a commissioner of Athens County in 1821, to the Ohio state legislature in 1824 and served as associate judge of the court of Common Pleas 1826 to 1833. He was a trustee of the Methodist Church many years. He died June 1, 1852 at The Plains.

3. BARUCH DORR[2] (MATTHEW[1])

Baruch Dorr (1778-1842) came with his parents to Marietta, Ohio, in 1795. Two years later he was one of the first party of settlers to arrive in what is now Athens County. In June of the same year his parents removed to Waterford up the Muskingum river.

It was there that Baruch Dorr met the attractive little Phoebe Ward (then only eleven years of age) daughter of Jonas and Phoebe Ward who came from Rockingham County, Virginia to Waterford on the Muskingum in 1797. (See #15 Deweese lineage. The husband of Elizabeth Deweese, (Jonas Ward, Jr.) was a brother of Phoebe Ward.)

Baruch and his brothers Edmund and William settled in Athens County and pursuaded their parents to remove there also which they did in 1798 and located near Wolf's Plains (now called "The Plains").

A few years later Jonas Ward removed with his family to Licking County, Ohio.

Baruch, unable to forget Phoebe, traced the Wards to Licking County and there he married her on June 1, 1809. She was born in Rockingham County, Virginia Feb. 21, 1788 and died at Westville, Porter County, Ind. on Apr. 22, 1877.

Baruch Dorr returned with his bride to Athens County where they resided until the autumn of 1835 when they journeyed overland to Porter County, Ind., where they resided until death.

They had twelve children, all of whom were born in Athens County, Ohio.

He died Mar. 4, 1842 and his will is of record in Porter County, Ind. Will book A pp 7 and 8 and is as follows:

"I Baruch Dorr, considering the uncertainty of this mortal life and being of sound mind and memory (blessed be Almighty God for the same) do make and publish this my last Will and Testament, in manner and form following that is to say:

First, I give and bequeath unto my beloved wife Phebe Dorr during her natural life, the use of my real and personal estate, Second, my three daughters, Helena, Julian and Lavina Dorr or either of them, shall receive equally of the avails of the above mentioned estate, during their remaining single and staying at home. The real estate shall belong eventually to my three youngest sons: Jonathan L, Jonas and Joseph Dorr, upon condition they continue cultivating the same, if either of them die, their share of the real estate shall be equally divided among my proper heirs, not leaving it in the power of either of them to sell or convey in any way any part of the real estate to any but one of the heirs.

Third I appoint Russell Dorr, Edward Dorr, Henry Herrold administrators in conjunction with my wife to transact business, give advice, set off dowers to any of my daughters at their discretion and settle disputes. This being my last Will and Testament, hereby revoking all former wills by me made. In witness whereof I have hereunto set my hand and seal this 20th day of August, in the year of our Lord one thousand eight hundred and thirty-nine.

Baruch Dorr

Filed, proven and recorded the 9th day of May A.D. 1842.

The children of Baruch and Phebe (Ward) Dorr were:

7. Helena Dorr b. 5 Mar. 1810, married 24 Mar. 1840 John Wornick of La Porte County, Ind. He died Aug. 1890 and she d. Aug. 10, 1894.
8. Russell Dorr b. 23 Dec. 1811.
9. Belinda Dorr b. 28 June 1814, married in April of 1835 Henry Herrold and resided in Westville, Ind., where she died Mar. 11, 1855.
10. Edward Dorr b. 6 Apr. 1816.
11. Julia Ann Dorr b. 2 Mar. 1818, married June 1853 L. N. Skinner and had one child, name not available. Julia A. Skinner died May 8, 1854.
12. Lavinia Dorr 1819-1845.
13. Harriet Dorr
14. Jane Dorr } twins b. 27 June 1822- d. y.
15. John L. Dorr 1824-1825.
16. Jonathan Lindley Dorr b. 4 June 1827.
17. Jonas Dorr
18. Joseph Dorr } twins b. 13 Aug. 1829.

4. LYDIA DORR[2] (MATTHEW[1])

Lydia Dorr (1780-1842) married June 19, 1806 Jacob Wolf (b. 13 Aug. 1784 in Westmoreland County, Penn., and died Apr. 15, 1851 in Porter County, Ind.) son of Andrew and Eve (Krebs) Wolf.

Theirs was a double wedding held in conjunction with that of her brother William Dorr to Jane Lyons.

Lydia Dorr Wolf died in Porter County, Ind. in 1842. Jacob Wolf married second Sarah_____(b. 1780 in Conn.) prior to 1850, who survived him. There was no issue by the second marriage. The children of Jacob and

Lydia Wolf were:
19. Edmond Dorr Wolf b. 30 Dec. 1807.
20. Elizabeth Wolf b. 25 Feb. 1809.
21. Rhoda Wolf b. 10 Jan. 1811 unm.
22. John Wolf b. 31 Oct. 1812.
23. Jacob Wolf b. 7 Feb. 1814.
24. Milton Wolf b. 25 Nov. 1816.
25. Amy Wolf b. 6 Dec. 1819.
26. Josephus Wolf b. 22 June 1822.

5. WILLIAM DORR[2] (MATTHEW[1])

William Dorr (1782-1832) farmer, resided on his father's home site near Sugar
Creek. He was one of the husky young lads
who accompanied the first band of pioneers
up the Hock-hocking river in 1797.

He married June 19, 1806 Jane Lyons
(b. Feb. 1787) in a double wedding with his
sister Lydia Dorr to Jacob Wolf. Jane Lyons
was a daughter of Joseph and Mary (Cary)
Lyons.

Joseph Lyons was a Revolutionary soldier
and pioneer settler in Athens County, Ohio.
(See Official Roster of Revolutionary Soldiers buried in Ohio - Vol. 1 p. 234.)

William Dorr died May 21, 1832 with
burial in The Plains cemetery.

Jane Lyons Dorr is said to have been
living as late as 1858 but her date of
death is unknown. Their children were:
27. Matthew Dorr b. 1808.
28. Lucy P. Dorr b. ca 1810.
29. Mary Dorr b. 1812, m. 1836 David Herrold.
30. Lydia Dorr b. Jan. 1814.
31. Joseph Dorr b. 1 June 1815.
32. Fanny Dorr b. 1827.
33. Edmond Dorr b. ca 1820.
34. Anne Dorr.

6. RHODA DORR[2] (MATTHEW[1])

Rhoda Dorr (1784-1845) married Mar. 20,
1804 Christopher Wolf (b. 23 Feb. 1780 in
Westmoreland County, Penn., and died Sept.
21, 1845 near Haydenville, Ohio. He was a
miller and stock dealer,a man of exceptional
generosity who (it is said) "gave away more
than all of Hocking County was worth."

A man once stole a cow from him and on
hearing of it, "Chris" told his hired-man to
hitch up a wagon and take over some feed,
"the cow has to have something to eat and I
reckon he doesn't have much feed," was his
only comment.

He was a son of Andrew and Eve (Krebs)
Wolf. Andrew Wolf came to America on the
ship "Hero" from Rotterdam in Oct. of 1764.
He was then about 21 years of ago. He married

Eve Krebs in Philadelphia, Penn., Aug. 8, 1769.
Rhoda Dorr Wolf died May 9, 1845 and is
buried with her husband in the family burial
lot on a hill at Haydenville. Their children
were:
35. William Wolf b. 1805.
36. Lydia Wolf b. ca 1808.
37. Andrew Wolf b. 19 July 1810.
38. Edmond D. Wolf b. 1811.
39. Matthew D. Wolf b. 17 Dec. 1812.
40. Baruch D. Wolf b. 1814, m. 19 Nov. 1836
    Eliza Johnson.
41. Rhoda Wolf.
42. Joseph Wolf b. 7 Jan. 1822.
43. Jonathan D. Wolf b. 1824.
44. Elizabeth Wolf b. 27 Oct. 1827.

8. RUSSELL DORR[3] (BARUCH[2], MATTHEW[1])

Russell Dorr (1811-1879) married Dec. 25,
1834 Emeline James (b. 1813 in Vermont) in
Athens County, Ohio. They removed to Porter
County, Ind., where he died Mar. 8, 1879.
Their children were:
45. Phebe J. Dorr b. 1847 in Ind.
46. Helena E. Dorr b. 1849 in Ind.

10. EDWARD DORR[3] (BARUCH[2], MATTHEW[1])

Edward Dorr (1816-1879) married in June
of 1846 Eliza Bull (b. 1827 in N. Y.) and resided in Portage township of Porter County,
Ind. He is said to have died there Oct. 14,
1879. They had at least six children:
47. Ophelia Dorr b. 1848 in Ind.
48. John E. Dorr b. 1850 in Ind.
49. William Dorr b. 1852 in Ind.
50. Ellen Dorr b. 1854 in Ind.
51. Lillian Dorr b. 1856 in Ind.
52. Oscar Dorr b. 1860 in Ind.

16. JONATHAN L. DORR[3] (BARUCH[2], MATTHEW[1])

Jonathan Lindley Dorr (1827-1909) married
at 20 Mile Prairie, Ind., on Nov. 17, 1853
Laura L. Underwood.

In the spring of 1858 they removed to
Valparaiso, Ind., where he was engaged in the
grocery business until 1865 when he removed
to DesMoines, Ia., at which place he died
Sept. 4, 1909. Their children were:
53. Frank Dorr m. Eliza Schiley.
54. Alfred Dorr. unm.
55. Jane Dorr m. Jasper Harvey.
56. Lovinia Dorr m. John H. Owens and resided
    at Peoria, Ill.
57. Phoebe Dorr, unm.

18. JOSEPH DORR³ (BARUCH², MATTHEW¹)

Joseph Dorr (b. 1829) married in 1856 Julietta Reynolds (b. 1833). He was an attorney at law and resided in DesMoines, Ia. They had issue but names are not available.

19. EDMOND D. WOLF³ (LYDIA², MATTHEW¹)

Edmond Dorr Wolf (b. 1807) married Oct. 29, 1826 Sylva Ann Wells (1807-1837) a daughter of Varnum G. and Sarah (Davis) Wells. They removed to Porter County, Ind. Their children were:
58. Jacob Clark Wolf b. 1829 in Ohio.
59. Sarah A. Wolf b. 1831 in Ohio.
60. Catherine Wolf b. 1834 in Ind.
61. Harriet Wolf b. 1835 in Mich.
62. Charles Wolf b. 1837 in Ind.
Edmond D. Wolf married second Dec. 26, 1838 Loisa Beebe (b. 1815 in N. Y.) and had issue:
63. Prentice Wolf b. 1840 in Ind.
64. Joseph Wolf b. 1842 in Ind.
65. Mary Wolf b. 1842 in Ind.
66. Annette Wolf b. 1846 in Ind.
67. Franklin Wolf b. 1848 in Ind. twins
68. Francis Wolf b. 1848 in Ind.
There may have been other children.

22. JOHN WOLF³ (LYDIA², MATTHEW¹)

John Wolf (b. 1812) married ca 1842 Martha F. _____ (b. 1826 in Ohio) and had issue:
69. Maryette Wolf b. 1843.
70. Myrum Wolf b. 1845.
71. Lydia A. Wolf b. 1848.
Probably there were other children.

26. JOSEPHUS WOLF³ (LYDIA², MATTHEW¹)

Josephus Wolf (b. 1822) married Sept. 30, 1852 Susan Young (b. 1830) and resided in Porter County, Ind., in 1860, at which time there were no children.

27. MATTHEW DORR³ (WM.², MATTHEW¹)

Matthew Dorr (1808-1882) married Dec. 31, 1835 Julia Coe (b. 7 Apr. 1814 and d. Sept. 14, 1904) a daughter of Josiah and Mary Ann (Beach) Coe (see Coe lineage).
Matthew Dorr was a man of powerful physique and the champion wrestler of Athens County. It is said that on one occasion a man who considered himself the champion of the state of Kentucky, walked all the way from his home to Athens in search of "Matt" Dorr, hoping to defeat him in a fight.

However "Matt" turned the tables and the defeated "Kentucky champ" returned home a sadder, wiser man.
Matthew Dorr died Mar. 22, 1882 and Julia Coe Dorr passed away Sept. 21, 1904 in her ninty-first year. Their children were:
72. William Dorr 1836-1838.
73. Adaline Dorr 1838-1888. unm.
74. Mary Ann Dorr 1840-1841.
75. Josephus Dorr b. 1 Dec. 1841.
76. Henry Lewis Dorr 1843-1844.
77. Edmond Dorr b. 31 Aug. 1845.
78. Charles Dorr b. 21 Dec. 1847.
79. Franklin Dorr b. 8 Nov. 1849.
80. Elizabeth Dorr b. 9 Dec. 1851.
81. Leander Dorr b. 1855.

28. LUCY P. DORR³ (WM.², MATTHEW¹)

Lucy P. Dorr (1810-1881) married Mar. 22, 1833 Woodruff Connett (b. 6 Mar. 1810) a son of Abner Connett who came to Ohio from Penn. in 1798. Lucy Dorr Connett died Jan. 22, 1881. They had at least two children:
82. Lydia Connett.
83. Hyrcanus Connett b. 26 Feb. 1844.

30. LYDIA DORR (WM., MATTHEW)

Lydia Dorr (1814-1865) married Nov. 24, 1836 George Connett and had at least three sons:
84. Andrew Connett.
85. Loring L. Connett.
86. Lewis William Connett.

31. JOSEPH DORR³ (WM.², MATTHEW¹)

Joseph Dorr (1815-1884) married Mar. 1, 1844 Dorcas Matheny (b. 11 Feb. 1827 and d. Mar. 22, 1896) a daughter of John and Rebecca (Benjamin) Matheny.
Joseph Dorr died June 14, 1884 with burial in the West Union street cemetery at Athens, Ohio.
Their children were:
87. Eber G. Dorr M. D. (b. 1848) of Menard Co., Texas.
88. Lucy C. Dorr b. 1850, m. David C. Casto of Wirt Co., W. Va.
89. Hadley King Dorr b. 10 Sept. 1852 - d. 1902, druggist.
90. Laura Frances Dorr 1853-1937 m. Mr. Wilson.

32. FANNY DORR³ (WM.², MATTHEW¹)

Fanny Dorr (b. 1827) married May 28, 1843 Charles Matheny (b. 1822) a son of John and Rebecca (Benjamin) Matheny. Their children were:

91. Hannah Matheny b. 1846.
92. Mallissa Matheny b. 1848.
93. Homer Matheny b. 1850 (living in Apr. 1883).
94. Charlotte Matheny b. 1852.
95. Indiana Matheny b. 1854.
96. Henry A. Matheny b. 1859.

33. EDMOND DORR³ (WM.², MATTHEW¹)

Edmond Dorr (b. 1820) married Feb. 9, 1845 Theresa P. Rowell and resided in Rome township of Athens County as late as Feb. 1870. Definite knowledge of their children is lacking but John Dorr who married in 1865 Elizabeth Hooper and Theora Dorr who married in 1868 E. M. Shotwell are thought to have been of that family.

35. WILLIAM WOLF³ (RHODA², MATTHEW¹)

William Wolf (b. 1805) married Mar. 14, 1825 Mary (Polly) Matheney (b. 1806 in Va.) daughter of Frederick and Jane Matheny who came from Hampshire County, Va., (now W. Va.) to Athens County.
William and Mary Wolf moved to Iowa and later to Porter County, Ind., but returned to Hocking County, Ohio prior to 1838. Their children were:
97. Christopher Wolf b. 1831 in Iowa.
98. Joseph Wolf b. 1 Jan. 1836 in Porter Co., Ind.
99. William Wolf, Jr., b. 3 Nov. 1838 in Ohio.
100. Jonathan Wolf b. 1840 in Ohio.
101. Henry H. Wolf b. 1842 in Ohio.
102. Baruch Wolf b. 1846 in Ohio, m. in 1868 Elizabeth Botts.

36. LYDIA WOLF³(RHODA², MATTHEW¹)

Lydia Wolf (b. 1808) married Feb. 26, 1829 Josiah H. Moore of Athens County, Ohio. Their children were:
103. Isaac Moore b. 1830.
104. Andrew Moore.
105. Wilson P. Moore.
106. Baruch W. Moore.
107. Caroline W. Moore.
108. Rhoda Moore.
109. Lydia Moore m. Mr. Westenhaver of Logan, Ohio.
110. Elizabeth H. Moore.

37. DR. ANDREW WOLF³ (RHODA², MATTHEW¹)

Andrew Wolf M.D. (1810-1896) graduated at Medical College of Castleton, Vt., in 1834. He went to McArthur, Ohio where he practiced medicine many years. He married in Renselver County, N. Y. Eliza Lottridge and had by her four children:
111. Sarah M. Wolf.
112. Anna D. Wolf.
113. Charles B. Wolf.
114. Lydia M. Wolf m. Dr. Rannels of McArthur, Ohio.
Eliza Wolf died in 1851 and he later married Pauline Bryan.

38. EDMOND D. WOLF³ (RHODA², MATTHEW¹)

Edmond Dorr Wolf (b. 1811) married June 4, 1844 Caroline Chapman (b. 1825 in N. Y.) and had at least two children:
115. Delilah Wolf b. 1847.
116. Lucy M. Wolf b. 1849.

39. MATTHEW D. WOLF³ (RHODA², MATTHEW¹)

Matthew Dorr Wolf (1812-1893) married Jan. 1, 1839 Chloe Green Brown (b. 8 May 1821 and d. Jan. 12, 1887) a daughter of Perley and Eliza (Hulburt) Brown.
Matthew Dorr Wolf died Jan. 17, 1893 and is buried in Green Lawn cemetery near Nelsonville, Ohio. Their children were:
117. Edmond D. Wolf b. 1840.
118. Rhoda Wolf b. 1842.
119. Lydia M. Wolf b. 1845.
120. Perley Brown Wolf b. 1848.
121. Joseph W. Wolf b. 1849.
122. John L. Wolf.
123. Lafayette W. Wolf b. 23 May 1852.
124. Corinda A. Wolf.
125. Christopher C. Wolf.
126. Phedora F. Wolf.
127. Andrew F. Wolf.
128. Charles P. Wolf.
129. Finley H. Wolf 1866-1926.
130. Loraine L. Wolf.

42. JOSEPH WOLF³ (RHODA² MATTHEW¹)

Joseph Wolf (1822-1858) married May 29, 1844 Mary Rice (b. 1823) a daughter of Col. Jonas Rice and his wife Tamar Culver. Col. Rice served in the War of 1812.
Joseph and Mary Wolf had the following children:
131. Sarah Wolf b. 1846, m. George Fry.
132. Lewis H. Wolf b. 27 Mar. 1848.
133. Mary M. Wolf b. 1849, m. Wm. N. England.
134. Helena T. Wolf b. 1851, m. Samuel England.
135. Andrew J. Wolf, went to Washington Territory
136. Fanny L. Wolf.
137. Effie H. Wolf.

43. JONATHAN WOLF³(RHODA², MATTHEW¹)

Jonathan D. Wolf (b. 1824) married Feb. 7, 1844 Minerva Callis (b. 1824 in Ohio) and resided in Hocking County, Ohio. They had at least one child:
138. Emeline Wolf b. 1847.

44. ELIZABETH WOLF³ (RHODA², MATTHEW¹)

Elizabeth Wolf (b. 1827) married ca 1848 Wilford Stires (b. 1824) and resided in Hocking County, Ohio. They had at least one son:
139. Vernon Stires b. 1849.

75. JOSEPHUS DORR⁴ (MATT³, WM², MATT¹)

Josephus Dorr (1841-1928) married Nancy E. _____ and resided in Mitchell, Rice County, Kan. They had at least one son:
140. William Dorr of Canadian, Texas.
Josephus Dorr died Aug. 24, 1928.

77. EDMOND DORR⁴ (MATT³, WM², MATT¹)

Edmond Dorr (1845-1922) married Apr. 22, 1880 Louisa Barrett (b. 20 Oct. 1857 and d. May 24, 1890) a daughter of William and Mary (McCoy) Barrett of Malvern, Ia.
They removed to Wabash, Cass County, Nebr. Their children were:
141. Della Louise Dorr b. 13 Mar. 1881.
142. Ralph Earle Dorr b. 4 Oct. 1885.
Edmond Dorr died May 19, 1922

78. CHARLES DORR⁴ (MATT³, WM², MATT¹)

Charles Dorr (1847-1926) served in the Civil War.
He married in Athens County, Ohio on Feb. 22, 1881 Effie E. Junod (b. 1848) a daughter of Frederick Lewis Junod (b. 1832 in Ohio) and his wife: Lydia Stephenson (b. 1834 in Ohio.) Charles Dorr died Oct. 28, 1926 survived by the following children:
143. Ralph J. Dorr of Toledo, Ohio.
144. Fred Edmond Dorr m. and has seven children.
145. William L. Dorr b. 11 Nov. 1886, m. 1915 Hazel G. Henry, no issue.
146. Bernice Dorr b. 12 Aug. 1891.
147. Ryland Charles Dorr b. 23 July 1894.
148. Russell Dorr b. 20 July 1899.

79. FRANKLIN DORR⁴ (MATT³, WM², MATT¹)

Franklin Dorr (1849-1886) went to Mills County, Iowa where he married Lorinda J._____.

Their children's names are not available. Franklin Dorr died Oct. 4, 1886.

80. ELIZABETH DORR⁴ (MATT³, WM², MATT¹)

Elizabeth Dorr (1851-1919) married Hugh A. Poston son of Hugh A. Poston Sr., and resided for several years in Mason County, W. Va. Their children were:
149. Frank Poston, preacher of Ironton, Ohio.
150. Albert Poston.
151. Jesse B. Poston b. 1882, m. 1904 Emma R. McDaniel.

81. LEANDER DORR⁴ (MATT³, WM², MATT¹)

Leander Dorr (1855-1935) farmer of near Chauncey, Ohio, married Apr. 25, 1888 Mary Harvey (d. 1914). Their children were:
152. Carlos French Dorr b. 15 May 1889.
153. Nellie Dorr b. 30 Apr. 1891.
154. James H. Dorr m. and had issue.
155. Lucy Dorr b. 14 Aug. 1896, m. Mr. Ferril.
156. Elmer H. Dorr b. 4 May 1898.
157. Helen Dorr m. Mr. Brown of Newark, Ohio.

83. HYRCANUS CONNETT⁴ (LUCY³, WM², MATT.¹)

Hyrcanus Connett (b. 1844) married Mar. 29, 1871 Elzina Bean, a daughter of Isaiah Bean. They had a daughter:
158. Della May Connet b. 1 May 1876, m. Dr. Hixon.

84. ANDREW W. CONNETT⁴ (LYDIA³⁾ WM², MATT.¹)

Andrew W. Connett married May 28, 1868 Sally Brown and had at least three children:
159. Mabel Connett 1871-1940. unm.
160. George Connett.
161. Raymond Connett b. 20 Apr. 1890, m. Irma Hill and had issue.

86. L. WILLIAM CONNETT⁴ (LYDIA³, WM², MATT.¹)

Lewis William Connett, florist of Athens, Ohio, married May 4, 1881 Mary W. Brown and had several children:
162. Harry Lewis Connett.
163. Dana Connett m. Jenny Silvus. No issue.
164. Loring G. Connett m. Ruth Haight and had issue.
165. William Connett m. Lottie Rose. No issue.
166. Mary Connett, instructor, Athens High School.
167. Elizabeth Connett m. 1915 Guy Don Estes and had issue.

96. HENRY A. MATHENY⁴ (FANNY³, WM².,
MATT.¹)

Henry A. Matheny (b. 1859) married
Sept. 4, 1884 Fanny Henry (b. 29 Nov. 1861
and died in 1940) a daughter of Parker C.
Henry and his wife Elizabeth Bean.
Henry A. Matheny died Oct. 18, 1926.
Their children were:
168. Letha Mame Matheny m. W. H. McClain.
169. Raymond Henry Matheny d. Nov. 8, 1908.

98. JOSEPH WOLF⁴ (WM³., RHODA², MATT.¹)

Joseph Wolf (b. 1836) married Nov. 15,
1857 Sarah N. Rogers a daughter of James
Rogers. Their children were:
170. Frank L. Wolf b. 1858.
171. Eugene Wolf b. 1860.
172. Charles J. Wolf b. 1862.
173. Sylvester E. Wolf b. 1864.
174. Elizabeth B. Wolf b. 1866, m. Riley
Andrews.
175. James M. Wolf b. 1868.
176. Dora Mary Wolf b. 1870, m. Wm. Phillips.
177. Cora Meade Wolf b. 1870, d. in inf.
178. Homer V. Wolf b. 14 July 1871.
179. Minnie Florence Wolf b. 1874, m. Wm.
Edward Humphrey.
180. Nellie B. Wolf m. Frank Bennett and had
issue.
181. Myrta A. Wolf m. Charles Bennett.

99. WILLIAM WOLF⁴ (WM³., RHODA², MATT.¹)

William Wolf (1838-1865) married Mary
Jane Parker and had several children:
182. Dora B. Wolf.
183. Albert P. Wolf.
184. Fanny P. Wolf.
185. James C. Wolf.
186. Robert V. Wolf.
187. Lillie M. Wolf.

100 JONATHAN WOLF⁴ (WM³., RHODA²,
MATT.¹)

Jonathan Wolf (b. 1840) married in 1865
Sarah Mintun (b. 1842 in OHIO) a daughter of
Thomas and Nancy Mintun. Their children were:
188. Lewis Wolf. b. 1866.
189. Charles Wolf. b. 1868.
190. Kirby Wolf b. 17 Apr. 1870.

109. LYDIA MOORE⁴ (LYDIA³, RHODA²,
MATT.¹)

Lydia Moore (1844-1939) married William
Westenhaver of near Logan, Ohio, and had six
children:

191. Alice Westenhaver m. Mr. Steinman.
192. Clara Westenhaver m. Mr. Campbell.
193. Ella Westenhaver m. Mr. Keynes.
194. Emma Westenhaver unm.'
195. Lucy Westenhaver m. H. W. Murphy of
Athens, O.
196. Arthur Westenhaver of Columbus, Ohio.

117. EDMOND D. WOLF⁴ (MATT³., RHODA²,
MATT.¹)

Edmond D. Wolf (b. 1840) married ca
1864 Nancy _____ (b. 1835 in Ohio), and had
at least one child:
197. William Wolf b. 1865.

123. LAFAYETTE W. WOLF⁴ (MATT³,
RHODA², MATT.¹)

Lafayette W. Wolf (b. 1852) married 1878
Florence Boudinot (d. 1882) a daughter of
Elias Boudinot and had a son:
198. Willis D. Wolf.

141. DELLA L. DORR⁵ (EDMOND⁴, MATT³,
WM²., MATT.¹)

Della Louise Dorr (b. 1881) married Nov.
5, 1905 G. Benjamin Root, a son of Dr. A. D.
Root of Crete, Nebr., and resides in
Alhambra, Calif. They had two sons:
199. Kenneth Dorr Root b. 23 Dec. 1906,
graduate of St. Joseph's College resides
in Portland, Ore.
200. Howard W. Root b. 3 Sept. 1908 in Okla.

142. RALPH E. DORR⁵ (EDMOND⁴, MATT³,
WM²., MATT.¹)

Ralph Earl Dorr (b. 1885) married Feb.
14, 1906 Jessie McCrory and had three
children:
201. Frances Marian Dorr b. 16 Mar. 1907,
graduate of the University of Nebr. and
teacher.
202. Edmond Neal Dorr b. 21 July 1911.
203. Russell Earl Dorr b. 20 Sept. 1914.

146. BERNICE DORR⁵ (CHAS⁴., MATT³,
WM²., MATT.¹)

Bernice Dorr married Nov. 6, 1912 Earl
Halbirt (b. 1890) a son of E. E. and Berta
(Burns) Halbirt. Their children were:
204. Donna Halbirt, teacher.
205. John E. Halbirt.
206. Roger Halbirt.
207. Philip Halbirt.

152. CARLOS F. DORR[5] (LEANDER[4], MATT[3], WM[2], MATT.[1])

Carlos French Dorr (b. 1889) married Nov. 27, 1913 Nora Ethel Everett (b. 1895) daughter of Lewis and Rebecca (Karns) Everett.

153. NELLIE DORR[5] (LEANDER[4], MATT[3], WM[2], MATT.[1])

Nellie Dorr (b. 1891) married June 20, 1917 C. L. Giesecke, son of Herman W. and Emma (Krietz) Giesecke. They have a daughter:
208. Mary Bernardine Giesecke, student at Ohio University.

200. HOWARD W. ROOT[6] (DELLA[5], EDM[4], MATT[3], WM[2], MATT.[1])

Howard W. Root (b. 1908) graduated at the University of Oregon where he was a member of Kappa Sigma Fraternity. He is engaged in radio and orchestral work in California.
Dec. 15, 1933 he married Lenore Lindholm at Portland, Ore., and they have a daughter:
209. Sally Dorr Root.

205. JOHN E. HALBIRT[6] (BERNICE[5], CHAS[4], MATT[3], WM[2], MATT.[1])

John Earl Halbirt married Dec. 7, 1938 Laura Margaret Plumly a daughter of G. E. and Laura (McGirr) Plumly of Beaumont, Texas.

They have a daughter:
210. Donna Margaret Halbirt b. 13 Dec. 1939.
Dorr or Dore is believed to have been a place name of French origin. The earliest appearance of the name in English records is found about 1271 A.D. in Lincolnshire.

Dorr Lineage Notes

Edward Dorr (1648-1734) came from England about 1670 and settled at Roxbury, Mass. His first wife was Elizabeth _____ (1756-1719). Her surname is unknown. Their son: Edmond Dorr (1692-1776) was a clothier by trade. He went to Lyme, Conn., where he met and married Mary Griswold (b. 1694) on Sept. 14, 1719. She was a daughter of Matthew and Phebe (Hyde) Griswold. Their son: Captain Matthew Dorr (1724-1801) was the Ohio pioneer.
This Dorr family was the type everyone is proud to claim as ancestors. They were always prominent in the community in which they lived and commanded the respect of all their contemporaries. They were likewise thrifty and frugal. One descendant loved to tell that when as a child she was wont to object to sitting up late at night or to getting up before daylight because it was necessary to burn oil in order to see to work, that the older members of the family would laugh and say: "that's the Dorr in her!"

1. JOSIAH COE

Josiah Coe was born at Stratford, Conn. on the 4th of March 1769. While living in the town of Canaan, Litchfield County, Conn., he purchased five hundred acres of land in the "Territory of the United States, northwest of the River Ohio" for which he paid one thousand dollars. This purchase was made the 12th of May in the year 1803.

Two years later he removed with his (third) wife and all his children, except the eldest daughter, to near Middletown (now Athens) Ohio.

He served on the first grand jury in Athens County and was frequently thereafter called to act in similar public service. When it was decided to raise funds by popular subscription to build a court house in the community, he was an early contributor.

As a progressive and industrious farmer he engaged in sending flatboats, laden with his farm produce, down the Hock-Hocking and Ohio rivers to the Cincinnati markets where he sold the cargo and then walked back home a distance of one hundred and fifty-five miles.

He had an unusually keen sense and accuracy of sight and when building a house or other structure never used a measuring rod or tape, instead he would walk along a piece of lumber, size it by sight and spit on the spot where he wanted to place a peg, saying as he did so: "Bore a hole there!" Walk on and spit again - "Bore there!"

It is said that his method was surprisingly accurate and that he was an excellent marksman!

Josiah Coe was a man of varied interests. In addition to agriculture he engaged in the milling business as owner of a grist mill. He bought and sold real estate, took an active interest in community affairs and was one of the nine founders of the Athens Presbyterian church which was established in 1809.

In the one hundred and thirty-five years that have elapsed since Josiah Coe settled in southeastern Ohio with his large family, they with their descendants have been the most desirable of citizens. Few families have equalled and none surpassed the splendid record of high moral integrity, industry and law-abiding citizenry which has characterized the Coe descendants through almost a century and a half of residence in the midwest.

Josiah Coe died Apr. 28, 1846. His Will was made upon his death-bed and bears evidence of having been made hurriedly and by one not accustomed to writing legal documents.

It was admitted to probate May 5, 1846 and is of record in Athens County Will Bk. 4 p. 287 and reads as follows:

"The last Will and Testament of Josiah Coe concerning the distribution of his property. First it is his request that his wife shall live with Joseph Robbins on the farm during her lifetime (that the said Robbins now lives on) and at her decease, for him to have the farm without any division among the other heirs and to have the same as his own. The said Robbins is to support my wife on the farm in a comfortable manner while she lives and this farm is for compensation for so doing and the balance of the estate real and personal is to be divided equally amont the other heirs except Joseph Robbins.

I also appoint James Coe, Isaac Coe, Joseph Brit and Joseph Robbins as my executors.

                              Josiah Coe
Witnessed by
G. T. Beaton
Parker Carpenter

Numerous interesting articles are listed in his inventory and sales, a few of which are given herewith:
1 Old desk at $1.00 - taken by the widow.
1 " bureau" "   "   " "   "
1 Looking glass "   "   " "   "
1 Trunk   .75¢   "   " "   "
1 Rocking chair 1.00   "   " N. Bates
1 Rifle, Gun Horn and pouch at $4.00 taken by Isaac Coe.
1 Bell and strap at $50. taken by James Coe.
1 Flax Hatchet at .75¢ taken by S. Gillet.
1 Salt dish   "   " Mrs. Coe.
3 Blue-edged plates at .25¢.
6 Pewter plates at $1.00.
1 Pewter platter " 1.00.
1 Bedstead and cord at .25¢.
1 Feather bed and pillows at $3.00.
1 Chest at .50¢.
12 Cows
80 Sheep
1 Horse at $20.
1 Yoke Oxen at $20.
16 Hogs and pigs.
1 Pair mill-stones.

Josiah Coe was four times married. His first wife was Esther Curtis (1769-1794) whom he married Christmas Eve in 1793 at Stratford, Conn. She died the following year leaving a thirteen day old baby daughter:
2. Esther Coe b. 3 Oct. 1794.

Josiah Coe married in Dec. 1795 Phoebe Beach (1774-1798) daughter of Nathaniel Beach and his wife Patience Peat. By her he had two sons:
3. John Coe b. 19 Oct. 1796 in Mass.
4. Beach Coe b. 10 Apr. 1798 in Mass.

Following the death of his wife Phoebe in Southwick, Mass., he returned to Stratford, Conn., with his baby sons and there on the 10th of March, 1799 he married Mary Ann Beach a cousin of his second wife. Mary Ann Beach was born at Stratford, Conn., the 28TH of Feb. 1776 and died at Nelsonville, Ohio on the 31st of Jan. 1818. She was the mother of eleven children:
5. James Coe b. 8 Jan. 1800 in Conn.
6. Isaac Coe b. 29 May 1801 in Conn.
7. Mary Ann Coe b. 28 Sept. 1802 in Conn.
8. Charles Coe 1804-1817.
9. Eunice Coe b. 12 Mar. 1806 in Ohio.
10. Lovey Coe b. May 1807 in Ohio.
11. Harry Coe unm (1810-1839) - killed by horse kick.
12. Harriet Coe b. 10 June 1810 (twin of Harry).
13. Salina Coe b. 16 Mar. 1812 in Ohio.
14. Julia Coe b. 7 Apr. 1814 in Ohio.
15. Caroline Coe b. 6 Sept. 1815 in Ohio.

Josiah Coe married a fourth time on June 11, 1818 Amelia Codner by whom he had no issue.

2. ESTHER COE[2] (JOSIAH[1])

Esther Coe (1794-1870) was left motherless when but thirteen days old and was reared by her mother's people. She married John Wells of Stratford, Conn., and had three children:
16. Nathan Wells (1818-1894) unm.
17. Hepsy Wells (1821-1885) m. Dr. Lewis.
18. Sarah Wells (1825-1905) m. Mr. Curtis.

3. JOHN COE[2] (Josiah[1])

John Coe (1796-1842) served in the War of 1812 as private in the companies of Capt. Jehiel Gregory, Jr. and Capt. Nehemiah Gregory in the second regiment of Ohio Milita. He enlisted Aug. 9, 1812 and served until Feb. 17, 1813.

He was a farmer and resided about three miles northwest of Athens, Ohio.

He married the 11th of June 1817 Nancy Armitage, a daughter of John and Nancy Armitage who came from Huntingdon County, Penn.

John Coe died Dec. 1, 1842 at Nelsonville, Ohio and is buried in The Plains cemetery.

Nancy Armitage Coe married July 16, 1845 Sylvanus Lamb. She died Sept. 25, 1868 and is buried by her first husband at The Plains. Their children were:
19. Elizabeth Coe b. 4 Apr. 1818.
20. John Coe Jr. b. ca 1820.
21. Josiah Coe b. 20 Jan. 1823.
22. George M. Coe (1824-1852) unm.
23. Nancy Emily Coe b. 9 Dec. 1826.
24. Hiram Coe (1828-1847) unm.
25. Wesley Coe b. 28 June 1834.

4. BEACH COE[2] (JOSIAH[1])

Beach Coe (1798-1836) miller of York township, Athens County, Ohio married the 20th of April 1819 Anna Dew a daughter of Thomas Dew (1776-1846) and his first wife Mary McDonald.

Beach Coe died the 7th of July 1836 and is buried in the Dew cemetery near Buchtel, Ohio. His widow married in 1840 Perry Bland.

The children of Beach Coe and Anna Dew were:
26. Thomas Coe b. 26 Aug. 1820.
27. Phoebe Coe b. 31 Mar. 1823.
28. Charles Coe b. 30 Nov. 1826.
29. John Coe b. 1831.
30. Mary Coe b. 1836 (posthumous)

5. JAMES COE[2] (JOSIAH[1])

James Coe (1800-1875) farmer, came to the Ohio Country with his parents when only five years old and was reared in true pioneer fashion.

He married June 20, 1822 Catherine Hurlburt who was born the 23rd of Jan. 1808 near Salt Lick in York township of Athens County. She was a daughter of Reuben and Rachel Hurlburt, believed to have been the first white settlers in what is now York township.

Reuben and Rachel Hurlbut removed to Porter County, Ind., where he died about 1843.

James Coe died the 27th of Feb. 1875 at Nelsonville, Ohio and is buried in the old Fort street cemetery on the hill. His wife survived him and went to Iowa (where some of her children resided) and died there Sept. 18, 1887.

5. James Coe

Catherine Hurlbut Coe

35. Josiah Coe

124. J. Gaston Coe

121. Sidney Coe

The children of James Coe and Catherine Hurlbut were:
31. Ebenezer Coe b. 25 Sept. 1823.
32. Mary Ann Coe b. 30 Jan. 1825.
33. Johnson Coe b. 5 Nov. 1826.
34. Jackson Coe (1828-1891) unm.
35. Josiah Coe b. 4 Mar. 1830.
36. Reuben Coe b. 30 June 1831.
37. Lovey Coe b. 3 May 1833.
38. Caroline Coe (1835-1851) unm.
39. Eliza Coe b. 24 Jan. 1840.
40. James Coe b. 1842 at Nelsonville, Ohio.
41. Catherine Coe b. 15 Dec. 1846.

6. ISAAC COE[2] (JOSIAH[1])

Isaac Coe (1801-1873) farmer resided about one mile west of Athens on the west side of Margaret's Creek for a number of years.

He married Apr. 17, 1825 Delilah Ward (b. 1801 and d. 10 Nov. 1843). Their children were:
42. Sarah Jane Coe b. 1827.
43. Amelia Codner Coe b. ca 1829.
44. Hiram Ward Coe b. 14 Apr. 1831.
45. Lucetta Quintella Coe b. ca 1834.
46. Maria Coe b. 1838.
47. Lovey Coe b. 1841 m. 10 Feb. 1863 Wm. Robinson.
48. Sylvester Coe
49. Sylvanus Coe } b. 10 July 1842.

Isaac Coe married a second time Sept. 20, 1845 Sarah Shry (b. 1810 in Ohio) and they had one daughter:
50. Diana Coe b. 1847.

On June 9, 1853 Isaac Coe married his third wife Margaret Sterling by whom he had one daughter:
51. Lucretia Ellen Coe b. 1857.
m. Elias W. Davis.

7. MARY A COE[2] (JOSIAH[1])

Mary Ann Coe (1802-1836) was married the 24th of Aug. 1821 to Michael Wearin who was an early settler in Starr township of Hocking County and who served on the first grand jury of that county in 1818. He was born in Virginia (now W. Va.) in 1791 and died in Mills County, Iowa in 1887.

They resided in Harrison County, Va. (now W. Va.) for a few years but removed back to Ohio in 1827.

Mary Ann Coe Wearin died July 30, 1836 leaving seven small children:
52. Josiah Coe Wearin b. 2 May 1824 in Va.
53. Otho Wearin b. 22 Mar. 1826 in Va.
54. Andrew Wearin b. ca 1828 in Ohio.
55. Harry Wearin b. ca 1830 in Ohio.

56. Experience Wearin d. y. (after 1847).
57. Mary Ann Wearin b. ca 1833 in Ohio.
58. Harriet Wearin b. ca 1835 in Ohio.

9. EUNICE COE[2] (JOSIAH[1])

Eunice Coe (1806-1898) was licensed to wed Nicholas Bates July 21, 1821. No record of the actual date of marriage is to be found in the county records, but the marriage is known to have occurred a few days later.

Nicholas Bates (son of Nicholas Bates, Sr.) was an early settler of Athens County and owned a farm where the Nelsonville brick factories are now located. He was born Sept. 3, 1798 in Rhode Island and died Jan. 6, 1870 in York township of Athens County, Ohio.

Eunice Coe Bates died the 6th of Sept. 1898 at Nelsonville. The children of Nicholas Bates and Eunice Coe were:
59. Charles Coe Bates b. 28 Apr. 1822.
60. John Coe Bates b. ca 1824 - d. y.
61. Eli Bates b. 15 July 1826.
62. Susan Ann Bates b. 27 Apr. 1830.
63. Caroline Bates b. 1 June 1832.
64. Joseph B. Bates b. 14 Nov. 1834.
65. Columbus Bates b. 1836 - d. y.
66. Salina Bates b. 4 Sept. 1838.
67. William Bates b. 1840 - d. y.
68. George Wesley Bates (1842-1863) unm.
   Served and died in Civil War at Louisville, Ky., 92nd Reg. O. V. I.

10. LOVEY COE[2] (JOSIAH[1])

Lovey Coe (1807-1857) married Jan. 28, 1826 Joseph Brett. The latter was born in Colchester, England July 11, 1800. He came to America in 1820 arriving at Philadelphia Oct. 1st. He served as Athens township trustee from 1851 to 1853, was a Justice of the Peace 1853-1862 and was postmaster at Nelsonville, Ohio 1857 to 1862. He died the 8th of Sept. 1863.

Lovey Coe Brett preceded him in death Apr. 19, 1857 and they are buried in the old Fort Street Cemetery at Nelsonville. They had one daughter:
69. Elizabeth Brett b. 25 Jan. 1840.

12. HARRIET COE[2] (Josiah[1])

Harriet Coe (1810-1899) married 31 May 1829 Joseph J. Robbins (a miller) who was born Apr. 10, 1803 in Mass. and died Oct. 20, 1873 in Athens County, Ohio. He was a son of Samuel Robbins (1771-1832) and his wife Nabby Putnam who came from near Boston, Mass. about 1819 and established the first tannery in York township. Through his mother Joseph

J. Robbins was a great grandson of General
Israel Putnam.

Harriet Coe Robbins died July 20, 1899.
Their children were:
70. Sarah Robbins b. 1830.
71. Charles Robbins b. 14 Sept. 1832 -
    merchant
72. Lewis Robbins b. 1835 - Went to Iowa.
73. Julia Laura Robbins b. Oct. 27, 1837.
74. George Porter Robbins b. 1840 d. y.
75. Henry Clay Robbins b. 9 Nov. 1843.
76. Mariah Robbins b. ca 1847 - d. y.
77. Harriet Elizabeth Robbins b. 1849 - d. y.
78. Joseph Robbins, Jr. d. y.
79. Franklin Robbins b. 1845 - d. 1932
    Malvern, Ia.
80. Ida Emma Robbins - d. y.

13. SALINA COE^2 (JOSIAH^1)

Salina Coe (1812-1901) married Dec. 29,
1832 Archibald C. Armitage (b. 1801 in
Huntingdon County, Pa. and died 1875 at
Columbus, Ohio). He was a son of John and
Nancy Armitage early settlers in Athens
County. Salina Coe Armitage died Feb. 11,
1901. They are buried at The Plains, Ohio.
Issue of this marriage:
81. Nancy E. Armitage b. 1836.
82. Caroline Armitage b. 1838 - unm.
83. Elizabeth Armitage b. 1840 - unm.
84. Mary Armitage 1841-1846.
85. John Armitage b. 1843.

14. JULIA COE^2 (JOSIAH^1)

Julia Coe (1814-1904) married
31 Dec. 1835 Matthew Dorr (see #27 Dorr
lineage)

15. CAROLINE COE^2 (JOSIAH^1)

Caroline Coe (1815-1898) married July 4,
1837 Samuel Putnam Robbins (b. 1809 in Mass.
and d. Apr. 8, 1889 in Porter County, Ind.)
He was a son of Samuel (1771-1832) and Nabby
Robbins and through his mother a great grandson of General Israel Putnam.

Samuel P. Robbins and his wife Caroline
Coe removed to Porter County, Ind. in 1837,
where she died Oct. 19, 1898. They had
issue:
86. Esther Robbins.
87. Andrew Robbins.
88. Lyman Robbins.
89. Amos Robbins b. 1841 in Ind.
90. Levi Robbins b. 1848 in Ind.
91. James B. Robbins b. 1851 in Ind.
92. Lewis H. Robbins b. 1853 in Ind.
93. Joseph D. Robbins b. 4 Dec. 1854.

(Five others whose names are not available)

19. ELIZABETH COE^3 (JOHN^2, JOSIAH^1)

Elizabeth Coe (1818-1851) married June
21, 1838 William Weatherby who was born in
Washington County, Ohio, Nov. 27, 1819, a son
of Isaac and Elizabeth Weatherby of Belpre.

Elizabeth Coe Weatherby died June 17,
1851 and is buried near The Plains, Ohio.
Their children were:
94. Salina Weatherby b. 24 Mar. 1839.
95. John Wesley Weatherby b. 17 Aug. 1840.
96. George Armitage Weatherby b. 24 July
    1845.
97. Emily Jane Weatherby b. 18 Aug. 1849.

20. JOHN COE JR.^{3} (JOHN^2, JOSIAH^1)

John Coe Jr., (b. ca 1820) married Aug.
9, 1840 Nancy Dawley and is said to have removed to Piatt County, Ill. Nothing is
known of his descendants.

21. JOSIAH COE^3 (JOHN^2, JOSIAH^1)

Josiah Coe (1823-1858) married Mar. 20,
1845 Sarah Ann Marlett (b. 1824) and resided
at Nelsonville, Ohio. They are said to have
had seven children but only two names are
available:
98. Augustus Coe b. 1846.
99. Augusta Coe b. 1848.

23. NANCY E. COE^3 (JOHN^2, JOSIAH^1)

Nancy Emily Coe (1826-1867) married the
11th of Dec. 1845 Ormond Gilbert Burge (b.
7 July 1820 in Litchfield, Conn., and d. 19th
Sept. 1903). He was a son of Orrin Burge who
came from near Cleveland, Ohio to Athens
County and settled near Chauncey.

Ormond Burge was a shoe merchant and
served as trustee of Dover township twelve
years and as assessor for five years.

Nancy Coe Burge died June 7, 1867 at
Chauncey, Ohio, survived by the following
children:
100. Lemuel Columbus Burge b. 20 Sept. 1846.
101. Caroline E. Burge b. 19 Jan. 1850.
102. Leanora H. Burge b. 21 June 1852.
103. William Wallace Burge b. 5 June 1854.
104. Clara Jane Burge b. 5 Aug. 1856.
105. Cora Belle Burge b. 5 Feb. 1859.

25. WESLEY COE^3 (JOHN^2, JOSIAH^1)

Wesley Coe (1834-1874) farmer of near
The Plains, Ohio, married June 16, 1869
Sophia Sheffield (b. 26 Nov. 1836) a

daughter of Ezekiel and Sophia Sheffield of Athens, Ohio.

Wesley Coe died Nov. 8, 1874 survived by one daughter:
106. Ida Mabel Coe b. 14 July, 1872.

26. THOMAS COE³ (BEACH², JOSIAH¹)

Thomas Coe (1820-1907) known familiarly as "Cap" Coe, lived near Jacksonville, Ohio. He married Nov. 6, 1845 Caroline Mansfield (b. 18 Mar. 1818 in Ohio and d. 13 May 1893).

Her grandfather Mansfield served in the Revolutionary War.

Thomas Coe died 8 Dec. 1907 and is buried in Dew cemetery near Buchtel, Ohio. They had issue:
107. Mary Ann Coe b. 1847.
108. Lorain Coe b. 1849.
109. Lewis Coe b. 1850.
110. John Coe b. 12 Sept. 1852 - d. 1880.
111. Maria Coe b. 1855.
112. James Coe b. 26 Mar. 1863 - d. 1905.

27. PHOEBE COE³ (BEACH², JOSIAH¹)

Phoebe Coe (1823-1848) married Mar. 12, 1840 Caleb Myrick (b. 1817) a son of James Myrick.

She died Mar. 31, 1848 leaving three small children:
113. Emeline Myrick b. 1841.
114. Thomas Coe Myrick b. 1844.
115. Edward V. Myrick b. 1847.

28. CHARLES COE³ (BEACH², JOSIAH¹)

Charles Coe (1826-1903) served in Co. F. of the 122nd Ohio Volunteer Infantry in the Civil War.

He married Feb. 4, 1848 Cynthia Galliton (b. 1829 in N. Y. and d. 1869).

Charles Coe died Dec. 15, 1903 and is buried in Dew cemetery near Buchtel.

They are said to have had five children but only one name is given:
116. Francis Coe b. 1849.

29. JOHN COE³ (BEACH², JOSIAH¹)

John Coe (1831-1910) married Feb. 20, 1852 Diadama Bridge (b. 29 Feb. 1834 and d. 16 Nov. 1903) a daughter of David and Phoebe (Lyons) Bridge.

John Coe served in the Civil War in Co. H., 18th Ohio Infantry.

He died Jan. 11, 1910 with burial at Green Lawn cemetery near Nelsonville, Ohio. Their children were:
117. John Beach Coe b. ca 1856.

117. John Beach Coe b. ca 1856.
118. Thomas G. Coe b. ca 1858.

31. EBENEZER COE³ (JAMES², JOSIAH¹)

Eben Coe (1823-1884) farmer of Canaan township, Athens County, Ohio, married Apr. 4, 1844 Elizabeth Gillet (b. 1821 in Conn. and d. 1908) daughter of Samuel Gillet (1785-1875) who came from Hartford, Conn. and established a tannery on Stroud's Run. His wife's name was Charlotte _____. The children of Eben and Elizabeth (Gillet) Coe were:
119. Elizabeth Coe b. 1846 at Nelsonville, O.
120. Dennis Coe b. 25 Apr. 1849   "   "
121. Sidney Coe b. 1 Aug. 1853, York tp.
122. Eunice Coe b. 1857 in York tp.
123. Samuel Coe b. 5 Feb. 1865 York tp.

32. MARY A. COE³ (JAMES², JOSIAH¹)

Mary Ann Coe (1825-1885) married 28 Jan. 1844 David Jackson of Nelsonville, Ohio. They removed to Cape Girardeau, Mo., and are said to have had six children, three of whom died in infancy, and are buried on the Coe lot in the Fort street cemetery at Nelsonville, Ohio. Nothing is known of the other descendants.

33. JOHNSON COE³ (JAMES², JOSIAH¹)

Johnson Coe (1826-1890) miller of Nelsonville, Ohio married June 24, 1852 Thankful Francis (b. 26 Apr. 1832 and died 19 Aug. 1858) see Bk. 1 p. 44 "Pioneer Families of the Midwest."

Johnson Coe died Feb. 8, 1890, survived by two children by his first wife:
124. James Gaston Coe b. 2 Sept. 1853.
125. George Coe b. 22 June 1855.

Johnson Coe married second Oct. 13, 1867 Mary J. Older and had issue:
126. Clarence Coe b. 20 May 1871.
127. Emma Coe b. 21 Jan. 1874.

34. JOSIAH COE³ (JAMES², JOSIAH¹)

Josiah Coe (1830-1915) emigrated from his native state of Ohio to Iowa in 1854. A letter to his son, written May 24, 1891 speaks graphically of his trip as follows: "Dear George,

I expected to write to you at least once in a week, but I have been thrown out of time and lost one week partly by un-controlable causes.

Last week I was called by my Brother

Jackson. His house was in ashes and the most of his effects so I felt it my duty to go and see him and holp start to build a new house.-------- We have had copious raines this week. It was very dry but everything is revived corn come about as last year with some replanting.

I see by your letter to Artie that you are quite lonely, no wonder a young growing boy, your first experience from home. But your first experience from home is far different from mine. It is true that I was older than you are. I was 24 years old when I first left my Parental Roof and with another young man shouldered our knapsacks and footed it to the Ohio river some 28 miles, then took (a) steam-boat down the Ohio - and up the Mississippi river to Keokuk, Iowa, then footed it across the state to Council Bluffs and up to Harrison County. Oh how I used to long to see Father and Mother, Brothers and sisters and school mates that I was brought up with. But my intention was when I started from home was to go to a new country and as Horace Greeley says Build or Grow up with the country. With that determination in view I have done the best that I could, I thank the Lord that He has Blessed me in so many ways both spiritual and tempural and I realize that the Earth is the Lord's and the fullness thereof and that I am only His steward and will have to give account of my stewardship--
from Father

Josiah Coe was actively engaged in farming for forty years in Harrison County, Iowa where by his industry, good judgment and progressive methods acquired a splendid estate of thirteen hundred acres.

In 1884 he founded and was made president of the First National Bank of Woodbine, Iowa. He retired from active farming about 1895 but continued as president of the bank until his death May 20, 1915.

He was an active member of the Woodbine church of Christ, having donated one third of the cost of a new edifice in 1905.

He married at Plattsmouth, Nebr., Mar. 20, 1865 Jessie Kinnis (b. in Perth, Scotland June 14, 1843) a daughter of Andrew and Mary (McLaren) Kinnis who came to America in 1854. She died Nov. 9, 1919.

Josiah Coe, pioneer of Iowa, like his grandfather Josiah Coe the Ohio pioneer, left "footprints in the sands of time" worthy of emulation by his many descendants. These were their children:
128. Jennie Ewing Coe b. 3 Mar. 1866.
129. Kate Mae Coe b. 20 July 1868.
130. Bertha Edith Coe b. 21 Oct. 1870.

131. George Washington Coe b. 28 Dec. 1872.
132. Mary Nettie Coe b. 2 Mar. 1875.
133. Arthur Josiah Coe b. 30 Mar. 1879.
134. Jessie Scott Coe b. 3 May 1886.
135. Amy Kinnis Coe b. 1889 - d. 1891.

36. REUBEN COE[3] (JAS[2], JOSIAH[1])

Reuben Coe (1831-1907) married 24 Aug. 1854 Susan Hyde. They removed to Memphis in Scotland County, Mo., where they died. They had at least two children:
136. Irene Coe.
137. Charles F. Coe b. 16 Mar. 1866 in Mo.

37. LOVEY COE[3] (JAS[2], JOSIAH[1])

Lovey Coe (1833-1907) married Dec. 25, 1857 Rev. Alfred Jolly a Presbyterian Minister of Ft. Scott, Kan.
They had no issue.

39. ELIZA COE[3] (JAMES[2], JOSIAH[1])

Eliza Coe (b. 1840) married Aug. 16, 1858 John Dixon (b. 28 Sept. 1840) of Hocking County, Ohio.

Eliza Coe was a school teacher before her marriage and John Dixon a teacher of singing schools. He served in the Civil War and worked in southeastern Ohio Mines following the War.

They removed to near Russell, Iowa about 1868. Their children were:
138. Robert C. Dixon m. Mary_____and had issue.
139. George Dixon m. Etta _____and had issue.
140. A. C. Dixon m. Ada _____and had issue.
141. Reuben Dixon m. Mary _____and had issue.
142. Grace Dixon m. Wm. Phippen and had issue.
143. Marcella Dixon m. Stephen Beatty and had issue.
144. Elbert Dixon m. Emma _____and had issue.
145. Mary Dixon.
There were five others, names unknown, three of whom died in infancy.

40. JAMES COE JR.[3] (JAMES[2], JOSIAH[1])

James Coe (b. 1842) married Rilla_____ and removed to Milton, Iowa. They had two children:
146. Allie Coe unm.
147. Ernest Coe.

41. CATHERINE COE[3] (JAMES[2], JOSIAH[1])

Catherine Lucy Coe (1846-1935) was a

teacher in the schools of Athens and Hocking Counties for six years prior to her marriage Aug. 14, 1870 to David Bramwell Cravens (d. 1940). They removed to Missouri in 1877 where she resided at Arbela at her death which occurred May 8, 1935. She was a member of the Methodist Church for seventy-four years.

Bramwell and Catherine Cravens had four children:
148. Frank Cravens.
149. Josiah Cravens.
150. Emma Cravens d. 1904.
151. Dow Cravens.

42. SARAH COE[3] (ISAAC[2], JOSIAH[1])

Sarah Jane Coe (1827-1847) married Jan. 1, 1846 John W. Pickett and died one year later on Jan. 7, 1847.

43. AMELIA C. COE[3] (ISAAC[2], JOSIAH[1])

Amelia Codner Coe (b. 1829) married June 24, 1849 Ira B. Goodspeed.
She is believed to have died young without heirs.

44. HIRAM W. COE[3] (ISAAC[2], JOSIAH[1])

Hiram Ward Coe (b. 1831) married Mar. 30, 1854 Lucretia Moore (1833-1861) daughter of David and Mary Moore. Hiram and Lucretia Coe had issue:
152. Phoebe Coe b. 1855.
153. Mary Coe b. 1856.
154. Lovey B. Coe b. 1860.
Following the death of his wife Hiram Coe married Harriet Robinson and removed to Johnson County, Kan. His children by the second marriage were:
155. Ira R. Coe b. 1866 - m. Henrietta Tuttle.
156. Irene M. Coe b. 1880.

46. MARIA COE[3] (ISAAC[2], JOSIAH[1])

Maria Coe (b. 1838) married William Robinson. She died prior to Oct. 1873. Their children were:
157. Mary Robinson b. ca 1855.
158. Edward Robinson b. ca 1857.
159. Sarah Robinson.
160. William Robinson.

48. SYLVESTER COE[3] (ISAAC[2], JOSIAH[1])

Sylvester Coe (1842-1872) went to Gardner, Johnson County, Kan., where he died about 1872. He married ca 1870 (name of wife unknown) and had one son:
161. John S. Coe b. 1871.

49. SYLVANUS COE[3] (ISAAC[2], JOSIAH[1])

Sylvanus Coe (1842-1922) married Mar. 20, 1866 Catherine Warren and second Aug. 8 1875 Susan Rodgers, in 1917 he married a third wife Mrs. Lucinda Guigerilla. He died Jan. 2, 1922 at Trimble, Ohio. Nothing is known of his children.

50. DIANA COE[3] (ISAAC[2], JOSIAH[1])

Diana Coe (b. 1847) married Joseph Redd and lived at McArthur, Ohio. Her children's names are not known.

52. JOSIAH C. WEARIN[3] (MARY A[2], JOSIAH[1])

Josiah Coe Wearin (1824-1881) went to Porter County, Ind. where he married Sept. 3, 1848 Olive Smith (b. 1828 near Rochester, N. Y.) daughter of James F. and India (Derby) Smith.
In 1854 they removed to Hastings, Ia. where he eventually acquired seven thousand acres of land on which he raised stock. He was vice president of the Mills National Bank of Malvern, Iowa.
He was killed in a railroad accident Nov. 8, 1881. Their children were:
162. Frances Wearin m. Mr. Benton.
163. Adelvert J. Wearin.
164. Caloma Wearin m. Mr. Hyde.
165. India Wearin m. Mr. Coffman.
166. Ida Wearin m. Mr. Fickel.
167. Olive Wearin.
168. Flora Wearin.

53. OTHO WEARIN[3] (MARY A[2], JOSIAH[1])

Otho Wearin (b. 1826) went to Porter County, Ind. about 1852 with his brother Josiah. In 1854 they went to Mills County, Iowa, walking most of the way.
Otho Wearin married Dec. 23, 1859 Martha Workman (1832-1862) and had four children:
169. Charles O. Wearin of Los Angeles, Calif.
170. Joseph A. Wearin m. Mary Donner.
171. William Henry Wearin
172. Mary V. Wearin.

59. CHARLES C. BATES[3] (EUNICE[2], JOSIAH[1])

Charles Coe Bates (1822-1909) married Apr. 9, 1848 Margaret A. Whitmore (b. 31 Jan.

1826 and d. Jan. 17, 1913). He preceded her in death Mar. 3, 1909. Their children were:
173. John Wesley Bates b. 17 Apr. 1849.
174. Elizabeth Bates b. ca 1852.
175. Lewis A. Bates b. ca 1854.
176. Harriet Bates b. 1861. d. y.

61. ELI BATES[3] (EUNICE[2], JOSIAH[1])

Eli Bates (b. 1826) married July 2, 1848 Ruth Amanda Hill (b. 1827 in Ohio) and had issue:
177. Harriet L. Bates b. 1849.
178. Lovel E. Bates b. 1855.
179. Clara J. Bates b. 1858 m. Al Brenholts.
180. William P. Bates b. 1860.
181. Walter Bates.
Eli Bates married second Lydia Devol.

62. SUSAN A. BATES[3] (EUNICE[2], JOSIAH[1])

Susan Ann Bates (1830-1878) married Jas. M. Martin of Nelsonville, Ohio.

63. CAROLINE BATES[3] (EUNICE[2], JOSIAH[1]) ·

Caroline Bates (b. 1832) married Mar. 14, 1852 Elijah Swackhamer (b. 1827 in Penn.). They removed to Frankfort, Ind.

64. JOSEPH B. BATES[3] (EUNICE[2], JOSIAH[1])

Joseph B. Bates (b. 1834) married Lydia M. Wolf and resided near Obetz Junction. He died Jan. 2, 1898.

66. SALINA BATES[3] (EUNICE[2], JOSIAH[1])

Salina Bates (1838-1914) married May 15, 1860 Joseph H. Wilson and had issue:
182. Fred Wilson m. 1st Miss Coakley.
    2nd Louise Jumiper.
183. Flora Wilson m. Winfield Poston.

69. ELIZABETH BRETT[3] (LOVEY[2], JOSIAH[1])

Elizabeth Brett (1840-1879) married John W. Scott of Nelsonville, Ohio. She died Sept. 3, 1879 and is buried in Fort street cemetery.

70. SARAH ROBBINS[3] (HARRIET[2], JOSIAH[1])

Sarah Robbins (b. 1830) married Mar. 23, 1851 John Cheshire.

73. JULIA L. ROBBINS[3] (HARRIET[2], JOSIAH[1])

Julia Laura Robbins (1837-1931) married Feb. 17, 1867 Dr. David Frame Baird (d. 1876)

of McArthur, Ohio and had several children:
184. Charles L. Baird d. Dec. 17, 1934 unm.
185. John C. Baird.
186. Harriet Baird of Nelsonville, Ohio.
187. Mary Baird m. Mr. Stuart of St. Paul, Minn.

75. HENRY C. ROBBINS[3] (HARRIET[2], JOSIAH[1])

Henry Clay Robbins (1843-1925) served in the Civil War in Co. A, 92nd. Reg. O. V. I. under Capt. Elmer Golden. He removed to Mills County, Iowa in 1865 where he later became president of a bank at Hastings, Ia. He married Feb. 2, 1869 Mary Jane Barrett daughter of Dr. Wm. Barrett and his wife Mary McCoy who came from England.
The children of Henry C. Robbins were:
188. William E. Robbins of Gage County, Nebr.
189. Joseph J. Robbins.

81. NANCY E. ARMITAGE[3] (SALINA[2], JOSIAH[1])

Nancy E. Armitage (b. 1836 in Ohio) married Jan. 26, 1869 William Warner.

85. JOHN ARMITAGE[3] (SALINA[2], JOSIAH[1])

John Armitage (b. 1843 in Ohio) married Oct. 10, 1871 Mary Alice Young and resided in Meigs County, Ohio.

93. JOSEPH D. ROBBINS[3] (CAROLINE[2], JOSIAH[1])

Joseph DeForest Robbins (b. 1854) attended Valparaiso College. He removed from Porter County, Ind. to Woodson County, Kan. where he was a large land holder and specialized in raising fine stock. He married about 1881 Harriet Gaylord daughter of Charles Gaylord and his wife Theodocia Sayles of Porter County, Ind. They had three children:
190. Ina Mae Robbins b. 1883.
191. Lewis Leroy Robbins b. 1887.
192. Fern Lynetta Robbins b. 1892.

94. SALINA WEATHERBY[4] (ELIZ[3], JOHN[2], JOS.[1])

Salina Weatherby (b. 1839) married 21 Nov. 1861 John A. Haines of York township, Athens County, Ohio.

95. JOHN W. WEATHERBY[4] (ELIZ[3], JOHN[2], JOS.[1])

John Wesley Weatherby (b. 1840) married

Sept. 14, 1866 Rachel M. Weatherby.

96. GEORGE A. WEATHERBY⁴ (ELIZ³, JOHN², JOS.¹)

George Armitage Weatherby (b. 1845) married Feb. 18, 1866 Mary Jane Weatherby and removed to Hardin County, Ill.

He served as private in Co. G., 63rd O. V. I. 1863 to 1865. He was described in his discharge papers as five feet, eleven inches in height, light complexioned with light hair and eyes.

97. EMILY J. WEATHERBY⁴ (ELIZ³, JOHN², JOS.¹)

Emily Jane Weatherby m. Augustus Coe (see number 98, this lineage)

98. AUGUSTUS COE⁴ (JOSIAH³, JOHN², JOS.¹)

Augustus Coe (b. 1846) married July 24, 1865 his cousin Emily Jane Weatherby (b. 1849) and had issue:
193. Orie Coe b. 1866.
194. Vinnie Mae Coe b. 20 Apr. 1881.

Augustus Coe married second ca 1885 Jennie Call and had by her at least one child:
194A-Sylvia Coe b. 21 June 1886.

100. LEMUEL C. BIRGE⁴ (NANCY³, JOHN², JOS.¹)

Lemuel Columbus Birge (1846-1886) served in the War of the Rebellion.

He married Nov. 24, 1866 Lucia L. Davis (b. 4 Nov. 1845 and d. 16 Mar. 1876) daughter of Edwin and Lucia Davis. Their children were:
195. Bertha E. Birge b. 8 July 1867.
196. Ida Minnette Birge b. 4 Nov. 1868.
197. Ormond E. Birge 1873-1874.
198. Nancy Lucina Birge b. 6 Dec. 1875.

Lemuel C. Birge married second on the 27th of Sept. 1877 Sarah Ellis (b. 15 Apr. 1851 and d. 13 Apr. 1936), daughter of Thomas Ellis (1817-1899) a native of Lincolnshire, Eng., and his wife Mary Ann White daughter of John S. White.

The children of Lemuel and Sarah (Ellis) Birge were:
199. Lemuel Ellis Birge b. 1879 unm.
200. Albert W. Birge b. 1880 unm.
201. Mary Bess Birge b. 25 Jan. 1884.

Lemuel C. Birge died Feb. 19, 1886.

101. CAROLINE BIRGE⁴ (NANCY³, JOHN², JOS.¹)

Caroline Birge (b. 1850) married Silas Stevenson and had issue:
202. Zina Stevenson.
203. Zella Stevenson.
204. Olive Stevenson.
205. Conrad Stevenson.
206. Clyde Stevenson.
207. Vance Stevenson.

102. LEANORA BIRGE⁴ (NANCY³, JOHN², JOS.¹)

Leanora Birge (1852-1884) married Sept. 28, 1873 Tobias Theodore Boudinot (b. 7 Aug. 1852 and d. 27 July 1931) and had issue:
208. Marcellus Lemuel Boudinot.
209. Orley Boudinot.
210. Gilbert Boudinot.
211. Fletcher Elias Boudinot.

103. WILLIAM W. BIRGE⁴ (NANCY³, JOHN², JOS.¹)

William Wallace Birge (1854-1924) married Aug. 31, 1879 Ida Lapham and had issue:
212. Gertrude Birge b. 8 Apr. 1880.
213. Clara M. Birge b. 13 Sept. 1881.
214. Ormond Simon Birge.
215. Ethel Birge.
216. Molly Birge.
217. Hazel Birge.
218. William Birge.
219. Lemuel C. Birge b. 2 May 1879.

104. CLARA J. BIRGE⁴ (NANCY³, JOHN², JOS.¹)

Clara Jane Birge (1856-1938) married Samuel Maxwell and removed to Shelby, Iowa. Their children were:
220. Ida Maxwell.
221. Nettie Maxwell.
222. Wallace Maxwell.
223. Charles Maxwell.

105. CORA B. BIRGE⁴ (NANCY³, JOHN², JOS.¹)

Cora Belle Birge (1859-1930) married Feb. 11, L880 James P. Orme. There was no issue:

107. MARY A. COE[4] (THOS[3],
BEACH[2], JOS.[1])

Mary Ann Coe (b. 1847) married William
H. Mosure and had at least one child:
224, Charles F. Mosure b 18 Jan. 1880.

108. LORAIN COE[4] (THOS[3],
BEACH[2], JOS.[1])

Lorain Coe (1849-1934) married Nancy
Embrey (d. 1929) but had no issue.

109. LEWIS COE[4] (THOS[3],
BEACH[2], JOS.[1])

Lewis Coe (1850-1919) married Mar. 10,
1871. Helen R. Ogg (b. 1847 and had issue:
225. Lewis Elsworth Coe b. 14 Jan. 1872.
226. Stella Coe m. 1st Frank Sharon -
2nd Bernard Powell.
227. Marcus Coe of Penn. - m. Blanche _____
228. Thomas Coe m. Patience_____
229. Oscar Coe 1886-1919.
230. Ida Coe m. Walter Cunningham.

117. J. BEACH COE[4] (JOHN[3],
BEACH[2], JOS.[1])

John Beach Coe (1856-1938) married
Feb. 22, 1873 Laura Matson (d. 1932). He
died at Columbus, Ohio Dec. 25, 1938. Their
children were:
231. Callie Coe b. 31 Dec. 1873 - m. Mr.
Welton.
232. Diadama Coe 1875 - 1903 unm.
233. John C. Coe b. 7 Apr. 1877 of Columbus,
Ohio.
234. Frederick Coe b. 24 July 1879 - m. Miss
Flagg.
235. Elza Coe m. Miss Niel.
236. Carl Coe.

118. THOMAS G. COE[4] (JOHN[3],
BEACH[2], JOS.[1])

Thomas G. Coe (b. 1858) popularly called
"Toy" Coe, married Feb. 20, 1873 Malissa Mays
and had issue:
237. Gertrude Coe b. 10 Feb. 1874 m. Mr.
Jenkins.
238. Grace G. Coe b. 23 Nov. 1876 m. Mr.
Williams.
239. James E. Coe b. 1 Feb. 1879.
240. Elizabeth M. Coe b. 28 Sept. 1881 m.
Mr. Druggins.
241. Emma Coe b. 29 July 1886 m. Mr. Teagarden
242. Roy Coe.

119. ELIZABETH COE[4] (EBEN[3], JAS[2],
JOS.[1])

Elizabeth Coe (b. 1846) married Sept.
27, 1877 Isaiah Winters and went to Iowa.
Their children were:
243. Harry D. Winters.
244. Frances M. Winters.

120. DENNIS COE[4] (EBEN[3], JAS[2], JOS.[1])

Dennis Coe (1849-1911) farmer, married
Aug. 21, 1872 Frances Cook (b. 8 Oct. 1857
and d. 31 Oct. 1928) daughter of Cyrus B.
Cook (d. ca 1901) of Hocking County, Ohio
and resided on a farm near Carbon Hill.
Their children were:
245. William E. Coe b. 22 Oct. 1873.
246. Gertrude L. Coe b. 18 Aug. 1875.
247. Rufus Coe b. Apr. 1877.
248. Emma J. Coe b. 17 Sept. 1879.

121. SIDNEY COE[4] (EBEN[3], JAS[2], JOS.[1])

Sidney Coe (1853-1938) farmer, removed
to Woodbine, Ia. in 1871. There he married
Feb. 24, 1879 Mary Mendenhal. Their children
were:
249. Fred Coe b. 9 July 1880.
250. Frank Coe b. 26 Feb. 1883 unm.
251. Nellie Coe b. 28 Feb. 1887.
252. Bessie Coe b. 11 June 1889 - d. 1891.
253. Glenn Coe b. 14 June 1893.
254. Carl Coe b. 22 Apr. 1898.

122. EUNICE COE[4] (EBEN[3], JAS[2], JOS[1])

Eunice Coe (b. 1857) married Sept. 15,
1891 Marion Everett of Canaan township,
Athens County, Ohio and had at least one
daughter:
254A. Hattie Everett b. 1894.

123. SAMUEL COE[4] (EBEN[3], JAS[2], JOS.[1])

Samuel Coe (b. 1865) farmer of Strouds
Run, married Oct. 9, 1888 Winnie Jane Tucker
(b. 1873) and had issue:
255. Frances Coe m. Wade Everett.
256. Mary E. Coe m. Edward Smith.
257. Nancy Coe m. Owen Wingo.
258. Carl C. Coe m. Edith Smith.
259. Basil Coe m. Anna Bolin.
Four others died in infancy.

124. J. GASTON COE[4] (JOHNSON[3],
JAS[2], JOS.[1])
James Gaston Coe (1853-1915) prominent

farmer of near Nelsonville, Ohio. Married Apr. 18, 1877 Isabelle Martin (b. 1853) daughter of Peter Fisher Martin and his first wife, Mary Ann Hoppock.

Gaston and Isabelle Coe had three children, one of whom died in infancy.
260. Celia Coe b. Jan. 12, 1878.
261. Letty Coe m. A. V. Hintz- no issue.

125. GEORGE COE[4] (JOHNSON[3], JAS[2], JOS.[1])

George Coe (b. 1855) farmer of near Chauncey, Ohio married 1879 Della Shafer and had one daughter:
262. Olive Coe b. 1885.

126. CLARENCE COE[4] (JOHNSON[3], JAS[2], JOS.[1])

Clarence Coe (b. 1871) removed from Nelsonville to Columbus, Ohio. He married Florence Shepherd, daughter of P. W. Shepherd and had three children:
263. Frank Coe.
264. William Coe.
265. Florence S. Coe m. 1940 Robert A. Bratton.

127. EMMA COE[4] (JOHNSON[3], JAS[2], JOS.[1])

Emma Coe (1874-1903) married William Powell and had issue:
266. Helen Powell m. Mr. Stage.
267. Mary Powell - lives in Texas.
268. Alma Powell - lives in Columbus, Ohio.
269. Emma Powell - d. y.

128. JENNIE E. COE[4] (JOSIAH[3], JAS[2], JOS.[1])

Jennie Ewing Coe (b. 1866) attended Drake University three years. She married Mar. 3, 1891 Charles F. Coe who died in 1903 (see #137 this lineage).

Jennie Coe married June 30, 1908 the Rev. Walter M. Jordan (1865-1927) prominent minister of Billings, Mont.

Mr. Jordan had at the time of his marriage three children by his first wife (a cousin of Jennie Coe): Merle (b. 1894), Marian Jean (b. 1897) and Derryl (1898-1916) who were mothered and reared as her own by Jennie Coe Jordan.

She has given many years of her life to work in the field of Christian missions, having served as county president of the Christian Womens' Board of Missions, also as district leader of the Young People's Work in the seventh district of the Iowa Christian Endeavor Union. In Montana she served eleven years as general state secretary under the Christian Woman's Board of Missions.

She now resides in Aurora, Nebr.

129. KATE M. COE[4] (JOSIAH[3], JAS[2], JOS.[1])

Kate Mae Coe (b. 1868) was educated at Drake University. She is a member of the state board of the Kansas Women's Christian Missionary Society and of the Topeka (Kan.) chapter of the Daughters of the American Revolution.

She married June 28, 1892 John William Wilson (b. 22 July 1864) son of David G. and Appalonia Wilson of Effingham, Kansas. He graduated from Drake University 1890 and was principal for fifteen years of the Atchinson County high school, served four years as county highway engineer at Warrensburg, Kan., and has been an elder in the Christian Church for forty-six years.

A letter from Kate Coe Wilson to her sister relates many graphic stories of their early life, some of which are herewith given:

"Do you remember Jeannie-------the long trek of Indians, braves, squaws and pappoose and their pretty spotted ponies and dogs, and their long wagons carrying their tepee and poles or wigwams?

They usually passed the farm in the fall going to some Indian reservation. They seemed harmless but I remember mother was always quite nervous about them. One time when we were all in the kitchen, one brave and squaw came in and reached out his hand to us for some "white man's money." Father was there so mother was brave and spoke up and said: "No! no white man's money, give white man's sugar - white man's flour."

So they took that and went off with a grunt. I remember so well, the old brave went around and shook hands with all of us and how small and soft his hand felt! You know they never did any hard work.

And do you remember the heavy snows that came in the fall and filled the lanes even with the fence tops - - how Father would hitch up the old bob-sled and we would sit on the bottom on hay and he would cover us with the buffalo robes - a large one and a small one. I do not know where he got them but I presume in Omaha on trade. Then he would take us across fields to the Crane school, right over the fence tops, packed so solid it never broke through.

Our noon-day lunches would be frozen hard.

And then the "March thaws" - how Father dreaded them! They came after an unusually hot spell of a day or two and melted the snow so it went off in a mad rush taking fences with it and letting out the cattle and hogs -- I remember Mother telling how Father would butcher hogs and perhaps a beef in the fall and later take his oxen team and load up the bob-sled and drive overland to Omaha (40 miles) to sell his meat and stock up with staple groceries - green coffee that had to be roasted, then ground, brown sugar, ginger snaps, tea, cheese, etc.

There was no real wagon road but he managed to drive some way straight with the sun.

On returning one time, there had been a heavy snow and he was lost, then he discovered some one had been ahead (of him) by the liberal splashes of tobacco juice along the route and so he finally made it home. Much to Mother's relief for she had become very anxious.

Do you remember Father's long cold trips to the timber in Bigler's Grove to get wood for winter use? The immense piles so neatly cut, in the wood shed and great piles outside. I have seen him start out in a bitter cold morning with just the frame of the old wagon, (no wagon box) and he would be seated on a folded blanket, his lunch, which was always frozen, in a dinner pail. He would drive to the timber and cut and saw wood all day, returning in the evening with a wagon load of long heavy logs he had cut. He usually was walking and swinging his arms to warm up his hands. - I was such a little girl then but I believe I fully sensed his efforts to provide for and make us comfortable.

On cold winter nights, if he heard a pig squealing or a cow bawling he would get up and go out to make them comfortable.

What great loads of wheat he took to the mill and return with sacks and sacks of flour which were emptied in the huge flour bin in the pantry! Then there had to be the annual barrel of sorghum - not a little bucket like we get now!

At the time of my wedding, it was the last of June - and hot! Father was making his last trip to town before the wedding and mother told him to get a few oranges and lemons to make a cold drink. When he came home he had a whole crate of lemons and a crate of oranges! The children of John W. and Kate Coe Wilson were:
270. Mildred Coe Wilson b. 7 Oct. 1895.
271. Donald M. Wilson b. 12 Feb. 1898.
271A.Mary Kinnis Wilson. b. 26 Jan. 1900.

A graduate of Missouri State Teachers' College, Kansas State College and Chicago University. She is a member of Pi Beta Phi and has traveled extensively in the U.S.A. and Europe. She is a kindergarten teacher in the schools of Topeka, Kan.

130. BERTHA E. COE[4] (JOSIAH[3], JAS[2], JOS.[1])

Bertha Edith Coe (b. 1870) graduated from Drake University in 1896. She taught two years in the Woodbine Normal College. In 1898 she married John W. Jacobs (b. 1871) son of Henry and Margaret (Lawrence) Jacobs of Lake City, Ia.

Mr. Jacobs is a graduate of Drake University and of the Iowa State University Law School and a member of the law firm of Jacobs and McCauley.

In 1908 he was elected representative in the Iowa legislature, serving several terms.

They have two adopted children Catherine Coe Jacobs (b. 1913) and Jean Louise Jacobs (b. 1918).

131. GEORGE W. COE[4] (JOSIAH[3], JAS[2], JOS.[1])

George Washington Coe (1872-1932) attended Iowa Business College and Drake University. He was for many years, cashier of the First National Bank at Woodbine, Iowa.

He married June 30, 1903 Ora Blanche Kibler (d. 1919) a highly talented and capable woman, a graduate of Cornell College and teacher of art and music.

George W. Coe died Jan. 25, 1932 without issue.

132. MARY N. COE[4] (JOSIAH[3], JAS[2], JOS.[1])

Mary Nettie Coe (b. 1875) was educated at the Woodbine Normal School and the Oberlin Conservatory of Music.

She married Apr. 2, 1902 Frank Eugene Edgerton (b. Sept. 29, 1875 at Woodbine, Iowa) son of Leroy A. and Mary E. Edgerton. He graduated from the Nebraska State University and from George Washington University Law School. He was principal of the Fremont, Nebr. high school two years, reporter for the "Daily Star" at Lincoln, Nebr., for the same length of time, served several years each as secretary to Hon. Norris Brown, U. S. senator from Nebr., and as assistant attorney general of Nebraska.

In 1915 he returned to the private

practice of law in Aurora, Nebr. They have three children:
272. Harold Eugene Edgerton b. 6 Apr. 1903.
273. Mary Ellen Edgerton b. 27 Oct. 1904.
274. Margaret Coe Edgerton b. 2 May 1912.

133. ARTHUR J. COE[4] (JOSIAH[3], JAS[2], JOS.[1])

Arthur Josiah Coe (b. 1879) received his education at Oberlin College and Drake University. He married Arlene Thurman daughter of John C. and Chloro (Williams) Thurman of Green Bay, Wis. on May 15, 1915.
He is engaged in the Insurance and Real Estate business.
They have two foster daughters, Nancy Jean (b. 1923) and Natalie Jane (b. 1924).

134. JESSIE S COE[4] (JOSIAH[3], JAS[2], JOS.[1])

Jessie Scott Coe (b. 1886) attended the Woodbine Normal and Drake University. She taught in the public schools of Woodbine for two years.
She married Samuel R. DeCou son of Isaac and Sarah (Porter) DeCou the 15th of Feb. 1911.
Samuel R. DeCou is a graduate of Woodbine Normal and the law school at Iowa City. He is cashier of the First National bank and president of the Pesgah Savings bank, the Harrison County bankers association, the Harrison County chapter of the American Red Cross and the County Wild Life Association.
Jessie Coe DeCou is a member of the Christian church board, the library board, former president of the Women's Club and served as first president of chapter F. B. P.E.D.
They have two adopted daughters Amy Elizabeth (b. 1925) and Audrey Ellen (b. 1927).

136. IRENE COE[4] (REUBEN[3], JAS[2], JOS.[1])

Irene Coe married Mr. Wainwright and had issue:
275. Clara Wainwright.
276. Jennie Wainwright.

137. CHARLES F. COE[4] (REUBEN[3], JAS[2], JOS.[1])

Charles F. Coe (1866-1903) married Mar. 3, 1891 Jennie E. Coe (see #128 this lineage). He died the 28th of Jan. 1903 in a railroad accident while on a business trip to Chicago, Ill.

163. ADELVERT J. WEARIN[4] (JOSIAH[3], MARY A[2], JOS.[1])

Adelvert J. Wearin was born in Porter County, Ind, but removed with his parents to Mills County, Iowa in 1854.
He was instrumental in establishing a bank at Hastings and one at Malvern, Iowa.
He married in Sept. of 1885 Mary J. Foster, daughter of William and Ruth Foster. They had at least two children, one of whom died in infancy.
277. Josiah F. Wearin b. 30 Sept. 1887.

173. JOHN W. BATES[4] (CHAS[3]., EUNICE[2], JOS.[1])

John Wesley Bates (1849-1928) married Oct. 4, 1875 Laura Isabelle Shepard (b. Feb. 4, 1853) daughter of Aaron H. Shepard (1820-1884) and his wife Elizabeth Jane Powell (1821-1905).
John W. Bates died Dec. 17, 1928 survived by two children:
278. Lena Madge Bates b. 19 Aug. 1876.
279. Carl Hartley Bates 1879-1914.

174. ELIZABETH BATES[4] (CHAS[3], EUNICE[2], JOS.[1])

Elizabeth Bates (b. 1852) married Dec. 30, 1874 Abner Juniper (b. 1853) son of Thomas and Charlotte Juniper. Their children were:
280. Clarence A. Juniper - unm.
281. Walter Juniper.
282. Guy Juniper went to Nevada.
283. Harley Juniper.

175. LEWIS BATES[4] (CHAS[3], EUNICE[2], JOS.[1])

Lewis A. Bates (b. ca 1854) married Jan. 3, 1877 Electa Friedline and had issue:
284. Maud Bates m. Dr. Mansfield.
285. Margaret Bates m. Dr. McPherson.
286. Roy Bates, killed by tractor in 1917.

189. JOSEPH J. ROBBINS[4] (HENRY C[3], HARRIET[2], JOS.[1])

Joseph J. Robbins married Lillian Gaston of Tabor, Ia., and had issue:
287. Thelma Robbins.
288. Ralph E. Robbins.
289. Frank Arthur Robbins.

195. BERTHA BIRGE[5] (LEMUEL[4], NANCY[3], JOHN[2], JOS.[1])

Bertha E. Birge (b. 1867) married Elmer Van Pelt and later Mr. McNeal of LaPorte, Tex.

196. IDA M. BIRGE[5] (LEMUEL[4], NANCY[3], JOHN[2], JOS.[1])

Ida Minnette Birge (b. 1868) married first Herbert White and second: Harvey Courtney. Her children were:
290. Florence Courtney m. Lloyd Pendergrass.
291. Gilbert Birge Courtney b. 6 Jan. 1893.
292. Clifford Courtney b. 24 Aug. 1894.
293. Clinton Courtney b. 24 Aug. 1894.
294. Paul Courtney b. 23 Mar. 1897.
295. Christine Courtney married Ralph Brown and had one son. Ralph Brown, Jr.

201. M. BESS BIRGE[5] (LEMUEL[4], NANCY[3], JOHN[2], JOS.[1])

Mary Bess Birge (b. 1884) married Apr. 28, 1909 Emory Elmer Jacobs (b. 5 Apr. 1880) and had one son:
296. Elmer Ellis Jacobs, attorney at law, graduate of Ohio State University School of Law. He married Sept. 7, 1940 Betty Lou Journay daughter of Arthur G. Journay of Lakewood, Ohio.

229. OSCAR COE[5] (LEWIS[4], THOS[3], BEACH[2], JOS.[1])

Oscar Coe (1886-1919) married Bessie Hostetter and had issue:
297. Ralph Coe.
298. Margaret Coe m. Mr. Wingett.

245. WILLIAM E. COE[5] (DENNIS[4], EBEN[3], JAS[2], JOS.[1])

William E. Coe (b. 1873) married Maggie Wilkinson and had issue:
299. Roy Coe unm. (deceased)
300. Elmer Coe m. Opal Keplar.
301. Ethel Coe.
302. Alice Coe m. Oakley Smith and had one son, William Robert Smith.

246. GERTRUDE COE[5] (DENNIS[4], EBEN[3], JAS[2], JOS.[1])

Gertrude Coe (b. 1875) married in July of 1900 William Young and had two children:
303. Velma Young b. 19 Sept. 1903.
304. Gilbert R. Young b. 15 May 1907.

247. RUFUS H. COE[5] (DENNIS[4], EBEN[3], JAS[2], JOS.[1])

Rufus Hayes Coe (b. 1877) married May 19, 1900 Maud Donahue (b. 1879) and had eight children:
305. Rufus Coe, Jr.

306. Gertrude Coe m. Lester Briley and had issue.
307. Donald Coe.
308. Delbert Coe m. Cora Belle Smith.
309. Thurma Coe.
310. Ulyais Coe d. y.
311. Gerald Coe d. y.
312. Thelma Coe.

248. EMMA J. COE[5] (DENNIS[4], EBEN[3], JAS[2], JOS.[1])

Emma Jane Coe (b. 1879) married Nov. 14, 1896 John Henry Joyce and had issue:
313. Hazel Marie Joyce.
314. Gladys May Joyce.
315. Mary Frances Joyce.
316. Harry Wm. Joyce deceased.
317. Doris Belle Joyce   "
318. Arthur Paul Joyce   "
319. Victor Herbert Joyce
320. Willard Lester Joyce
321. Leonard Jackson Joyce
322. Beatrice Evelyn Joyce m. Wm. Bennett.

249. FRED COE[5] (SIDNEY[4], EBEN[3], JAS[2], JOS.[1])

Fred W. Coe (b. 1880) married Mar. 12, 1901 Estella Wells (d. 20 Apr. 1915) and had three children, one of whom (a son) passed away in infancy.
323. Lyla Coe b. 28 July 1905.
324. Lela Coe b. 7 July 1907.
On Mar. 3, 1921 Fred Coe married Mary Tuttle of Logan, Ia., and had issue:
325. Fred Coe, Jr., 1922-1925.
326. Richard Dean Coe b. 17 June 1927.

251. NELLIE COE (SIDNEY[4], EBEN[3], JAS[2], JOS.[1])

Nellie Coe married William Condron in 1904 and had issue:
327. Eva Joy Condron b. May 1905.
328. Clair Condron b. May 1907.

253. GLENN COE[5] (SIDNEY[4], EBEN[3], JAS[2], JOS.[1])

Glenn Coe (b. 1893) married in 1912 Ola Tiffy of Logan, Ia. and had seven children:
329. Lyle Coe b. 26 Aug. 1913.
330. Marjorie Coe b. 30 Oct. 1915.
331. Glenadine Coe b. 18 Nov. 1917.
332. Alvin Coe b. 26 June 1919.
333. Nina Fern Coe b. 10 Nov. 1922.
334. George Coe b. 19 Feb. 1925.
335. Max Coe b. 15 May 1927.

254. CARL COE⁵ (SIDNEY⁴, EBEN³, JAS²,
    JOS.¹)

Carl Coe (b. 1898) married in Jan. 1916
Mattie Siler and had three children:
336. Delva Carlos Coe b. Oct. 1917.
337. Lawrence Sidney Coe b. Oct. 1919.
338. Dorothy Fern Coe b. Feb. 1922.

260. CELIA COE⁵ (GASTON⁴, JOHNSON³,
    JAS², JOS.¹)

Celia Coe (b. 1878) married Nov. 27,
1901 John Thomas Hope, Jr. (b. 1878) son of
John T. Hope, Sr. and Mary Ellen Boal his
wife of Athens, Ohio (see Bk. 1, Hope and
Boal lineages in "Pioneer Families of the
Midwest." John T. Hope is commissioner of
Athens County and is engaged in the dairy
business. The children of John and Celia
(Coe) Hope were:
339. Geraldine Coe Hope b. 15 Sept. 1902,
    she was educated at Ohio University and
    is assistant to the Alumni Secretary of
    that institution, is president of the
    Athens chapter of the National or-
    ganization of the Business and Profes-
    sional Women's Club and past Ohio state
    treasurer of the same organization.
340. Alton R. Hope b. 1904 m. Mary E.
    Woodburn. They have two children,
    Barbara and Betty.
341. Harry Allen Hope b. 28 Dec. 1911 is a
    graduate of Athens High School and at-
    tended Ohio University. He is a Master
    Mason and member of the order of Knight
    Templar. He is engaged with his father
    and brothers in the dairy business at
    Athens, Ohio.
342. Carol Frances Hope b. 2 Aug. 1913,
    married Max Heston of Amesville, Ohio
    and has a son John William b. 13 July
    1938.
343. Warren Harding Hope b. 9 July 1920 is
    a graduate of Athens High School and a
    student at Ohio University.

262. OLIVE COE⁵ (GEORGE⁴, JOHNSON³,
    JAS², JOS.¹)

Ollie Coe (b. 1885) married Dec. 24,
1903 Charles A. Daugherty and had three
children:
344. Elwood Daugherty b. 10 Feb. 1906.
345. Pauline Daugherty b. 14 Jan. 1910.
346. Coe Daugherty b. 22 Oct. 1912.

270. MILDRED C. WILSON⁵ (KATE⁴,
    JOSIAH³, JAS², JOS.¹)

Mildred Coe Wilson (b. 1895) graduated

at Missouri State Teachers' College and
Columbia University, a kindergarten teacher in
Kansas City, Mo. for twelve years. She married
Sept. 22, 1936 Dwight Moody Davis, son of
Samuel B. and Lucie (Seeley) Davis of Edina,
Mo. Dwight M. Davis is a graduate of Leland
Stanford University, a member of Phi Delta
Phi, legal fraternity. They reside in Kansas
City, Mo.

271. DONALD M. WILSON⁵ (KATE⁴ JOSIAH³,
    JAS², JOS.¹)

Donald M. Wilson (b. 1898) graduate of
Kansas State College Engineering School. He
served in the World War with the marines and
was honorably discharged Jan. 14, 1919. He
is a successful contractor in state and federal
highway works. He married June 11, 1927
Nora Goder daughter of John King Goder and
his wife Lissa Ann (Sinex) Goder of Harvey
County, Kans.
She is a graduate of Kansas State College
and teacher of French and Spanish in Manhattan
High School, a member of Pi Beta Phi and Phi
Kappa Phi sororities. They have two children:
347. Donald King Wilson b. 3 July, 1928.
348. John Coe Wilson b. 16 July 1931.

272. HAROLD E. EDGERTON⁵ (MARY N⁴,
    JOS³, JAS², JOS.¹)

Harold Eugene Edgerton (b. 1903) graduate
of the University of Nebraska in electrical
engineering received his doctor's degree from
the Massachusetts Institute of Technology in
1931. He is associate professor of Electrical Measurements, an expert in the use of
stroboscope and rapid photography, author of
numerous magazine articles and the book
"Flash."
He married Feb. 25, 1928 Esther Garrett
(b. 8 Sept. 1903) graduate of Nebraska State
University and Boston Conservatory of Music.
They have three children:
349. Mary Louise Edgerton b. 21 Apr. 1931.
350. William Eugene Edgerton b. 9 Aug. 1933.
351. Robert Frank Edgerton b. 10 May 1935.

273. MARY E. EDGERTON⁵ (MARY N⁴,
    JOS³, JAS², JOS.¹)

Mary Ellen Edgerton (b. 1904) graduate
of Nebraska University 1926. She married
Sept. 8, 1926 Lloyd Welch graduate of University of Nebraska 1924 and of Harvard University
Law School 1927. He practiced law in Boston,
Mass., and is now a member of the general
council of Civil Aeronautics Authority. They
have two children:
352. Richard Welch b. 26 Apr. 1928.

353. William Lloyd Welch b. 17 Nov. 1932.

274. MARGARET C. EDGERTON[5] (MARY N[4]., JOS[3]., JAS[2]., JOS.[1])

Margaret Coe Edgerton (b. 1912) gradu- ated in Journalism from the University of Missouri in 1934. She married Aug. 18, 1934 Tremain Fisher Robinson journalist of Washington, D. C. He graduated from Mitchell, S. D. High School and the University of Missouri. They have a child:
354. Janice Lynn Robinson b. 26 July 1939.

278. L. MADGE BATES[5] (JOHN W[4]., CHAS. C[3]., EUNICE[2], JOS[1].)

Lena Madge Bates (b. 1876) married 17 Dec. 1889 Perley Willis Hickman (b. 8 Mar. 1876 and d. 28 Feb. 1937) graduate of the University of Michigan. He served in the Spanish-American War, was postmaster of Nelsonville, Ohio during the Taft administra- tion, was a Masonic lodge member and a pharmacist of Nelsonville for many years. They had one son:
355. John Willis Hickman b. 27 Dec. 1903, He m. 30 June 1933 Lawretta Fielder (b. 1911) and they have two children: Martha Ellen b. 1934 and Willis Benja- min b. 1937.

281. WALTER JUNIPER[5] (ELIZABETH[4], CHAS[4]., EUNICE[2], JOS.[1])

Walter Juniper married Lucina Howard and had issue:
356. Howard Juniper, instructor in languages at Ohio State University.
357. Ralph Juniper, student.

391. GILBERT COURTNEY[6] (IDA[5], LEM[4]., NANCY[3], JOHN[2], JAS.[1])

Rev. Gilbert Courtney was educated at Ohio University. He is pastor of four Christian Churches in the Chauncey, Ohio area and is one of the most influential men in southeastern Ohio. He married Helen Bradfield, daughter of Charles Bradfield, Sr. and had issue:
358. Betty Jane Courtney.
359. Isabel Courtney.
360. Marguerite Courtney d. ae 8 yrs.
361. Charles Harvey Courtney.
362. Gilbert Courtney, Jr.

301. ETHEL COE[6] (WM[5]., DENNIS[4], EBEN[3], JAS[2], JOS.[1])

Ethel Coe married Edward Levins and had

two children:
363. Evelyn Levins.
364. Elizabeth Ann Levins.

303. VELMA YOUNG[6] (GERTRUDE[5], DENNIS[4], EBEN[3], JAS[2]., JOS.[1])

Velma Young (b. 1903) married William Bream White of Montgomery, W. Va. June 29, 1932 and had a son:
365. William Bream White Jr., b. 24 Mar. 1933.

.304. GILBERT YOUNG[6] (GERTRUDE[5], DENNIS[4], EBEN[3], JAS[2]., JOS.[1])

Gilbert Young (b. 1907) married 17 June 1934 Rosemary Ucker of Nelsonville, Ohio and had one child.
366. John William Young b. 3 Sept. 1936.

313. HAZEL JOYCE[6] (EMMA[5], DENNIS[4], EBEN[3], JAS[2]., JOS.[1])

Hazel Marie Joyce married Haskel Garri- son and had a daughter.
367. Donna Virgine Garrison.

314. GLADYS JOYCE[6] (EMMA[5], DENNIS[4], EBEN[3], JAS[2]., JOS.[1])

Gladys May Joyce married Russell Dupler and had issue:
368. Garland Jay Dupler.
369. Forest Rex Dupler.
370. Glenford Dupler - deceased.
371. Leonard Wayne Dupler.
372. Robert Leland Dupler.

315. MARY F. JOYCE[6] (EMMA[5], DENNIS[4], EBEN[3], JAS[2]., JOS.[1])

Mary Frances Joyce married Selva Stover and had issue:
373. Beatrice Evelyn Stover.
374. Emma Mae Stover.
375. Eileen Virginia Stover.
376. Selva Stover, Jr.
377. Joyce Marie Stover.

319. VICTOR JOYCE[6] (EMMA[5], DENNIS[4], EBEN[3], JAS[2]., JOS.[1])

Victor Herbert Joyce married Gertrude Pickrell and had a daughter:
378. Doris Mae Joyce.

323. LYLA COE[6] (FRED[5], SIDNEY[4], EBEN[3], JAS[2]., JOS.[1])

Lyla Coe (b. 1905) married W. T. Kennel

of Middletown and had a daughter.
379. Joan Kennel b. 31 Oct. 1932.

324. LELA COE[6] (FRED[5], SIDNEY[4], EBEN[3], JAS[2], JOS.[1])

Lela Coe (b. 1907) married H. A. Johnson of Pomeroy, Ia., and had a son.
380. William John Johnson b. 26 Aug. 1931.

331. GLENADINE COE[6] (GLENN[5], SIDNEY[4], EBEN[3], JAS[2], JOS.[1])

Glenadine Coe (b. 1917) married Lyle Sellick and had issue:
381. Janice Jean Sellick.

336. DELVA C. COE[6] (CARL[5], SIDNEY[4], EBEN[3], JAS[2], JOS.[1])

Delva Carlos Coe (b. 1917) married Lawrence Major in 1937 and had issue.
382. Charlotte Ann Coe.

344. ELWOOD DAUGHERTY[6] (OLLIE[5], GEO[4], JOHNSON[3], JOS.[1])

Elwood Daugherty (b. 1906) married Oct. 30, 1931 Dorothy Rees and had issue.
383. Robert Daugherty b. 4 Oct. 1933.
384. Donald Daugherty b. 16 Nov. 1936.
385. Carolyn Sue Daugherty b. 20 July 1938.

305. RUFUS COE JR[6], (RUFUS[5], DENNIS[4], EBEN[3], JAS[2], JOS.[1])

Rufus Coe Jr. married Frances Stover and had two children.
386. Gerald Coe.
387. Doloris Coe.

307. DONALD COE[6] (RUFUS[5], DENNIS[4], EBEN[3], JAS[2], JOS.[1])

Donald Coe married Anna Pommel and had issue.
388. Jean Coe.
389. Shirley Coe.
390. Robert Rex Coe.

The Name

The surname "Coe" is a place name designating the place at which the family lived as: John atte Coo. Apparently of Dutch origin it has gone through many variations since its adoption as a name, such as Kew, Coo, Koko, Coco, Coa and Coe.

Coe Lineage Notes

The "Coe" or "Coo" family of Essex and Suffolk counties in England emerged from the obscurity of the middle ages to prominence through the valor of John Coo in the battle of San Gullo (1364) in Italy.

He received the spurs of Knighthood, acquired extensive estates and retired to his native shire and spent his later life as a country gentleman.

This Sir John Coo (1341-1415) resided at Gestingthorpe and his descendant of the ninth generation: Robert Coe (b. 1596) became the emigrant ancestor of the Ohio Coe family by removing with his family to New England in America in 1634. The line is

1. Robert Coe m. ca 1623 Marie_____
   b. 1596 - d. ____ b. ca 1600 - d. 1628.
   of Weathersfield, Conn.

2. Robert Coe Jr. m. ca 1650 Hannah Mitchell
   b. 1626 - d. 1659 b. 1631 - d. 1702
   of Stratford, Conn. dau. of Matthew Mitchell and his wife Susan Butterfield who came to America 1636.

3. Capt. John Coe m. 20 Dec. 1682 Mary Hawley
   b. 1658 - d. 1741 b. 1663 - d. 1731
   Miller and Innkeeper dau. of Lieut. Joseph
   Served as Lieutenant, Ensign Hawley and his wife
   and Captain in French and Catherine Birdsey.
   Indian War. Joseph Hawley served as Lieut. in French and Indian War.

4. Capt. Ebenezer Coe m. 18 Dec. 1728 Mary Blakeman
   b. 1704 - d. 1766 b. 1705 - d. 1773
   Served with local militia dau. of Zachariah
   against the Indians. Blakeman and his wife
   Man of distinction in the Elizabeth Denman and
   religious, social and great granddaughter
   military life of Strat- of the Rev. Adam
   ford, Conn. Blakeman the first minister at Stratford, Conn. 1639.

5. James Coe - m. 30 Oct. 1766 Huldah Wilcoxin
   b. 3 Feb. 1741, Stratford, b. 14 Oct. 1739
   Conn. d. 17 Nov. 1813
   d. 31 July 1790 " dau. of Josiah
   Conn. Wilcoxin and his wife
   Served 18 days as private Elizabeth Hubbell of
   in Capt. Jas. Booth's com- White Hills, Hunting-
   pany of Guards in the 4th ton, Conn.
   Conn. Regt. (Ref. Conn. Hist.
   Soc. Coll. Vol. 8 p. 181 & 219.

6. Josiah Coe b. 1769 - d. 1843 in Ohio
   See text.

Beach Lineage Notes

1. John Beach m.   Mary _____
   b. ca 1623 - d. 1677
   Was in New Haven, Conn.,
   in 1643, took the Oath
   of Fidelity 1 July 1644.
   Was an original proprietor
   of Wallingford. Elected
   "Town Crier" 1671.

2. Nathaniel Beach m. 29 Apr. 1686 Sarah Porter
   b. 1662 - d. 1747   b. 1678 - d. 1738
       dau. of Nathaniel Por-
       ter and his wife Sarah
       Groves, and grand-
       daughter of John Por-
       ter (1590-1648) and
       Anna (White) Porter.

3. Israel Beach m. 1 July 1731 Hannah Burritt
   b. 1707 - d. 1792   dau. of Joseph and
   Served in the French   Mary (Wakeley) Burritt.
   and Indian War.

4. Nathaniel Beach m. 22 Mar. 1758 Patience Peat
   b. 1735 - d. 1818   b. 1735 - d. 1792
       dau. of David Peat
       and his wife Mary
       Titharton

5. Phebe Beach m. 24 Dec. 1795 Josiah Coe
   b. 1774 - d. 1798   See Text.
   See Text.

Lineage of Mary Ann Beach

1. John Beach m.   Mary _____
   (Same as foregoing)

2. Nathaniel Beach m. 29 Apr. 1686 Sarah Porter
   (Same as foregoing)

3. David Beach m. ca 1716 Hannah Sherman
   b. 1692 - d. 1735   b. 1695 - d. 1772
       dau. of Matthew Sherman

4. David Beach Jr. m. 30 Nov. 1748 Ruth Hawley
   b. 1727 - d. 1797   dau. of John Hawley
   Served in Revolutionary War   and his wife Sarah
   (Conn. troops)   Walker

5. Eunice Beach m. 26 Oct. 1775 Ebenezer Beach
       b. 1751
       Served in Revolutionary
       War as Sgt. in 8th Co.
       of 5th Regt. Conn.
       troops
       Son of Israel Beach and
       Hannah Burritt (as
       above)

6. Mary Ann Beach m. 10 Mar. 1799 Josiah Coe
   b. 28 Feb. 1776 - d 31 Jan. 1818   See Text

References

1. National Archives - Washington, D. C.
2. Court, cemetery and family records for
   Washington, Hocking and Athens Counties, O.
3. Robert Coe, Puritan
4. Beach Family Magazine
5. County histories, family genealogies, etc.

1. RESOLVED FULLER

Resolved Fuller was born on the 16th of Sept. in the year 1780 at Pomfret, Conn. In 1796, when but sixteen years of age he left his native state in company with another young man for the Northwest Territory on foot. The only roads were not much more than wagon ruts through the forests and their shoes soon wore out so they were obliged to travel much of the way barefoot. When he arrived at the Marietta settlement he had only 37 1/2 cents left.

It speaks well for his industry and thrift that in less than a year later (Apr. 17, 1797) he was able to purchase a sizable tract of land, from the Ohio company, in Adams township of Washington County.

He married Apr. 3, 1806 Elizabeth V. Nash (b. 22 May 1786 and d. 17 July 1825) daughter of Samuel Nash and his first wife Vashti Pierre.

In 1813 they removed to Dover township, Athens County, Ohio where he purchased all that district where Chauncey and Millfield now stand.

He established the first salt-works in the County, there in 1838. He likewise owned a general store and at the time of his death (Aug. 14, 1850) the inventory of his large estate covered many pages in the record books of Athens County.

His Will is of record in Bk. 5, p. 313 and reads as follows:

"Know all men by these presents that I, Resolved Fuller of Millfield in the County of Athens and state of Ohio, being of sound disposing mind and memory do make and publish this my last Will and Testament.

1st. I give an bequeath to my son Russell N. Fuller's heirs a certain Bankstock in the Branch Bank of Ohio in Athens, said Bank stock to remain in Bank until the dividends pay up the thirty per cent before he draws on said stock (which) is not transferable in any way.

2nd. I give and bequeath to William F. Harmon son of R. G. Harmon a certain Lot of Land in Dover township, Athens County and state of Ohio, said Lot of Land was reserved by me when I sold and conveyed my farm to Ewing Vinton and company containing fifteen acres more or less. Also two hundred and fifty Dollars in money to be paid when he becomes of age.

3rd. I give and bequeath to Alace M. Harmon daughter of R. G. Harmon two Lots and House in the Town of Nelsonville, County and state aforesaid being Lots No. 103 and 104 also Two hundred and fifty Dollars in money.

4th. I give and bequeath to my daughter Lovina Grant and her heirs one thousand dollars to be paid out of the Mortgage given to Resolved Fuller by Wm. P. Cutler.

5th. It is also my wish that Austin Fuller and Hiram Fuller be my administrators or executors of my estate and further that I appoint Resolved Fuller Jr. agent for the property I will to William F. Harmon and Austin True to be agent of the property I will Alace M. Harmon. In testimony whereof I have hereunto set my hand and seal this 10th day of August 1850.
                                    Resolved Fuller
Signed, sealed, published and declared by the said Resolved Fuller as and for his Last Will and Testament in the presence of us who in the presence of each other and at his request have hereunto subscribed our names as witnesses."
Joel Sanders
Henry Brown
Thomas Ellis

Proved in court Aug. 19, 1850.

Resolved Fuller was a man much respected in the community and was elected Dover township trustee on several occasions and many times served on grand and petit juries through the first half century of the history of Athens County.

At the time of his death he was engaged in mercantile business and among the multudinous listings in the inventory were cashmere, red flannel, gingham, muslin, towels, tablecloth, sheeting, mustard, pencils, hose, buckets, dippers, candlesticks, teaspoons, chisels, dishes, silk, etc.

Among those owing debts to Resolved Fuller and their rating were:
D. W. Weethee - good
Daniel Curtis - uncollectable
David Eggleston -   "
Shep Tinker - doubtful
Elizabeth Tinker - doubtful
Edwin Davis - good
Isaiah Davis - good
James Davis - doubtful
R. G. Harmon - doubtful
John Chadwell - good
Samuel Chadwell - good
Austin True - good

Josiah True - good

The estate amounted to $13,439.94 exclusive of large acreages which he had previously transferred by deeds to his various children. His children by Elizabeth Nash his first wife were:
2. Almira Fuller b. 27 Sept. 1807.
3. Eveline Fuller b. 16 Apr. 1809.
4. Ira Fuller 1810-1825.
5. Hiram Fuller b. 22 Feb. 1812.
6. Austin Fuller b. 14 May 1814.
7. Russell Nash Fuller b. 13 Jan. 1817.
8. Lovina Fuller b. 5 Apr. 1818.
9. Elizabeth Fuller b. 3 May 1820
10. Resolved Fuller Jr. b. 10 Aug. 1823.

Resolved Fuller Sr. married second Oct. 15, 1825 Nancy Bachelder (b. Belfast, Maine Sept. 4, 1797 and d. Oct. 29, 1870) daughter of Benjamin Bachelder Jr. (b. 1773 in N. H. and d. 1859 Elkhart County, Ind.) and Olive Leighton his wife. The Bachelders came to Ohio through the influence of glowing letters sent them by the Dorr family who had been their neighbors at one time.

By Nancy Bachelder, his wife, Resolved Fuller had one daughter.
11. Jane Fuller b. 16 Sept. 1826.

The Fullers, their children with exception of Lovina Grant, Resolved Jr. and possibly Elizabeth Harmon are buried in Nye cemetery at Chauncey.

2. ALMIRA FULLER[2] (RESOLVED[1])

Almira Fuller (1807-1875) married Dec. 12, 1827 Charles S. Tinker (b. 5 May 1804 in Hampshire Co. Mass. and d. 7 Apr. 1884) a son of Elisha and Lydia (Shepherd) Tinker of Perry County, Ohio.

Almira Fuller Tinker d. Feb. 16, 1875. Her children were:
12. Charles H. Tinker b. 1829.
13. Elizabeth L. Tinker b. 1831.
14. Almyra Roxanna Tinker b. 1833.
15. Eugene A. Tinker b. 1835 - went to Topeka, Kan.
16. Resolved W. Tinker b. 1843.
17. Frances A. Tinker m. 1869 Thos. R. Myers - 2nd H. Pierce of Kan.
18. Austin H. Tinker b. 1846 - Went to Ross Co. Ohio.
19. Elisha W. Tinker M.D. b. 1843.
20. Bethnia Adeline Tinker b. 1837.

3. EVELINE FULLER[2] (RESOLVED[1])

Eveline Fuller (1809-1843) married 30 Mar. 1830 Daniel W. Weethee (b. 12 Jan. 1804 and d. 4 Sept. 1879) son of Daniel Weethee Jr.

(1779-1846) and his wife Lucy Wilkins (1779-1833) who came from Milford, N. H. in 1798 and settled first at Marietta and in 1802 came to Ames township of Athens County, Ohio. Eveline Fuller Weethee died 28 Apr. 1843 with burial at Nye cemetery. They had issue:
21. Lucy J. Weethee b. 1831.
22. Laura W. Weethee b. 1833 - m. 1859 J. S. Jennings.
23. Lavinia Weethee b. 1834 - m. 1863 James F Henry.
24. Daniel F. Weethee 1837-1865 - unm. of Trimble, Ohio.
25. Marcellus Weethee 1841-1844.
26. Eveline B. Weethee b. 1843 - m. 1870 Albert Moorehead.

5. HIRAM FULLER[2] (RESOLVED[1])

Hiram Fuller (1812-1888) jeweler of Chauncey, Ohio, married 13 Aug. 1833 Eleanor G. Conn (b. 27 July 1810 in Pa. and d. 12 Aug. 1873).

He served Athens County as Justice of the Peace 1846 to 1868. He died June 17, 1888. Their children were:
27. Mary Jane Fuller b. 1834.
28. Ira R. Fuller b. 3 June 1838.
29. Caroline Fuller b. 1839.
30. Susannah Fuller b. 1840.
31. Charles Fuller b. 1842 d. y.

Hiram Fuller married Nov. 25, 1874 Mrs. Sarah (Musgrave) Rice. She was born in Va. 1822 and died at Millfield, Ohio Aug. 15 1906.

6. AUSTIN FULLER[2] (RESOLVED)

Austin Fuller (1814-1876) farmer of near Chauncey, Ohio married Oct. 16, 1835 Mary Pratt (b. 19 Jan. 1817 and died 31 Mar. 1889) daughter of Azariah Pratt (1769-1836) and his wife Sarah C. Nye (1777-1857) who were married in Marietta, Ohio, May 4, 1797.

He served Dover township as trustee from 1850 to 1862. He died July 15, 1876 leaving the following children:
32. George Fuller b. 1837.
33. Flavius Fuller b. 1838.
34. Sarah Elizabeth Fuller b. 18 Jan. 1840.
35. Abigail Fuller b. 1841.
36. Resolved E. Fuller b. 1843.
37. Melzer N. Fuller b. 16 Dec. 1844.
38. Dudley D. Fuller b. 4 Mar. 1847.
39. Mary P. Fuller 1849-1919 - unm.
40. Eveline Fuller b. 1851.
41. Amy M. Fuller b. 1854 - d. y.
42. Carlin Fuller b. 1862.

7. RUSSELL N. FULLER[2] (RESOLVED[1])

Russell Nash Fuller M.D. (1817-1899) married 19 Apr. 1840 Eliza Buckingham Cooley (b. 31 Oct. 1820 and d. 21 May 1903) daughter of Caleb Cooley and his wife Matilda Buckingham of Coolville, Ohio.

Dr. Fuller practiced the profession of medicine many years in Athens and Meigs Counties. At one time he served Dover township as treasurer and as trustee.

In appearance he was courtly and distinguished, always wore a high silk hat and frock-coat and had white hair and beard. He died Jan. 31, 1899 leaving the following children:
43. Charles Resolved Fuller b. 5 Mar. 1841.
44. Mary Ella Fuller b. 6 Nov. 1844 in Meigs County, Ohio.
45. Emma Fuller (1846-1923) m. Elias James - no issue.
46. Milton Cooley Fuller b. 27 June 1848.
47. Susan Kate Fuller b. 13 Aug. 1850.
48. John Russell Fuller b. 26 Aug. 1852.
49. Henry Herbert Fuller b. 23 Nov. 1855.
50. Adela Esther Fuller b. 23 Nov. 1855. twins

8. LOVINIA FULLER[2] (RESOLVED[1])

Lovinia Fuller (1818-1846) married July 16, 1834 Royal C. Grant and removed to Middleport, Meigs County, Ohio. They had at least six children who survived her and also their grandfather Fuller and were living in Oct. of 1853 when his estate was settled. They were:
51. James Fuller Grant b. 1835.
52. Elbert Clark Grant b. ca 1837.
53. Edmond Sehon Grant b. ca 1839.
54. Eveline Grant b. ca 1841.
55. Lydia Augusta Grant b. ca 1843.
56. Emerson R. Grant b. ca 1845.

There was possibly a daughter Elizabeth who died in infancy.

9. ELIZABETH FULLER[2] (RESOLVED)

Elizabeth Fuller (1820 - ca 1844) married June 11, 1841 Robert G. Harmon (d. 1856) and had two children:
57. Alice W. Harmon b. 1842.
58. William F. Harmon b. 1843.

10. RESOLVED FULLER[2] JR. (RESOLVED[1])

Resolved Fuller Jr. (b. 1823) married Nov. 23, 1845 Olthenia Curtis (b. 1827) and removed to Iowa. Their children were:
59. Nancy Jane Fuller b. 7 Feb. 1847 d. 1875 in Kan.
60. Mary Porter Fuller b. 11 Feb. 1849 at Dover, Ohio.
61. Henry Nash Fuller b. 4 July 1851 - m. Sarah Ellen Thompson.
62. Hiram Allen Fuller b. 9 Feb. 1853 - Des Moines, Ia.
63. James Dixon Fuller b. 7 Oct. 1855 - Dallas Co., Ia.
64. Elizabeth Caroline Fuller b. 20 June 1858 - Shawnee Co., Ia.
65. Joseph Curtis Fuller b. 26 Feb. 1861 - Jefferson Co., Ia.
66. Eva Almira Olthenia Fuller 1863-1865.

11. JANE FULLER[2] (RESOLVED[1])

Jane Fuller (1826-1853) married Feb. 11, 1844 Austin True (b. 6 Mar. 1818 and. d. 12 Jan. 1906) a son of Josiah True, soldier of the War of 1812 and his wife Almira Tuttle, the latter a daughter of Capt. Solomon Tuttle who served in the Revolutionary War. (See "Official Roster of Revolutionary Soldiers Buried in Ohio," Vol. 1 p. 375) and his first wife Deborah Strong.)

Jane (Fuller) True died Oct. 17, 1853, children surviving were:
67. Hiram L. True b. 4 June 1845.
68. Sarah Edith True b. 27 June 1848.
69. John W. True b. 18 Oct. 1850.
69A. Thomas True d. in inf.

12. CHARLES H. TINKER[3] (ALMIRA[2], (RESOLVED[1])

Charles H. Tinker (b. 1829) farmer of near Trimble, Ohio married 11 Mar. 1851 Jane F. Watkins (b. 1834) and had issue:
70. Lavinia Tinker b. 1852.
71. Roxanna Tinker b. 1854, m. Mr. White.
72. Alvah Tinker b. 1857.
73. Emma Tinker b. 1862.
74. Frances Tinker b. 1865.
75. Jeannette A. Tinker (1867-1940) m. Albert Snow.
76. Charles A. Tinker b. 1869.

13. ELIZABETH TINKER[3] (ALMIRA[2], (RESOLVED[1])

Elizabeth L. Tinker (1831-1856) married June 19, 1851 Christopher H. Woodworth (1830-1897) and had issue:
77. Charles Christopher Woodworth (1852-1874)

14. ROXANNA TINKER[3] (ALMIRA[2], RESOLVED[1])

Roxanna Tinker (b. 1833) married Henry Freeman on Nov. 1, 1851 and had a large family. Her residence and names of her children are not available.

16. RESOLVED W. TINKER³ (ALMIRA², RESOLVED¹)

Resolved W. Tinker (b. 1843) married ca 1868 Mary F. Martin (b. 1849) and had issue:
78. Lewis M. Tinker b. 1869.
79. Elisha A. Tinker b. 28 Apr. 1871.
At least one other child b. 1877, name not given.

21. LUCY J. WEETHEE³ (EVELINE², RESOLVED¹)

Lucy Jane Weethee (b. 1831) married 28 Feb. 1850 Wm. H. Reeves of Perry County, Ohio.

27. MARY JANE FULLER³ (HIRAM², RESOLVED¹)

Mary Jane Fuller (b. 1834) married 4 July 1854 Algernon B. White.

28. IRA R. FULLER³ (HIRAM², RESOLVED¹)

Ira R. Fuller (1838-1922) married 16 Dec. 1861. Adaline Deshler (b. 1841) and had
80. Charlotte Fuller b. 1865.
81. Alice Fuller b, 1867.
Probably other children
He married 2nd Dec. 8, 1885 Anna C. Uhl. Ira R. Fuller died the 18th of Aug. 1922 at Chauncey, Ohio.

30. SUSANNAH FULLER³ (HIRAM², RESOLVED¹)

Susan R. Fuller (b. 1840) married 4 July 1859 John W. Brawley (b. 1831) son of James Brawley and had
82. Nellie Brawley m. George Merry
83. Clarence Brawley
84. Ida Brawley
85. Mary Brawley

32. GEORGE FULLER³ (AUSTIN², RESOLVED¹)

George Fuller (b. 1837) carpenter, married Nov. 28, 1858 Katherine James (b. 1837) and had one child
86. Austin Fuller II b. 1862.

33. FLAVIUS J. FULLER³ (AUSTIN², RESOLVED¹)

Flavius J. Fuller (b. 1838) merchant married 23 Sept. 1860 Martha C. Nesmith (b. 1844) and had issue:
87. Arthur Fuller b. 1862.
88. Herman Fuller b. 1865.

89. Almira Fuller b. 18, June 1868 at Millfield, Ohio

34. SARAH E. FULLER³ (AUSTIN², RESOLVED¹)

Sarah Elizabeth Fuller (1840-1876) married Dec. 25, 1855 W. P. Wyatt (d.ca 1868/9). She died Aug. 10, 1876 and is buried in Nye cemetery at Chauncey, Ohio. Their children were:
90. Daniel H. Wyatt b. 1862.
91. Minnie H. Wyatt b. 1864.
92. Charlotte H. Wyatt b. 1866 unm.
93. Sarah E. Wyatt b. 1868.

35. ABIGAIL FULLER³ (AUSTIN², RESOLVED¹)

Abigail Fuller (b. 1841) married 8 Aug. 1861 Rev. Ephraim C. Wayman of Chillicothe, Ill.

36. RESOLVED E. FULLER³ (AUSTIN², RESOLVED¹)

Resolved E. Fuller (1843-1887) merchant, married 23 May 1867 Henrietta Chadwell (b. 1849) eldest daughter of Samuel and Mary (Courtney) Chadwell. Resolved Fuller served in the Civil War and died Feb. 28, 1887 from infection incurred in the service. Their children were:
94. Adda F. Fuller b. 1868.
95. Jeannetta Fuller b. Jan. 17, 1870.
96. Florence Fuller d. y.
97. Nellie F. Fuller 1877-1940 m. H. Bahrman.

37. MELZER N. FULLER³ (AUSTIN², RESOLVED¹)

Melzer N. Fuller (1844-1875) married May 26, 1870 Mary Ellis (b. 7 Mar. 1849 and d. 4 Mar. 1901) daughter of Thomas and Mary (White) Ellis of Chauncey, Ohio.
Melzer Fuller died Apr. 6, 1876 survived by the following children:
98. Sarah Elizabeth Fuller b. 20 Aug. 1872.
99. Mary Pauline Fuller b. 20 Jan. 1875
100. Melzer Thomas Ellis Fuller b. 10 July 1876.
Furniture merchant. He married Addie Preston - no issue.

38. DUDLEY D. FULLER³ (AUSTIN², RESOLVED¹)

Dudley D. Fuller (b. 1847) served in the Civil War in Co. A, O.V.I. 129th Regt. He was a merchant and postmaster of Millfield, Ohio.

He married Oct. 8, 1876 Mary J. Wyatt, daughter of George Wyatt. They had one daughter.
101. Edith Alma Fuller b. 8 Nov. 1879.

40. EVELINE FULLER[3] (AUSTIN[2], RESOLVED[1])

Eveline Fuller (b. 1851) married 22 June 1873 Rev. Samuel W. Brown of Washington, Penn. and had one son who later lived in Vincennes, Ind.

42. CARL FULLER[3] (AUSTIN[2], RESOLVED[1])

Carl Fuller (1862-1935) secretary of the Athens, Ohio brick company and merchant married 1909 Dana Frances Brooks, daughter of William H. Brooks. Carl Fuller died July 30, 1935. They had two children:
102. Carolyn Fuller m. Robert Wickham.
103. Francis Fuller, photographer

43. CHARLES R. FULLER[3] (RUSSELL[2], RESOLVED[1])

. Charles Resolved Fuller (b. 1841) married Feb. 9, 1863 Lucetta Haning and had issue:
104. Willis Fuller
Charles R. Fuller married second Apr. 5, 1877 Anna Botkin and had two daughters:
105. Mary Eliza Fuller - lives in Calif.
106. Emma Lovina Fuller - lives in Los Angeles.

44. MARY E. FULLER[3] (RUSSELL[2], RESOLVED[1])

Mary Ella Fuller (1844-1922) married Oct. 19, 1862 Adam Kutz (b. 24 Dec. 1832 in Somerset Co. Penn. and d. 18 Mar. 1913 in Columbus, Ohio) son of David and Margaret (Levan) Kutz. Their children were:
107. Elizabeth May Kutz b. 11 May 1865 - unm.
108. Daisy Marie Kutz b. 28 Apr. 1867 - m. Edward Barnes.
109. William Parker Kutz b. 23 Sept. 1870 - unm.
110. Emma Adela Kutz b. 23 Sept. 1870.
111. Mabel Levan Kutz b. 2 Sept. 1878.

46. MILTON C. FULLER[3] (RUSSELL[2], RESOLVED[1])

Milton Cooley Fuller (1848-1893) married Apr. 23, 1888 Ida Hunter, daughter of John and Delilah (Cohenour) Hunter of New Marshfield, Ohio. He died at Millfield 18 Jan. 1893. Their children were:

112. Dell Buckingham Fuller b. 1889 - d. y.
113. William Henry Fuller b. 13 July 1892.

47. SUSAN K. FULLER[3] (RUSSELL[2], RESOLVED[1])

Susan Kate Fuller (1850-1937) married Dec. 13, 1869 David Jones son of John and Sarah (Levan) Jones and had issue:
114. Herbert Russell Jones 1873-1887.
115. Emma Katherine Jones b. 21 Feb. 1875.
116. Luella May Jones 1879-1887.
117. Laura Jones b. 23 Feb. 1890.

48. JOHN R. FULLER[3] (RUSSELL[2], RESOLVED[1])

John Russell Fuller (1852-1940) married 7 Sept. 1883 Mary Williams Kirby daughter of William and Elizabeth (Warford) Kirby of Fayette, Mo.
Mary Kirby Fuller died Feb. 3, 1902 at Millfield, Ohio. Their children were:
118. Helen Fuller b. 4 Oct. 1885 m. Paul Henderson of Akron, Ohio.
119. Kate Cooley Fuller b. 4 May 1887.
120. Jane Buckingham Fuller b. 16 June 1890.
121. Kirby Russell Fuller b. 25 Jan. 1893.
122. John William Fuller b. 21 June 1897.

49. H. HERBERT FULLER[3] (RUSSELL[2], RESOLVED[1])

Henry Herbert Fuller (1854-1895) married Dec. 30, 1880 Lilla Allen daughter of David and Mary Jane (Wilkins) Allen. He died in Athens, Ohio Oct. 18, 1895 leaving three young children:
123. Herbert Earl Fuller 1881-1904.
124. Josiah Allen Fuller b. 11 Feb. 1886.
125. Russell Nash Fuller b. 5 Nov. 1891

50. ADELA ESTHER FULLER[3] (RUSSELL[2], RESOLVED[1])

Adela Esther Fuller (1854-1939) married Mar. 22, 1877 George Metteer Gardner (b. 27 Oct. 1848 at Buffalo, Scott County, Iowa and d. 7 Dec. 1934 at Columbus, Ohio) a son of Caleb Harry Gardner and his wife Mary Stone Davis. One daughter was born to them.
126. Mary Cooley Gardner b. 2 Apr. 1879 Millfield, Ohio.

54. EVELINE GRANT[3] (LOVINA[2], RESOLVED[1])

Eveline Grant (b. 1841) married Dr. Davis of Middleport, Ohio and had several children among whom were
127. Eva Davis

128. Connie Davis.

67. HIRAM TRUE[3] (JANE[2] RESOLVED[1])

Dr. Hiram L. True, physician, scientist and author of the book: "The Cause of the Glacial Period" resided at McConnelsville, Ohio. He served in company A, 129th regiment of the Ohio volunteer infantry during the Civil War.

He married Nov. 8, 1865 Julia Weethee (b. 14 Oct. 1844 and d. Jan. 23, 1869) a daughter of Laurentius and Lucy (Nye) Weethee. They had one son:
129. Marcus W. True 1867-1887.

Hiram True married second Apr. 29, 1874 Helen Moore (b. 11 Nov. 1846 and d. Nov. 9, 1885) daughter of the Hon. James Moore and Rebecca McConnell his wife and granddaughter of Gen. Robert McConnell the founder of McConnelsville, Ohio. They had two daughters:
130. Evelyn True b. Jan. 26, 1875.
131. Augusta True b. May 21, 1877.

Dr. Hiram True died Oct. 22, 1912 at McConnelsville, Ohio.

68. SARAH E. TRUE[3] (JANE[2], RESOLVED[1])

Sarah E. True (b. 1848) married Oct. 21, 1866 Levi Allen Sprague (b. 24 Dec. 1844 and died 1933) a son of Wm. P. and Mary (Turner) Sprague. In their later years they resided in Athens, Ohio where they both died at advanced ages. Their children were:
132. Florence Sprague.
133. Wiley True Sprague.
134. Warran V. Sprague.
135. Myra G. Sprague m. Albert Watkins.
136. Jennie E. Sprague.
137. John R. Sprague.

69. JOHN TRUE[3] (JANE[2], RESOLVED[1])

John True (1850-1899) married Jan. 27, 1873 Martha Ann Maxwell (b. 4 Sept. 1853 at Athens, Ohio and d. June 1938 at Basil, Ohio). Their children were:
138. Effie True b. Oct. 1874, m. Arthur G. Brown and resides at Pueblo, Colo.
139. Laura E. True b. ca 1876, m. Wm. H. Gilmore of Croton, Ohio.
140. Lydia Olive True b. 13 Aug. 1879 at Millfield, Ohio.
141. Austin R. True m. Nellie Geiger and resides at Gore, Ohio.
142. Minnie Edith True m. Clifford R. Jolly of Basil, Ohio.

91. MINNIE WYATT[4] (SARAH[3], AUSTIN[2], RESOLVED[1])

Minnie M. Wyatt (b. 1864) married Burley Headley, bookkeeper and later a lumber dealer. They resided in Athens and Columbus, Ohio. Their children were:
143. Ross Headley of Columbus, Ohio.
144. Dean Headley of Columbus, Ohio.
145. Mary Headley.
146. Esther Headley.

94. ADDIE FULLER[4] (RESOLVED[3], AUSTIN[2], RESOLVED[1])

Addie Fuller (b. 1868) married Clayton Phillips of Hornell, N. Y. Their children were:
147. Bessie Phillips d. y.
148. Helen Phillips, assistant professor of English at N. Y. State Teachers' College at Albany, N. Y.

95. JEANNETTA FULLER[4] (RESOLVED[3], AUSTIN[2], RESOLVED[1])

Jeannetta Fuller (1870-1940) married Joshua Sands, surveyor of Athens, Ohio, and had one son:
149. Willis Sands.

98. ELIZABETH FULLER[4] (MELZER[3], AUSTIN[2], RESOLVED[1])

Sarah Elizabeth Fuller (1872-1938) married Apr. 27, 1892 Reuben Christopher Miller Hastings, furniture merchant and inventor of Athens and Columbus, Ohio.) He was a son of William and Mary J. Hastings who came from Pennsylvania to southeastern Ohio. Educated at Ohio University, he was a member there of Delta Tau Delta fraternity. They were active members of the Church of Christ. They had three daughters:
150. Lucile Fuller Hastings b. 22 June 1894.
151. Mildred Irene Hastings m. Neil Rumsey.
152. Mary Esther Hastings b. Mar. 1907.

99. MARY P. FULLER[4] (MELZER[3], AJSTIN[2], RESOLVED[1])

Mary Pauline Fuller (b. 1875) married June 27, 1900 Erwin C. Woodworth (b. 1873 - d. 1937) owner of the Athens Printing Co. He served as Athens County treasurer, as representative in the Ohio State legislature and as mayor of Athens. Their children were:

153. Ellis Woodworth m. Lucille Grandy.
154. Elizabeth Woodworth m. Everett M. Maguire.
155. Dorothy Woodworth.

101. EDITH A. FULLER[4] (DUDLEY[3], AUSTIN[2], RESOLVED[1])

Edith Alma Fuller (b. 1879) married Oct. 2, 1901 Alba Theodore Lawhead (b. 1878) son of Theodore and Rebecca (Hammond) Lawhead. Their children were
156. Mary Frances Lawhead m. John Rood.
157. Theodora Lawhead m. Peter Good and had sons John and Peter Jr.

110. EMMA A. KUTZ[4] (MARY E[3], RUSSELL[2], RESOLVED[1])

Emma Adela Kutz (b. 1870) married Oct. 21, 1906 Martin Morrison of Columbus, Ohio and had
158. Robert Parker Morrison b. Feb. 25, 1908 m. Frances Lloyd.
159. Frederick Kutz Morrison b. Apr. 9, 1912.

113. WILLIAM H. FULLER[4] (MILTON C[3], RUSSELL[2], RESOLVED[1])

William Henry Fuller (b. 1892) served in the World War and died soon after. He married Ethel _____ and had one son:
160. Francis Fuller b. ca 1918.

115. EMMA K. JONES[4] (SUSAN K[3], RUSSELL[2], RESOLVED[1])

Emma Katherine Jones (b. 1875) married Feb. 24, 1893 Elmer E. Learned (d. May 24, 1935) son of Dr. A. J. Learned (b. July 28, 1843- d. 1940) Civil War veteran of Millfiled, Ohio (Co. C-18th O.V.I.) They had issue:
161. Donald E. Learned b. Dec. 30, 1894.
162. Russell Learned b. Jan. 29, 1897.

117. LAURA JONES[4] (SUSAN K[3], RUSSELL[2], RESOLVED[1])

Laura Jones (b. 1890) graduate nurse, served over-seas in the World War, married Jack Holden of Los Angeles, Calif. and had one son:
163. Jack Holden Jr. b. Dec. 1925.

119. KATE C. FULLER[4] (JOHN R[3], RUSSELL[2], RESOLVED[1])

Kate Cooley Fuller (b. 1887) married July 4, 1910 Louis R. Russell of Milwaukee, Wis. and had issue:

164. Gerald Albert Russell b. Mar. 31, 1911.
165. Carol Raymond Russell b. Mar. 22, 1912.

120. JANE B. FULLER[4] (JOHN R[3], RUSSELL[2], RESOLVED[1])

Jane Buckingham Fuller (b. 1890) married Aug. 15, 1908 Edward J. Neutzling (b. June 19, 1886) of Mansfield, Ohio.

121. KIRBY R. FULLER[4] (JOHN R[3], RUSSELL[2], RESOLVED[1])

Kirby Russell Fuller (b. 1893) married Jan. 4, 1933 Grace Vess (b. Sept. 15, 1894) and had issue:
166. Ruth Ann Fuller b. May 1935, London, Ohio

124. JOSIAH A. FULLER[4] (HERBERT[3], RUSSELL[2], RESOLVED[1])

Josiah Allen Fuller (b. 1886) married Mrs. Mary Quinn Berry and had one son:
167. Stephen Herbert Fuller b. Feb. 4, 1920, was educated at Ohio University, a member of Delta Tau Delta fraternity.

125. RUSSELL FULLER[4] (HERBERT[3], RUSSELL[2], RESOLVED[1])

Russell Nash Fuller (b. 1891) married Gladys Miller and resides at Akron, Ohio. They have two children:
168. Anne Fuller.
169. William Fuller.

126. MARY C. GARDNER[4] (ESTHER[3], RUSSELL[2], RESOLVED[1])

Mary Cooley Gardner (b. 1879) married Dec. 11, 1897 Robert Wilmot Jones, son of Will S. and Harriet Call (Marshall) Jones of New Smyra Beach, Fla. Their children were:
170. Ruth A. Jones b. Jan. 19, 1900.
171. Marshall Gardner Jones b. Oct. 1, 1901.

130. EVELYN M. TRUE[4] (HIRAM[3], JANE[2], RESOLVED[1])

Evelyn Moore True (b. 1875) married Dec. 16, 1902 at Manila, P. I., Capt. Frank Rodman Button (b. Westport, Ky.) son of Richard W. and Elizabeth (McWilliams) Button. Capt. Button served in the Spanish-American and World Wars. They had two daughters:
171-A. Augusta True Button b. 9 May 1905 at Manila, R. I.
171-B. Helen Shawmut Button b. Oct. 7, 1906 on Pacific Ocean.

133. WILEY T. SPRAGUE[4] (SARAH[3], JANE[2], RESOLVED[1])

Wiley True Sprague M.D. (b. 1871) married Aug. 23, 1893 Royal Dent, daughter of R. S. Dent and had issue:
172. Allen Dent Spraque b. 1897.
173. Gerald True Sprague M.D. b. 1899.
174. Marian Sprague m. Mr. Snyder of Blanchester, Ohio.

134. WARREN V. SPRAGUE[4] (SARAH[3], JANE[2], RESOLVED[1])

Warren V. Sprague M.D. married and had at least three children:
175. Lenore A. Sprague D.D.S.
176. Lindley V. Sprague M.D.
177. Floride J. Sprague.

136. JENNIE SPRAGUE[4] (SARAH[3], JANE[2], RESOLVED[1])

Jennie E. Sprague married H. S. Shrigley D.D.S. of Athens, Ohio, and had two sons:
178. John H. Srigley D.D.S.
179. Robert Srigley M.D.

137. JOHN R. SPRAGUE[4] (SARAH[3], JANE[2], RESOLVED[1])

John R. Sprague M.D. married Miss Devlin and had issue:
180. John True Sprague M.D., m. Emily Liddell and had issue.
181. Bernardine Sprague m. Robert Main and had issue.
182. Edward Allen Sprague - student at Notre Dame University
183. William Sprague twins
184. Robert Sprague

140. LYDIA OLIVE TRUE[4] (JOHN[3], JANE[2], RESOLVED[1])

Lydia Olive True (b. 1879) married Dec. 8, 1901 Austin V. Myers at Basil, Ohio. They resided in Cleveland, Ohio and later at Wilmington, Del. Their children were:
184A. Austin Leland Myers b. 16 Apr. 1906, at Cleveland, Ohio.
184B. Robert True Myers b. 5 Mar. 1915 at Lakewood, Ohio.

143. ROSS HEADLEY (MINNIE[4], SARAH[3], AUSTIN[2], RESOLVED[1])

Ross Headley (b. ca 1898) married Pearl Robinson daughter of Wm. D. and Ina (Smith) Robinson and had three children:

185. Harold Eugene Headley b. 1920.
186. William Headley.
187. Martha Jane Headley.

149. WILLIS SANDS[5] (JEANETTA[4], RESOLVED[3], AUSTIN[2], RESOLVED[1])

Willis Sands married Helen Parker of Barberton, Ohio and had issue:
188. Richard Sands.
189. Willis Sands, Jr.
190. John Sands.
191. Joshua Roger Sands.

150. LUCILE HASTINGS[5] (ELIZABETH[4], MELZER[3], AUSTIN[2], RESOLVED[1])

Lucile Fuller Hastings (b. 1894) married Clarence Parks Lauderbaugh of Columbus, Ohio, and had two sons:
192. Clarence Parks Lauderbaugh, Jr. (1920-1934).
193. Thomas Ellis Lauderbaugh b. 1925.

152. MARY E. HASTINGS[5] (ELIZABETH[4], MELZER[3], AUSTIN[2], RESOLVED[1])

Mary Esther Hastings married Alfred Weisheimer of Columbus, Ohio, and had two children:
194. Charles Hastings Weisheimer.
195. Mary Alice Weisheimer.

155. DOROTHY WOODWORTH[5] (MARY[4], MELZER[3], AUSTIN[2], RESOLVED[1])

Dorothy Woodworth married Earl Shaffer of Athens, Ohio and had
196. Ellis Lee Shaffer.

161. DONALD LEARNED[5] (EMMA K.[4], SUSAN K.[3], RUSSELL[2], RESOLVED[1])

Donald Learned (b. 1894) married Leona Miles and had issue:
197. Lee Learned.
198. Julia Dorothy Learned.
199. Allen Learned.
200. Elaine Learned.

162. RUSSELL LEARNED[5] (EMMA K.[4], SUSAN K.[3], RUSSEL[2], RESOLVED[1])

Russell Learned (b. 1897) married Margaret _____ and had one daughter:
201. Marjorie Lorraine Learned.

170. RUTH JONES[5] (MARY C.[3], ESTHER[3], RUSSELL[2], RESOLVED[1])

Ruth Jones (b. 1900) married Nov. 19,

1920 Walter M. Miller of New Smyrna Beach, Fla, and had one son:
202. Walter M. Miller, Jr.

171. MARSHALL G. JONES[5] (MARY C.[4], ESTHER[3], RUSSELL[2], RESOLVED[1])

Marshall Gardner Jones (b. 1901) married Oct. 3, 1926 Mary Anne Adamson in Challis, Idaho. They reside in St. Lawrence County, N. Y., and have one daughter:
203. Ann Marshall Jones b. 3 May 1931.

171A. AUGUSTA T. BUTTON[5] (EVELYN[4], HIRAM[3], JANE[2], RESOLVED[1])

Augusta True Button married June 29, 1929 in Chicago, Ill. Alfred Storm Jameson (b. Dec. 29, 1900 at Whitby, Eng.) son of Capt. Alfred and Susan (Sanderson) Jameson. They have twin daughters:
204. Evelyn Storm Jameson
205. Dorothy True Jameson b. 5 July 1934 at Chicago.

171B. HELEN S. BUTTON[5] (EVELYN[4], HIRAM[3], JANE[2], RESOLVED[1])

Helen Shawmut Button (b. 1906) married June 8, 1932 at McConnelsville, Ohio, Louis R. O'Neill (b. 15 July, 1905 at Charlevoix, Mich.) son of Edward R. and Eve (Hamlin) O'Neill. They have a son:
206. Edward True O'Neill b. 20 July 1940 at Charlevoix, Michigan.

175. LENORE SPRAGUE[5] (WARREN[4], SARAH[3], JANE[2], RESOLVED[1])

Lenore Sprague D.D.S. married Charles E. Stack, merchant of Athens, Ohio and has two sons:
207. John Stack.
208. Charles Stack.

184A. AUSTIN L. MYERS[5] (OLIVE[4], JOHN[3], JANE[2], RESOLVED[1])

Austin Leland Myers (b. 1906) married Apr. 30, 1932 at Toledo, Ohio Mary Allison Young (b. 8 Oct. 1910 at Pittsburg, Penn.) and they have two children:
209. Carol Lee Myers b. 10 Dec. 1935 at Clarksburg, W. Va.
210. David True Myers b. and d. 1939 at Hammond, Ind.

The Name

Fuller is believed to have originated in France as a surname, first as Fouiller (Fowler) and to designate one from a certain place.

Fuller Lineage Notes

1. Lt. Thomas Fuller - m. 13 June 1643 Elizabeth Tidd
born - 1618   of Woburn, Mass.
died - June 1698
Came from Eng. 1638

2. Benjamin Fuller - m. 15 Dec. 1685 - Sarah Bacon
b. - 1660 in Woburn, Mass.   b. 1663
Removed to Ashford, Conn.,   a daughter of
where he died Oct. 5, 1754.   Michael and Sarah
                                    (Richardson)
                                    Bacon

3. Samuel Fuller - m. Apr. 1710 - Mary Littlefield
born - 1689 at Salem, Mass.   a daughter of James
                                    and Katherine (Heard)
                                    Littlefield

4. Capt. James Fuller - m. 4 Dec.   Abigail Ruewee
                        1738   a daughter of John
died ca 1786   Ruewee of Dudley,
Said to have served in the   Mass.
French and Indian Wars.

5. Job Fuller - m. 5 Nov. 1752 - Susannah Russell
born 1751   born - 18 Nov. 1750.
died ca 1794   died - 18 June 1833.
Served in War of the American
Revolution, in Capt. Samuel Chandlers Co. in 11th
Reg. Conn. troops

6. Resolved Fuller (1780-1850) see text.

Russell Lineage Notes

1. John Russell m. 30 Mar. 1710 - Elizabeth Pattin
born - ca 1686 in Mass.   born - ca 1684
died - Dec. 1762   died - 1754
at Thompson, Conn.   a daughter of
                                Nathaniel Pattin

2. Daniel Russell m. 13 July 1737 - Phebe Roberts
died 10 June 1776.   a daughter of David
                                Roberts of Woburn.

3. Susannah Russell m. 5 Nov. 1772 - Job Fuller
born - 18 Nov. 1750   bapt. 9 Aug. 1752

4. Resolved Fuller (1780-1850) See Text.

Nash Lineage Notes

1. Thomas Nash - m. -   Margery Baker
born in Eng.   died ca 1656
died 1658 at New Haven,   a daughter of Nicholis
Conn.   and Mary (Hodgetts) Baker
                            from Hertfordshire in Eng.

2. Lt. Timothy Nash m.
   born 1626
   Rebecca Stone
   a daughter of the
   Rev. Samuel Stone of
   Hartford, Conn.

3. Ephraim Nash - m.
   born - 1682 at Hadley, Mass.
   died - 9 Nov 1759
   Joanna Smith
   born 1686
   a daughter of
   Deacon John and
   Joanna (Kellogg)
   Smith of Hadley and
   Granby, Mass.

4. Elisha Nash - m
   born - 1729
   died - 1814
   Served in the War of the
   American Revolution
   Lois Frost
   died 1820
   See Frost Lineage
   Notes

5. Samuel Nash - m. ca 1784
   born 1760
   died 1823
   Served in the Revolutionary
   War in Capt. Dickinson's Co.,
   Col. Ruggles Woodbridge's Reg.
   of Mass. troops
   (P. 269 "Official Roster of Soldiers of American
   Revolution" by Dailey
   Vashti Pierre
   born 11 July 1763
   died 31 July 1820

Frost Lineage Notes

1. Edmund Frost - m.
   born - 1610 in Eng.
   Came to America from
   Suffolk, Eng. 1635.
   Thomasine _____
   died ca 1652.

2. Dr. Samuel Frost - m.
   born - 1638 at Cambridge, Mass.
   died Jan. 1712 at Billerica,
   Mass.
   Mary Cole

3. Samuel Frost - m.
   born 1664 in Mass.
   died 1739 in Conn.
   Experience Miller
   died 1731 in Conn.

4. Samuel Frost - m.
   born 1692 Springfield, Mass.
   died 1767
   Elected collector of rates
   and assessments and served
   in Capt. Eben Moulton's
   company in Col. Pomeroy's
   regiment in the Crown Point
   Expedition 1755.
   Deliverance _____

5. Lois Frost - m.   Elisha Nash
   died 1820

See Nash Lineage Notes

Batchelder Lineage Notes

1. Nathaniel Batchelder - m. 10 Dec.
   1656
   born 1630
   died 1709
   Deborah Smith
   died 1675

2. Benjamin Batchelder m. 25 Dec.
   1696
   born 1673
   died ca 1717
   Served in Indian Wars
   Susannah Page
   born 1674

3. Lt. Joseph Batchelder m. 19 Nov.
   1745
   born 1699
   Mrs. Miriam (Jones)
   Ring
   born ca 1718
   a daughter of
   Samuel and Sarah
   (Barnard) Jones

4. Capt. Benjamin Batchelder - m.
   born 1746
   died 1818 at Belfast
   Esther _____
   born 1747
   died 1799

5. Benjamin Batchelder - m.
   born 1773
   died 1859
   Olive Leighton
   born 1780
   died 8 Sept. 1838

6. Nancy Batchelder - m.
   born 1797
   died 1870
   Resolved Fuller
   See Text

References

1. Court records of Athens, Washington and
   Hocking Counties in Ohio.
2. New England Historical Register.
3. Nash Genealogy.
4. Fuller Genealogy.
5. Russell Genealogy
6. Family records.

1. REV. JOSHUA DEWEESE

Joshua Deweese was born in Kent County, state of Delaware May 3, 1742. He enlisted in the War of the American Revolution Nov. 23rd (year not given) and served in Capt. Richard Dalliner's company. His brothers Cornelius and Samuel enlisted the same day, another brother John having joined that company, a few days earlier (on Nov. 17th, see Delaware Archives Vol. 2, p. 766).

Joshua Deweese was with Gen. Washington's army at Valley Forge and suffered frozen feet from the excessive cold of that winter, losing a portion of one foot as a result.

His parents were Presbyterians and he was reared in that faith but in 1772 he affiliated with the Cowmarsh Baptist Church and was ordained for the ministry in that denomination on the 26th of Dec. 1785.

He served the Cowmarsh Church as one of its earliest ministers and was likewise the first minister of the church at Mispillion which was formed about 1781.

The swamp country of Delaware was exceedingly unhealthy and Rev. Deweese contracted tuberculosis.

Rev. Morgan Edwards, in his history of the Baptists in Delaware, written in March of 1791 refers to the intended emigration of Rev. Joshua Deweese in May (1791) to the "western world" --- "the reason of his going to the backwoods was that he might have land for his great family"--- and he continues: "Mr. Deweese's transition from a state of nature to a state of grace was tedious and distressing; his account of that transition put me in mind of what John Bunyan saith of himself in his Grace Abounding" but it will not be long before he make another transit from a state of Grace to a state of Glory for his lungs are wasting fast." (Penn. Mag. Vol. 9 pp. 197 to 213).

The exact date on which the Deweese family left Delaware is not known but on May 22, 1791 Rev. Deweese sold his plantation in Kent County to William Burroughs, Jr. for £250. The said plantation adjoined that of his deceased father-in-law, Thomas Bowman.

From Mispillion Hundred in Kent County, they removed to Wharton township, Fayette County, state of Pennsylvania.

The caravan included not only all the children of Joshua Deweese but his brother John and all his family. It was an arduous journey over the mountains, fording rivers and the health of Joshua Deweese grew steadily worse. They settled temporarily in the mountains of Wharton township and Rev. Deweese purchased land in the wilderness in what is now Monongehela County, W. Va. at the Pennsylvania line.

Before a home could be erected on the land he died in December of 1791. His Will is of record in Fayette County, Pennsylvania and reads as follows:

"In the Name of God Amen. I, Joshua Deweese late of Kent County and state of Delaware, now residing in Fayette County and State of Pennsylvania, being sick and weak in body but of perfect mind and memory, thanks be given unto God.

Calling unto mind the mortality of my body and knowing that it is appointed for all men once to Die, Do make and ordain this my Last Will and Testament that is to say principall and first of all I give and recommend my soul unto the hands of Almighty God that gave it and my body I recommend to the Earth to be buried in decent Christian Burial at the discretion of my Executors, nothing doubting but at the General Resurrection I shall receive the same again by the Mighty power of God and as touching such worldy Estate wherewith it has pleased God to bless me with in this Life I give and dispose of the same in the following manner and form.

Imprimis my will is that the money now in my possession or ten pounds be applyed towards the improving my Lands which I lately purchased in Mononghalia County and State of Virginia, likewise five and thirty pounds of the money due me in the Delaware state to be applyed in like manner at the discretion of my executors hereafter to be appointed.

Item I give and bequeath unto my beloved wife Elizabeth one third of all my moveable Estate to be taken in such articles as she shall choose out of the appraisement of my Estate. I likewise devise unto my said wife one half of the profits arising from my Lands above mentioned with the principle Dwelling house which shall be erected on the said lands with the money appropriated to that use by this my last Will and Testament, with half the other buildings which shall be erected thereon during the term of (her) natural life.

Item I give and bequeath one other third of my moveable Estate and the profits arising from the other half of my Lands to the support, cloathing and Schooling of my young children Joshua, Elizabeth and Mary until Mary the youngest shall arrive to the term of ten years old.

Item I give and bequeath the remaining third part of my moveable Estate to be equally divided between my Seven Sons, the money appropriated for the improvements above mentioned to be deducted out of the moveable Estate before it is divided and the residue to remain in the hands of the executors for the term of One Year.

Item my Will is that when my youngest daughter Mary arrives to the age of ten years that the half of my lands applyd to the support of my three youngest children shall be for the use and benefit of all my seven sons alike.

Item I give and bequeath unto my daughter Elizabeth ten pounds to be paid her by my Executors when she arrives at the age of eighteen years.

Item I give and bequeath unto my Daughter Mary ten pounds to be paid her by my Executors when she arrives at the age of eighteen years old and it is my will that after the decease of my beloved wife my whole Estate Real and Personal be equally divided (between) Thomas, Lewis, Samuel, William, James, Jethro and Joshua and I do hereby bequeath it to my said seven sons and their heirs forever.

And I do hereby ordain, constitute and appoint my beloved wife Elizabeth Executrix and my beloved Son Lewis Executor of this my Last Will and Testament. In testimony whereof I

have hereunto set my Hand and Seal this fourth day of December Anno Domini One thousand seven hundred and Ninety one 1791.

Josua Deweese   Seal

Signed, sealed and delivered in presence of us:

Isaac Griffin
Davis Merydith   Proved Jan. 4, 1792.
John Deweese

15. Elizabeth Deweese Ward

Joshua Deweese married first in 1765 Elizabeth Bowman (1745-1774) daughter of Thomas and Sarah Bowman of Mispillion Hundred, Kent County, Delaware and had by her four children:

2. Anna Deweese b. ca 1766.
3. Thomas Deweese b. 25 Dec. 1767.
4. Lewis Deweese b. 11 Oct. 1769.
5. Samuel Deweese b. 1772.

About 1774 he married second Hannah Birch and by her, had one son:

6. William Deweese b. ca 1775 (who is believed to have died unmarried between June 1797 and Oct. of 1802).

The date of marriage of Joshua Deweese to his third wife Elizabeth New, daughter of John New (d. 1776/7) has not been definitely established but it was evidently prior to Apr. 1777 when he administered his said father-in-law's estate as "next of kin." The children of Joshua and Elizabeth (New) Deweese were:

7. James Deweese b. 1778.
8. Jethro Deweese b. ca 1780.
9. Joshua Deweese Jr. b. ca 1783.
10. Elizabeth Deweese b. ca 1785.
11. Mary Deweese b. ca 1788 (probably d. y., no further mention).

Elizabeth New Deweese had a life estate

in the land left by her husband and since a
settlement was made by deeds Oct. 11, 1802
and were not signed by Elizabeth Deweese, it
is believed that she died in 1802 prior to
Oct. 11th.

2. ANNA DEWEESE[2] (JOSHUA[1])

Anna Deweese (b. 1766) married ca 1789
George Brandel (d. 1790) and had a son:
12. Charles Brandel b. ca 1790.

Since no further
data has been found
regarding Anna
Brandel, it is
thought that she
died following her
husband's death and
prior to the removal
of her father's
family to Fayette
County, Penn.

Joshua Deweese
administered the
estate of George
Brandel and turned
over the money,
which fell into his
hands amounting to
53.11.8 to
Hezekiah Cullen
named guardian for
Charles Brandel in
Feb. of 1791.

3. THOMAS DEWEESE[2] (JOSHUA[1])

Thomas Deweese
(1767-1837) was born
in Kent County, Del.
He married there
about 1790 Catherine
Spencer (b. 4 May
1764 and d. 17 Apr.
1842). They removed
with the Deweese
emigration late in
May of 1791 to Fayette
County, Penn. and early
in 1792 into what is now Monongehela County
of W. Va.

On the final payment, by the heirs of
Joshua Deweese June 12, 1797, David Scott Jr.
and Rachel his wife deeded to the said heirs,
namely: "Thomas, Lewis, Samuel, William,
James, Jethro and Joshua Deweese" of the
County of Monongehela and commonwealth of
Virginia."

On the 11th day of October 1802 Thomas

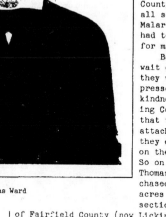

Jonas Ward

Deweese and Cate his wife, Samuel Deweese
and Sarah his wife, James Deweese and
Elizabeth his wife and Jethro Deweese, all of
the County of Monongehela and commonwealth
of Virginia" sold their shares in one tract
of land which their late father, Joshua
Deweese left, to their brother Lewis Deweese
(Deeds bk. 2 p. 503) and all five sold their
shares in another tract to Jacob Pindell the
same day, thus making a final settlement of
the real estate formerly belonging to their
father.

In October of
1804 Thomas Deweese
and his wife Catherine
sold their planta-
tion in Monongehela
County and in com-
pany with his
brother Jethro
Deweese and family
and others set out
overland for a set-
tlement at what is
now Columbus, Ohio.

By the time
they got as far as
Fairfield County
(the section now
called Licking
County) they were
all so ill with
Malaria that they
had to remain there
for many weeks.

Barely able to
wait on one another,
they were so im-
pressed with the
kindness of the Lick-
ing County settlers
that they became so
attached to the place
they decided to stay
on there permanently.
So on Dec. 2, 1804
Thomas Deweese pur-
chased two hundred
acres in township 2,
section 3, range 11
of Fairfield County (now Licking) and Jethro
Deweese purchased on adjoining one hundred
acres the same day.

Thomas Deweese was for more than thirty-
two years a prominent citizen and one of the
largest landholders in Madison township. He
died there Mar. 6, 1837 and Catherine Spencer
Deweese likewise died there Apr. 17, 1842 and
they were buried in a family cemetery on their
farm.

Some years later when a cemetary was laid out at Kirkersville, their son William Deweese purchased two lots and had those buried in the family lot reinterred there.

Thomas and Catherine Deweese had at least four children:

13. Sarah Deweese who married and had issue, name of her husband and children not now known.
14. Samuel Deweese b. 7 May 1793 in Va.
15. Elizabeth Deweese b. 1796 in Va.
16. William Deweese b. 25 Jan. 1799 in Va.

4. LEWIS DEWEESE[2] (JOSHUA[1])

Lewis Deweese (1769-1840) tanner and farmer, married probably in Fayette County, Penn. about 1795 Mary McKelvey (?) b. 18 Jan. 1772 and d. Aug. 14, 1847. They both joined the Baptist Church in 1795 and remained in that faith until their deaths.

On Feb. 9, 1807 they sold their plantation in Monongehela County Va. (now W. Va.) and removed in company with his brothers, James, Samuel and their families and their sister Elizabeth to western Ohio (see #7 James Deweese for full account).

He died at Fort Staunton, Ohio the 27th of Aug. 1840 and his wife Mary Deweese died there on Aug. 14, 1847. Both are buried in the old Staunton cemetery.

Their children were:

17. Anna Deweese b. 1796 in Va.
18. Margaret Deweese b. 21 Oct. 1799 in Va.
19. John M. Deweese b. 14 Sept. 1799 " "
20. Thomas M. Deweese b. 8 Dec. 1800 " "
21. Lewis Deweese Jr. b. ca 1802 " "
22. Samuel M. Deweese b. ca 1804 " "
23. William Deweese b. Jan. 1805 " "
24. James Deweese b. 14 Jan. 1807 " "
25. Elizabeth Deweese b. ca 1809. m. Jacob Haney
26. David Deweese b. ca 1811 in Ohio.
27. Jethro Deweese b. ca 1813 " "

5. REV. SAMUEL DEWEESE[2] (JOSHUA[1])

Samuel Deweese (1772-1819) married about 1793 Sarah MacDougal probably in Fayette County, Penn. She was born in 1775 and died in Miami County, Ohio, Apr. 10, 1821.

Samuel Deweese entered the Baptist Ministry early in life and actively engaged in organizing churches of that denomination in Virginia, Pennsylvania, and Ohio. He was organizing minister of the Fort Staunton Baptist Church near Troy, Ohio and served it until his death in March of 1819.

His children were:

28. Joshua Deweese b. 4 Dec. 1796 in Pa.

29. John Deweese b. ca 1798 in Va.
30. Elizabeth Deweese b. ca 1800 in Va.
31. Catherine Deweese b. 1802 " "
32. Samuel Deweese Jr. b. 3 Mar. 1804 in Va.
33. Margaret Deweese b. 1806 in Va.
34. Mary Deweese b. 11 Dec. 1808 in Ohio.
35. Ann Deweese b. ca 1810 in Ohio.
36. Sarah Deweese b. ca 1812 " "

5. WILLIAM DEWEESE[2] (JOSHUA[1])

The aforesaid William Deweese is believed to have died young as previously stated because no deed, assignment or other legal steps were taken to settle his share of his father's estate. However a William Deweese who died in Miami County in 1837 remains unidentified. The similarity of his children's names would seem to indicate a connection viz: Thomas, John, Catherine, Mary J., Stacey (or Tracey) William and Hannah. He may have been a son of Joshua Deweese but is believed to have been a son of John, brother of Joshua.

7. JAMES DEWEESE[2] (JOSHUA[1])

James Deweese (1778-1852) blacksmith and farmer, married probably in southern Fayette County, Penn. or Monongehela County, Virginia (now W. Va.) about 1800, Elizabeth Whitlow who came from England alone, at the age of sixteen to make her home with relatives in Virginia. The old oak chest in which she brought her clothing to America and later from Virginia to Ohio, is still in possession of a descendant.

In the spring of 1807 James Deweese and his wife Elizabeth and their children, together with his brothers Samuel and Lewis and their families and their sister Elizabeth (then unmarried) set out for Wheeling on the Ohio river. There they built a large flat boat, loaded their household equipment thereon and floated down the river. They took ample provisions including livestock. One of the pigs they were bringing persisted in falling into the water whereupon it (being valuable cargo) would have to be rescued.

They were enroute probably several weeks, overland to Wheeling, thence down the Ohio to the mouth of the Great Miami river, at which place they sold or abandoned their large boat and built or purchased small boats for the trip up the Miami river to Dutch Station (later called Fort Staunton) near the present site of Troy, Ohio on the opposite side of the river.

James Deweese is said to have been the first blacksmith in what is now Miami County.

He is likewise said to have served on a

grand jury there in 1805, deliberations held in a French fur traders store at Dutch Station. If that is correct James Deweese preceded his family there two or more years, probably to prepare a home before taking them into the new settlement. The Deweese family went well-provisioned and did not suffer the great privations endured by many of the early settlers.

James Deweese died June 3, 1852 in Shelby County, Ohio.

Elizabeth Whitlow Deweese, long survived her husband and made her home with her daughter Elizabeth Dye. They are said to be buried at the Port Jefferson cemetery.

The children of James Deweese and his wife Elizabeth Whitlow were:
37. Michael Deweese b. ca 1801.
38. Jesse Deweese b. ca 1804.
39. Elizabeth Deweese b. 30 Dec. 1808.
40. Lydia Deweese (see #27 this lineage).
41. Eliza Deweese b. 13 June 1812.
42. Lewis Deweese b. 6 Dec. 1813.
43. Nancy Deweese.
44. Christiana Deweese b. 16 Nov. 1822.
45. Diadama Deweese b. 1825.
(Probably others who died young).

8. JETHRO DEWEESE² (JOSHUA¹)

Jethro Deweese (b. ca 1780) went as a young lad with his parents to Pennsylvania, thence into Virginia and in October of 1804 to Licking County, Ohio with his oldest half-brother Thomas Deweese.

He served as a private in the War of 1812 with Ohio troops.

He married in Monongehela County, Va. (now W. Va.) the 16th of Nov. 1802 Margaret Baker a daughter of James Baker (d. 1822) of Hardy County, Va.

Prior to Oct. of 1822 Jethro Deweese removed with his family to Hardy County, Va. where he with other heirs of James Baker, executed a deed disposing of land formerly owned by his wife's father James Baker, on Oct. 8, 1822.

No further record is found there and it is believed that he removed to some other locality shortly thereafter.

His children's names are not known.

9. JOSHUA DEWEESE JR² (JOSHUA¹)

Joshua Deweese Jr. (b. ca 1783) is believed to have died unmarried between the dates of June 12, 1797 when David Scott Jr. made a deed to the heirs of Joshua Deweese, thus fulfilling the contract made by the late James Scott and Joshua Deweese late of

Fayette County, Penn., and Oct. 11, 1802 when the heirs of Joshua Deweese made a final settlement of their father's estate by executing several deeds which were not signed by the said Joshua Jr.

However the name Joshua Deweese appears in Hardy County, Virginia records as early as 1809 when Mary Peacock grants him power of attorney to dispose of her property there. The same Joshua Deweese was living there Nov. 18, 1813 when he purchased land in Monongehela County, Va.

This Joshua Deweese is thought to be probably the son of John Deweese (brother of Rev. Joshua Deweese Sr.) who died in Fayette County, Penn. survived by a son Joshua.

10. ELIZABETH DEWEESE² (JOSHUA¹)

Elizabeth Deweese (b. ca 1785) went with her parents to Fayette County, Penn. in 1791, thence to Monongehela County, Va. and in the spring of 1807 with her brothers and their families to Miami County, Ohio.

She married Aug. 26, 1810 Jonathan Smith at Dutch Station (later called Fort Staunton) near Troy, Ohio. The ceremony was performed by her brother the Rev. Samuel Deweese.

Her children's names are not known but it is thought that Lewis D. Smith (who married Nov. 21, 1837 Elizabeth Blue) was a son.

14. SAMUEL DEWEESE³ (THOMAS², JOSHUA¹)

Samuel Deweese (1793-1856) farmer of Madison township, Licking County, Ohio, served in the War of 1812 as a private. He was called Oct. 1, 1812 to Capt. Joseph Sutton's company of Colonel Miller's regiment. For his service he was granted bounty land.

He married Aug. 31, 1815 at Newark, Ohio Mary Dugan (b. 1793) and had by her six children.

He died Jan. 25, 1856 survived by his wife and children:
46. Alonzo Deweese b. 1816.
47. William Deweese b. 1818.
48. James L. Deweese b. 1824.
49. Towle Deweese b. 1824.

The other two were probably daughters, their names are unknown.

15. ELIZABETH DEWEESE³ (THOMAS², JOSHUA¹)

Elizabeth Deweese (1796-1872) married Sept. 22, 1814 Jonas Ward Jr., a son of Jonas Ward Sr. (a soldier of the American Revolution) and his wife Phoebe Ward who came from Rockingham County, Va. to Marietta, Ohio in

1797, thence to Licking County, Ohio in 1807 where they settled in Hanover township, at which place Jonas Ward Sr. died in 1812.

Jonas Ward Jr. was a prominent citizen of Newark, Ohio for many years. In 1836 he was elected a ruling elder in the second Presbyterian Church.

A brief history of his life is given in a letter published in a Newark, Ohio, newspaper at the time of his death:

Winterset, Madison Co., Ia.
Dec. 30, 1873.

Hon. Isaac Smucker

Dear Sir,

One of the early settlers of Licking County died in this County on the 10th inst. I refer to Jonas Ward, He died at the residence of his son Josiah S. Ward from an affection of the kidneys after about twelve hours illness.

From a conversation with the deceased a couple of weeks before his death and from information given me by Mr. J. S. Ward his son, I am enabled to give you the following facts pertaining to his personal history.

He was born in Rockingham County, Va. on the 10th day of Feb. 1790 and removed with his father Jonas Ward Sr. into Ohio in 1798, stopping about a year at Marietta, then moving up the Muskingum to Waterford and afterwards in 1805 settling in Licking County where his father died in the year 1812. The deceased was a soldier in the War of 1812, having enlisted soon after war was declared, in Capt. Bradley Buckingham's company of "Minute Men," also serving in Col. Lewis Cass' regiment. Among other expeditions in which he took part during the War, was that of Greentown on the Mohegan, near Mansfield where a part of his company went to protect the citizens from attacks by the Indians. In the spring of 1813, he was in the expedition that went to the relief of Ft. Meigs.

On the 22nd day of Sept. 1814 he married Elizabeth Deweese, daughter of Thomas Deweese who resided near Newark. After his marriage he located on a farm about two miles south of Newark, where he resided until 1848, when he removed to Crawford County, Illinois and in 1860 he removed from the latter place to Story County, Iowa and remained there until about two months before his death at which time he came to live with his son in this county. His wife died in Story County on the 14th day of Feb. 1872 after a wedded life of nearly fifty-eight years, dropping dead while apparently in sound health.

Jonas Ward was a man of great firmness

of character - very decided in his opinions.

He espoused the cause of Gen. Jackson as early as 1824 and held tenaciously to the Jacksonian view of politics until his death.

As early as 1820 he became a member of the Presbyterian Church in Newark and was a deacon therein for many years. When the division in the Presbyterian Church took place he was an ardent supporter of the New School and remained in that faith until his death.

He raised a family of six children, two sons and four daughters, who all survive him.

He had succeeded in accumulating considerable property, the most of which he had distributed among his children.

What a span in the history of this country his life has reached over and what great historical events have transpired in that time!"

The children of Jonas and Elizabeth (Deweese) Ward were:
50. Josiah S. Ward.
51. Jerusha Elizabeth Ward.
52. Jonas Lutellas Ward b. 29 Nov. 1821.
53. Fidelia Ward.

There were two other daughters one of whom is said to have been named Cummings, probably the surname of the man she married. No data has been found available concerning them.

16. WILLIAM DEWEESE[3] (THOMAS[2], JOSHUA[1])

William Deweese (1799-1861) farmer of near Kirkersville, Ohio, married July 11, 1820 Margaret Sproul (b. 9 Aug. 1798 in Penn. and d. Aug. 16, 1860) a teacher in Licking County prior to her marriage.

William Deweese died Apr. 7, 1861 survived by the following children:
54. Frances Deweese b. 17 Apr. 1822.
55. Samuel Deweese b. 20 Dec. 1824.
56. James Deweese 1827-1858 unm.
57. Sarah Catherine Deweese b. 12 Mar. 1830.
58. Elizabeth M. Deweese b. 3 Apr. 1834.
59. William Spencer Deweese 1837-1863 - No issue.

17. ANNA DEWEESE[3] (LEWIS[2], JOSHUA[1])

Anna Deweese (b. 1796) married Feb. 26, 1818 John Lloyd (b. 1790 in Penn.) a son of David and Isabell Lloyd and resided in Miami County, Ohio. The children of John and Anna (Deweese) Lloyd were:
60. David Lloyd b. 1820.
61. Isabell Lloyd b. 1825.
62. Rachel Lloyd b. 1827.
63. Ruth Lloyd b. 1829.
64. Hetty Lloyd b. 1830.

65. Uriah Lloyd b. 1833.
66. Henry Lloyd b. 1836.
67. Hannah Lloyd b. 1838.
   There may have been other children
especially among the older issue.

18. MARGARET DEWEESE³ (LEWIS², JOSHUA¹)

   Margaret Deweese (b. 1797) married first
Jan. 4, 1816 John Garrard. He died and she
married Oct. 20, 1820 Uriah Blue (Jr.).

19. JOHN M. DEWEESE³ (LEWIS², JOSHUA¹)

   John M. Deweese (1799-1857) married Apr.
18, 1823 Elizabeth Blue (b. 7 Mar. 1800 and
d. Sept. 12, 1854). He died 9 Feb. 1857 and
both are buried in the old Staunton cemetery.

18. THOMAS M. DEWEESE³ (LEWIS², JOSHUA¹)

   Thomas M. Deweese (1800-1838) married 30
May 1822 Ruth Dye (b. 1802 in Pa.) daughter of
John M. Dye (1774-1842) and his wife Elizabeth
(1776-1852) of Staunton.
   Thomas M. Deweese died the 17th of Feb.
1838. His children were:
68. John D. Deweese b. ca 1823.
69. Mary Deweese b. 1825.
70. Andrew Deweese b. Sept. 1827.
71. Elizabeth Deweese b. Jan. 1831.
72. David Deweese b. Mar. 1833.
73. Catherine Deweese 1834-1839.
74. Melissa Deweese b. Aug. 1835.
75. Thomas L. Deweese b. Apr. 1837.

21. LEWIS DEWEESE³ (LEWIS², JOSHUA¹)

   Lewis Deweese Jr. (1802-1834) married Apr.
10, 1823 Hannah Clyne (d. 22 Jan. 1884) and
had issue:
76. Isaac Deweese b. and d. in 1824.
77. William Deweese b. 31 May 1827.
78. Olive Deweese 1829-1850 unm.
79. Jacob Deweese 1831-1833.
80. James Deweese b. 7 June 1833.

22. SAMUEL M. DEWEESE³ (LEWIS², JOSHUA¹)

   Samuel M. Deweese (b. ca 1804) married
16 Feb. 1825 Mary Howell.
   He was living in Miami County at the time
his father's estate was settled as he was then
guardian for his brother Lewis' minor
children.

23. WILLIAM DEWEESE³ (LEWIS², JOSHUA¹)

   William Deweese (b. 1805 in Va. and d.
Feb. 17, 1874) married Feb. 26, 1829 Susannah

McDowell (b. 6 July 1805 in Ohio and d. 16 Dec.
1873). Their children were:
81. Belinda Deweese b. 5 Dec. 1829.
82. David Deweese 1830-1831.
83. Mark Deweese b. and d. in 1833.
84. Thomas Deweese 1834-1855 unm.
85. Henry W. Deweese b. 25 Aug. 1836.
86. Elizabeth Jane Deweese 1838-1865 unm.
87. John M. Deweese b. 20 Feb. 1841 - d. 1927.
88. William H. Deweese b. 7 July 1843.
89. Mary Ann Deweese b. 22 Aug. 1845.
90. Harriet Deweese b. 2 Jan. 1848.

24. JAMES R. DEWEESE³ (LEWIS², JOSHUA¹)

   James Robinson Deweese (1807-1876)
married Mar. 15, 1829 Rebecca Blue (b. 28
June 1811 and d. 20 Apr. 1869) and resided at
Dayton, Ohio. They had several children, it
is said but the name of only one is available:
91. Francis Marion Deweese.

26. DAVID DEWEESE³ (LEWIS², JOSHUA¹)

   David Deweese (b. ca 1811) married Mar.
6, 1834 Mahetable Stinchcomb.
   They probably removed from Miami County
prior to 1850 as nothing further was found in
the records there.

25. JETHRO DEWEESE³ (LEWIS², JOSHUA¹)

   Jethro Deweese (b. ca 1813) married Dec.
25, 1834 his cousin Lydia Deweese (b. ca 1815)
daughter of James and Elizabeth (Whitlow)
Deweese. (See #40 this lineage.) They lived
near Port Jefferson in Shelby County, Ohio
and had several children, most of whom died
young of tuberculosis, the great Nemesis of
the Deweese clan!

28. REV. JOSHUA DEWEESE³ (SAMUEL², JOSHUA¹)

   Joshua Deweese (1796-1859) is said to have
followed his father as the second minister of
the Ft. Staunton Baptist Church. He was
licensed to preach and perform weddings in
the year 1824.
   He is said to have served in the War of
1812.
   On Apr. 9, 1818 he married Mary Gerard
(b. 21 Apr. 1800) who is claimed to have been
the first white child born in Miami County.
She was a daughter of Henry Gerard one of
Miami County's earliest pioneers.
   Joshua Deweese is said to have died in
May of 1859. Their children were:
92. Samuel McDougal Deweese b. 1819.
93. Martha Deweese b. 1821 - m. Daniel C.
   Hathaway

94. Sarah Deveese b. 27 Apr. 1822 m. 1844 Este Simon
95. Catherine Deweese b. 16 Feb. 1824 - m. 1842 Ebenezer G. Hathaway
96. Henry Gerard Deveese b. Jan. 1827.
97. George Washington Deweese b. 1828 d. y.
98. Rachel Deweese b. 1829 - m. 1849 Thos. Weatherhead.
99. John B. Deweese b. 1832.
100. Joshua H. Deweese b. ca 1834.
101. Mary Ann Deweese 1836-1839.
102. Joseph Deweese b. 1837-
103. Thomas W. Deweese b. 1839.
104. Mary Deweese b. 1840 - d. y.
105. James Watts Deweese b. 1842.
106. Mary Ann Deweese b. ca 1850.

29. JOHN DEWEESE³ (SAMUEL², JOSHUA¹)

John Deweese (b. ca 1798) married 13 March 1824 Susannah Blue.

30. ELIZABETH DEWEESE³ (SAMUEL², JOSHUA¹)

Elizabeth Deweese (b. ca 1800) married Dec. 19, 1822 Lewis Rodgers.

31. CATHERINE DEWEESE³ (SAMUEL², JOSHUA¹)

Catherine Deweese (b. 1802) married Mar. 30, 1824 Jesse Kerr. She died June 15, 1847 aged 45 years and 21 days. They had several children among whom were:
107. Joshua A. Kerr 1835-1845.
108. Mary Ann Kerr d. y.

32. SAMUEL M. DEWEESE³ (SAMUEL², JOSHUA¹)

Samuel M. Deweese (b..3 Mar. 1804 in Va. and d. 4 Dec. 1862) married Jan. 7, 1830 Elizabeth McDowell (b. 5 Mar. 1804 and d. 20 Apr. 1880) and had issue:
109. Alexander Deweese b. 1833.
110. Mary Deweese b. 1837.
111. Thomas Deweese b. 1839.
112. Harvey Deweese b. 1841.
113. James Deweese b. 1843.

33. MARGARET DEWEESE³ (SAMUEL², JOSHUA¹)

Margaret Deweese (b. 1806) married Apr. 12, 1826 John Murphy.

34. MARY DEWEESE³ (SAMUEL², JOSHUA¹)

Mary Deweese (b. 1808) married Aug. 22, 1832 Thomas R. Webb (b. 11 Mar. 1808 and d. 5 Sept. 1865). She died Oct. 8, 1838. They are buried in Lost Creek cemetery in Miami County, Ohio.

35. ANNA DEWEESE³ (SAMUEL², JOSHUA¹)

Anna Deweese (b. 1810) married Oct. 19, 1831 Jesse T. Webb.

37. MICHAEL DEWEESE³ (JAMES², JOSHUA¹)

Michael Deweese (b. ca 1801 in Va.) married Feb. 14, 1822 Delilah Jackson in Miami County, Ohio and had issue but names are not available. He died about 1864 near Lost Creek.

38. JESSE DEWEESE³ (JAMES², JOSHUA¹)

Jesse Deweese (b. ca 1804) married Nov. 3, 1825 Amy Blue, daughter of Michael Blue (1784-1875) a soldier of the War of 1812 and his wife Ann Chaney, and a granddaughter of Uriah Blue (1752-1829) a soldier of the American Revolution.
They had a large family and lived near Logansport, Ind.

39. ELIZABETH DEWEESE³ (JAMES², JOSHUA¹)

Elizabeth Deweese (b. 1808) married Dec. 10, 1829 Rev. Jacob J. Dye (b. 1810) and resided at Columbus, Grove, Ohio where she died Oct. 25, 1877. They are said to have had at least eight children.

41. ELIZA DEWEESE³ (JAMES², JOSHUA¹)

Eliza Deweese (b. 1812) married in March of 1837 George W. Barnes (b. in Ire. and d. Sept. 1838) and had one daughter, name unknown.
Eliza Barnes married second Thomas R. Webb (1808-1865) as his second wife and had several children who died young.
She died Mar. 15, 1862 and is buried in Lost Creek cemetery.

42. LEWIS DEWEESE³ (JAMES², JOSHUA¹)

Lewis Deweese (b. 1813) married Oct. 14, 1837 Rebecca Smalley (b. 13 Aug. 1813). He died Sept. 7, 1848 of typhoid, survived by five children.
114. Sylvester C. Deweese b. 10 Sept. 1838.
115. James Alford Deweese b. 13 Jan. 1840.
116. Melinda Irene Deweese b. 18 Oct. 1841.
117. David Marion Deweese b. 30 July 1845.
118. Sarah Diadema Deweese b. 1847.
119. George Lewis Deweese b. and d. 1848.

43. NANCY DEWEESE³ (JAMES², JOSHUA¹)

Nancy Deweese married Sept. 4, 1838 William S. Barnes (b. in Ire. and d. in

Des Moines, Ia.) and had four children.
Nancy Deweese Barnes died at the advanced age of 97 years.

44. CHRISTIANA M. DEWEESE[3] (JAMES[2], JOSHUA[1])

Christiana Deweese (1822-1882) married Dec. 25, 1845 Rev. Jesse Everett Davis (b. 3 Nov. 1821 and d. 18 July 1863) as his second wife.
They resided first in Miami County, Ohio but later removed to Wells County, Ind. where they both died. Her death occurred Mar. 7, 1882. Their children were:
120. Melville Davis b. 29 Jan. 1847 at Casstown, Ohio.
121. James Oscar Davis b. 21 Jan. 1854 at Arcanum, Ohio.
122. Sarah Elizabeth Davis b. 10 Mar. 1856 in Wells County, Ind.

45. DIADEMA DEWEESE[3] (JAMES[2], JOSHUA[1])

Diadema Deweese (1825-1919) married Sept. 29, 1850 Garrett Miller Davis (1827-1867) a half-brother of Rev. Jesse E. Davis who married her sister, Christiana.
They removed to Adams County, Ind, where he died in 1867. She married second Mr. McLeod.
There were five children by her first husband but names are not available.
She died at Decatur, Ind. in 1919 and is buried by her husband at Greenville, Ohio.

46. ALONZO DEWEESE[4] (SAM'L[3], THOS[2], JOSH.[1])

Alonzo Deweese (b. 1816) married Sarah Carlin (b. 1824 in Md.) and had issue:
123. Leroy Deweese b. 1840.
124. John W. Deweese b. 1842.
125. Mary J. Deweese b. 1844.
126. George W. Deweese b. 1849.
Probably other children.

47. WILLIAM DEWEESE[4] (SAM'L[3], THOS[2], JOSH.[1])

William Deweese (b. 1818) married Effa_____ (b. 1818 in Ohio) and had
127. Perry Deweese b. 1840.
128. Alfred Deweese b. 1844.
129. Arris Deweese b. 1847.
Probably other children.

48. JAMES L. DEWEESE[4] (SAM'L[3], THOS[2], JOSH.[1])

James L. Deweese (b. 1824) married

Eliza J. _____ (b. 1831 in Ohio) and had at least one child:
130. Mary A. Deweese b. 1850.

49. TOWLE DEWEESE[4] (SAM'L[3], THOS[2], JOSH.[1])

Towle Deweese (b. 1824) married Hannah _____ (b. 1830) and resided in Licking County, Ohio. They had at least one child:
131. Joel Deweese b. 1849.

50. JOSIAH S. WARD[4] (ELIZABETH[3], THOS[2], JOSH.[1])

Josiah S. Ward Esq. was living in Crawford County, Ill., in 1852. He removed to Winterset, Iowa where he was living in 1873 when his father Jonas Ward died there in his home. Nothing is now known of his descendants.

51. JERUSHA E. WARD[4] (ELIZABETH[3], THOS[2], JOSH.[1])

Jerusha Elizabeth Ward married Dr. Wesley Park and had at least three sons:
132. Arthur Park.
133. George Park of Godfrey, Ill.
134. Fred Park,

52. DR. JONAS L. WARD[4] (ELIZ[3], THOS[2], JOSH.[1])

Jonas Lutellas Ward M.D. (b. 1821) graduated in 1848 at the Ohio Medical College at Cincinnati.
In 1849 he removed to Crawford County, Ill. where he practiced medicine about seven years, then he removed to Clay County and later to Jerseyville in Calhoun County, Ill. where he died May 4, 1884.
He married Mar. 3, 1853 at Robinson, Ill. Mrs. Margaret (Bockhoven) Selby (b. 1823 in N. J.) in Crawford County, Ill. She died Apr. 9, 1882 at Jerseyville. Their children were:
135. Florence Ward b. 29 Mar. 1856.
136. Margaret Ward m. Perry Sparkman.
137. Mary Ward m. Frank Snowden.
138. Charles Ward.
139. Jonas Ward Jr. - d. in a well accident.

54. FRANCES DEWEESE[4] (WM[3], THOS[2], JOSH[1])

Frances Deweese (1822-1842) married James Hedden. She died Oct. 17, 1842.

55. SAMUEL DEWEESE[4] (WM[3], THOS[2], JOSH[1])

Samuel Deweese (1824-1884) farmer of

Licking County, Ohio married Jan. 22, 1856
Maria Lighty (b. 25 Sept. 1832 and d. 2 Mar.
1873).

Samuel Deweese died Oct. 15, 1884 survived by several children:
140. Luther James Deweese b. 8 Nov. 1857 - d.
1923.
141. Laura Ellen Deweese b. 16 June 1859 - d.
1921.
142. Emma Alice Deweese b. 19 Sept. 1860.
143. Mary Idella Deweese b. 26 Mar. 1862 - d.
1863.
144. William O. Deweese b. 3 Sept. 1863 - d.
1883.
145. John F. Deweese b. 1 Jan. 1865.
146. Albert Deweese b. ca 1869 - d. 25 Dec.
1889.
147. Charles Edward Deweese b. 20 June 1870 -
d. 1900.

57. SARAH C. DEWEES⁴ (WM³, THOS²,
JOSH.¹)

Sarah Catherine Dewees (1830-1855) married in 1849 Harvey Turner. She died Apr. 3,
1855 leaving at least one little daughter:
148. Elizabeth Turner b. 1850.

58. ELIZABETH M. DEWEES⁴ (WM³, THOS²,
JOSH.¹)

Elizabeth Margaret Dewees (1834-1912)
married Francis Jackson. She died Dec. 28,
1912.

60. DAVID LLOYD⁴ (ANNA³, LEWIS², JOSH¹)

David Lloyd (b. 1820) married ca 1848
Sarah _____ (b. 1827 in Ohio) and had
issue:
149. Samuel D. Lloyd 1848-1849.
150. Alwilda J. Lloyd b. 1850.
151. Rosillia Lloyd b. 1853.
152. Martha Lloyd b. 1858.

68. JOHN D. DEWEESE⁴ (THOS., M³,
LEWIS,² JOSH.¹)

John D. Deweese (1823-1883) married in
1845 Martha _____ (b. 1822 in Ohio) and
had issue:
153. William Deweese b. 1846.
154. Mathias Deweese b. 1848 - d. y.
155. Andrew G. Deweese b. 1850 went to
Pettis County, Mo.
156. Perry L. Deweese b. 1852.
157. Ruth Deweese b. 1859 - d. y.

70. ANDREW DEWEESE⁴ (THOS. M³,
LEWIS,² JOSH.¹)

Andrew Deweese (1827-1896) married
Sept. 4, 1866 Elizabeth Hart but had no
issue.

72. DAVID DEWEESE⁴ (THOS. M³,
LEWIS², JOSH.¹)

David Deweese (1833-1912) married after
1870 Lydia _____ but had no issue. He
died in Dec. 1912.

80. JAMES DEWEESE⁴ (LEWIS³,
LEWIS², JOSH.¹)

James Deweese (1833-1895) married Dec.
30, 1858 Frances Yaste (b. 1837 in Md.)
and had three children, two of whom died in
infancy. James Deweese died Apr. 22, 1895.
158. Albert Deweese b. 30 June 1864.

81. BELINDA DEWEESE⁴ (WM³, LEWIS²
JOSH.¹)

Belinda Deweese (b. 1829) married ca
1850 John L. Pence (b. 1821 in Va.)

91. FRANCIS M. DEWEESE⁴ (JAS. R³,
LEWIS², JOSH.¹)

Francis Marion Deweese is said to have
married and had at least two children:
159. Kathryn Deweese m. Peter Blosser.
160. Earl Deweese (d. 1924) m. 1897 Beatrice
Davis.

92. SAMUEL M. DEWEESE⁴ (JOSHUA³,
SAM'L², JOSH.¹)

Samuel McDougal Deweese (b. 1819)
married Jan. 19, 1843 Rachel Cornell (b. 1824
in Ohio) and resided in Concord township of
Miami County, Ohio. Their children were:
161. Joshua Deweese b. 1845.
162. Albert Deweese b. 1851 of Troy, Ohio.
163. Edward Deweese b. 1853 of Philadelphia,
Pa.
164. Allen Deweese b. 1855 of Pleasant Hill,
Ohio.
165. Judson Deweese b. 1857 of Decatur, Ala.
166. Azena Deweese b. 1859.
167. Arthur Deweese of Tippecanoe City, Ohio.
168. Flenthan Deweese.
169. Cresta Deweese.
170. Marion Deweese.

96. HENRY G. DEWEESE[4] (JOSHUA[3], SAM'L[2], JOSH.[1])

Henry Gerard Deweese (1827-1904) married Aug. 25, 1848 Lucy Ann Este (b. 1827 in Ohio). Their children were:
171. Arminta J. Deweese b. 1849 m. Mr. Moore.
172. Zelia Deweese b. 1850.
173. Jotham Deweese b. 1852.
174. Franklin Deweese b. 1854.
175. Harrison Deweese b. 1856.
176. Lucy M. Deweese b. 1860.
177. Florence Deweese b. 1862.
178. Docia Deweese b. 1869 - m. Mr. Wilson.
179. Alva Deweese.

99. JOHN B. DEWEESE[4] (JOSHUA[3], SAM'L[2], JOSH.[1])

John B. Deweese (b. 1832) lawyer of Miami County, Ohio - married Oct. 13, 1852 Caroline Hosier and had issue:
180. Charles W. Deweese b. 1857.
181. Caroline Deweese b. 1859.

109. ALEXANDER DEWEESE[4] (SAM'L M[3], SAM'L[2] JOSH.[1])

Alexander M. Deweese (1833-1903) married Sept. 7, 1865 Sarah E. Sayers (b. 1845 in Ohio) and had issue:
182. William H. Deweese b. 1866.
183. Ora J. Deweese m. Mr. Updike.

112. HARVEY DEWEESE[4] (SAM'L M[3], SAM'L[2], JOSH.[1])

Harvey Deweese (1841-1915) married Nancy J. _____ and resided at Pique, Ohio. They had a daughter:
184. Arminta Deweese m. Wm. R. Doup and had issue.

114. SYLVESTER DEWEESE[4] (LEWIS[3], JAS[2], JOSH.[1])

Sylvester C. Deweese (1838-1919) of Piqua, Ohio married June 7, 1866 Mary Miller and had at least two children:
185. Phinian Deweese.
186. Ida Deweese m. Mr. Galloway.

120. MELVILLE DAVIS[4] (CHRISTIANA[3], JAS[2], JOSH.[1])

Melville Davis (1847-1927) merchant of Bluffton, Ind. married Sept. 19, 1869 Almira Merriman (d. 1882) and had five children.
On Mar. 28, 1886 he married Sarah Jane Garrison (b. 1866) by whom he is said to have had two children.
Melville Davis died Apr. 20, 1927 at Bluffton, Ind.

121. JAMES O. DAVIS[4] (CHRISTIANA[3], JAS[2], JOSH.[1])

James Oscar Davis (1854-1915) merchant of Bluffton, Ind. married Apr. 14, 1884 Margaret Jane Lanning (b. 16 May 1859 in Wells County, Ind. and d. at Kokomo, Ind. 13 Jan. 1918). He died at Bluffton, Ind. Aug. 2, 1915. They had three children:
187. Charles Davis.
188. Fred Davis.
189. Eva Mae Davis b. 8 Feb. 1896 m. 1929 Lewis W. Appelquist.

122. SARAH E. DAVIS[4] (CHRISTIANA[3], JAS[2], JOSH.[1])

Sarah Elizabeth Davis (b. 1856) married Arthur M. Shady (b. 1853) Sept. 2, 1874 and resided at Larned, Kan.
They had seven children.

135. FLORENCE WARD[5] (JONAS L[4], ELIZ[3], THOS[2], JOSH.[1])

Florence Ward (1856-1932) married first William Richardson and had:
190. Helen Richardson m. Luther Crosby and had issue.
191. Jennie Richardson m. John Killebrew and had issue. She married second Aug. 23, 1880 Henry King (b. Sept. 28, 1859 at Fieldon, Ill.) and had issue:
192. Ward King m. Josephine _____ and had one son.
193. Paul King m. and had a son, Gerald King.
194. Florence King b. 18 Dec. 1889 at Fieldon, Ill.
195. Margaret King b. 1 Dec. 1893.
196. Edith King d. y.
197. Fred King m. Hulda Johnson and had issue.
198. Freda King m. Roy Clark and had issue.

142. EMMA A. DEWEES[5] (SAM'L[4], WM[3], THOS[2], JOSH.[1])

Emma Alice Dewees (1860-1889) married Perry Tygard and had two children:
199. Charles Tygard b. 1880 m. Carrie Cusac.
200. Marinda Tygard b. 1883 m. William Edwards.

194. FLORENCE KING[6] (FLORENCE[5], JONAS L[4], ELIZ[3], THOS[2], JOSH.[1])

Florence King (1889----) married Jan. 25,

1904 Culvert Killebrew (b. 1 Apr. 1878 at Belleview Ill.) and had issue:
201. Margaret Killebrew b. Aug. 4, 1905.
202. Alice Killebrew b. July 24, 1909.

Florence King Killebrew married second David Long (d. 1924) and had a son:
203. John David Long b. 10 Apr. 1917.

Florence K. K. Long married third K. D. Chissom, no issue by the third marriage.

195. MARGARET KING[6] (FLORENCE[5], JONAS[4], ELIZ[3], THOS[2], JOSH.[1])

Margaret King (b. 1893) married Oct. 22, 1910 Walter Ross Kelly (d. 27 Mar. 1933) and had issue:
204. Ronald Earl Kelly b. 14 Aug. 1911.
205. Doris Vivian Kelly b. 14 June 1913.
206. Walter Robert Kelly b. 19 Mar. 1916.
207. Raymond Leroy Kelly b. 2 Feb. 1921.

201. MARGARET KILLEBREW[7] (FLORENCE[6], FLORENCE[5], JONAS[4], ELIZ[3], THOS[2], JOSH.[1])

Margaret Killebrew (b. 1905) married Aug. 30, 1933 Richard Nesti (b. 25 Mar. 1903) instructor, and has one daughter:
208. Mary Alice Nesti b. 23 Dec. 1937.

204. RONALD E. KELLY[7] (MARGARET[6], FLORENCE[5], JONAS[4], ELIZ[3], THOS[2], JOSH.[1])

Ronald Earl Kelly (b. 1911) married Dec. 25, 1937 Helen June Sewell and had one child:
209. Demetria Ann Kelly b. 16 Oct. 1938.

205. DORIS V. KELLY[7] (MARGARET[6], FLORENCE[5], JONAS[4], ELIZ[3], THOS[2], JOSH.[1])

Doris Vivian Kelly (b. 1913) married in Jan. 1930 Stonewall Dearen Bassett and have two children:
210. William Walter Bassett b. 24 Nov. 1931.
211. David Edward Bassett b. 11 Nov. 1933.

206. WALTER R. KELLEY[7] (MARGARET[6], FLORENCE[5], JONAS[4], ELIZ[3], THOS[2], JOSH.[1])

Walter Robert Kelly (b. 1916) enlisted in the U. S. Army Aug. 26, 1934, 9th Engs. and is stationed at Fort Riley, Kan. He married Dec. 31, 1937 Arlene Josephine Fengel and has one daughter:
212. Patricia Lee Kelly b. 30 Dec. 1938.

Apparently of Dutch origin, the name Deweese, meaning the orphan as Hendrik de vees (Henry the orphan) first came into use about the twelfth century.

Adrian de Wees of Amsterdam, Holland (thirteenth century) is claimed to have been descended from the ancient lords of Kessel. His son Gerrard (Garret) went to England during the reign of Henry VIII and established there the English "D'Ewes" family which was the surname of the Earl of Warwick whose Coat of Arms was visited 1709.

Deweese Lineage Notes

The earliest settlers of the name in America were Gerrard Hendricks De Wees, his wife Zytian and his children: Wilhelmina, William, Cornelius, Lewis, and Johannes. There may also have been another daughter Sarah. They came about 1688 and settled first at New Amsterdam, removing the following year to Germantown, Penn. where on Mar. 1, 1690 "Gerrie Hendriks De Wees purchased of Herman Epden Graff, attorney of Dirck Sipman of Crefeld in Germany a certain lot of land--- in the inhabited part of Germantown."

Lewis De Wees said to have been the youngest son of Garrett Hendriks De Wees was a weaver by trade and followed that occupation for some years in Philadelphia. Early in 1727 he removed with his family to what is now Kent County, Delaware and purchased Feb. 22, 1727 three hundred acres on the north side of Fishing Creek where he lived until his death in the early spring of 1743.

The name of his wife is not known. He had several children among whom was Samuel Deweese b. ca 1713 in Philadelphia, Penn. He married ca 1735 Mary _____ in Kent County, Del. He died in Oct. of 1753.

His son Joshua Deweese was born in Kent County, May 3, 1742 (See text.)

Bowman Lineage Notes

The Bowman family is one of the oldest in Delaware.

On the 6th day of the 12th month 1681 Henry Bowman purchased "on Ceedar Creeke of a Plantacon House and one thousand acres of land." Some of his land was purchased from the Indians who made claim in court that the said Henry Bowman had failed to pay "two match cootes" part of the purchase price (presumably meaning two matched colts).

Henry Bowman was made "Ranger" for Sussex County in 1685.

INDEX

BRANDEL, Anna 109, Charles 109, George 109.
BRAWLEY, Clarence 100, Ida 100, John 100, Mary 100,
    Nellie 100.
BRETT, Elizabeth 81,86, Joseph 79,81.
BREWSTER, Ann 41, Frank 40,41, Henry 40, John 40,
    Nancy 40, Pauline 40, Ruth 40, Sherman 40,
    Virginia 40.
BRIDGE, David 83, Diadama 83, Phoebe 83.
BRIGGS, Archibald 16,17, Charles 20,24, Clara 20,
    Eliza 16, Elizabeth 20,24, Esther 24, Fergus 24,
    Glenn 24, Ida 20,24, Jackson 17,20, James 16,
    John 16,17,20, Laura 20, Mary 16,20, Matilda 17,
    Melissa 17,20, Myrtle 20, Sarah 16, Susanna 24,
    Velma 24, William 24.
BRIGHT, Mary 49.
BROWN, Anna 40, Arthur 102, Chloe 75, Eliza 75,
    Helen 76, Henry 97, Mary 10,76, Maude 25, Perley
    75, Sally 76, Samuel 101, Ralph 92.
BUCKINGHAM, Matilda 99.
BUKER, Israel 19, Melissa 19,23.
BURCHER, Albert 54, Ethel 54, Fonda 59, Mary 54,
    Montford 54, Paul 59, R.L. 54, Ronald 59.
BURGE, Caroline 82,87, Cora 82,87, Leanora 82,87,
    Orrin 82.
BURKHART, Gladys 27, Rexford 27.
BURR, Alcinda 38, Alfred 38,40, Edward 40, Elizabeth
    38, Emma 38, George 39,40, Laura 40, William 38.
BUTTON, Augusta, 103,105, Elizabeth 103, Helen 103,105,
    Frank 103, Rich. 103.

CALDWELL, Alexander 4, James 4, Maria 5.
CAMPBELL, Nettie 62,67, Oliver 62.
CARPENTER, George 11, Nettie 11, Parker 79.
CARTER, Aaron 32, Alice 53, Clara 54, Elmer 53, Emmett
    54, Fenton 54, Frances 50,54, Harry 54, James 50,
    54, John 50,54, Joseph 50, Lloyd 54, Ray 54, Ruth
    28,50,54, Samuel 50, Sarah 50,54, Thomas 50,53,
    Truman 54, William 50,54.
CHADWELL, Henrietta 100, John 97, Mary 100, Samuel 97,
    100.
CHASE, Faith 65, Fern 65, Walter 65.
CHIDESTER, Guinevere 41, John 41, Ida 41.
CHURCH, Bessie 61, Iza 61, Theo 61, Zala 61.
CLARK, Eleanor 40, Roy 117.
CLARNO, Herman 68, Keith 68.
CLAWSON, Henry 26, Ruth 26.
COE, Alice 92, Allie 84, Alvin 92, Amelia 81,85,
    Amy 81, Augusta 82, Augustus 82,87, Arthur 84,91,
    Basil 88, Beach 80,88, Bertha 84,90, Bessie 88,
    Callie 88, Carl 88,93, Caroline 80,81,82,
    Catherine 81,84, Celia 32,46,89,93, Charles 80,82,
    83,84,89,91, Charlotte 95, Clarence 83,89, Delbert
    92, Delva 93,95, Dennis 83,88, Diadama 88, Diana
    81,85, Doloris 95, Donald 92,95, Dorothy 93,
    Ebenezer 81,83, Eliza 81,84, Elizabeth 80,82,83,
    88, Elmer 92, Elza 88, Emma 83,88,89,92, Ernest
    84, Esther 80, Ethel 92,94, Eunice 80,81,83,88,
    Florence 89, Francis 83,88, Frank 88, Fred 88,92,
    Frederick 88, Gaston 44,46,83,88,89, George 44,46,
    80,83,84,89,90,92, Gerald 92,95, Gertrude 88,92,

Glenadine 92,95, Glenn 88,92, Grace 88, Harriet 80,
81, Harry 80, Hiram 80,81,85, Ida 83,88, Ira 85,
Irene 84,85,91, Isaac 79,80,81, Jackson 81,84,
James 44,79,80,81,83,84,88, Jean 95, Jennie 84,89,
91, Jessie 84,91, John 80,82,83,85,88, Johnson 44,
81,83, Josiah 74,79,80,81,82,84, Julia 74,80,82,
Kate 84,89, Lawrence 93, Lela 92,95, Letty 46,89,
Lewis 83,88, Lorain 83,88, Lovey 80,81,84,85,
Lucetta 81, Lucretia 81,85, Lyla 92,94, Lyle 92,
Marcus 88, Maria 81,83,85, Marjorie 92, Margaret
92, Max 92, Mary 80,83,84,85,88,90, Mary Ann 74,
80,81,83,88, Nancy 80,82,88, Nellie 88,92, Nina 92,
Olive 46,89,93, Orie 87, Oscar 88,92, Phoebe 80,
82,83,85, Ralph 92, Reuben 81,84, Richard 92,
Robert 44,95, Roy 88,92, Rufus 88,92,95, Salina
80,82, Samuel 83,88, Sarah 81,85, Shirley 95,
Sidney 83,88, Stella 88, Sylvanus 81,85, Sylvester
81,85, Sylvia 85, Thelma 92, Thomas 80,83,88,
Thurma 92, Ulysis 92, Vinnie 87, Wesley 80,82,83,
William 88,89,92.
COIT, Alonzo 56, Earl 56, Ella 56,62, Fred 56, George
56, Harry 56, John 56, May 56,62.
CONDRON, Clair 92, Eva 92, William 92.
CONN, Eleanor 98.
CONNETT, Abner 74, Andrew 74,76, Dana 76, Della 76,
    Elizabeth 76, George 74,76, Harry 76, Hyrcanus 74,
    76, Loring 74,76, Lucy 74, Lydia 74, Mabel 76,
    Mary 76, Raymond 76, Woodruff 74.
COOK, Albert 33, Ann 2, Cyrus 88, Frances 88, Maxine 33.
COOLEY, Caleb 99, Eliza 99.
COULSON, Bernice 59, Charles 59, Leah 59,64.
COURTNEY, Betty 94, Charles 94, Clifford 92, Clinton 92,
    Christina 92, Florence 92, Gilbert 92,94, Harvey
    92, Isabel 94, Paul 92.
CRALEY, Fred 10, Martha 10.
CRANE, Virginia 25, William 25.
CRAVENS, Bramwell 85, Catherine 85, Dow 85, Emma 85,
    Frank 85, Josiah 85.
CRAWFORD, A.E. 61, Arthur 61, Edna 12,61,66, Lyle 61,
    Mabel 61,66, Vira 61,66.
CREESY, Emily 39.
CUMMINS, Adam 22, Addie 22,27, David 22, Fred 22,
    Minnie 22,27, William 22.
CUNNINGHAM, Asbury 58, Charles 4, Clarence 58, Edward
    58, Frank 58, Fred 58, Elmira 4, Jessie 58, Mary 4,
    58, Ottie 58, Walter 88.
CURTIS, Daniel 45,97, Esther 80, Frank 45, Olthenia 99.

DALTON, Anna 21, Charles 21, John 21, Lulu 21.
DAUGHERTY, Carolyn 95, Charles 46,93, Clarence 68,
    Coe 93, Donald 95, Dora 68, Elwood 93,95, Mae 68,
    Minnie 68, Pauline 93, Robert 95, R.P. 68, Rose
    68, Walter 68.
DAVIS, Beatrice 116, Bonnie 14, Charles 117, Connie
    102, Dwight 93, Edwin 87,97, Elias 81, Eva 117,
    Fred 117, Garrett 115, Isaiah 97, James 97,115,
    117, Jesse 115, John 57, Lucia 87, Lucy 93, Mary
    101, Melville 115,117, Samuel 93, Sarah 115,117.
DE COU, Isaac 91, Jessie 91, Samuel 91, Sarah 91.
DELONG, Andrew 10, Catherine 8,10, George 10, Rhoda 10,
    Sarah 9,10.

FULLER, Russel 97,98,99,101,103, Ruth 103, Sarah 98,100, 102, Susan 98, 101, Susannah 98,100, Stephen 103, William 101,103, Willis 101.

GAMMAGE, Fred 64, Gloria 64.
GARDNER, Caleb, 101, Duane 69, Erwin 69, George 101, Lester 26, Mary 101,103, Robert 69.
GARRETT, Anson 17,20, Emma 59, Emza 17,20, Ermina 25, Esther 93, Georgia 17,20, James 17, Jane 17, John 17, Louise 17,20, Luther 20, Mary 20, Sydnor 20, Wm. 20,25.
GARRISON, Donna 94, Haskel 94, Sarah 117.
GAYLORD, Charles 86, Harriet 86, Theodocia 86.
GERARD, Henry 113, John 113, Mary 113.
GIESECKE, C. L. 78, Emma 78, Herman 78, Mary 78.
GILLET, Charlotte 83, Elizabeth 83, Samuel 79,83.
GOOD, John 103, Peter 103.
GRANT, Edmond 99, Elbert 99, Emerson 99, Eveline 99,101, James 99, Lovina 97,98, Lydia 99, Royal 99.
GRAY, Combe 44, Elizabeth 44.
GREATHOUSE, Helen 27, Leora 27, Mary 27, Walter 27, Wilford 27.
GREEN, Dell 54, Sarah 37.
GREGG, Caleb 39, John 54, Martha 39, Millicent 39.
GRIEST, Elizabeth 12, Isaac 12, Robert 12.
GRIM, Amos 30, Daniel 30,31, Mary 31.
GRIMES, Anna 38, Benjamin 37,38, Bertha 38, Charles 38, Catherine 37, Esther 37,38, George 38, Hannah 37, 39, Joanna 37, Margaret 37, Mary 38, Owen 37,38 Samuel 37,38.
GRISWOLD, Carrie 6, Charles 6, Ellen 6, Hoyt 6, Luzerne 6, Mary 78, Mathew 78, Phebe 78.

HALBIRT, Berta 77, Earl 77, Donna 77,78, John 77,78, Phillip 77, Roger 77.
HALL, Abraham 63, Audrey 63, Fern 63, Grace Ina 63, Leona 63, Macelline 68, Maud 63, Melba 63, Myrtle 63, Purley 63,68.
HALLEY, Martha 23, William 23.
HALLOWAY, Emma 10, William 10.
HAPGOOD, Belle 62, Loretta 62,67, May 62,67.
HARDGROVE, Charles 22, Fred 22, George 22, Rolland 22, Shelby 22, Stella 22, Walter 22.
HARMON, Alice 97,99 Elizabeth 98, Harry 57, Maud 57, R.G. 97, Robert 99, Roxie 57, Ruth 57, William 97,99.
HARPER, Adaline 3, Albert 2,3, Alexander 1,2,3,4, Amanda 3,4,5, Amelia 3,5, Amy 4, Ann 2, Asenath 2, Benjamin 2, 4, Catherine 5, Charles 1,2,4,6, Christiana 1,2,3,4, Clarence 5, Clarissa 2, Cyrus 4,5, David 5, Derastus 2,3, Edmond 4, Edwin 66, Eliphalet 4,5, Elsie 66, Eliza 3,4,5, Elizabeth 1,2,3 Emily 4, F.A. 3, Fanny 1,2, Frank 66, George 3, Hamilton 4, Helen 66, Henderson 5, Hester 3, Isabelle 1,2, Isadore 5,6, James 2,3,4, John 1,2,3, Joseph 4, Leo 5, Lora 5, Lydia 32, Martha 4,5, Mary 3,4,5,6, Myron 5, Netti 5, Persocia 3, Rebecca 4, Robert 2,3,4,5, Roderick 3, Sarah 2, Sarepta 5,6, Susan 4, Theron 2,3, Vesta 5, Vinton 5, Willard 66,

HARRIS, Dixie 32, Jonathan 36.
HASTINGS, Lucile 102,104, Mary 102,104, Mildred 102, R.C.M. 102, William 102.
HATHAWAY, Ebenezer 114, Daniel 113.
HAWES, Cyrus 9, Frances 9, Luther 9, Lydia 9, Mary 9, Orpha 9, Permelia 9, Sarah 9, Ursala 9.
HEADLEY, Burley 102, Esther 102, Dean 102, Harold 104, Martha 104, Mary 102, Ross 102,104, William 104.
HEAD, Gertrude 62, Ollie 58.
HENRY, F.A. 11, Fanny 76, Hazel 76, James 98, Nina 14, Parker 77, Sarah 11.
HERCOCK, Beverly 26, Billy 26, Delbert 26, Ethel 26, Norma 26, Ray 26, Robert 26.
HERROLD, Daniel 4, Franklin 4, Henry 72, Sophia 4.
HESTON, John 93, Max 93.
HICKMAN, John 94, Martha 94, Perley 94, Willis 94.
HINTZ, A.V. 46, 89, Letty 46.
HIVNOR, Albert 26, Archibald 26, Charles 26, Clarence 26, Ella 21,26, Forrest 26, Frank 21, Harry 21,26, Martha 26, Ona 21,26, Raymond 26, Robert 26, Sidney 21,26, Walter 26.
HOLDEN, Jack 103.
HOMROLD, Harold 24, Henry 24.
HOODLET, Charles 34, Constance 34.
HOPE, Addie 31, Alton 32,34,93, Alvira 6,31,58, Amanda 30, Anna 30, Barbara 34,93, Bernard 29, 30, 31,33 Bernice 31, Bertha 31, Betty 33,34,93, Burwell 32, Carol 32,93, Charles Clarinda 31,32, Dora 32,34, Doris 33, Dulcia 32, Earl 32,34, Edward 33, Eliza 30, Elizabeth 29,31,32,33,34,39, Elmer 32, Erma 31,33, Frank 32,33, George 29,30,31,32, Geraldine 32,93, Harley 30,31,33, Harold 33,34, Harry 32,34, 93, Hazel 31,32, Henry 35, Howard 32,34, Helen 32, 33,34, Ida 32, Isaiah 30,31, James 29, J. Garfield 31,33,58, Jane 29, Jean 31, Jeannette 32, John 29, 31,32,34, Joyce 34, Juanita 34, John Thomas 22,29, 30,31,32,46,58,93, Kermit 32, Lau Dell 32,34 Leona 32, Lesley 31,33, Mabel 32,34, Margaret 32, Margretta 30, Marie 32,33, Marvin 34, Maurice 32, Mary 35, Mary Elizabeth 29,30,31,35,58,64, Mazie 31,33, Milton 30,31, Nellie 31,32, Noah 31, Norma 31,33, Oswald 33, Paul 31,32, Pearl 32, Peyton 22, 29,30,35,58, Philip 34, Ralph 34, Raymond 33,34, Richard 32, Rita 32, Rhoda 31,58, Robert 34, Ronda 32, Russell 29,30,31, Ruth 34, Terrence 33, Vincent 32, Virginia 34, Walter 31, Warren 33,93, William 31,34, Worley Alvadore 31,32.
HOWALD, Charles 12, George 12.
HOWARD, Anery Eichner 61.
HUGHES, Margaret 41, Sarah 8.
HUMMEL, Alfred 50,55,60, Alice 54, Archie 55, Audrey 60, Cecil 55,60, Charles 54, Clarence 55,60, Cora 54, Effie 54, Ethel 55,60, Ellen 50,55, Errol 60,65, Elizabeth 50,55,65, Fay 60, George 55, Isaac 50,54, James 50,55, John 55, Joseph 54, Julia 50,54, Laura 54, Lavina 54, Lewis 50,55, Lida 55, Martha 50,55,65, Mary 50,55, Mildred 60, Nancy 65, Olive 54, Sarah 50,55, Wm. 50,55.
HUMPHREY, Don 64, E.D. 64, Joe 64, Nellie 64, Thomas 62, William 77.

McLEAN, Lydia 71, Robert 45.
McNALL, Athol 62, Donna 67, Edward 62, J.M. 63, Lura 62,
    Mary 62, Murray 63, Reah 63, Theo 62,67.
MERRYMAN, Almira 117, Earl 39, George 39, Nicholis 39,
    William 39.
MILLER, Anna 11, Charles 55, George 55,60, Gladys 103,
    Iva 55, James 60, Jennie 55, Maggie 55, Mary 55,
    Susannah 17, Walter 105, William 55.
MINTUN, Nancy 77, Sarah 77, Thomas 77.
MOODY, Chester 59, Clyde 59, John 50, Leonard 59,
    Parker 59.
MOORE, Andrew 75, Arlie 58, Baruch 75, Caroline 75,
    David 85, Elizabeth 75, Flora 11, Helen 102,
    Isaac 75, James 102, Josiah 75, Lucretia 85,
    Lydia 75,77, Martin 59, Mary 85, Wilson 75,
MORRIS, Bishop 5, Diana 4, Sarah 16.
MORRISON, Frederick 103, Martin 103, Robert 103.
MOSURE, Charles 88, William 88.
MURREY, George 10, Nellie 10.
MULLIGAN, Elizabeth 65, Gertrude 65, Hugh 65.
MYERS, Alice 11, Austin 104,105, Boyd 25, Carol 105,
    Emma 25, Harold 25, Hazel 25, Leroy 25, Lyle 25,
    Robert 104, Thelma 25, Thomas 98.
MYRICK, Caleb 83, Edward 83, Emeline 83, Thomas 83.

NASH, Elizabeth 97,98, Samuel 97.
NAYLOR, Archie 55, Isaac 55.
NELSON, Carrie 65, Charles 27, Dolph 27, Emma 21,
    Henry 9, Isaac 9, John 9,27, Mildred 27, Nancy 8,
    Robert 9, Seth 9.
NEWMAN, Easter 58, Jane 53, George 52, Lethinda 52.
NESTI, Mary Alice 118, Richard 118.
NICKLE, Robert 69, Ronald 69, Sarah 22.
NONNEMAN, Barbara 65, Raymond 65.

O'NEIL, Edward 105, Eve 105, Louis 105.
OWENS, Eliza 4, John 83, Sarah 56.

PARKER, Edmund 54, Harrison 53, Mary 77.
PARSONS, Alva 27, Daniel 27, Eldon 27, Emeline 27,
    Joseph 55, Lavinia 55,59, Luke 27, Mark 27, Mary
    55,59, Oceanna 55,59, Viola 27.
PASOLD, David 66, Ferman 66.
PATRICK, Carrie 53, Jan 53, Nancy 53, Sarah 53,
    William 53.
PATTISON, Frank 53, Jasper 53.
PETTY, Katherine 28, Sally 38.
PHILLIPS, Clayton 102, Daniel 43, Helen 102, John 47,
    Martha 43, Thankful 43, Wm. 77.
PICKETT, Charlotte 67, Elizabeth 3, James 3, John 85.
PIDGEON, John 54,59, Mary 59, Viola 59.
PLUMLY, Hope 39, G.E. 78, Laura 78, Margaret 78.
PORTER, Dorothy 68, Edgar 45, Emma 44, Ethel 68,
    Frances 45, Frank 44, Georgia 45, Henry 68, James
    68, Joseph 45, William 45.
POSTON, Albert 76, Frank 76, Hugh 76, Jesse 76, Win-
    field 76.
POWELL, Bernard 88, Elizabeth 91, Alma 89, Emma 89,
    Helen 89, Mary 89, Wm. 89.
PRATT. Azariah 98. Mary 98.

PROCTOR, George 49, Jane 53.
PUGSLEY, Charles 44, Frances 44, George 44, Georgiana
    44, James 44, Laura 44, Marcellus 44.
PURVIANCE, Amanda 38,39, Edward 40, Eleanor 38,39,
    Elizabeth 37, Elsworth 38, Emily 38,39,40,
    Ernest 40, Esther 37,38,39, George 36,37,38,
    Harriet 38, Helen 40, Isaac 37,38, James 38,
    John 38,40, Mabel 40, Martha 37,38, Mary 37,38,39,
    Nathan 37,38, Orville 40, Owen 37,38, Plummer 38,
    40, Rachel 38,39, Richard 37,38, Samuel 37.

PUTNAM, Israel 82, Nabby 81, Rufus 71.

RAINEY, Albert 9,11,12, Alice 10, Alma 11, Amos 8,10,
    Anna 7,8,9,12,16, Archie 12, Arlene 14, Armedia
    11, Atta 10, Bertha 11, Bessie 11,13, Carl 12,14,
    Carolyn 14, Carroll 14, Cecil 12,14, Charles 10,
    12,14, Charlotte 8,10, Clara 10,12, Clarence 12,
    Cleo 13, Clyde 12,14, Delbert 11,13, Della 12,
    Doris 14, Duane 14, Edna 14, Edward 8,12, Edwin
    9,10, Effie 12, Eldon 13,14, Eli 9,10,11,12,52,
    Elizabeth 9,10,12,14,52, Ella 12, Elvin 14, Emma
    10,12, Estell 11,13, Eunice 9,11, Eva 10, Flora
    11,12, Florence 12, Frank 12,14, Frederick 10,12,
    Geraldine 13, George 10, Gifford 14, Harold 12,
    Hattie 12, Hazel 12, Howard 12,14, Hubert 13, Ilah
    14, Isaac 7,8,9,10,52, Jackson 9, James 7,8,9,10,
    11,12, Jane 7,8,9, Jennie 10, Jennet 7,8,9,10,
    John 7,8,9,10,11,12,14, Joseph 10, Julius 9,12,
    Kenneth 14, Leland 14, Leone 12, Lewis 10, Lottie
    11, Lovinia 9,11,52, Lowell 14, Lucinda 10, Lydia
    8,10, Mabel 12, Marguerite 12, Maria 7,8,9,16,
    Martha 8,9,10, Matilda 8,9, Mary 7,8,9,10,11,12,
    Milan 11, Nellie 10, Nettie 11, Norman 14, Ora 11,
    Philip 14, Priscilla 8, Rhoda 8,9,10,12, Robert
    7,8,9,10,13, Rosetta 9, Roy 11,12,13,14, Ruth 13,
    14, Sarah 9,10,11,12, Schyler 10, Silvanus 9,11,
    Stella 12, Warren 14, William 7,8,9,12.
RASMUSSENT, James 33, Janet 33.
RATHBUN, Gideon 43, Mercy 43,44.
RENSHAW, Alberta 20,25, George 20, Joyce 20, Mabel 20,
    Ransom 20.
RICE, Charles 62, Elizabeth 62,66, Elsie 62,66, Fred
    62, Grace 62,66, Jonas 75, Louis 62, Mary 75,
    Ruth 62,66, Sarah 62,66,98, Thomas 62, William 62.
RICHARDS, Charles 27, Dean 27, Elizabeth 41, Margaret
    41, Mildred 27, Owen 41, William 41.
RICHARDSON, Helen 117, Jennie 117, William 117.
ROBBINS, Amos 82, Andrew 82, Charles 82, Esther 82,
    Fern 86, Frank 91, Franklin 82, George 82,
    Harriet 82, Henry 82,86, Ina 86, James 82, Joseph
    79,81,82,86,91, Julia 82,86, Levi 82, Lewis 82,86,
    Lyman 82, Nabby 82, Ralph 91, Samuel 81,82, Sarah
    82,86, Thelma 91, Wm. 86.
ROBERTS, Clarence 39, Ella 39, Lenna 39, Nathan 39,
    Wylie 39.
ROBINSON, Edward 85, Harriet 85, Ina 104, Janice 94,
    Mary 85, Pearl 104, Sarah 85, Tremain 94, Wm. 81,
    85,104.
ROGERS, Doloris 66, Donald 66, James 77, Rachel 31,

ROGERS, Sarah 77, Susan 85, William 31.
ROOT, A.D. 77, Benjamin 77, Howard 77,78, Kenneth 77.
ROUANZOIN, Elizabeth 48,49,55, Katherine 55.
RUEK, Agnes 63, Olga 63.
RUSSELL, Carol 103, Gerald 103, Louis 103, Sarah 5,
   William 4.

SALZER, Betty 64, Delbert 64, Richard 64.
SANDERS, Benjamin 22, Emeline 22, 52, Joel 97.
SANDS, Joshua 102,104, Richard 104, Thomas 104, Willis
   102,104.
SARGENT, Arlie 58, Bartlett 52,57, Florence 58, Guirney
   66, Jesse 57, John 52,57, Lee 57, Lucretia 52,
   Marcellus 52,57, Marie 66, May 58, Newton 52,
   Serena 52,58.
SAWYER, Claud 12, R.C. 39.
SCHADT, Lois 63, Rudolph 63.
SCHAEFFER, Fred 56, Grace 56,62, Hattie 56,62.
SCHANG, Clifton 67, Harold 67, Lyle 67.
SCHULTZ, Frank 67, Genevieve 67, Phyllis 67.
SCOTT, Amelia 37, Amos 38, Anna 38, Cora 38, Esther 38,
   George 38, Henrietta 38, Isaac 38, Julia 50, Levi
   38, Lewis 38, Martha 38, Sarah 38, William 38,
   John 86.
SEAY, John 23, Winifred 23.
SELLECK, Janice 95, Lyle 95.
SERVICE, Evelyn 59, Newell 59, Roscoe 59, Vivian 59,64.
SHAFFER, Della 46,89, Earl 104, Ellis 104, Matilda 59.
SHEFFIELD, Ezekiel 83, Sophia 83.
SHEPHERD, Aaron 91, Charles 32, Florence 89, Laura 91,
   P.W. 89.
SHIELDS, Frank 68, Lewis 68, Thomas 68.
SIX, Catherine 5, George 5, William 42,43.
SKINNER, Julia 72, L.N. 72, Nat 18.
SMITH, Aaron 49,51,56,57,63, Albert 10,58,64, Alexander
   52, Alice 62, Amanda 50,52, Amy 49,58, Ann 47,69,
   Annis 51,57, Arthur 49,56,63, Arwilda 56,63,
   Asbury 52, August 40, Bartlett 51,56, Beatrice 61,
   Belle 56,62, Benjamin 47,48, Bernice 57,59, Bert,
   61,65, Bertha 58, Betty 65, Blanche 58, Bonnie 58,
   64, Burgess 56, 60, Caroline 56,61, Carrie 56,63,
   Carver 61, Catherine 50, Charlotte 65, Clara 53,
   57,59,63, Clarence 53,59, Clifford 65, Cora 92,
   Corintha 54, Dale 58, Daphne 56, David 50,52,57,63,
   69, Delbert 63, Delilah 50, Don 64, Donna 64,
   Doris 65, Druzilla 50, Earl 56,63, Edith 58,61,88,
   Edward 53,59,88, Edna 61, Eldora 56,61, Eli 9, 18,
   48,49,51,52,53,55,56,58, Eliphalet 69, Eliza 51,
   56,57,60, Elizabeth 48,49,51,52,56,60, Ellen 49,
   52, Ellis 60, Elva 57,63, Emma 56,62, Emmett 65,
   Ephraim 61, Ernest 56, Ervin 56, Eugenia 62,
   Evelyn 63, Florence 58,64, Floyd 63, Forest 58,64,
   65, Frank 58, Fred 58, Freda 59,64, F. W. 20,
   George 49,51,52,57, Georjane 51,57, Grace 57,62,
   Harold 57,61,63,65, Harrison 52,58, Harry 56, Harvey 51, Hazel 58, Helen 65, Henry 52, Hiram 51,57,
   Homer 60, Howard 58, India 85, Irene 62, Israel 69,
   Iva 58, Jane 53, Janice 64, James 51,52,56,58,65,
   85, Jeannette 63,68, Jerry 65, John 50,51,52,54,56,
   58,61,64, Jonathan 48,111, Judith 65, Kenneth 63,

Kitty 58, Lady 56,63, Lavinia 49,50,52, Leemoy
   56,62, Lee 58,64, Leland 65, Lela 61,65, Leonard
   59, Lewis 61,65,111, Louise 63, Lucinda 10, Mabel
   58, Maria 52, Marjorie 63,64, Margaret 50,51,52,
   56,57,60,65, Martha 57,64, Mary 48,50,53,56,58,62,
   May 57, Michael 69, Myrtle 56,62, Nancy 47,48,
   Nellie 56,58,62, Nelson 61, Newton 57, Oakley 92,
   O.K. 56,63, Olive 40,58,85, Opal 65, Ora 31,48,
   Paul 65, Purley 51,56,57, Raymond 63,64, Rhoda 18,
   49,52,57, Robert 64, Russell 61,65, Ruth 57,63,64,
   Samuel 48,49,50,54,69, Sarah 9,49,50,51,52,53,56,
   Seth 53,58, Solomon 49,52,53,58, Susannah 52,58,
   Sophronia 56, Tad 58, Thaddeus 47,69, Thelma 61,
   65, Thurman 57, Temperance 69, Ulah 56,63, Valeria
   60, Vivian 62, Warren 63, Washington 49,52, Wil-
   liam 48,49,50,53,56,57,59,61,62,92, William Hall
   56,61, Zophar 48.
SNOWDEN, Dorothy 60, Frank 115.
SNYDER, Carver 60, Charles 60, Christina 60, Edith 61,
   Ernest 60, Ervin 13, Herbert 63, John 60.
SPEAR, Byron 61,65, Caroline 65, Donna 65, Edna 61,
   Iowa 61, Jas. 65, Margaret 65, Norma 65, Samuel 61.
SPRAGG, Anna 24, F.C. 19.
SPRAGUE, Allen 104, Bernardine 104, Edward 104, Florence
   102, Floride 104, Gerald 104, John 102,104, Jennie
   102,104, Lenore 104,105, Levi 102, Lindley 104,
   Marion 104, Mary 102, Myra 102, Robert 104, Warren
   102,104, Wiley 102,104, William 102,104.
SPUNG, Lemuel 26, Mabel 26, Margaret 26, Verna 26.
SPURRIER, Alice 60, Ernest 60, Ernestine 60, Forest 60,
   Gertrude 60, Mae 60, Mary 60, Omar 60, Ross 60,
   Thomas 60, Woodrow 60.
SRIGLEY, H. S. 104, John 104, Robert 104.
STACK, Charles 105, John 105.
STERRETT, Erva 67, Ethel 67, John 67, Margaret 18,
   Robert 67, Verla 67,69, William 67.
STEVENSON, Clyde 87, Conrad, 87, Lydia 76, Olive 87,
   Silas 87, Vance 87, Zella 87, Zina 87.
STEWART, Alice 67, Allen 40, Columbus 2, Fern 25,
   Martha 2, Sarah 50.
STIRES, Vernon 76, Wilford 76.
STOLTE, Helen 66, William 66.
STONE, Arnold 68, George 68, Florence 68.
STOVER, Beatice 94, Eileen 94, Emma 94, Frances 95,
   Joyce 94, Selva 94.
STRIBLEY, Evaline 67, Louise 67, William 67.
STRONG, Deborah 99, Isabelle 17, Martha 17.

TATE, Paul 66, Sarah 66, Verna 66.
TEETERS, Edson 27, Gladys 27, Guy 22,27, Plyly 22,
   Vernon 27, Virgil 27.
THARP, Jerusha 49, Owen 13, Ronald 13, Ruth 13, Spencer
   13, Wallace 13.
THEW, Alice 66,69, Amy 67, Clifton 62, Chester 67,
   Edith 62,67, Elaine 69, Erma 67, Eunice 62,67,
   Frank 62,67, Gladys 67,69, Harold 66,67,69,
   Katherine 66, Lois 67, Lula 62,67, Margaret 69,
   Melvin 69, Oliver 62,67, Robert 66,69, Ruth 66,
   Stephen 62,66,69, Stewart 66,69, Violet 62,67.
THISSELLE, Benjamin 58, Laura 58, Samuel 58.

THOMASON, Dale 67, Gary 67, Rex 67.
THOMPSON, Edna 34, John 54, Laura 11,52, Lavinia 54,
    Madeleine 34, Manley 54, Maude 24, Mary 54,
    Oliver 33, Prudence 54, Rosella 54, Solomon 54.
THURMAN, Arlene 91, Chloro 91, John 91.
TINGLE, Anna 11, Benoni 9, Elias 11, Ellen 11, Elnora
    11, Hannah 11, Hubert 11, James 11, Libbie 11,
    Lewis 11, Phebe 11, Robert 9,11, William 7,9,11
TINKER, Almira 98, Alvah 99, Austin 98, Bethnia 98,
    Elisha 98,100, Emma 99, Eugene 98, Frances 98,
    99, Charles 98,99, Jeannette 99, Lavinia 99,
    Lewis 100, Lydia 98, Resolved 98, Roxana 99,
    Elizabeth 97,98,99, Shepherd 97.
TOM, Marybelle 24, Stephen 24.
TRUE, Augusta 102, Austin 97,99,102, Effie 102, Evelyn
    102,103, Hiram 99,102, Josiah 98,99, Laura 102,
    Lydia 102,104, Marcus 102, Minnie 102, John 99,
    102, Sarah 99,102.
TUCKER, Joel 49, William 49, Winnie 88.
TURNER, Elizabeth 116, Harvey 116.
TUTTLE, Almira 99, Henrietta 85, Mary 92, Solomon 99.
TYGARD, Charles 117, Marinda 117, Perry 117.

UPDIKE, Aaron 48,50, Albert 50, Alice 50,53, Anne 48,
    49, Charles 53, Clarissa 50,53, Delilah 48,49,
    Elijah 48,50, Emeline 50, Emily 50,53, Estella
    53,59, Florence 50, Frank 50, Gilbreath 50,53,
    Grace 53,59, Harrison 48,50, Henry 49, Isaac 48,
    49,50,53, John 48,49,50,53, Joseph 49,53, Levi 49,
    Lutitia 48, Mabel 53, Margaret 50,53, Martha 49,
    50, Mary 49,50, Mollie 50, Monroe 50, Nancy 49,
    50, Ora 117, Peter 48,49,50, Ruth 48, Samuel 48,
    49,50,53, Sarah 50, Victoria 50, Virgil 48,50,53,
    William 50, Wesley 49.

VAN SICKLE, Belle 60,65, Frank 60, Henry 60, Maizie 61.
VAUGHN, Arthur 58, Mary 58, Serena 58.
VERNON, Clyde 24, Haamen 24.
VESEY, Alice 23, James 67.
VEST, Alta 32, Edmund 32, Eldon 32, Lloyd 32.
VINSEL, Corra 19, Emeline 19, Hagar 19, John 19, Otis
    19, Mary 19,24, William 19.
VON ESSEN, Arnold 68, Joan 68.

WAINWRIGHT, Clara 91, Jennie 91.
WALDEN, Blanche 64, Clara 39, Flora 37, George 39,
    Harry 39, Hester 64, Marion 64, Samuel 39,
    William 31,39,64.
WALKER, Sarah 46, Stella 64.
WARD, Charles 115, Cora 34, Delilah 81, Florence 115,
    117, Fidelia 112, Jonas 72,111,112,115, Jerusha
    112,115, Josiah 36,112,115, Margaret 115, Mary 115,
    Phebe 72,111.
WARNER, Charles 61, Ellen 48, F.L. 61, Florence 61,
    Fred 61, William 61.
WARREN, Agnes 25, Andrea 25, Carl 25, Carrie 21,25,
    Catherine 85, Clarence 25, Clyde 66, Cora 17,21
    Dale 25, Donald 25,26, Donna 66, Doris 66,68,
    Florence 21,26 Gladys 21,25, Guy 21,25, Harry 21,
    Helen 26, Herbert 21,25, Isaac 17, John 17,21,
    Julian 25, Lester 21,26, Lois 66, Lucy 17,21, Mary

21, Oma 25, Ona 21, Opal 25, Orvie 21,26, Paul 25,
    Robert 25, Samuel 17,21.
WASHINGTON, Laura 57, Margaret 57.
WASS, Florence 19, John 19, Laura 19, Mary 19, Munsel 19.
WATKINS, Albert 102, Jane 99.
WAXLER, Carrie 27, Fenton 27.
WEARIN, Adalvert 85,91, Andrew 81, Caloma 85, Charles 85,
    Flora 85, Frances 85, Harriet 81, Harry 81, Ida 85,
    India 85, Joseph 85,91, Josiah 81,85, Mary 81,85,
    Michael 81, Olive 85, Otho 81,85, William 85.
WEATHERBY, Elizabeth 82, Emily 82,87, George 82,87,
    Isaac 82, John 82,86, Mary 87, Rachel 87, Salina 82,
    William 82.
WEBB, Jessie 114, Thomas 114.
WEETHEE, Daniel 97,98, Eveline 98, Julia 102, Laura 98,
    Laurentius 102, Lavinia 98, Lucy 98,100,102.
WEISHEIMER, Alfred 104, Charles 104, Mary Alice 104.
WELCH, Lloyd 93, Mary 4, Richard 93, William 93.
WELLS, Estella 92, Hepsy 80, John 80, Nathan 80, Sarah
    74,80, Sylva 74, Varnum 74.
WESTENHAVER, Alice 77, Arthur 77, Clara 77, Ella 77,
    Emma 77, Lucy 77, William 77.
WETER, Carl 21, Frank 21, Grant 21, Lucy 21,26, Ruth 21.
WHARTON, Anastasia 18, Charles 18, James 18, John 18,
    Elsworth 18, Fred 18, Mae 18, Minnie 18, Myrtle 18,
    Paul 18, Robert 18, Samuel 18.
WHITE, Algernon 100, Almond 39, Bernice 64,68, Betty 26,
    Carie 64,68, Elsie 64,68, Evelyn 64,68, Galen 68,
    Herbert 92, Howard 64, Ilah 68, Iola 68, John 87,
    Lillian 26, Lucille 26, Marguerite 26, Marian 26,
    Mary 87, Melvin 64,68, Ralph 68, Rhoda 64, Thomas
    64, William 26,94.
WHITMER, Dora 34, Richard 34, Rolland 34.
WILDS, George 44, James 44, Mariah 44, Mary 44, Rachel
    44, Thomas 44.
WILLIAMS, Emeline 30, Jeremiah 21, Lucy 12,21, Margaret
    21.
WILLS, Joy 62, L.Z. 62.
WILSON, Amos 5, Annabelle 34, Appalonia 89, Caleb 39,
    David 89, Daniel 37,39, Delbert 61, Donald 90,93,
    Flora 86, Fred 86, John 89,90,93, Joseph 86, Kate
    89,90, Laura 74, Margaret 37, Mary 90, Mildred 90,
    93, Rachel 37, Sally 29, Owen 37, Thomas 37.
WININGER, Charles 11, Henry 11, Libbie 10, Sabra 11.
WINTERS, Frances 88, Harry 88, Isaiah 88.
WOLF, Albert 77, Amy 72, Andrew 72,73,75, Anna 75,
    Annette 74, Baruch 73,75, Catherine 74, Christopher
    73,75, Charles 74,75,77, Corinda 75, Delilah 75,
    Dora 77, Edmond 73,74,75,77, Eliza 75, Effie 75,
    Elizabeth 73,76,77, Emeline 76, Eugene 77, Eve 72,
    73, Fanny 75,77, Francis 74, Franklin 74, Frank 77,
    Finley 75, Harriet 74, Helena 75, Henry 75, Homer
    77, Jacob 72,73,74, James 77, Jonathan 73,75,76,77,
    John 73,74,75, Joseph 73,74,75,77, Josephus 73,74,
    Kirby 77, Lafayette 75,77, Lewis 75,77, Lillie 77,
    Loraine 75, Lucy 75, Lydia 73,75,86, Mathew 73,75,
    Martha 74, Mary 74,75, Maryette 74, Milton 73,
    Minnie 77, Myrum 74, Nellie 77, Myrta 77, Perley
    75, Phedora 75, Prentice 74, Rhoda 73,75, Robert 77,
    Sarah 72,74,75, Sylvester 77, William 73,75,77,
    Willis 77.

PIONEER FAMILIES
OF THE MIDWEST

By
BLANCHE L. WALDEN

3

FOREWORD

It is not the aim of this publication to furnish complete genealogies of the families presented, but rather to bridge the earlier records in order that descendants may trace their own lines without great difficulty. Every year fire, time and flood take their toll of our heritage of old Bible records, portraits, court records, etc., so it has been thought best to preserve these left to us, for future generations.

In each of the families included in this series, the pioneer father is given the number 1, the eldest child is number 2 etc., so each individual member of a family has a number given to only one member of that family. Thus it is a very simple matter for a descendant to trace his line back to the pioneer by following the numbering. His parent's number appears as the head of a family and again as a child on an earlier page, his grandparent will head the family in which his parent's name appears as a child, etc.

Abbreviations used with meanings are:

b. - born	m. - married
d. - died	unm. - unmarried
d.y. - died young	ca - about
d. in inf. - died in infancy	

The compiler wishes to here express gratitude to all those who have so graciously aided and made possible this publication by supplying data from records in their possession and especially to Marie C. Jones, Lydia D. Johnson, Panthea Pratt, Grace P. Eaton, G. E. Plumly, Elizabeth Plumly Doudna, S. O. Godman, Eva Smith Holloway and Edith Cole Brian, for invaluable contributions of family portraits and records.

B. L. Walden

PORTRAITS

TABLE OF CONTENTS

1. JONATHAN ALLEN

Jonathan Allen was born the 28th of July 1771 in Woodstock, Conn. He married March 24, 1796 Susannah Fuller (b. Nov. 1777 and died the 19th of Aug. 1835) a daughter of Job and Susannah (Russell) Fuller.

They removed in 1816 to Athens County, Ohio and settled in Dover township where they purchased land on Nov. 14th of the same year, in a location near that of Resolved Fuller (a brother of Susannah Fuller Allen) who had preceded them to Ohio by nineteen years.

Jonathan Allen served on Athens County grand juries in 1823, 1824 and was a trustee of Dover township in 1826.

He died Oct. 1, 1826 and is buried in Nye Cemetery near Chauncey, Ohio. His Will is on record in book 1, p. 81 in Athens County records and reads as follows:

"To all whom this may concern I, Jonathan Allen being in my sound mind and at the same time believing life to be uncertain, make this my last Will and Testament:

First, I will to Clarray my eldest child one cow which will make her equal with Wilmarth and David my two sons. One hundred and thirty dollars I will to Joseph my son. The land on Monday Creek east of David's land I will to my son Samuel. My daughter Martha is to have one hundred dollars when of age. My son George is to have one hundred and thirty dollars when of age.

Furthermore I appoint my wife and my son Joseph as my lawful administrators in the full settlement and management of all my temporal affairs.

After my wife's decease I wish to have the balance of my estate equally divided among all my lawful heirs. The above is made (in) sincerity in the name of God, Amen.
                                    Jonathan Allen
Witnesses: Samuel Porter, Resolved Fuller, Lydia Nye.

The children of Jonathan and Susannah (Fuller) Allen were:
2. Clarissa Allen b. 18 Feb. 1797 in Conn.
3. Wilmarth Allen b. 10 Dec. 1798 in Conn.
4. David Allen b. 26 Apr. 1801 in Conn.
5. Jonathan Allen, Jr. 1803-1812.
6. Joseph F. Allen b. 13 Oct. 1805 in Conn.
7. Samuel Allen b. 24 Feb. 1809 in Conn.
8. Martha Allen b. 1811 in Conn.
9. George Allen b. 1816 in Conn.

2. CLARISSA ALLEN[2] (JONATHAN[1])

Clarissa Allen (1797-1871) married the 12th of April 1821 John Herrold (1798-1823) a son of Christopher and Martha (Cable) Herrold and had one son:
10. John Herrold, Jr. b. 30 Aug. 1822.

Clarissa Allen Herrold married Feb. 14, 1825 Rufus Putnam Davis (1799-1837) son of Rev. Nehemiah Davis and his second wife Phebe Dorr. (See Davis lineage for descendants).

For her third husband Clarissa Allen Herrold Davis married Aug. 20, 1842 Cyrus Catlin by whom there was no issue.

She died the 7th of Oct. 1874 at Nelsonville, O. and is buried in Nye Cemetery at Chauncey.

3. WILMARTH ALLEN[2] (JONATHAN[1])

Wilmarth Allen (1799-   ) came with his parents to Athens County in 1816. He married the 6th of Feb. 1823 Betsey Woodbury (b. 11 July 1802 and died the 18th of Feb. 1840) a daughter of Nathan and Betsey Woodbury early settlers of Athens County, Ohio.

The children of Wilmarth and Betsey (Woodbury) Allen were:
11. John Woodbury Allen b. 19 July 1827.
12. Melissa Ann Allen b.   1829
13. Malinda A. Allen b.   1833
14. Johiel Allen b.   1835

Wilmarth Allen married second Jan. 9, 1842 Mrs. Judith Davis Nesmith (b. 10 June 1805 in Washington County, Ohio) a daughter of Rev. Nehemiah Davis and his second wife Phebe Dore. (See Davis lineage). They had two daughters:
14A-Phebe Susannah Allen b. 1843.
14B-Mary J. Allen b. 1845.

Wilmarth Allen was interested in public improvements and was a subscriber in 1827 to the first bridge built across the Hockhocking river. He served at different times from 1836 to 1847 on Athens County juries.

4. DAVID ALLEN[2] ESQ. (JONATHAN[1])

David Allen (1801-1842) married Mar. 9, 1826 Amanda Fuller (b. 1809) daughter of Joseph and Anna (Davis) Fuller and granddaughter of Rev. Nehemiah Davis and his first wife Elizabeth Marston.

Davis Allen served on Athens County juries in 1833 and was elected a Justice of the Peace in 1840, in which office he served until his death on the 23rd. of Dec., 1842.

Bills listed in his estate settlement as paid included:

Funeral expenses at	$1.00
Coffin "	4.00
Dr. L. K. McLaughlin	9.12
Dr. J. D. Davis and	
Dr. W. Pettit	17.62
Dr. J. D. Holcomb	13.25
Grave stones	11.00

David and Amanda Allen had four children:
15. Joseph F. Allen b. 1830
16. David Allen b. 1831 unm.
17. Joel J. Allen b. 1836
18. Jonathan Allen b. 16 Aug. 1839.

Amanda Fuller Allen married second in 1845 Chester Woodworth by whom she had one son Earl Woodworth.

6. JOSEPH F. ALLEN² (JONATHAN¹)

Joseph F. Allen (1806-1852) married Dec. 4, 1832 Sally Davis (b. 1815) and resided at Trimble, Ohio. .

He served many times on juries in the County from 1831 to 1850.

He left no will but his inventory taken Apr. 7th 1852 mentions many items among them the following:

103 head of sheep	at	$125.00
1 gray mare (19 years old)		15.00
1 bay horse (6 years old)		65.00
10 hogs (1400 lbs.)		42.00
850 bu. of corn		170.00
1 mantle clock		3.00
1 Bureau		8.00

Articles taken by the widow included 1 loom, 3 spinning wheels, family Bible, 1 cooking stove and some school books.

The children of Joseph F. and Sally Allen were:
19. Emily J. Allen b. 1834.
20. Horace R. Allen b. 1835.
21. Mary Catherine Allen b. 1836.
22. Jonathan Allen b. 1839.
23. Eleanor Elizabeth Allen b. 1 Apr. 1841.
24. Reuben D. Allen 1844-1864 unm.
25. Sarah Minerva Allen b. 13 Dec. 1848.

7. SAMUEL ALLEN² (JONATHAN¹)

Samuel Allen (b. 1803 in Conn.) married Apr. 24, 1842 Sophia J. Eggleston (b. 1824 in N. Y.) a daughter of David and Rebecca Eggleston (the former a native of N. Y. and the latter of Vt.) of Trimble township, Athens County.

Samuel and Sophia Allen went to Hocking County where they were residing in 1850. Their children were:
26. Aaron W. Allen b. 1846.
27. Rebecca Allen b. 1848.
Probably other children.

8. MARTHA ALLEN² (JONATHAN¹)

Martha Allen (b. 1811 in Conn.) married Nov. 3, 1844 Oliver Hyde and removed to Lee County, Iowa. Nothing is known of her descendants.

9. GEORGE ALLEN² (JONATHAN¹)

George Allen (b. 1816 in Conn.) married Dec. 13, 1842 Anna M. Wells (b. 1823) a daughter of Varnum G. Wells and Sarah Davis his wife. (See Davis lineage. George and Anna (Wells) Allen had at least three daughters:
28. Lauretta Allen b. 1845 in Ohio. She m. 29 May 1863 James H. Rhinehart.
29. Louisa Allen b. 1847 in Ohio.
30. Sophia Allen b. 1854 in Ohio.
They are said to have removed to Kansas.

10. JOHN HERROLD JR.³ (CLARISSA², JONATHAN¹)

John Herrold (1822-1875) married Apr. 14, 1842 Lucretia Ann Davis (see Davis lineage) and had four children:
31. Emily S. Herrold b. 1844.
32. Sarah L. Herrold b. 1846.
33. Mary E. Herrold b. 1851, d. y.
34. Nancy L. Herrold b. 1853.

John Herrold married second Sally I. True (1833-1855) by whom there was no surviving issue.

He married third June 3, 1856 Nancy B. Dean (b. 1825) a daughter of William T. Dean (d. 1867) and had issue:
35. Ella L. Herrold b. 1857.
36. Minnie Herrold b. 1863, d. y.

John Herrold died Mar. 18, 1875 with burial at Nye Cemetery in Chauncey, Ohio.

11. JOHN W. ALLEN³ (WILMARTH², JONATHAN¹)

John Woodbury Allen (1827-1903) married Dec. 28, 1851 Elizabeth E. Davis (b. 1828 in Penn. and d. Aug. 25, 1919) a daughter of Nehemiah Davis Jr. (see Davis lineage)

John W. Davis died July 7, 1903 at Glouster, Ohio survived by his wife and the following children:
37. Asher A. Allen b. 1853.
38. Wilmarth E. Allen b. 1856.
39. Mary E. Allen b. 29 Apr. 1860.
40. John Grant Allen b. 1864.
41. Elizabeth J. Allen b. 1869 unm.
42. Olive Alzina Allen 1871-1905 unm.

12. MELISSA A. ALLAN³ (WILMARTH², JONATHAN¹)

Melissa Ann Allen (b. 1829) married May

4, 1852 Enoch McKee (b. 1824 in Ohio) son of
Andrew and Nancy McKee who came to Athens
County, Ohio from Pennsylvania. The children
of Enoch and Melissa McKee were:
43. Almira J. McKee b. 1854.
44. Alice McKee b. 1856.
45. Aaron M. McKee b. 1860.

13. MALINDA ALLEN³ (WILMARTH², JONATHAN¹)

Malinda A. Allen (b. 1833) married Dec.
6, 1857 Sollomon J. Harter and resided at
New Madison (Dark County) Ohio in 1881. They
had at least two children:
46. Emma Harter
A son (name not known) who died of "damp"
while cleaning out a well.

14. JOHIEL ALLEN³ (WILMARTH², JONATHAN¹)

Johiel Allen (1834-1917) merchant of
Glouster, Ohio, served in the Civil War with
company G, 141st Reg. O.V.I.
He married Dec. 7, 1857 Hannah E. Hadley
(b. June 7, 1838 and d. 24th of April 1926)
a daughter of William and Jane Hadley who
came from New Hampshire to Ohio. Hannah Hadley was a school teacher and later served as
postmistress of Glouster from 1876 to 1883.
Her brothers started the famous Bowery
Mission in New York City which still func-
tions.
The children of Johiel and Hannah Allen
were:
47. Clifton Allen b. 1859.
48. William Allen b. 1862, d. y.
49. Lulu F. Allen b. 1864.
50. John Harrison Allen b. 16 Oct. 1867.
51. Carrie Allen b. 14 Dec. 1869.
52. Myra Allen b. ca 1871.

14A. PHEBE S. ALLEN³ (WILMARTH², JONATHAN¹)

Phebe Susannah Allen (b. 1843) a teacher
of Trimble, O. married May 30, 1876 James
Davis Gardner (1841-1879).
She married second Ira Ullom.

14B. MARY J. ALLEN³ (WILMARTH², JONATHAN¹)

Mary J. Allen (b. 1845) married the 25th
of Dec. 1866 Joseph M. Russell and resided in
Waxford County, Mich.

15. JOSEPH F. ALLEN³ (DAVID², JONATHAN¹)

Joseph F. Allen (1830-1890) married Feb.
23, 1851 Ann Mariah Nesmith (1831-1919) daughter of Benjamin Nesmith Jr. (1802-1835) and
his wife Judith Davis (who married second (as

his second wife) Wilmarth Allen). See also
Davis lineage.
Joseph F. and Mariah (Nesmith) Allen had
five children:
53. Judith N. Allen b. 1852, m. Mr. McDaniel
and lived in Wisconsin.
54. Esther M. Allen b. 1854.
55. Augusta J. Allen b. 1857.
56. John Orlando Allen b. 1859.
57. Adela Allen b. 1866 (Apr. 25).

17. JOEL J. ALLEN³ (DAVID², JONATHAN¹)

Joel J. Allen (b. 1836) served as a
corporal in company G of the 141st. Regiment
for one hundred days in the Civil War. His
discharge describes him as five feet, nine and
one half inches tall, dark complexioned with
gray eyes and black hair.
He married in Perry County, Ohio Amanda
Fowler (b. 1835) and had issue:
58. Josiah Allen b. 13 Aug. 1859.
59. Clara Allen b. 1861.
60. Myrtle Allen b. 1864.
61. Charles Allen b. 1867.
62. Carley M. Allen b. 6 Oct. 1871.
63. Harlin Allen b. 22 Jan. 1878.
64. Lilly Allen b. 6 Oct. 1871.
65. William G. Allen b. 21 May 1880.

18. JONATHAN ALLEN³ (DAVID², JONATHAN¹)

Jonathan R. Allen (1839-1894) merchant of
Glouster, Ohio, served as sergeant in company
B of the 75th regiment O.V.I. (from Dec. 10,
1861 to Dec. 22, 1864). His discharge states
he was five feet, nine and one quarter inches
in height, was light complexioned with blue
eyes and light hair.
He married Hannah M. Hill (b. 12 Mar.
1842 in Penn. and d. Dec. 7, 1900) and had issue:
66. Halley Allen 1869-1871.
67. Claude M. Allen b. ca 1871.
68. Albert Bertram Allen b. 22 Mar. 1874 in
Republic County, Kansas.
69. Lulu E. Allen b. 16 Oct. 1875, d. y.
70. Lancelot Wade Allen b. 19 Sept. 1878.

19. EMILY J. ALLEN³ (JOSEPH F², JONATHAN¹)

Emily J. Allen (b. 1834) married Sept.
13, 1860 Samuel Rankin and removed to Gallia
County, Ohio where they were living in Sept.
of 1864.

20. HORACE R. ALLEN³ (JOSEPH², JONATHAN¹)

Horace R. Allen (b. 1835) married Harriet Elizabeth Shepherd daughter of Silas M.

Shepherd and Sophia Fox his wife and granddaughter of Enoch Shepherd a Revolutionary
soldier who died at Marietta, Ohio. Horace
R. and Harriet E. Allen were residing in
Athens County Ohio in Sept. of 1857.

21. MARY C. ALLEN³ (JOSEPH², JONATHAN¹)

Mary Catherine Allen (b. 1836) married
Feb. 4, 1857 Thomas D. Mintun (1834-1905) son
of Thos. L. Mintun (1809-1887), grandson of
John Mintun a soldier of the War of 1812 and
a great grandson of John Mintun (1752-1826) a
soldier of the American Revolution. They had
issue:
71. Frank L. Mintun b. 1858 in Ohio.
72. Joseph Allen Minton b. 20 June 1861 in
    Ohio.
    Probably other children.

23. ELEANOR E. ALLEN³ (JOSEPH², JONATHAN¹)

Eleanor Elizabeth Allen (b. 1841) married
July 18, 1861 Isaac B. Bradrack and removed to
Pickaway County, Ohio, where they were resid-
ing in Sept. of 1864.

31. EMILY S. HERROLD⁴ (JOHN³, CLARISSA², JONA¹)

Emily S. Herrold (b. 1844) married Apr.
25, 1866 Elliott Gardner and resided at Nelsonville, Ohio. Their children were:
73. Mabel E. Gardner b. 25 July 1875.
74. Lelia Gardner b. 24 May 1880.

32. SARAH L. HERROLD⁴ (JOHN³, CLARISSA², JONA¹)

Sarah L. Herrold (b. 1846) married Jan.
22, 1867 Dow L. Poston of Athens County, Ohio.

34. NANCY L. HERROLD⁴ (JOHN³, CLARISSA², JONA¹)

Nancy L. Herrold (b. 1853 and died Mar.
20, 1876) married Oct. 21, 1874 A. D. Smith.
She is buried in Nye Cemetery at Chauncey,
Ohio.

35. ELLA L. HERROLD⁴ (JOHN³, CLARISSA², JONA¹)

Ella L. Herrold (b. 1857) married Mar. 31,
1879 Frederick L. Preston and had three children:
75. John Preston m. Miss Merritt and had issue
76. Perry Preston d. y.
77. Dix Preston died without issue.

37. ASHER A. ALLEN⁴ (JOHN³, WILM², JONA¹)

Asher A. Allen (b. 1853) postmaster at
Glouster, Ohio (1883-1886). He married Sept.

23, 1882 Nettie B. Hadley. He died in Apr.
of 1926 survived by two daughters:
78. Grace Hadley Allen b. 4 June 1885.
79. Estella Allen, married and resides in
    Alabama.

38. WILMARTH E. ALLEN⁴ (JOHN³, WILM², JONA¹)

Wilmarth E. Allen (b. 1856) married Feb.
13, 1883 Cynthia A. Posey (1854-1911). There
was no issue.

39. MARY ALLEN⁴ (JOHN³, WILM², JONA¹)

Mary E. Allen (1860-1898) married Dec.
19, 1886 Dr. E. F. Danford (1856-1934) of
Glouster, Ohio. Their children were:
80. Gladys Danford b. 1887, m. Rev. Miles
    Hoon.
81. Lalla R. Danford, teacher of Glouster,
    Ohio.
82. Dorothy Adene Danford b. 1893, m. Thos.
    Gibson.
83. Mary E. Danford, b. 1898.

40. J. GRANT ALLEN⁴ (JOHN³, WILM², JONA¹)

John Grant Allen (b. 1864) married
Sarah _____ and resided in Illinois.

43. ALMIRA J. McKEE⁴ (MALISSA³, WILM², JONA¹)

Almira J. McKee (b. 1854) married Dec.
7, 1873 John D. Andrews in Athens County,
Ohio and had issue:
84. Royal A. Andrews b. 16 Oct. 1875.
85. Clara G. Andrews b. 7 Dec. 1877.
86. Richard M. Andrews b. 6 Nov. 1879.

45. AARON M. McKEE⁴ (MALISSA³, WILM², JONA¹)

Aaron M. McKee (b. 1860) married Aug. 2,
1888 Elizabeth Shell. They had a daughter:
87. Lulie E. McKee b. 31 Dec. 1889.

46. EMMA HARTER⁴ (MALINDA³, WILM², JONA¹)

Emma Harter married May 19, 1888 George
Edward Faires and had:
88. Stella M. Faires b. 17 Feb. 1890.
89. Fred W. Faires b. 15 Apr. 1893.
90. Ernest D. Faires b. 27 Feb. 1895.
91. Ray Dale Faires b. 25 Oct. 1898.

49. LULU F. ALLEN⁴ (JOHIEL³, WILM², JONA¹)

Lulu F. Allen (1864-1885) married Feb.
17, 1884 Sanford L. Alderman and had one daughter:
92. Lola Florence Alderman b. 11 Oct. 1885.

50. JOHN HARRISON ALLEN[4] (JOHIEL[3], WILM[2], JONA[1])

John Harrison Allen (1867-1940) married Jan. 2, 1890 Anna Hope (b. Oct. 2, 1870 and d. Mar. 4, 1891) daughter of John T. Hope and his wife Mary Ellen Boal. They had one child:
93. Maude Allen b. and d. 1891.
Harry Allen married second in 1893 Almeda Murphey (1869-1939) and had issue:
94. Harold H. Allen b. 2 June 1894.
95. William R. Allen b. 17 Dec. 1895.
96. Lucy Allen d. y.
97. George Allen b. 12 Jan. 1901.
98. Hannah Jane Allen b. 12 Sept. 1907.

51. CARRIE ALLEN[4] (JOHIEL[3], WILM[2], JONA[1])

Carrie Allen (1869-1941) married Mar. 7, 1889 Samuel S. Carpenter and had issue:
99. Oril A. Carpenter b. 26 Mar. 1890.
100. Alfred Carpenter b. 18 Feb. 1893.

52. MYRA ALLEN[4] (JOHIEL[3], WILM[2], JONA[1])

Myra Allen (1871-1936) married June 14, 1893 William Crombie and had issue:
101. Hannah E. Crombie b. 19 Mar. 1894.
102. Russell Crombie b. ca 1895.
103. Eva Crombie.
104. Carrie Crombie.

54. ESTHER ALLEN[4] (JOSEPH[3], DAVID[2], JONA[1])

Esther Allen (b. 1854) married Apr. 1, 1877 Edward N. Moorehead and had issue:
105. Grace L. Moorehead M.D. b. 1878.

55. AUGUSTA ALLEN[4] (JOSEPH[3], DAVID[2], JONA[1])

Augusta Allen (1856-1933) married Jan. 4, 1877 George W. Duffee (1853-1911) a son of James and Mary Ann Duffee and had issue:
106. Bertha Duffee d. y.
107. Jannette Duffee b. 10 Aug. 1883.
108. Lucille Duffee, graduate of Ohio Univ. 1926 and Instructor in Athens (O). Junior high school.

56. ORLANDO ALLEN[4] (JOSEPH[3], DAVID[2], JONA[1])

Orlando Allen (b. 1859) married Clara _____ and had two sons:
109. Cecil Allen
110. Harold Allen, deceased.

57. ADELA ALLEN[4] (JOSEPH[4], DAVID[2], JONA[1])

Adela Myra Allen (1866-1927) was born at Marshall, Ohio. She married Milton Lobingier and resided at Chester, Nebr. Her death occurred March 9, 1927. Their children were:
111. Elsie Blanche Lobingier b. 31 Aug. 1885.
112. George Fred Lobingier b. 25 Jan. 1892.
113. Arthur Dwight Lobingier b. 1 May 1894.
114. Grace Evelyn Lobingier b. 1 July 1906.

58. JOSIAH ALLEN[4] (JOEL[3], DAVID[2], JONA[1])

Hon. Josiah Allen (b. 1859) served as Athens County representative in the Ohio State Legislature.
He married Sarah L. Jones and had at least two children:
115. Elizabeth Allen.
116. Frank Allen.

59. CLARA ALLEN[4] (JOEL[3], DAVID[2], JONA[1])

Clara Allen (b. 1861) married John Davis and had issue (see Davis lineage).

60. MYRTLE ALLEN[4] (JOEL[3], DAVID[2], JONA[1])

Myrtle Allen (b. 1864) married Dec. 24, 1882 Clinton D. Amos and had at least one daughter:
117. Lillie Dell Amos b. 14 Dec. 1885.

61. CHARLES ALLEN[4] (JOEL[3], DAVID[2], JONA[1])

Charles Allen (b. 1867) married Apr. 19, 1888 Addie Wyatt and had issue:
118. a son b. Jan. 26, 1889.
119. a son b. Jan. 26, 1890.
120. Arnold Allen b. Sept. 30, 1893.
121. Elizabeth Allen b. Nov. 22, 1905.

68. ALBERT B. ALLEN[4] (JONA[3], DAVID[2], JONA[1])

Dr. Albert Bertram Allen (b. 1874) married Apr. 1, 1896 Gwenllian Williams and had at least one child:
122. Harold Russell Allen b. Nov. 23, 1899.

92. LOLA ALDERMAN[5] (LULU[4], JOHIEL[3], WILM[2], JONA[1])

Lola Florence Alderman (b. 1885) married

Sept. 20, 1908 Rev. Everett Pedicord and had four daughters. They removed to Indiana.

107. JANNETTE DUFFEE[5] (AUGUSTA[4], JOSEPH[3], DAVID[2], JONA[1])

Jannette Duffee (1883-1918) married Dec. 23, 1905 Milford M. Russell (b. Sept. 26, 1877 in W. Va.) a son of Newton and Eliza (Bolton) Russell. They had three daughters:

123. Mary Virginia Russell m. Emmett J. Wilson.

124. Esther Russell m. Darryl W. Watkins.

125. Catherine Russell m. John Kessie.

111. ELSIE B. LOBINGIER[5] (ADELA[4], JOS[3], DAVID[2], JONA[1])

Elsie Blanche Lobingier (b. 1885) married in San Francisco, Calif., on July 3rd 1905 John Robert Bales.

They removed to the Rio Grande Valley where they operate citrus orchards and a stock ranch.

They have four children, all of whom reside in the Rio Grande Valley.

126. Murrell Kenneth Bales b. 25 May 1906.

127. Richard Carvel Bales b. 9 Oct. 1907.

128. Hazel Adela Bales b. 24 Dec. 1915.

129. John Lobingier Bales b. 3 Apr. 1921.

112. GEORGE F. LOBINGIER[5] (ADELA[4], JOS[3], DAVID[2], JONA[1])

George Fred Lobingier was born in Loveland, Colo. in 1892. He served in the World War (no. 1), has since married and resides in California. He has no children.

113. ARTHUR D. LOBINGIER[5] (ADELA[4], JOS[3], DAVID[2], JONA[1])

Arthur Dwight Lobingier was born in Loveland, Colo. in 1894. He served overseas in the World War. On Dec. 25, 1920 he married Alta Thomas and they have two children:

130. Thomas Lobingier.

131. Francis Adell Lobingier.

126. MURRELL K. BALES[6] (ELSIE B[5], ADELA[4], JOS[3], DAVID[2], JONA[1])

Murrell Kenneth Bales (b. 1906) married Apr. 5, 1937 Mamie Francis of Missouri. They reside in Texas.

127. RICHARD C. BALES[6] (ELSIE B[5], ADELA[4], JOS[3], DAVID[2], JONA[1])

Richard Carvel Bales (b. 1907) married Esther Parsons Apr. 15, 1933. They have three daughters.

128. HAZEL A. BALES[6] (ELSIE B[5], ADELA[4], JOS[3], DAVID[2], JONA[1])

Hazel Adela Bales (b. 1915) married Francis W. Arterberry of Ill. on Dec. 24 1934.

The Name

Allen is a place name of very ancient origin. It is found in the "Domesday Book" (1086 A.D.) in the form of Alan.

Allen Lineage Notes

Jonathan Allen was a son of Jonathan Allen Sr. (b. Apr. 4, 1730 and d. Oct. 25, 1788 in Woodstock, Conn.). The latter was of the fourth generation from James Allen (the immigrant ancestor) who came from Norfolk, Eng. ca 1637.

Fuller Lineage Notes

Susannah Fuller, wife of Jonathan Allen was a daughter of Job Fuller (1751-1794) who married Nov. 5, 1772 Susannah Russell (1750-1833) of Connecticut.

Job Fuller served in the American Revolution in Capt. Samuel Chandler's company in the 11th regiment of Conn. troops.

References

Athens County, Ohio Court Records, Woodstock, Conn. Vital Statistics. U. S. Census of 1850, 1860 and 1870. U. S. War Records.

1. AZARIAH PRATT

Azariah Pratt, a silver-smith by trade, was born Dec. 10, 1767 at Saybrook, Conn.

In the spring of 1788 he accompanied the vanguard of pioneers who started from Connecticut to make the first settlement in the Northwest Territory at what is now Marietta, Ohio. Later the same year he returned to Saybrook where he remained until after the Indian war in 1793 at which time he returned to the Marietta settlement.

He married at Marietta on May 4, 1797 Sarah C. Nye (born Feb. 21, 1777 at Tolland, Conn. and died Nov. 9, 1857 in Dover township of Athens County, Ohio).

In the year of 1819 Azariah Pratt purchased a quarter section of land in Athens County and in 1821 removed with his growing family to the new home near the present site of Millfield.

The land grant is of record in Deed book 9 p. 822 of Athens County records and is as follows:

"James Monroe, President of the United States of America, To all to whom these Presents shall come, Greeting: Know ye that Azariah Pratt of Marietta having deposited in the General Land Office a certificate of the Register of the land office at Marietta whereby it appears that full payment has been made for the Southwest quarter of section seven in township ten of range fourteen of the land directed to be sold at Marietta by Act of Congress, entitled:

"An Act Providing for the Sale of the Lands of the United States in the Territory North West of the Ohio and above the Mouth of the Kentucky River." And of the Acts Amandatory to the same there is granted by the United States unto the said Azariah Pratt the quarter Lot and Section of Land above described: To have and to hold the said quarter lot or section of land with the appurtenances unto the said Azariah Pratt his heirs and assigns forever. In testimony whereof I have caused these letters to be made Patent and the Seal of the General Land Office to be hereunto affixed. Given under my hand at the City of Washington, the tenth day of February in the year of our Lord one thousand eight hundred and Nineteen and of the Independence of the United States of America the forty-third.

By the President   James Monroe.

Sarah Nye Pratt lived with her parents in the block-house at Marietta during the Indian war and witnessed the attempt of the Indians to kill George Meigs.

Azariah Pratt served on various county juries in the years 1824 and 1836. He was an original incorporator of the Dover Library Association established by an act of the Ohio State Legislature Dec. 21, 1830 and named as one of the first three directors of the association. He died intestate Nov. 2, 1836 and is buried at Nye Cemetery in Chauncey, Ohio.

The children of Azariah and Sarah (Nye) Pratt were all born at Marietta, Ohio, and were named:

2. Elisha Pratt b. 18 Feb. 1798.
3. Lucinda Pratt b. 2 Oct. 1799.
4. George Pratt b. 30 Sept. 1801.
5. Seth Pratt (M.D.) b. 29 Sept. 1804.
6. Lucy Pratt (1806-1820).
7. Azariah Pratt Jr. b. 30 Jan. 1809.
8. Abigail Pratt (1811-1855- unm.
9. Ebenezer Pratt b. 20 June 1813.
10. Mary Pratt b. 19 Jan. 1817.
11. Lewis Pratt b. 1820, d. ae 6 mo.

2. ELISHA PRATT[2] (AZARIAH[1])

Elisha Pratt (1798-1857) married at Marietta, Ohio Apr. 6, 1826 Lydia B. Smith (b. in 1800 and died at Marietta in 1851). They had one child:
12. Sarah M. Pratt b. ca 1827.

Elisha Pratt married second Apr. 4, 1853 Martha Moore.

3. LUCINDA PRATT[2] (AZARIAH[1])

Lucinda Pratt (b. 1799, living 1862) married in Athens County, Dec. 8, 1822 James Fuller (born Mar. 13, 1797 and died Oct. 8, 18-2 with burial at Nye Cemetery). They had one child:
13. Seth Fuller b. 5 July 1827.

4. GEORGE PRATT[2] (AZARIAH[1])

George Pratt (1801-1835) married in Athens County, O. on Nov. 5, 1826 Martha H. Nesmith (d. 1843).

He served on juries in 1824 and 1833. His death on Jan. 18, 1835 cut short a useful

---

life and he is buried in Nye Cemetery. One son survived him:

14. George Oliver Pratt b. Mar. 23, 1830.

5. AZARIAH PRATT JR.², (AZARIAH¹)

Azariah Pratt Jr., (b. 1809) married Mar. 19, 1845 Mrs. Harriet Crouse (b. 1813 in Conn.) a young widow with two children and they resided at Millfield.

He served at various times on Athens County juries in 1846 and in that year was elected Dover township trustee, a post he held for twelve years.

Their children were:

15. Horace Pratt b. 1846 in Dover township.
16. Azariah Pratt III b. 1848 in Dover township.
17. Mary Pratt b. 1850 at Millfield.

There were probably other children.

9. EBENEZER PRATT² (AZARIAH¹)

Ebenezer Pratt (1813-1899) married Dec. 31, 1835 Susanna Wells (b. Dec. 4, 1813 and d. Feb. 8, 1889) a daughter of Varnum G. and Sarah Davis Wells (see Davis lineage).

Ebenezer Pratt served as Dover township trustee in 1862 and 1868. He died Sept. 10, 1899 and is buried in Nye Cemetery. Their children were:

18. Edward Pratt (1836 1837).
19. Lucy Pratt b. 1838 in Athens County.
20. Mary Pratt b. 1840 in Athens County.
21. Minerva J. Pratt b. 1843, m. 1876 Chester Woodworth.
22. Panthea Pratt b. 1846, unm. (Living 1941).
23. Sarah Pratt b. 1852 in Athens County.

10. MARY PRATT² (AZARIAH¹)

Mary Pratt (1817-1889) married the 16th of Oct. 1835 Austin Fuller (b. May 14, 1814 and d. July 15, 1876) a son of Resolved and Elizabeth (Nash) Fuller. Their children were:

24. George Fuller b. 1837 in Dover township.
25. Flavius Fuller b. 1838 in Dover township.
26. Sarah E. Fuller b. 1840 - d. 1876, m. W. P. Wyatt.
27. Abigail Fuller b. 1841, m. E. C. Wayman.
28. Resolved E. Fuller 1843-1887 m. Henrietta Chadwell.
29. Melzer N. Fuller 1844-1875 m. Mary Ellis.
30. Dudley D. Fuller b. 1847, m. Mary J. Wyatt.
31. Mary P. Fuller 1849-1919, unm.
32. Eveline Fuller b. 1851, m Samuel Brown.
33. Amy M. Fuller b. 1854, d. y.

34. Carlin Fuller 1862-1935, m. Miss Dana Brooks.

See Fuller family in Book 2 for descendants.

12. SARAH M. PRATT³ (ELISHA², AZARIAH¹)

Sarah M. Pratt (b. ca. 1827) married in 1852 at Marietta, Ohio Alexander McGirr (b. 1825) a son of Arthur Jr. and Elizabeth McGirr.

Alexander McGirr served as sergeant in company A, 148th Regt. O.V.I. during the Civil War.

They had four children.

13. SETH FULLER³ (LUCINDA², AZARIAH¹)

Seth Pratt (b. 1827) married Dec. 11, 1843 Theresa M. Dean (b. 1824 in Ohio) a daughter of John N. Dean (d. 1874).

He served as Dover township trustee in 1853 and 1854.

Their children were:

35. James Fuller b. 1844 in Athens County.
36. Mary Fuller b. 1846 in Athens County.
37. Joseph Fuller b. 1848 in Dover township.
38. John Fuller b. 1850 in Dover township.
39. Edward Fuller b. 1853 in Dover township.
40. Mariah Fuller b. 1854 in Dover township.

14. GEORGE O. PRATT³ (GEORGE², AZARIAH¹)

George Oliver Pratt (b. 1830) merchant, married Sally Nesmith and resided in Wood County, W. Va. They had several children.

19. LUCY PRATT³ (EBENEZER², AZARIAH¹)

Lucy A. Pratt (1838-1881) married June 5, 1862 S. C. Gillespie of Zanesville, Ohio, and had issue:

41. Alice S. Gillespie.
42. Mary W. Gillespie, m. Mr. Worstell.
43. Hugh N. Gillespie.
44. J. Clinton Gillespie.
45. Lewis Gillespie.
46. Ralph R. Gillespie.
47. Roy P. Gillespie.
48. Helen J. Gillespie.
49. Eben Gillespie.

20. MARY PRATT³ (EBENEZER², AZARIAH¹)

Mary F. Pratt (b. 1840) married Oct. 20, 1859 Hiram C. Wyatt and went to Butler in Bates County, Mo. They had at least one son:

50. George J. Wyatt b. May 26, 1869.

Probably other children.

23. SARAH PRATT^3 (EBEN^2, AZARIAH^1)

Sarah Pratt (b. 1852) married Mr. Merrifield and resided at Boone Grove, Ind. in 1899.

The Name

Pratt is a personal name. It appeared as a surname in Gloucestershire, England as early as 1273 A.D.

Pratt Lineage Notes

Azariah Pratt was a son of Seth Pratt and his wife Abigail Tully (a daughter of William) of Saybrook, Conn. Seth Pratt served in the American Revolution with Conn. troops.

The immigrant ancestor was William Pratt (1622-1678) who came from England in 1636 with the Rev. Thomas Hooker and settled first at Hartford.

In 1645 he removed to Saybrook and served there in the Pequot War. He married Elizabeth Clark, a daughter of John Clark one of the nineteen Patentees named in the Royal Charter from King Charles II.

Nye Lineage Notes

Sarah Nye Pratt was a daughter of Ebenezer Nye (b. Oct. 21, 1750 at Tolland, Conn. and died in Washington County, Ohio on Feb. 28, 1823, and his wife Desire Sawyer (b. at Litchfield, Conn. May 6, 1757 and d. Feb. 7, 1800 in Washington County), whom he married in March of 1776.

Ebenezer Nye served in the Revolutionary War with Conn. troops (see Connecticut Men In The Revolution p. 331 and Official Roster of Revolutionary Soldiers buried in Ohio, Vol. 1 p. 274).

The immigrant ancestor was Benjamin Nye (b. 1620 in Kent, England) who came in the ship "Abigail" in 1635. In the year 1640 he married Catherine Tupper, a daughter of Rev. Thomas Tupper who likewise came on the same ship.

References

Athens County Court Records.
Washington County Court Records.
Pratt Genealogy.
Nye Genealogy.
Compendium of American Genealogy.
U. S. War and Pension Records.
U. S. Land Office Records.

1. ELDER NEHEMIAH DAVIS

Nehemiah Davis was born 'the 3rd of May 1755 near Kingston, N. H.   He served as a private in Capt. Abraham French's New Hampshire regiment in the Revolutionary War, his name appearing on a return dated Nov. 5, 1775 signed by Capt. French on Great Island.

In 1781 he removed to York   County, Maine where he was ordained an elder in the Baptist Church and in the same year was instrumental in organizing the first Baptist Church at Shapleigh, Me., near which place he resided on a farm.

In the year of 1797 he determined to remove to the Northwest Territory and set out in the early fall with his large family and in company with his brother Reuben and his family they journied through the wilderness, fording streams and over the rugged mountains of western Pennsylvania, arriving at Marietta in November.

There, Nehemiah Davis worked as a clerk while preaching on Sundays at various backwoods settlements. He is credited with having organized the first Baptist Church in what is now the state of Ohio at a place called "Rainbow" located in Washington County on the Muskingum river.

December 30, 1797, he purchased of Samuel Fulsom of Marietta, a tract of land containing one hundred acres "on the northeasterly bank of the Muskingum river" the said land lying in the "Big Run" district.

He resided there several   years, later removing to Ames township (now Dover) of Athens County in the year 1802.

He married at Hawke, N. H., Aug. 7, 1777 Elizabeth (Betty) Marston (b. Dec. 1, 1755 and d. Nov. 4, 1792 at Shapleigh, Me.) of Brentwood, N. H., a daughter of Elisha and Anna (Philbrick) Marston. He had by her five children:

2. Elisha Marston Davis b. Dec. 23, 1778 at Poplin, N. H.

3. Benjamin Davis b. Jan. 25, 1780 at Poplin, N. H.
4. Anna Davis b. 16 May 1783 near Shapleigh, Me.
5. Sarah Davis b. 20 Apr. 1785 near Shapleigh, Me.
6. Nehemiah Davis, Jr. b. 12 Oct. 1787 near Shapleigh, Me.

He married second July 15, 1793 Phebe Dore (b. ca 1770 at Lebanon, Me. and d. May 1, 1849 near Chauncy, Ohio) a daughter of James and Hannah (Hussey) Dore and had issue:

7. James Dore Davis b. 19 Nov. 1795 at Shapleigh, Me.
8. Isaiah Davis b. 8 July 1796 at Shapleigh, Me.
9. Rufus Putnam Davis b. in 1799 at Big Run, Ohio.
10. Hannah Davis b. 14 June 1803, d. y.
11. Judith Pettingell Davis b. 10 June 1805 in Athens Co., Ohio.
12. Reuben Davis b. 1807, living 1832.
13. Phebe G.Davis b. 1809 in Dover tp. of Athens Co. Ohio.
14. Mary Stone Davis b. 16 May 1811 near Chauncey, Ohio.

Elder Nehemiah Davis died Aug. 23,   1823 and is buried in Nye Cemetery at Chauncey, Ohio

2. ELISHA M. DAVIS (NEHEMIAH[1])

Elisha Marston Davis (b.   1778) came to the Northwest Territory with his father and numerous relatives in 1797. He purchased a farm from his brother Benjamin Davis May 13, 1803, located in Adams township of Washington County.

He married Jan. 17, 1805 Nancy (or Agnes) Allison and they are said to have had several children including:

15. Nehemiah Davis b. 1816.
16. Emily Davis.

Elisha M. Davis removed to Marion County, Ohio where he purchased a farm about twelve miles from Marion.

An Elisha Davis married in Washington County on Oct. 22, 1820 Susanna Mason but whether this was Elisha, son of Nehemiah or another is not clear.

3. BENJAMIN DAVIS² (NEHEMIAH¹)

Benjamin Davis (b. 1780) farmer, miller and innkeeper came with his father and family to Washington County, Ohio in 1797. He purchased one parcel of land in Adams township in 1802 and sold it to his brother in 1803.

He went to Ames township of Athens County where he met and married about 1804 Anna Strine (or Strain) a daughter of Mrs. Jacob Boyles by a former marriage.

On Sept. 17, 1806 he purchased from Upton Farmer, one hundred acres of land "lying in the township of Ames" where he resided for some years.

Benjamin Davis was active in community affairs serving Ames township as trustee in 1807 and as clerk in 1819 and 1822.

He served on juries in 1807 and 1818, as election clerk in 1808 (for which he was paid seventy-five cents) and was elected a justice of the peace in 1810.

About 1822 he removed to Marion, Ohio where he kept an inn. Both Benjamin Davis Esq. and his wife Anna Strine Davis died at Marion but dates are not available. Their children were:
17. Loisa Decker Davis b. 1 Nov. 1807.
18. Anna Strine Davis b. 13 July. 1812.
19. Achsah Wyatt Davis.
20. Minerva M. Davis b. 25 Feb. 1822.
21. Princess Davis.

There was, according to tradition, an infant son whose name and dates of birth and death are now unknown.

4. ANNA DAVIS² (NEHEMIAH¹)

Anna Davis (b. 1783) married Mar. 15, 1801 Joseph Fuller (d. ca 1835) and resided in Washington County until about 1816 when they removed to Dover township in Athens County. Their children were:
22. James Fuller.
23. Amanda Fuller b. 1809, m. in Athens County Mar. 9, 1826 David Allen (see Allen Family).
24. Elizabeth (Betsey) Fuller m. 24 Feb. 1824 Thomas Camby.
25. Joel Fuller.
26. Levi Fuller.
27. Hannah Fuller.

Anna Davis Fuller and her four youngest children removed about 1841 to Tippecanoe County, Ind.

5. SARAH DAVIS² (NEHEMIAH¹)

Sarah Davis (1785-1825) married Nov. 7, 1805 Varnum G. Wells (b. Aug. 4, 1782 and d. 16 Oct. 1828) of Chauncey, Ohio.

She died the 5th of Sept. 1825 and is buried in Nye Cemetery. Their children were:
28. Benjamin D. Wells b. 29 June 1806.
29. Sylva Ann Wells b. 18 Dec. 1807.
30. Orin M. Wells b. 19 Oct. 1809, licensed to preach May 1, 1832 (Church of Christ) went to Tippicanoe County, Ind.
31. Sally Wells b. 21 Jan. 1812.
32. Susannah Wells b. 4 Dec. 1813, m. 1835 Ebenezer Pratt (see Pratt family).
33. Marcia Wells b. 18 Nov. 1815, m. 30 Sept. 1830 Wm. P. Williams.
34. Rufus Wells b. 5 Dec. 1817, went to Tippicanoe County, Indiana.
35. Harlow M. Wells b. 1 Dec. 1819, went to Tippecanoe County, Ind.
36. Joseph Wells b. 29 Oct. 1821, unm., educated at Princeton as a Presbyterian Minister, located in Wisconsin.
37. Anna Wells b. 1824, m. 1842 George Allen. (See Allen family).

6. NEHEMIAH DAVIS² (NEHEMIAH¹)

Nehemiah Davis Jr. (1787-1840) married in Lycoming County, Pa. in 1819 Christiana Jane Cornes (b. 12 Mar. 1794 in N. J. and d. about 1835 in Washington County, Ohio) a daughter of Joseph and Anna (DeWitt) Cornes. They are said to be buried in the Layman Cemetery three miles west of Barlow in unmarked graves. Their children were:
38. Elias Davis b. ca 1821 in Penn. m. and resided York tp., had sons John and Charles.
39. Lucretia Ann Davis b. 1823 in Penn.
40. Nehemiah Davis III, d. y.
41. Joseph Davis b. 1827 in Ohio, living in 1850.
42. Elizabeth Davis b. 1828 in Pa., m. 1851 John W. Allen (See Allen family).
43. Mary Davis b. 1830 in Ohio.
44. Phebe Davis d. ae 4 yrs.
45. Elvina Davis b. 1833, d. ae 26 yrs., unm.
46. Asher Davis d. ae 5 yrs.
47. Jane Eleanor Davis b. 1832 in Ohio.

7. JAMES D. DAVIS² (NEHEMIAH¹)

James Dore Davis, M.D. (1795-1871) a successful physician of Dover township, Athens County, Ohio, married May 14, 1815 Martha Pugsley (b. May 13, 1797 and d. Mar.

9, 1832) a daughter of Abraham Pugsley, pioneer settler of Athens County.

The children of Dr. Jas. D. Davis and Martha Pugsley Davis were:
48. Edwin Davis b. Mar. 6, 1816.
49. Lewis L. Davis b. Oct. 17, 1817.
50. Nehemiah W. Davis b. Oct. 12, 1819.
51. Phebe Davis b. Apr. 9, 1821.
52. Susannah Davis b. Dec. 18, 1822.
53. Sarah J. Davis b. July 2, 1824.
54. James Davis b. Oct. 7, 1826.
55. Hiram Dore Davis b. July 15, 1827.
56. John R. Davis b. Mar. 21, 1829.
57. Joel Davis b. Jan. 25, 1831, d. 1844, unm.

Dr. James D. Davis married second Jan. 28, 1833 Marcia James (b. July 18, 1809 in Maine and died Mar. 27, 1856) a daughter of Samuel and Mary James, and had issue:
58. Samuel W. Davis b. Oct. 19, 1833.
59. Eli J. Davis b. Feb. 23, 1835.
60. Mary J. Davis b. Sept. 8, 1836, m. Mr. Cowrin.
61. Anna E. Davis 1838-1845, unm.
62. Rufus P. Davis b. Mar. 25, 1840, d. Nov. 1872.
63. Infant 1841-1842.
64. William H. Davis b. Apr. 24, 1843.
65. Eunice Davis b. May 14, 1845.
66. Isaiah Davis 1847-1848, unm.
67. Hettie Davis b. June 8, 1850, d. Sept. 3, 1879.

Dr. Davis died Oct. 7, 1871 with burial in Nye Cemetery.

8. ISAIAH DAVIS² (NEHEMIAH¹)

Isaiah Davis (1796-1863) farmer of Dover township, married Feb. 26, 1834 Anna James (b. 1815 in Maine) a daughter of Samuel and Mary James who emigrated from Maine to Ohio about 1818 and settled in Dover township.

Isaiah Davis died Apr. 17, 1863 with burial in Nye Cemetery. His widow was living in 1888 but her date of death is not known. Their children were:
68. Reuben A. Davis b. Dec. 1834.
69. Francis J. Davis b. 1838.
70. Orin W. Davis b. 1842.
71. Lorinda E. Davis b. 1849, teacher.

9. RUFUS P. DAVIS² (NEHEMIAH¹)

Rufus Putnam Davis (1799-1837) married Feb. 20, 1825 Mrs. Clarissa (Allen) Herrold (1797-1871) a daughter of Jonathan and Susannah Allen and widow of John Herrold. (See Allen Family). Rufus P. Davis died July 26, 1837 survived by three children:
72. Joseph Davis b. 1 Dec. 1825.

73. Orin Davis 1830-1846.
74. Susannah Davis b. 10 July 1833, unm.

11. JUDITH P. DAVIS² (NEHEMIAH¹)

Judith Pettingell Davis (b. 1805) married Feb. 5, 1828 Benjamin Nesmith, Jr. (b. 1802 in Maine and d. Sept. 17, 1835) a son of Benjamin and Hannah Nesmith. They had three children:
75. James Nesmith 1829-1851.
76. Ann Maria Nesmith b. 1830, m. Joseph F. Allen (See Allen Family).
77. John Nesmith b. 1833.

Judith Davis Nesmith married second as his second wife Wilmarth Allen on Jan. 9, 1842. They had two daughters:
78. Phebe Susannah Allen b. 1843.
79. Mary J. Allen b. 1845.
(See Allen family for descendants).

13. PHEBE DAVIS² (NEHEMIAH¹)

Phebe G. Davis (b. 1809) married Jan. 4, 1835 Elisha James in Athens County, Ohio.

14. MARY S. DAVIS² (NEHEMIAH¹)

Mary Stone Davis (1811-1891) married Aug. 5, 1832 Caleb Harry Gardner (1800-1855) a son of Caleb and Lydia (Thurston) Gardner, pioneers of Meigs County, Ohio.

They removed to Clarks Ferry now Buffalo, Iowa where he was postmaster in 1847.

She died Aug. 31, 1891 in Kansas. Their children were:
80. Orrin A. A. Gardner b. Sept. 1, 1833.
81. Phebe Ann Gardner m. W. G. Church.
82. James Davis Gardner b. Oct. 24, 1841.
83. Charles Oregon Gardner b. Mar. 4, 1844.
84. George Metteer Gardner b. Oct. 27, 1848.

15. NEHEMIAH DAVIS³³(ELISHA², NEHEMIAH¹)

Nehemiah Davis (b. 1816) farmer of Grand township, Marion County, Ohio, married ca 1844 Mary _____ (b. 1820 in Ohio) and had issue:
85. William Davis b. 1845 in Ohio.
86. Hugh V. Davis b. 1847 in Ohio.
87. Harrison Davis.
There may have been other children.

17. LOISA D. DAVIS³ (BENJ²., NEHEMIAH¹)

Loisa Decker Davis (1807-1885) married Jan. 6, 1825 Rev. George W. Baker (b. Oct. 22, 1803 in Maine and died at Marion, Ohio,

Oct. 11, 1881) a son of Eber and Lydia
(Smith) Baker. They had the following children:
88. Oscar E. Baker b. 9 Jan. 1826 at Marion, Ohio.
89. Allen D. Baker b. 5 Feb. 1828 at Marion, Ohio.
90. Lydia Ann Baker b. 29 June 1831 at Marion, Ohio.
91. Louisa Jane Baker b. 22 May 1836 at Marion, Ohio.
92. Eber S. Baker b. 13 Nov. 1838 at Marion, Ohio.
93. Princess Amanda Baker b. 6 May 1842 at Marion, Ohio.
    Loisa Davis Baker died Dec. 11, 1885 at
Marion, Ohio.

18. ANNA S. DAVIS^3 (BENJ^2, NEHEMIAH^1)

Anna Strine Davis (1812-1873) married
Nov. 27, 1828 James Harper Godman (b. Oct. 19,
1808 in Berkeley County, Va. and d. Oct. 4,
1891) an eminent lawyer of Marion, Ohio. He
was appointed Major of Volunteers, 4th Ohio
Infantry in May of 1861 Lieut. Colonel in
Jan. of 1862, Colonel in May 1863 and General
Mar. 13, 1865. He was severely wounded at
the battle of Fredericksburg. He was elected
state Auditor of Ohio and served some years
in that office. He was a son of William and
Hannah (Harper) Godman and a great grandson
of Capt. William Godman (b. 1754 in Frederick
County, Md. and died July 10, 1825) who enlisted Jan. 24, 1776 in Capt. Nathaniel
Smith's Company of Artillery. Capt. Godman's
wife was Allena Gartrell.
    The children of Gen. Jas. H. Godman and
Anna Strine Davis Godman were:
94. William Davis Godman b. 8 Sept. 1829.
95. Henry Clay Godman b. 1831.
96. James Mortimer Godman b. ca 1834 - d. 1845.
97. John Marshall Godman 1840-1910 of Cleveland, Ohio, m. Sarah C. Leonard and had issue:
98. Ann Eliza Godman d. in inf.
99. Charles Carroll Godman 1842-1917, of Kansas City, Mo., m. twice and had issue.
100. James Harper Godman Jr. 1846-1914 resided in Chicago, Ill. in 1910.

19. ACHSAH W. DAVIS^3 (BENJ^2, NEHEMIAH^1)

Achsah Wyatt Davis married Oct. 14, 1832
Elisha Jolly at Marion, Ohio. They had at
least two children:
101. Davis Jolly, merchant of Morgan City, Iowa.
102. Princess Anna Jolly (some doubt about this name).

20. MINERVA DAVIS^3 (BENJ^2, NEHEMIAH^1)

Minerva M. Davis (1822-1844) married
John J. Williams of Marion, Ohio, the 24th
of Nov. 1841. There were no children.

21. PRINCESS DAVIS^3 (BENJ^2, NEHEMIAH^1)

Princess Davis married Apr. 17, 1844
Rodney Spaulding and had two children both of
whom died in infancy

29. SYLVA A. WELLS^3 (SARAH^2 NEHEMIAH^1)

Sylva Ann Wells (1807-1837) married
Oct. 29, 1826 Edmond D. Wolf (b. 1807) a son
of Jacob and Lydia (Dorr) Wolf and removed
to Porter County, Ind. where she died. Their
children were:
103. Jacob Clark Wolf b. 1829 in Ohio.
104. Sarah A. Wolf b. 1831 in Ohio.
105. Catherine Wolf b. 1834 in Ind.
106. Harriet Wolf b. 1835 in Mich.
107. Charles Wolf b. 1837 in Ind.
    (See also Dorr family in Book 2).

31. SALLY DAVIS^3 (SARAH^2, NEHEMIAH^1)

Sally Davis (b. 1812) married Feb. 11,
1830 Francis P. James a son of Samuel and
Mary James who came from Maine to Ohio in
1818. They went to Iowa and no data is
available on descendants.

39. LUCRETIA A. DAVIS^3 (NEHEMIAH^2, NEHEMIAH^1)

Lucretia Ann Davis (1823-1853) married
Apr. 14, 1842 John Herrold (1822-1875) son of
John and Clarissa (Allen) Herrold. (See Allen
Family). Their children were:
108. Emily S. Herrold b. 1844, m. Elliott Gardner.
109. Sarah L. Herrold b. 1846, m. Mr. Poston.
110. Mary E. Herrold b. 1851, d. y.
111. Nancy L. Herrold b. 1853.
    Lucretia Ann Davis Herrold died Apr. 10,
1853.

43. MARY DAVIS^3 (NEHEMIAH^2, NEHEMIAH^1)

Mary Davis (1837-1918) married Mar. 24,
1858 Daniel Canfield (1828-1899) and resided
near Barlow, Ohio. They had several children
among whom were:
112. Sewella Jane Canfield 1858-1889.

113. Mary Frances Canfield 1863-1882.
114. Betsey Richards Canfield 1871-1889.

47. JANE E. DAVIS[3] (NEHEMIAH[2], NEHEMIAH[1])

Jane Eleanor Davis (b. 1832) married ca 1854 Peter G. Hibbard and resided in Dover township. They had several children:
114a. Mary E. Hibbard b. 1855.
114b. Emma J. Hibbard b. 1856.
114c. Charles H. Hibbard b. 1858.
      There were probably others.

48. EDWIN DAVIS[3] (JAS. D[2]., NEHEMIAH[1])

Edwin Davis (1816-1885) carpenter lived in both Trimble and York townships of Athens County. He married Oct. 7, 1841 Lucina B. Woodworth (b. Jan. 20, 1818 in Windham County, Conn., and died June 6, 1851 with burial in True Cemetery) a daughter of Chester and Lucia Woodworth. Edwin and Lucina Davis had
115. Lucia Lucina Davis b. Nov. 4, 1845.
116. Rebecca Dean Davis b. Mar. 19, 1849.
117. Charles Edwin Davis b. Apr. 11, 1851, d. in inf.
Edwin Davis married second Cynthia J. Cook the 10th of Feb. 1852. She was born in Yates County, N. Y. May 9, 1826 and died Aug. 29, 1909 with burial in Nye Cemetery. They had three daughters:
118. Lydia Florence Davis b. Feb. 14, 1857.
119. Effie May Davis b. Dec. 13, 1863.
120. Mary Gardner Davis b. Mar. 27, 1866.
     m. July 17, 1889 Hugh S. James (1867-1934). m. 2nd Mr. Harry Betts.

49. LEWIS L. DAVIS[3] (JAS. D[2]., NEHEMIAH[1])

Lewis L. Davis (1817-1903) blacksmith, married July 26, 1846 Mary Gilliland (b. 1826 in Ohio) and had issue:
121. Sarah Davis b. 1850.
122. Betsey J. Davis b. 1853.
123. Edmund H. Davis b. 1855.
124. Joseph L. Davis b. 1857.
125. Charles L. Davis b. 1860.
126. Celestia Davis b. 1862.
126A. Elmer G. Davis b. 1869.
      There may have been other children.

50. NEHEMIAH W. DAVIS[3] (JAS. D[2]., NEHEMIAH[1])

Nehemiah W. Davis (1819-1898) carpenter of Trimble township, Athens County, Ohio,

married Feb. 4, 1843 Polly D. Andrews and had one child:
127. Jeremiah Davis b. 1846 teacher, m. May. 1, 1872 Ellen Moody.
Nehemiah W. Davis married second Apr. 6, 1848 Sarah J. Love (b. 1829 in Ohio) and had issue:
128. Thomas Davis b. 1849.
129. Louisa J. Davis b. 1852.
130. Franklin P. Davis b. 1854.
131. Clarissa A. Davis b. 1856.
132. Dexter M. Davis b. 1858.
133. Parkinson J. Davis b. 1859.
134. Charles Davis b. 1862.
135. Effie Davis b. 1864, m. 1st Mr. Finley m. 2nd Mr. Lamborn.

51. PHEBE DAVIS[3] (JAS. D[2]., NEHEMIAH[1])

Phebe Davis (1821-1902) married July 5, 1846 Henry Ryan.
Phebe Davis Ryan married second Mr. McKee.

52. SUSANNAH DAVIS[3] (JAS. D., NEHEMIAH[1])

Susannah Davis (1822-1895) married Dec. 23, 1842 Samuel N. Andrews (b. Sept. 25, 1818 and d. Oct. 1, 1860) and had issue:
136. John D. Andrews b. ca 1853.
137. Sarah F. Andrews b. 1860.
     Probably other children.
Susannah Davis Andrews married second Mr. McKee. She died Dec. 8, 1895.

53. SARAH J. DAVIS[3] (JAS. D[2]., NEHEMIAH[1])

Sarah J. Davis (1824-1892) married July 10, 1845 Nathan Wallace.
She died June 21, 1892.

54. JAMES DAVIS[3] (JAS. D[2]., NEHEMIAH[1])

James Davis (1826-1891) married Nov. 26, 1847 Eunice Stevens. He died Sept. 13, 1891.

55. HIRAM D. DAVIS[3] (JAS. D[2]., NEHEMIAH[1])

Hiram Dore Davis (1827-1891) married in 1852 Margaret Lee Collins and resided in Missouri. He died Oct. 13, 1891. They had a daughter:
138. Hortense Davis m. 1878 George P. Collins and had a son Atty. George Gordon Collins (1882-1940) of St. Louis, Mo.

58. SAMUEL W. DAVIS[3] (JAS. D., NEHEMIAH[1])

Samuel W. Davis (1833-1872) farmer of

Chauncey, Ohio served three years as a private in the Civil War. His discharge papers given Sept. 19, 1864 describes him as being 5 ft. 8 in. tall, having fair hair and complexion, with gray eyes.

59. Eli J. Davis[3] (JAS. D[2]., NEHEMIAH[1])

Eli J. Davis (1835-1892) married July 24, 1859 Louisa Watkins and had at least one child:
139. Lewis H. Davis b. 1860.
They are said to have removed to a western state but were living in Trimble township in the summer of 1860.

64. WILLIAM H. DAVIS[3] (JAS. D[2]., NEHEMIAH[1])

William H. Davis (1843-1903) married Mar. 10, 1864 Rhoda Cass. He died June 9, 1903.

65. EUNICE DAVIS[3] (JAS. D[2]., NEHEMIAH[1])

Eunice Davis (1845-1881) married Feb. 9, 1868 Harmon J. Fulton.

68. REUBEN A. DAVIS[3] (ISAIAH[2], NEHEMIAH[1])

Reuben A. Davis (1834-1903) married Kate _____ after 1870. He died at Nelsonville, Ohio. One child:
139A. Lucy Davis, m. Mr. Welling.

69. FRANCIS J. DAVIS[3] (ISAIAH[2], NEHEMIAH[1])

Elder Frank J. Davis (b. 1838) married three times and had issue.

71. LORINDA DAVIS[3] (ISAIAH[2], NEHEMIAH[1])

Lorinda Davis (b. 1849) married Mr. Wallace and had issue.

72. JOSEPH DAVIS[3] (RUFUS, NEHEMIAH[1])

Joseph Davis (1825-1866) farmer, married Oct. 24, 1850 Alvira Judd (d. 1873) a daughter of Arunah Judd and had issue:
140. Elizabeth Davis.
141. Charles J. Davis.
142. Seth P. Davis, d. y.
143. Susan Davis d. y.
144. Edward Homer Davis b. 15 Apr. 1859.
145. John F. Davis b. 4 Sept. 1861.
146. Clinton L. Davis b. 1863.

80. ORRIN GARDNER[3] (MARY[2], NEHEMIAH[1])

Orrin Adolphus Augustus Gardner (1833-1915) married first Louisa West, Second: Emma Beauchamp. He died Apr. 27, 1915.

82. JAMES D. GARDNER[3] (MARY[2], NEHEMIAH[1])

James Davis Gardner (1841-1879) married May 30, 1876 Phebe Susannah Allen, a daughter of Wilmarth and Judith (Davis) Allen. (See Allen family.)

84. GEORGE M. GARDNER[3] (MARY[2], NEHEMIAH[1])

George Metteer Gardner (1848-1934) married Mar. 22, 1877 Adela Esther Fuller (b. Nov. 23, 1854 and d. Apr. 24, 1939) a daughter of Dr. Russell Nash Fuller and wife Eliza B. (Cooley) Fuller. (See Fuller family in book 2). George M. Gardner died Dec. 7, 1934 survived by one daughter.
147. Mary Cooley Gardner b. Apr. 2, 1879.

88. OSCAR E. BAKER[4] (LOISA[3], BENJ[2]., NEHEMIAH[1])

Rev. Oscar E. Baker (1826-1893) married Oct. 13, 1850 Jane E. Powell (b. Jan. 2, 1828 and d. Oct. 8, 1859).
He was a clergyman of the Free Will Baptist Church in Marion, Ohio and Waterloo, Iowa. They had two children:
148. George P. Baker b. Dec. 6, 1854, d. 1873.
149. Jennie L. Baker b. Apr. 12, 1858, d. 1879.
Rev. Baker married Oct. 4, 1860 Augusta Wilson (b. Oct. 8, 1830). They had one daughter:
150. Louisa A. Baker b. Feb. 6, 1863.

89. ALLEN D. BAKER[4] (LOISA[3], BENJ[2]., NEHEMIAH[1])

Allen D. Baker (1828-1906) served in the 136th O.V.I. of the Civil War. He married Feb. 22, 1849 Alida Van Osten (b. July 17, 1828 and d. July 30, 1858) and had issue:
151. Oscar Albertus Baker b. Feb. 17, 1850.
Allen D. Baker married Feb. 16, 1859 Elsie A. Dockey (b. Sept. 20, 1840) and had:
152. Louisa A. Baker 1859-1867.
153. Ella P. Baker 1861-1867.
154. William H. Baker 1863-1864.
Allen D. Baker married third Feb. 28, 1867 Lucinda F. Fowler (b. July 10, 1837 and d. Sept. 15, 1904) and had issue:
155. Flora A. Baker b. Jan. 1, 1868.

90. LYDIA A. BAKER[4] (LOISA[3], BENJ[2]., NEHEMIAH[1])

Lydia Ann Baker (1831-1863) married Aug. 6,

1854 William A. Clark (b. Nov. 21, 1830) and had issue:
156. Elden b. and d. 1855.
157. Louisa 1858-1874.
158. Princess L. Clark b. Feb. 17, 1862.

91. LOUISA J. BAKER⁴ (LOISA³, BENJ², NEHEMIAH¹)

Louisa Jane Baker (b. 1836) married Oct. 19, 1856 John C. Johnstone of Van Wert, O. (b. 1829 and d. 1906) attorney-at-law. Served in the Civil War and was mayor of Marion, Ohio for several years. They had three children.
159. Geneora E. Johnstone b. Nov. 12, 1857,
160. Orlando W. Johnstone b. Sept. 23, 1859.
161. Homer C. Johnstone b. May 21, 1868.

92. EBER S. BAKER⁴ (LOISA³, BENJ², NEHEMIAH¹)

Eber S. Baker (b. 1838) served in the Civil War in company H., 4th O.U.I. and was in the battle of Gettysburg where he was taken prisoner and confined in Libby Prison where he almost lost his life. He married Oct. 22, 1864 Mary E. Trimble and had:
162. Herman E. Baker b. Nov. 15, 1865.
163. Beatrice Baker b. Feb. 18, 1877, m. Oct. 22, 1913 Wm. H. Marsh.

93. PRINCESS A. BAKER⁴ (LOISA³, BENJ², NEHEMIAH¹)

Princess Amanda Baker (1842-1899) married Dec. 17, 1861 O. C. Smith of Toledo, Ohio (b. 1833 and d. Dec. 28, 1907 at Chicago, Ill. She died in Chicago Dec. 15, 1899. Their children were:
164. Burton D. Smith b. Feb. 24, 1870.
165. Clement E. Smith 1876-1881.

94. WILLIAM D. GODMAN⁴ (ANNA³, BEN², NEHEMIAH¹)

Dr. William D. Godman (1829-1908) graduated at Ohio Wesleyan Univ. 1849 and received his D.D. in 1867. Was professor of Greek at Northwestern University, of Mathematics and Theology at Ohio Wesleyan and President of Baldwin University 1875-1878 and of Gilbert Academy and Agricultural College in Louisiana (1878-1908). He married Susan H. Porter and had issue:
167. Anna Fidelia Godman, m. Rev. I. K. Pittinger and had issue.
Dr. Godman married second Margaret McClintock, no issue.
He married third Augusta Dexter and had issue:

168. Inez Augusta Godman b. 10 Aug. 1865.

95. HENRY C. GODMAN⁴ (ANNA³, BENJ², NEHEMIAH¹)

Henry Clay Godman (1831-1907) attorney-at-law, married Sept. 23, 1852 Katherine L. Copeland of Marion, Ohio, (she d. 1910 at Columbus, Ohio) and had:
169. James Copeland Godman b. 1853.
170. William Guild Godman b. 1855.
171. Anna Catherine Godman b. 1858.
172. Alice Godman b. 1863.

115. LUCIA L. DAVIS⁴ (EDWIN³, JAS², NEHEMIAH¹)

Lucia Lucina Davis (1845-1876) married Nov. 4, 1866 Lemuel C. Birge and had issue:
173. Bertha E. Birge b. July 8. 1867.
174. Ida M. Birge b. Nov. 4, 1868.
175. Ormond Birge b. 1873 d. 1874.
176. Nancy Lucina Birge b. Dec. 6, 1875.

116. REBECCA D. DAVIS⁴ (EDWIN³, JAS², NEHEMIAH¹)

Rebecca Dean Davis (1849-1881) married Jan. 27, 1870 Robert Brookins.

118. LYDIA F. DAVIS⁴ (EDWIN³, JAS², NEHEMIAH¹)

Lydia Florence Davis (b. 1857) married Dec. 25, 1882 DR. John Walker Johnson (b. Feb. 16, 1851 and d. July 1, 1914) and had issue:
177. Helen Almarine Johnson b. 20 Feb. 1887.
178. John Edwin Johnson b. 27 Oct. 1893.

119. EFFIE M. DAVIS⁴ (EDWIN³, JAS², NEHEMIAH¹)

Effie May Davis (1863-1930) married Dec. 17, 1884 D. S. Anderson (d. Aug. 18, 1936) and resided in Guthrie County, Iowa where she died Oct. 19, 1930. Their children were:
179. Harold Anderson.
180. Howard Anderson.
181. Neil Anderson.

147. MARY C. GARDNER (GEO., MARY, NEHEMIAH)

Mary (Marie C.) Cooley Gardner (b. 1879) married Dec. 11, 1897 Robert Wilmot Jones, a son of Will S. Jones and his wife Harriet C. (Marshall) Jones.
The children of R. W. Jones and Mary C.

Gardner his wife were
182. Ruth A. Jones b. 19 Jan. 1900.
183. Marshall Gardner Jones b. 1 Oct. 1901.

177. HELEN A. JOHNSON[5] (LYDIA[4], EDWIN[3], JAS[2], NEHEMIAH[1])

Helen Johnson (b. 1887) married Sept. 2, 1915 Dano Elmer Starr D.D.S. (d. Apr. 28, 1933 at Mt. Sterling, Ohio) a son of Clayton and Lula (Smith) Starr of Athens, Ohio, and had issue:
184. Clayton Johnson Starr b. Aug. 12, 1916, m. 1940 Ruth Ellen Gerhart.
185. Hugh Sawyer Starr b. Nov. 20, 1917.
186. Rupert Dano Starr b. July 16, 1922.

178. J. EDWIN JOHNSON[5] (LYDIA[4], EDWIN[3], JAS[2], NEHEMIAH[1])

John Edwin Johnson (b. 1893) married Dec. 30, 1916 Nellie Grace Ceope and had issue:
187. Edith Almarine Johnson 1917-1938.
188. John Wesley Johnson b. Oct. 1, 1919.
189. Pauline Ruth Johnson b. Dec. 8, 1923.

182. RUTH JONES (MARY[4] C., GEO[3], MARY[2], NEHEMIAH[1])

Ruth Jones (b. 1900) married Nov. 19, 1920 Walter M. Miller and had issue:
190. Walter Mitchell Miller, Jr. b. 23 Jan. 1923.

183. MARSHALL G. JONES[5] (MARY C[4], GEO[3], MARY[2], NEHEMIAH[1])

Marshall Gardner Jones (b. 1901) married Oct. 3, 1926 Mary Anne Adamson and had issue:
191. Ann Marshall Jones b. 3 May 1931.

DAVIS LINEAGE

1. Francis Davis m. ca 1650 Gertrude Emerson
   b. ca 1626   b. ca 1630
   From Eng. to Mass.
   1638 in the "Confidence"

2. Francis Davis Jr. m. Jan. 20, 1673 Mary Taylor
   b. 1655   daughter of
   of Amesbury, Mass.   Walter and
   Oath of Fidelity Dec. 20, 1677   Alice

3. John Davis m. Dec. 22, 1707 Mrs. Ruth (Badger) Jewell
   b. 1674, d. 1742   daughter of
   of W. Amesbury   Sergt. John
   a "joiner"   Badger and
                                Hannah (Swett)
                                Badger

4. Timothy Davis m. Nov. 18, 1736 Judith Pettingell
   b. Feb. 1, 1712   b. Oct. 28, 1711,
   a "turner" of   a daughter of Mathew
   Amesbury, Mass.   and Joanna (French)
   and Salisbury, Removed   Pettingell.
   1738 to Kingston, N.H.

5. Nehemiah Davis - m. 1st. Elizabeth Marston
   (1755-1823)   m. 2nd. Phebe Dore
   See Text.

MARSTON LINEAGE

1. William Marston m. in Eng., wife's name unknown.
   b. in Eng. ca 1590.
   To Salem, Mass. 1634,
   To Hampton, N. H. 1638.

2. Thomas Marston m. ca. 1647 Mary Estow
   b. ca 1617 in Eng.   a daughter of
   came with father 1634   William Estow of
   To Hampton, N.H.   Ormesby

3. Ephraim Marston m. 19 Feb. 1677 Abial Sanborn
   b. Aug. 8, 1654 at   b. Feb. 25, 1653
   Hampton, N. H.   a daughter of
   Rep. to General Court   Lieut. John and Mary
   for several years.   (Tuck) Sanborn.
   He d. Oct. 10, 1742.   Abial Marston d. Jan. 3, 1743.

4. Capt. Jeremiah Marston m. 23 Mar. 1720 Mary Smith
   b. Nov. 5, 1691 in N. H.
   Killed in "French and
   Indian War" at seige of
   Louisburg, Cape Breton
   May 29, 1745.

5. Elisha Marston m. 5 Dec. 1754 Anna Phibrick
   b. 16 Mar. 1730 at Hampton,   b. 9 June 1732.
   N. H. Went to Brentwood
   where he d. Dec. 11, 1765

6. Elizabeth Marston m.   Nehemiah Davis
   b. Dec. 1, 1755   See Text.

DORE LINEAGE

1. Richard Dore m. Tamsen _____
   d. ca 1715
   of Portsmouth, N. H.

2. Philip Dore m. May 20, 1708 Sarah Child of Newington, N. H.

3. Philip Dore m. Lydia Mason.
   b. ca 1728
   d. 1796 at
   Shapleigh, Me.

4. James Dore m. Aug. 3, 1769 Hannah Hussey
   bapt. Aug. 20, 1749   daughter of Richard
                               and Phebe (Varney)
                               Hussey

5. Phebe Dore m. Aug. 7, 1777 Rev. Nehemiah Davis

1. JOSIAH TRUE ESQ.

Josiah True was born Oct. 25, 1776 in New Hampshire. He came in the year 1798 from Milford, N. H., to Marietta on the Ohio river and in company with Daniel Weethee to what is now Dover township in Athens County the following year (1799).

He married in 1803/4 Almira Tuttle (b. 1788 in Vt. and d. Oct. 22, 1853) a daughter of Capt. Solomon and Deborah Tuttle, first settlers of Trimble township.

Josiah True was public-spirited to an unusual degree having been the founder of the "Coon-skin Library" established at Amesville as the "Western Library Association" in 1804 and of which he served as director from 1816 to 1820.

He was elected lieutenant of militia in 1803, served on many juries from 1810 until his death, listed taxes in 1805, served as postmaster of Millfield in 1836 and 1837, elected "Overseer of the Poor" in 1802, township trustee in 1805, 1827, 1828 to 1850, a justice of the peace from 1815 to 1851, was one of the original incorporators of the Dover Library Association incorporated by the Ohio State Legislature in 1830.

He was an original landholder of one hundred and thirty-seven acres of land in what is now Dover township (Athens County) as well as an original landholder in the "Donation Tract" (Washington County, Ohio) of one hundred acres.

Josiah True was a great hunter and it is told that once he and his brother-in-law Cyrus Tuttle chased a bear into a cave and shot it. On being certain that it was dead, they entered and attempted to remove the carcass but another bear which had been hiding in the rear of the cave, rushed by them knocking Mr. True to the floor in its effort to escape.

He is said to have been the first to bring a spinning wheel into the county, having taken an accumulated supply of bear and deer skins on his back, afoot to Zanesville market and purchased the spinning wheel which he carried on his back on the return trip, in all a distance of about eighty miles round trip which he accomplished in two days.

He is also credited with having planted the first apple orchard in the county.

He served in the War of 1812 in Capt. George Ewings Company, the second regiment of the first brigade in the third division.

He died Sept. 16, 1855 and is buried in True Cemetery. His Will is of record in book 7, p. 109 of Athens County records and is as follows:

"I Josiah True of Dover township in the County of Athens and State of Ohio, do make and publish this my last Will and Testament:

First: It is my Will that my just debts and all charges be paid out of my personal property.

Second: I give and bequeath to my beloved wife the use of one third of all my estate real and personal during her natural life.

Third: To my son Mason I give the southwest quarter of section 24 in township 10 of range 14.

To my son Austin True I give the southeast quarter of section 24, township 10 range 14.

Fourth: I also give to my son Austin the home place being 137 acres of land in section 18, township 10, range 14 upon condition that he shall pay therefore twelve hundred dollars to my children: Lydia Porter, Almira Woodworth, Mary Jane True, Lucy W. Fulton, Mason True and my granddaughter Sally True in such proportions that my said children shall have equal shares and my said granddaughter Sally shall have one third as much as either of my said children.

Fifth: I give and bequeath to my children Lydia Porter, Almira Woodworth, Mary Jane True, Lucy W. Fulton, Mason True and my granddaughter Sally True in equal proportions the northwest quarter of section 24, township 10 of range 14.

Sixth: In case of the death of my son Austin True previous to my decease I give and bequeath to his heirs-at-law the house recently built by him west of my house together with a half acre of ground about said house in such form as may be convenient for the use of the house.

Seventh: I hereby name and appoint my son Austin executor of this my last Will and Testament with full authority to compromise, adjust, release and discharge in such manner as may seem best the debts and claims due to me, also if necessary to pay my debts, to sell by private sale or in such manner and upon such terms of credit as he may think proper all or any part of my real estate and deeds to purchasers to execute, acknowledge and deliver in fee simple and I revoke all former wills made my me. In testimony whereof I have hereunto set my hand and Seal this 8th day of Sept. A.D. 1851.
                    Josiah True
Witnesses
Henry T. Brown   Filed Sept. 29, 1855

The children of Josiah and Almira Tuttle True were:
2. John True b. 1806.
3. Lydia True b. 1809.
4. Josiah E. True b. 1816 - d. 1848, unm.
5. Austin True b. 6 Mar. 1818.
6. Mason True b. 1821.
7. Almira True b. 9 Feb. 1823.
8. Lucy W. True b. 1825.
9. Mary Jane Ture b. 1827.
Several children died in infancy.

2. JOHN TRUE² (JOSIAH¹)

John True (1806-1839) married Dec. 23, 1830 Sally Irene Eggleston (b. June 25, 1817 and d. Mar. 10, 1833) a daughter of David and Rebecca Eggleston. There was one daughter born to .hem:
10. Sally Irene True b. Mar. 7, 1833.
John True married second Feb. 25, 1835 Mary Ann Eggleston a sister of his first wife and had one son:
11. William Henry Harrison True.
John True died Apr. 10, 1839.

3. LYDIA TRUE² (JOSIAH¹)

Lydia True (b. 1809) married Dec. 1, 1831 Samuel Porter (b. 1806 in N. Y.) and resided in Wayne County, Iowa.
Their children were:
12. John Porter b. 1833 in Ohio.
13. Sally A. Porter b. 1835 in Ohio.
14. Isaac Porter b. 1837 in Ohio.
15. Austin Porter b. 1843 in Ohio.
16. Charles Porter b. 1846 in Ohio.

5. AUSTIN TRUE² (JOSIAH¹)

Austin True (1818-1906) married Feb. 11, 1844 Jane Fuller (b. Sept. 16, 1826 and d. Oct. 17, 1853) a daughter of Resolved and Nancy (Bachelder) Fuller the former a native of Conn. and the latter of the state of Maine. (See Bk. 2 p. 105 and 106 for ancestral notes). Austin True died Jan. 12, 1906 survived by the following children.
17. Hiram L. True b. June 4, 1845.
18. Sarah E. True b. June 27, 1848.
19. John W. True b. Oct. 18, 1850.
20. Thomas True d. in inf.

6. MASON TRUE² (JOSIAH¹)

Mason True (b. 1821) married Mar. 2, 1843 Esther B. Campbell (b. 1823 in Ohio) and removed to Mercer County, Missouri where they were living in 1857. They had several children among whom were:

21. Solan True b. 1845 in Ohio.
22. Sylvanus True b. 1847 in Ohio.
23. Lawrence True b. 1849 in Ohio.

7. ALMIRA TRUE² (JOSIAH¹)

Almira True (1823-1851) married Oct. 30, 1842 Bennett Woodworth and had several children most of whom died in infancy. They were:
24. Almyra Jane Woodworth b. 10 Jan. 1846.
25. Josiah B. Woodworth d. in inf.
26. Eaton Woodworth d. in inf.
27. Mary Woodworth d. in inf.
28. Ada Woodworth d. in inf.
29. Henry Woodworth d. in inf.
Almira True Woodworth died Oct. 20, 1851.

8. LUCY TRUE² (JOSIAH¹)

Lucy True (b. 1825) married Dec. 24, 1846 Daniel Fulton (b. 1822 in Athens County, Ohio) and had issue:
30. Harmon Fulton b. 1848 in Dover tp.
31. Mary J. Fulton b. 1849 in Dover tp.
32. Lydia E. Fulton B. 1849 in Dover tp.
33. Lucy Fulton b. 1859 in Dover tp.
34. Sarah I. Fulton
35. John A. Fulton

9. MARY JANE TRUE² (JOSIAH¹)

Mary Jane True (b. 1827) married Nov. 11, 1855 John Fulton and went to Wayne County, Iowa.

10. SALLY I. TRUE³ (JOHN², JOSIAH¹)

Sally Irena True (b. 1833) married Jan. 17, 1855 John Herrold (1822-1875) as his second wife. She died Nov. 20, 1855 and is buried in Nye Cemetery. No surviving issue.

17. HIRAM L. TRUE³ (AUSTIN², JOSIAH¹)

Dr. Hiram L. True (1845-1912) served in company A, 129th regiment of the O.V.I. during the War between the States.
He married the 8th of Nov. 1865 Julia Weethee (1844-1869) and had one son:
36. Marcus W. True 1867-1887.
Hiram True married second Apr. 29, 1874 Helen Moore and had two daughters.
37. Evelyn True b. 26 Jan. 1875.
38. Augusta True b. 21 May 1877.
Dr. True died the 22nd of October in 1812. He was described as light complexioned with gray eyes and light hair in his army discharge.

18. SARAH E. TRUE[3] (AUSTIN[2], JOSIAH[1])

Sarah E. True (b. 1848) married Oct. 21, 1866 Levi A. Sprague (1844-1933). Their children were:
39. Florence Sprague
40. Wiley T. Sprague, M.D.
41. Warren V. Sprague, M.D.
42. Myra G. Sprague
43. Jennie E. Sprague
44. John R. Sprague, M.D.

19. JOHN W. TRUE[3] (AUSTIN[2], JOSIAH[1])

John W. True (1850-1899) married Jan. 27, 1873 Martha Ann Maxwell (1853-1938) and resided at Basil, Ohio. Their children were:
45. Effie True b. Oct. 1874.
46. Laura True b. Mar. 16, 1877 in Dover tp.
47. Lydia Olive True b. Aug. 13, 1879 at Millfield, Ohio
48. Austin R. True of Gore, Ohio
49. Minnie Edith True m. C. R. Jolly

47. LYDIA O. TRUE[4] (JOHN[3], AUSTIN[2], JOSIAH[1])

Lydia Olive True (b. 1879) married Austin V. Myers at Basil, Ohio on Dec. 8, 1901. Their children were:
50. Austin Leland Myers b. Apr. 16, 1906.
51. Robert True Myers b. Mar. 5, 1915.

50. A. LELAND MYERS (LYDIA O[4], JOHN[3], AUSTIN[2], JOSIAH[1])

Austin Leland Myers (b. 1906) married Apr. 30, 1932 Mary A. Young (b. 1910) and had three children:
52. Carol Lee Myers b. Dec. 10, 1935.
53. Davis True Myers b. and d. 1939.
54. Marilyn Jane Myers b. Dec. 16, 1940.

The Name

True became a surname through its use first as a nickname as "John the true" (a trustworthy person) about 1273 A.D. in Bedfordshire, Eng.

True Lineage

1. Henry Trew m. 1644 Israel Pike (d. prior to 1659) From Eng. ca 1644 to Salem, Mass., a founder of Salisbury, Mass. — (d. 1699) a daughter of John Pike from Eng. to Newbury 1635 on the "James."

2. Henry True m. 1688 (1645-1735) Ensign in 1682, Lient. in 1691, Capt. in 1703/4 Represented Salisbury in Mass. General Court 1689 to 1695 and 1707. — Jane Bradbury (1645-1700) daughter of Thomas Bradbury (1611-1694) teacher, clerk justice. Mass. Gen. ct. 1651, 52, 56, 57, 60, 61, 66. Capt. of Militia, Associate Judge. m. Jane Perkins

3. John True m. 1702 (1698-1754) — Martha Merrill

4. John True m. (b. 1704) — Mary Brown

5. Ephraim True m. 1775 b. 21 Dec. 1756 at Salisbury, Mass. Went to Saybrook, N. H. And in 1798 to Washington County, Ohio where he died Aug. 17, 1835. Served in the Revolutionary War. — Martha Eaton daughter of Thomas Eaton

6. Josiah True (see text)

1. REV. WILLIAM ARGO

William Argo was born in Sussex County, Delaware Aug. 12, 1763. He prepared for the ministry and for many years was a "circuit rider" in Pennsylvania and in Jefferson and Harrison Counties in Ohio. In April of 1809 he produced credentials in the Common Pleas Court of Jefferson County proving that he was an ordained minister of the Methodist Episcopal Church and was granted certification to perform marriages in Ohio. He served on Jefferson County juries many times from Mar. of 1808 through the following quarter of a century.

He married about 1788 near Milford, Del. Nancy Crabbich. They removed about 1790 to western Pennsylvania and lived at frontier settlements. At one time they erected a home on some land they purchased in the back woods some distance from a settlement.

Rev. Argo was away from home and she was alone with her two babies: Anna and Jeremiah (an infant). She saw a band of Indians approaching and quickly snatched up her two babies and run into the woods back of the house where she hid the sleeping baby in a hollow log and ran with the other child to the nearest settlement for help.

The settlers returned with her and found the baby still asleep and unharmed and the Marauding Indians gone.

She preceded him in death (but after 1830) and is probably buried in Warren township of Jefferson County. Rev. Argo died intestate Feb. 26, 1846 at the home of his son-in-law John Ralston in Harrison County, Ohio with burial on the Ralston lot in the old Bethel Graveyard.

Their children were:

2. Anna Argo b. ca 1789 probably in Northampton Co. Pa.
3. Jeremiah Argo b. 1791 in Washington Co. Pa.
4. Susannah Argo b. ca. 1795 in Pa.
5. William Argo, Jr. b. ca 1797 in Pa.
6. Margaret Argo
7. Elizabeth Argo
8. Eleanor Argo
9. Leusintha Argo b. 8 Dec. 1807 in Jefferson County, Ohio.
10. Julia Ann Argo b. 1810 in Jefferson Co. Ohio.
11. Joseph Argo b. ca 1815 in Jefferson Co. Ohio.
There may have been another son born ca 1820.

2. ANNA ARGO[2] (WILLIAM[1])

Anna Argo (b. 1789) married Oct. 2, 1807 to John H. Smith (b. the 27th of May 1788 in Sussex County, Del. and d. at Kewanee, Ill. about 1868).

He states in a brief preface to a little book of his own poems that his father and grandfather were slave-holders and that he was left an orphan at the age of eighteen months (presumably the death of his mother). When fifteen years of age he was apprenticed to a blacksmith whose establishment was connected with a tavern where he remained eight years. About 1812 he was converted upon hearing of the "happy and extraordinary death of his father" and became a preacher. He was a violinist and wrote several pamphlets of verse mostly on religious themes in the style of the times.

John and Anna Argo Smith went to Kewanee, Ill. prior to 1857. They had twelve children, five of whom are believed to have died young. Names available are:

12. Jesse Smith b. 1810.
13. Nancy Smith.
14. Maria Smith b. 14 May 1815 in Va.
15. Harrison Smith.
16. Salathiel Smith unm.
17. Aaron Smith.
18. John Smith Jr. b. 18 Oct. 1831.

3. JEREMIAH ARGO[2] (WILLIAM[1])

Jeremiah Argo (b. 1791 in Pa.) served as a corporal in Capt. Alexander's company of Ohio volunteer militia in the War of 1812 in which service his health suffered through an arduous trip down the river on ice to capture some Indians.

He married Aug. 26, 1813 Ann Oxley (b. 1787 in Va.) and resided on a farm in Warren township of Jefferson County for several years.

On Oct. 1, 1824 he together with Everett Oxley (probably his father-in-law) received a U. S. land grant signed by President James Monroe for 158 acres located in Muskingum County, Ohio.

Everett Oxley and Rachel his wife of Belmont County gave a quit-claim deed to Jeremiah Argo for their share in 1828.

In 1850 Jeremiah and Ann Argo were living in Blue Rock township of Muskingum County. She died there prior to 1862.

He removed to Inland, Cedar County, Iowa

where he was living in 1871. He died at the age of 90 years Apr. 18, 1881 at Tipton, Iowa. Their children were:
19. John W. Argo b. 1814 in Jefferson County, Ohio.
20. Linia Argo b. 1827 in Muskingum County.
21. William Argo b. 1829 in Muskingum. County.
22. Marinda Argo b. 1832 in Muskingum County.
23. Everett Argo b. 1836 in Muskingum County.
    There were other children but names are not known.

4. SUSANNAH ARGO[2] (WILLIAM[1])

Susannah Argo (b. ca 1795) married on July 13, 1815 in Jefferson County, Ohio, Thomas Marshall.

5. WILLIAM ARGO[2] (WILLIAM[1])

William Argo, Jr. (b. ca 1797) married June 18, 1818 Jane Marshall in Jefferson County, Ohio. They were residing in Warren township in 1820 with two infant sons.

6. MARGARET ARGO[2] (WILLIAM[1])

Margaret Argo (b. ca 1799 in Pa.) married Oct. 15, 1819 Samuel Todd in Jefferson County, Ohio.

7. ELIZABETH ARGO[2] (WILLIAM[1])

Elizabeth Argo (b. ca 1801) married May 3, 1821 Micajah Runyon of Jefferson County. About 1837 they sold their farm and removed from the county.

8. ELEANOR ARGO[2] (WILLIAM[1])

Eleanor Argo (b. ca 1803) married Feb. 12, 1822 David Runyon. Samuel Runyon who was married June 14, 1845 to Sarah Jane Moore by William Argo M.G. is believed to have been their son.

9. LEUSINTHA ARGO[2] (WILLIAM[1])

Leusintha Argo (1807-1846) married Mar. 16, 1826 John Ralston (b. July 13, 1799 in Adams County, Pa. and d. Oct. 24, 1881). They removed to Harrison County, Ohio and resided about one mile out of Cadiz. She died there Jan. 13, 1846 and is buried in Bethel Church Yard. They had three children:
24. Emily Ralston b. 1830 in Jefferson County, Ohio.
25. Margaret A. Ralston b. 1837 in Harrison County, Ohio.
26. Joseph F. Ralston b. 1840 in Harrison County, Ohio.

10. JULIA ANN ARGO[2] (WILLIAM[1])

Julia Ann Argo (1810-1850) married Oct. 26, 1826 John O. Walden (b. Sept. 11, 1807 at Unionport, Ohio, and d. Dec. 7, 1868 at Torch, Ohio with burial in the Baptist Church yard) a son of Francis and Nancy (Pettit) Walden of Unionport, Ohio.

They resided on a farm near Unionport until about 1836 when they removed to Athens County but in 1848 sold their farm near Frost, Ohio and went to German township of Harrison County where she died in the fall of 1850.

The children of John O. Walden and Julia Ann Argo his wife were:
27. Cynthia Ann Walden b. 1830.
28. Mary A. Walden b. 24 Nov. 1834.
29. Sarah E. Walden b. 31 Aug. 1836.
30. William Milphard Walden b. 6 Dec. 1838.
31. Francis Walden 1840-1844 at Frost, Ohio.
32. Infant whose name and dates of birth and death are unknown. These two children were buried at Frost but no stones were found.
33. Martha M. Walden b. 20 Nov. 1844.
34. Permelia Walden b. 21 Feb. 1848.

11. JOSEPH ARGO[2] (WILLIAM[1])

Joseph Argo (b. ca 1815) married in Athens County, Ohio Aug. 10, 1837 Martha Alexander.

12. JESSE SMITH[3] (ANNA[2], WILLIAM[1])

Jesse Smith (1810-1878) married first Phoebe Pierson (b. Sept. 27, 1812 and d. Apr. 9, 1860 at Wethersfield, Ill.) and had issue:
35. Isaac Smith.
36. Elizabeth Smith.
37. Jane Smith.
38. William P. Smith.
39. Cynthia Smith.
40. Lavina Smith.
41. John Solomon Smith.
42. Hannah Smith.
    Jesse Smith married second Rachel Thompson (1822-1901) and had one child:
43. Albinas Smith.

14. MARIA SMITH[3] (ANNA[2], WILLIAM[1])

Maria Smith (1815-1891) married Ezekiel Cole (b. May 20, 1814 in Jefferson County, Ohio and d. Nov. 28, 1859 at Wethersfield, Ill.) They had several children:
44. Joshua Cole b. Oct. 29, 1837 in Athens County, Ohio.
45. Sarah Cole b. ca 1839 in Athens County, Ohio.

46. John Cole b. June 27, 1841 in Athens County, Ohio.
47. Thomas Cole b. Jan. 10, 1842 in Athens County, Ohio.
48. Harrison Cole b. Aug. 10, 1844 in Athens County, Ohio.
49. Mary Jane Cole b. Apr. 1, 1846 in Athens County, Ohio.
50. Ezekiel Cole b. Dec. 20, 1847 in Athens County, Ohio.
51. Maria Cole b. Mar. 10, 1851 in Athens County, Ohio.

15. HARRISON SMITH[3] (ANNA[2], WILLIAM[1])

Harrison Smith taught "singing schools." He married Eliza_____ and removed to Missouri. Enroute to church one night he stopped at a house to get out of a storm and was struck by lightning and killed. They had two children:
52. Emily (or Eliza) Smith m. Mr. Preshaw.
53. George Smith, a carpenter.

17. AARON SMITH[3] (ANNA[2], WILLIAM[1])

Aaron Smith (d. ca 1862) married in Stark County, Ill. Dec. 9, 1858 Lydia Dalrymple and had one son:
54. Aaron Smith, Jr. b. 3 Oct. 1861.

18. JOHN SMITH[3] (ANNA[2], WILLIAM[1])

John Smith (1831-1868) married ca 1858 Emeline Hoppock (b. Jan. 11, 1835 and d. Apr. 6, 1900) and resided in Henry County, Ill., and had issue:
55. William Harrison Smith 1859-1934, unm.
56. Emily Ann Smith b. 6 Jan. 1861.
57. Sarah Eva Smith b. 7 Feb. 1862.
58. Ella May Smith b. 24 Apr. 1865.
59. Sheridan Smith b. 1 May 1866.
60. Minnie Edith Smith b. 4 Sept. 1867.

19. JOHN W. ARGO[3] (JEREMIAH[2], WM.[1])

John W. Argo (b. 1814) "harness Marker" married ca 1837 in Blue Rock township of Muskingum County, Ohio, Elizabeth _____ (b. 1817 in Ohio). About 1855 they removed to Springfield township, Cedar County, Iowa. Their children:
61. Elisha S. Argo b. 1838 in Muskingum County.
62. Salva P. Argo b. 1842 in Muskingum County.
63. Margaret Argo b. 1844 in Muskingum County.
64. Jeremiah E. Argo b. 1846 in Muskingum County.
65. Ann M. Argo b. 1848 in Muskingum County.
66. John W. Argo b. 1852 in Muskingum County.
67. Nancy E. Argo b. 1854 in Muskingum County.

21. WILLIAM ARGO[3] (JEREMIAH[2], WM.[1])

William Argo (b. 1829) farmer of Blue Rock township, Muskingum County, Ohio, married ca 1851 Sarah _____ (b. 1829 in Ohio), and had issue:
68. Lewis H. Argo b. 1852, lived in Morgan County, Ohio.
69. Elizabeth A. Argo b. 1854 in Ohio.
70. William A. Argo b. 1856 in Ohio, was living in Morgan County, Ohio in 1888.
71. Anna Eliza Argo b. 1859 in Ohio.
Probably other children.

24. EMILY RALSTON[3] (LEUSINTHA[2], WM.[1])

Emily Ralston (b. 1830) married in Harrison County, Ohio (prior to 1869) Robert Masten.

25. MARGARET RALSTON[3] (LEUSINTHA[2], WM.[1])

Margaret Ralston (b. 1837) married Mr. Copeland in Harrison County, Ohio. She died prior to 1869 survived by two children:
72. Henry F. Copeland.
73. Laura Bell Copeland.

26. JOSEPH F. RALSTON[3] (LEUSINTHA[2], Wm.[1])

Joseph F. Ralston (b. 1840) married Aug. 8, 1861 Isabella Gilbert in Harrison County, Ohio.

27. CYNTHIA ANN WALDEN[3] (JULIA[2], WM.[1])

Cynthia Ann Walden (b. ca 1830) married in Athens County, Ohio, Sept. 23, 1847 Ephraim Foreman of Harrison County, Ohio, as his second wife. They removed to Virginia.

28. MARY WALDEN[3] (JULIA A.[2], WM.[1])

Mary Walden (1834-1922) married June 7, 1855 John Allensworth (b. May 8, 1827 and d. Mar. 11, 1910) and resided at Doylestown, Ohio. She died there Dec. 2, 1922 survived by:
74. Samuel Allensworth b. 8 Mar. 1859.
75. William Allensworth b. 1 Jan. 1862.
76. Carrie Allensworth b. 5 Aug. 1875.
77. George Allensworth, went to Casper, Wyo.
Probably others who died young.

29. SARAH WALDEN[3] (JULIA A[2]., Wm.[1])

Sarah E. Walden (1836-1916) married
Dec. 2, 1856 Samuel Lewis (b. June 1822 and
d. July 12, 1864) and resided at Akron, Ohio.
Their children:
78. Caroline Lewis b. Dec. 15, 1857.
79. Anna Mary Lewis b. May 8, 1861, m. Chas.
    Tuttle, contractor of San Gabriel, Calif.
    Sarah Walden Lewis married second in
Akron, Ohio, Joseph Ryan (b. Kildare, Ire.)
merchant and they removed to New Decatur, Ala.
Their children were:
80. Martha Ryan 1866-1868.
81. Clarence J. Ryan b. 1868.
82. Emeline Ryan b. 22 Apr. 1872.
83. Claudine Ryan 1874-1892, unm.
84. Adella Ryan b. 1876.

30. WILLIAM M. WALDEN[3] (JULIA A[2].,
    WM.[1])

William Milphard Walden (1838-1918) married in Jefferson County, Ohio Nov. 25, 1862
Hester Mariah Purviance (b. July 16, 1845 and
d. Feb. 8, 1906) a daughter of Samuel and
Amelia (Scott) Purviance of Smithfield, Ohio.
He died at Coolville, Ohio, May 13, 1918.
Their children were:
85. John Samuel Walden b. 31 Mar. 1864.
86. Flora Walden b. 26 Jan. 1867.
87. William L. Walden b. 5 Feb. 1869.
88. Clara M. Walden b. 2 Feb. 1871.
89. Rachel E. Walden 1874-1878.
90. George H. Walden b. 14 July 1876.
91. Harry M. Walden b. 11. Aug. 1885.

33. MARTHA M. WALDEN[3] (JULIA A[2].,
    Wm.[1])

Martha M. Walden (1844-1891) married
Nov. 17, 1867 Thomas Taylor (b. Sept. 26, 1842
and d. Mar. 19, 1890 and resided at Akron,
Ohio. Their children were:
92. Lillie O. Taylor b. 21 Aug. 1868, m. J. M.
    Willard.
93. Blanche Taylor b. 2 Dec. 1871, m. R. B.
    Koontz.
94. William Taylor 1875-1878.
95. George Taylor 1878-1882.
    Martha Taylor died May 21, 1891.

34. PERMELIA WALDEN[3] (JULIA A[2]., WM[1].)

Permelia Walden (1848-1881) married Feb.
20, 1869 Harvey Baker (b. May 26, 1832 and
d. Nov. 27, 1902) and resided at Torch, Ohio.
She died there Oct. 21, 1881 survived by four
children:
96. Anna O. Baker (1869-1917) m. S. S. Winters.

97. Nora Baker m. E. E. James.
98. Asa Baker unm.
99. John Baker 1878-1884.

44. JOSHUA COLE[4] (MARIA[3], ANNA[2],
    WM.[1])

Joshua Cole (1837-1917) married in
Henry County, Ill. Feb. 6, 1860 Susan Hoppock
and had issue:
100. Mary Cole.
101. Joseph Cole.
102. Elton Cole.
103. Martha Cole.
104. William Cole.
105. Wesley Cole.
106. Otis Cole.
107. Ernest Cole.

45. SARAH COLE[4] (MARIA[3], ANNA[2],
    WM.[1])

Sarah Ann Cole (b. 1839) married Nov. 6,
1859 Phelix Inman in Stark County, Ill., and
removed to Iowa. They had:
108. Talbert Inman.
109. Charles Inman.
110. Clara Inman, d. y.
111. Lilly Inman, d. y.

46. JOHN COLE[4] (MARIA[3], ANNA[2],
    WM.[1])

John W. Cole (1841-1912) married at
Portage, Wis., Feb. 14, 1861 Zulia Ann
Dutton (b. Wyoming Co. N. Y., June 30, 1840
and d. May 6, 1903 at Toulon, Ill.) and had
issue:
112. Izella Cole.
113. Frank Cole, b. Dec. 16, 1862.
114. Efena Cole.
115. Flavia Cole.
116. Alfred Cole.
117. Edna Cole.
118. Esta Cole.
119. John Mara Cole.
120. Rolla Henry Cole.

47. THOMAS COLE[3] (ANNA[2], WM.[1])

Thomas Cole (b. 1842) married Lydia
Stewart (b. Aug. 23, 1847 Ontario, Canada)
and had issue:
121. Ellen Cole.
122. Arvilla Cole.
123. Harrison Cole.
124. Thomas Cole.
125. John Cole.
126. Nettie Cole.
127. Anna Cole.

128. Lucy Cole.
130. William Cole.
131. Bert Cole.
132. Ada Cole.

54. AARON SMITH[4] (AARON[3], ANNA[2], WM.[1])

Rev. Aaron Smith (b. 1861) married Aug. 29, 1889 Hattie G. Sheppard (b. May 4, 1867 and d. Mar. 21, 1904) and had issue:
132a. Vera Myrtle Smith b. 1894.
132b. Alpha Edson Smith b. 1896.
133c. Marion Russell Smith b. 1898.
133d. Roland Sheppard Smith b. 1901.
Rev. Smith married Oct. 10, 1905 Mollie Counts (b. Jan. 2, 1871 and d. June 6, 1917) and had issue:
134a. Waunetta Smith m. Joseph Stetson.
134b. Flora Smith m. Tobias Sprinke.

57. EVA SMITH[4] (JOHN[3], ANNA[2], WM.[1])

Sarah Eva Smith (b. 1862) married in 1888 Carl Mayfield and had issue:
140. Ernest Earl Mayfield b. May 26, 1889.
141. Leonard Leroy Mayfield b. 1891.
142. Lura Ellen Mayfield b. Apr. 10, 1893.
143. William Jennings Mayfield b. and d. 1897.

64. JEREMIAH ARGO[4] (JOHN[3], JEREMIAH[2], WM.[1])

Jeremiah E. Argo (b. 1846) married in Springfield township of Cedar County, Iowa ca 1858 Anna _____ (b. 1830 in Ohio) and had issue:
132. Tabitha Argo b. 1860 in Iowa.
133. Homer Argo b. 1863 in Iowa.
134. Lewis Argo b. 1866 in Iowa.
135. Oran Argo b. 1870 in Iowa.
136. Emma Argo b. 1872 in Iowa.

Jeremiah E. Argo died before 1880.

66. JOHN W. ARGO[4] (JOHN[3], JEREMIAH[2], WM.[1])

John W. Argo (b. 1852 in Ohio) married ca 1870 Ida_____ (b. 1850 in Iowa) and resided in Fairfield township of Cedar County, Iowa. They had issue:
137. Mary Argo b. 1871 in Iowa.
138. Anna Argo b. 1877 in Iowa.
139. Edith Argo b. 1879 in Iowa.
Probably other children.

113. FRANK COLE[5] (JOHN[4], MARIA[3], ANNA[2], WM.[1])

Frank E. Cole (1862-1933) married Feb. 18, 1885 Samantha White (b. Mar. 7, 1863 and d. Dec. 31, 1920) and had issue:
151. Edith Cole m. F. B. Brian Atty-at-Law.

The Name

Argo is of Greek derivation and a very ancient surname meaning bright. The name is quite common in Scotland in the vicinity of Aberdeen and is believed to have been brought into the country with the arrival of invading Greeks on the ship "Argo" at an extremely early date.

Argo Lineage Notes

The Argo family was located in Sussex County, Delaware as early as 1746. The first ancestor was Alexander Argo who died there in 1777. His wife's maiden name was Sarah Tharpe. Their children were Joseph, David, George, Alexander, Jr., Alice and Robert.
The partentage of William Argo has not been definitely established but Joseph and Sarah (Say) Argo are probably his line.

1. WILLIAM PLUMLY

William Plumly was born in lower Bucks County, Pennsylvania on the 24th day of the tenth month of the year 1777, a birth-right member of the society of Friends. He married in Bucks County about 1805 Ann Stackhouse (b. 3.18.1789) a daughter of Thomas and Hannah (White) Stackhouse.

In the year of 1819 they came with their children in a covered wagon over the mountains of western Pennsylvania to Belmont County, Ohio where they settled in Somerset township near the little town of Somerton, where they spent the remainder of their lives.

William Plumly died Mar. 30, 1862 and his will is or record in book I, p. 458 of Belmont probate records:

"I, William Plumly of Belmont County in the State of Ohio, in perfect health of body and of sound and deserning mind, memory and understanding,

considering the certainty of death and the uncertainty of the time thereof and being desirous to settle my worldly affairs, do therefore make and publish this my last Will and testament hereby revoking all former wills by me made in manner and form following that is to say:

First, It is my Will that after my death all my just debts and funeral charges shall be paid.

Second, I give, devise and bequeath unto my beloved wife Ann Plumly all the rest, residue and remainder of my estate real and personal during her natural life should she remain a widow, if she should not remain my widow I give, devise and bequeath it to her during widowhood, it having been chiefly acquired by the joint interest of my dear wife

and myself and further I desire and will that no appraisement of my real or person property be taken at my death.

Third, At the death or should she marry at the termination of her widowhood I devise and bequeath all the real and personal Estate to my daughter Ann S. Plumly and my grandson Marius R. Plumly to be equally divided between them share and share alike and that I also will that neither sell without the consent of the other. I desire it must be mutual to have and to hold the same to them, their heirs and assigns forever. The reason I do not hereby provide for my other children is that I consider them already provided for equally with my daughter and grandson above as named.

And lastly, I do hereby constitute and appoint my said daughter Ann S. Plumly and Marius R. Plumly my grandson to be the Executrix and Executor of this my last Will and Testament, revoking and annulling all others and confirming this and no other to be my last Will and Testament and it being so it is my will and desire that they the within named Executor and Executrix avoid all appeal to Court or law and that no security be required of them in settlement of the estate but execute this Will avoiding all such expenses. They having the same within their power as heirs and Executrix and Executor of my estate.

In testimony whereof I William Plumly have hereunto set my hand and seal this third day of the twelfth month in the year of Our Lord one thousand eight hundred and fifty nine.

William Plumly

Witnesses
Solomon Hogue
John Mead
William Stanton

Filed for probate Aug. 27, 1862. The children of William and Ann (Stackhouse) Plumly were:

2. Jonathan Stackhouse Plumly b. Oct. 29, 1806.
3. Joseph W. Plumly b. 1809 in Penn.
4. Osborne Plumly b. ca 1811 in Penn.
5. A son of whom nothing is known.
6. Thomas Plumly b. 1816 in Penn.
7. Aaron Plumly b. 1818 in Penn.
8. Evan Griffith Plumly b. Nov. 29, 1820 in Belmont Co. Ohio.
9. Mary Plumly b. 1822 in Belmont County.
10. Hannah Plumly b. 1828 in Belmont County.
11. Ann S. Plumly b. 1830 in Belmont County.
   Three children died in infancy, (two of measles).

2. JONATHAN S. PLUMLY[2] (WILLIAM[1])

Jonathan Stackhouse Plumly (1806-1892) farmer of Belmont and later of Washington County, Ohio, married Oct. 12, 1828 Rebecca Nickolson (b. Oct. 10, 1808 in Belmont County and died Aug. 26, 1890) Their children were:
12. Jacob Nickolson Plumly b. Nov. 29, 1829.
13. William D. Plumly b. 1832 in Ohio.
14. Mary Ann Plumly (1833-1909) m. Aug. 29, 1875 Adam Matheny. no issue.
15. Clarkson Plumly (1835-1859) m. Nov. 20, 1858 Sarah Stanton. no issue.
16. Peaslee Plumly (1838-1857)
17. John Plumly (1840-1940) m. 21 Mar. 1878 Imogene Cliton, no issue.
18. Jane Plumly (1842-1940) unm.
19. Job Osborn Plumly b. May 22, 1844.
20. Hannah Elizabeth Plumly b. July 5, 1849.

3. JOSEPH PLUMLY[2] (WILLIAM[1])

Joseph W. Plumly (b. 1809) married Jan. 1, 1833 Charlotte Stanton (b. 1811 in Belmont County, Ohio) a daughter of Borden and Charlotte Stanton.
   They removed to Washington County, Ohio and later to Williamstown, W. Va. Their children were:
21. Borden Stanton Plumly b. 1834 in Belmont County.
22. Edward Plumly b. 1835 in Belmont County.
23. Aaron Plumly b. 1836 in Belmont County.
24. Henry Wright Plumly b. 1840 in Washington, County.

4. OSBORN PLUMLY[2] (WILLIAM[1])

Osborn Plumly (1811-1839) married ca 1837 Hannah _____ and removed from Belmont to Morgan County (Marion township) Ohio. They had a son:
25. Marius Plumly b. 1838, m. Sarah _____ and had issue.

6. THOMAS PLUMLY[2] (WILLIAM[1])

Thomas Plumly (1816-1890) married May 26, 1840 Elizabeth Way (b. 1817 in Ohio, d. ca 1852) and resided in Athens County, Ohio where he purchased a farm in 1844. Their children were:
26. Mary Jane Plumly b. 1842, m. Mr. Morris of Wolf Creek, Ohio.
27. George B. Plumly b. 1845.
28. Hannah Ann Plumly b. 1847, m. Jas. M. Graham of Bartlett, Ohio.
29. William Henry Plumly b. 1849.
   Thomas Plumly married second Nov. 28, 1856 Iva Basin (d. before 1860) and had issue:
30. Lucy Plumly b. ca 1857, unm.
   Thomas Plumly married third Dec. 2, 1862 Mrs. Catherine Coll and had issue:
31. Flora M. Plumly b. ca 1864, m. Mr. McNich of Gridley, Kan.
   Thomas Plumly married fourth Aug. 4, 1887 Aurilla M. Steenrod who survived him at his death which occurred Mar. 22, 1890 in Perry County, Ohio. There was no issue by the fourth wife.

7. AARON PLUMLY[2] (WILLIAM[1])

Dr. Aaron Plumly (1818-1894) read medicine with Dr. Schooley of Mt. Pleasant, Ohio

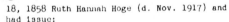

and later graduated from Starling Medical College with highest honors in 1853. He practiced medicine in Cumberland, Ohio and was the first mayor of that town. Later he practiced in Bristol, Malta and Barnesville, Ohio.

Dr. Plumly was public-spirited, serving many years on the schoolboard and for thirty-five years as president of the official board of the first M.E. Church at Barnesville.

He was a man of strong principles and especially active in the cause of temperance. He refused to write prescriptions for liquor and was known by his contemporaries as a Christian gentleman.

Dr. Plumly married first Sept. 25, 1845 Rebecca Trilby in Washington County, Ohio. She died early without issue and he married second Elizabeth Jane Devett on Aug. 6, 1853 in Morgan County, Ohio.

To this union was born two children:
32. James William Plumly 1856-1887.
33. Ella Plumly b. 2 May 1858. d. 18 Oct. 1921.

Dr. Plumly married third Elizabeth Virginia Cox (b. July 13, 1838 and d. Mar. 24, 1912) a daughter of Peter Pressley Cox and Ann Maria Leland his wife. Their children were:
34. Anna Leland Plumly b. Mar. 24, 186-
35. Roberta Plumly d. in inf.
36. Clarence Plumly d. in inf.
37. Park Pressley Plumly b. May 24, 1868, d. 1891.
38. Edward Cox Plumly b. Sept. 6, 1870.
39. Grace Augusta Plumly b. Dec. 20, 1872.
40. Dwight Arthur Plumly b. June 25, 1875.

Dr. Plumly died at Barnesville, Ohio. Jan. 23, 1894.

8. EVAN G. PLUMLY[2] (WILLIAM[1])

Evan Griffith Plumly (1820-1902) farmer of near Barnesville, Ohio, married Oct. 27, 1847 Abigail Bailey (b. 1824 in Ohio) She died without issue. He married second Mar.

18, 1858 Ruth Hannah Hoge (d. Nov. 1917) and had issue:
41. Elizabeth Plumly b. July 2, 1861.
42. Clyde Hoge Plumly b. Dec. 5, 1870.

9. MARY PLUMLY[2] (WILLIAM[1])

Mary Plumly (b. 1822) married Dec. 1, 1846 Thomas Whitacre (b. 1811 in Ohio) a son of Thomas Whitacre who came from Loudoun County, Virginia to Ohio prior to 1811. The latter was born 1777 in Virginia. They resided near Barnesville and had two daughters:
43. Maria Whitacre (b. 1852) m. Wm. McKinley.
44. Florence Whitacre m. Grant Keyser.

11. ANN S. PLUMLY[2] (WILLIAM[1])

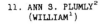

Ann S. Plumly (b. 1830) married Nov. 5, 1868 Charles Thornton Whitacre (a cousin of Thos. Jr. who married her sister Mary) and resided near Barnesville, They had two children:
45. Amos William Whitacre, no issue.
46. Howard Anderson Whitacre, had one son who resides in N. Y.

12. JACOB N. PLUMLY[3] (JONATHAN[2], WM.[1])

Jacob Nicholson Plumly (1829-1898) farmer and Millwright of Washington County, Ohio, married Nov. 10, 1853 Emily Shotwell (1835-1855/6) a daughter of Isaac and Hope (Stanton) Shotwell.

Jacob N. Plumly married second May 17, 1857 Susan Jane Shotwell (1839-1921) a sister of his first wife. Their children were:
47. Fremont Plumly 1858-1870.
48. Emily Shotwell Plumly b. June 30, 1860.
49. Martha Ellen Plumly b. July 31, 1863.
50. Clarkson W. Plumly b. Apr. 13, 1866.
51. Elmer Ezra Plumly b. Dec. 31, 1871.
52. Hope Ruth Plumly b. Nov. 9, 1873.
53. Cora Lenore Plumly b. Oct. 13, 1875.
54. Guy Elias Plumly b. Dec. 15, 1822.

19. J. OSBORN PLUMLY[3] (JONATHAN[2], WM.[1])

Job Osborn Plumly (1844-1922) married Aug. 23, 1870 Melinda Basom and had issue:
55. Ora Plumly
56. Sarah Jane Plumly b. Aug. 13, 1875, m. 1899 Edwin H. Stout.
57. Otis Plumly m. 23 Mar. 1898 Orinda Root.
Osborn Plumly died Mar. 19, 1922.

20. HANNAH E. PLUMLY[3] (JONATHAN[2], WM.[1])

Hannah Elizabeth Plumly (1849-1931) married in Nov. of 1875 Frank Nicholson and had two children:
58. Mary Nicholson.
59. Laura Nicholson.

21. BORDEN S. PLUMLY[3] (JOSEPH[2], WM.[1])

Borden Stanton Plumly (1834-1896) railroad agent, married Nov. 10, 1857 Lucy Fuller (b. 1836 in Ohio) at Marietta, Ohio. She died prior to 1870 survived by a son:
60. George Wright Plumly b. 1860.
Borden S. Plumly married May 9, 1871 Jane F. Miller in Washington County, Ohio, and had issue:
61. Lottie Plumly 1872-1892.
62. Roberta Ruth Plumly b. June 2, 1874.
63. Charles Plumly b. Sept. 15, 1876.
Borden S. Plumly married Oct. 5, 1881 Margaret Harper who survived him at his death May 20, 1896 at Stewart, Ohio.

23. AARON PLUMLY[3] (JOSEPH[2], WM.[1])

Aaron Plumly (b. 1836) married in Washington County, Ohio Feb. 19, 1857 Phebe Moore of Belpre township. They removed to Muscatan, Iowa.

24. HENRY W. PLUMLY[3] (JOSEPH[2], WM.[1])

Henry Wright Plumly (1840-1904) married Oct. 26, 1863 Ellen F. Waterman (b. 1843) a daughter of Dr. Waterman of Coolville, Ohio. They had a son:
64. William S. Plumly.

27. GEORGE B. PLUMLY[3] (THOS[2]., WM[1].)

George B. Plumly (b. 1845) married Rhoda A. Cowell and resided at Dunbar, Ohio. They had at least one child:
65. Charles Plumly b. Jan. 21, 1879, m. Nov. 28, 1903 Ella M. Root a daughter of Isaac Root.

29. WILLIAM H. PLUMLY[3] (THOS[2]., WM.[1])

William Henry Plumly (b. 1849) married Sept. 9, 1875 Mary S. Bennett and resided at Roxbury, Ohio. They had at least one son:
66. Henry Leonard Plumly b. Jan. 13, 1881, m. Aug. 31, 1904 Florence Spears a daughter of Charles and Sadie (Lynn) Spears.

34. ANNA L. PLUMLY[3] (AARON[2], WM.[1])

Anna Leland Plumly (b. ca 1864) married Joseph G. Norrall and had issue:
67. William Leland Norrall b. 3 Oct. 1896.
68. I. Edward Norrall b. 5 Feb. 1902.

38. EDWARD C. PLUMLY[3] (AARON[2], Wm.[1])

Edward Cox Plumly (b. 1870) married ca 1914 Helen G. Shirley of Chicago, Ill.

39. GRACE A. PLUMLY[3] (AARON[2], WM.[1])

Grace Augusta Plumly (b. 1872) married May 23, 1900 Ross Barton Eaton and had issue:
69. Elizabeth Virginia Eaton b. 10 Apr. 1902.
70. Joseph Ross Eaton b. 22 Feb. 1904.
71. John Plumly Eaton b. 19 June 1906.
72. Ruth Eaton b. 20 Apr. 1908.
73. Grace Lee Eaton b. 6 May 1910.

40. DWIGHT A. PLUMLY[3] (AARON[2], WM[1].)

Dwight Arthur Plumly (1875-1941) married Katherine _____ and resided in Berkeley,

Calif. They had issue:
74. Elizabeth Plumley.
75. Beatrice Plumly.
76. Carol Plumly.

41. ELIZABETH PLUMLY[3] (EVAN[2], WM.[1])

Elizabeth Plumly (b. 1861) married Edwin J. Doudna and resided in Kentucky. They had one daughter:
77. Clara Thalia Doudna.

42. CLYDE H. PLUMLY[3] (EVAN[2], WM.[1])

Clyde Hoge Plumly (b. 1870) married and resides in Belmont County, Ohio. He had five sons:
78. Park W. Plumly
79. Mansel Plumly
80. Cecil Evan Plumly
81. Harold Plumly
82. Willard Plumly

48. EMILY S. PLUMLY[4] (JACOB[3], JONA[2], WM.[1])

Emily Shotwell Plumly (b. 1860) married Thomas McPherson of Little Hocking, Ohio and had issue:
83. William McPherson
84. Edwin McPherson
85. Ellen McPherson

49. MARTHA E. PLUMLY[4] (JACOB[3], JONA[2], WM.[1])

Martha Ellen Plumly (1863-1907) married Apr. 4, 1889 Sandy A. Cassidy of near Belpre, Ohio and had issue:
86. Ray Cassidy.
87. Clyde Cassidy.
88. Cora Cassidy.
89. Gladys Cassidy.
90. Ernest Cassidy.
91. Bernice Cassidy.
92. Forest Cassidy.

50. CLARKSON PLUMLY[4] (JACOB[3], JONA[2]., WM.[1])

Clarkson William Plumly (b. 1866) married Sept. 12, 1888 Metta R. Chick (d. 1921) and had one son:

93. Leon Jacob Plumly of Ft. Worth, Texas.

51. ELMER E. PLUMLY[4] (JACOB[3], JONA[2], WM.[1])

Elmer Ezra Plumly (1871-1936) married June 24, 1897 Blanche Laura Curtis a daughter of Henry Curtis of Little Hocking, Ohio., and had issue:
94. Henry Curtis Plumly.
95. Donald Elmer Plumly d. y.
96. Edward Cedric Plumly d. 1937.

52. HOPE R. PLUMLY[4] (JACOB[3], JONA[2], WM.[1])

Hope Ruth Plumly (b. 1873) married Nov. 9, 1891 John Samuel Walden (1864-19 (See #85 in Argo lineage) and had issue:
97. Lawrence M. Walden m. Rilla Green
98. Kenneth P. Walden d. y.
99. Annie L. Walden R. N.
100. Raymond G. Walden m. Marian Meredith
101. Mabel Walden m. Orville Brandelberry.
105. John S. Walden m. Doris Bingman
106. Dora Walden m. Carl Lockhart.

53. CORA L. PLUMLY[4] (JACOB[3], JONA[2], WM.[1])

Cora Lenore Plumly (b. 1875) married Aug. 14, 1902 C. Stuart Simpson (b. Dec. 19, 1874) son of Robert D. and Betsey (Botkin) Simpson and had issue:
107. Carl William Simpson b. 6 May 1905.
108. Susan Simpson b. 27 May 1907.
109. Robert Jacob Simpson b. 19 Dec. 1908.
110. Lou Simpson b. 22 Nov. 1910.
111. George Arthur Simpson b. 19 May 1912.

54. GUY E. PLUMLY[4] (JACOB[3], JONA[2], WM.[1])

Guy Elias Plumly (b. 1882) married Dec. 7, 1904 Laura McGirr a daughter of Franklin and Mary J. (Bean) McGirr of Little Hicking, Ohio and had issue:

112. Kenneth Franklin Plumly d. in inf.
113. Laura Margaret Plumly b. 5 July 1918

60. GEORGE W. PLUMLY[4] (BORDEN[3], JOSEPH[2], WM.[1])

George Wright Plumly (b. 1860) married Mary Graham and resided in Chillicothe, Ohio. They had at least one son:
114. C. A. Plumly b. Mar. 8, 1882 at Stewart, Ohio.

64. WILLIAM S. PLUMLY[4] (HENRY[3], JOSEPH[2], WM.[1])

William S. Plumly married Iona Johnson and had issue:
115. Ellen Florence Plumly m. Mr. Augustson.
116. Jean Plumly.

67. W. LELAND NORRALL[4] (ANNA[3], AARON[2], WM.[1])

William Leland Norrall (b. 1896) married Jane_____ and had:

117. John L. Norrall b. 19 Nov. 1926.
118. Donald G. Norrall b. 4 Nov. 1930.
119. Marianne Jane Norrall b. 15 Nov. 1932.

69. E. VIRGINIA EATON[4] (GRACE[3], AARON[2], WM.[1])

Elizabeth Virginia Eaton (b. 1902) married Oct. 18, 1924 A. Lloyd Billingsley and had issue:
120. William Ross Billingsley b. 21 Feb. 1930.
121. Lloyd Eaton Billingsley b. 27 Nov. 1934
122. James Robert Billingsley b. 23 July 1936.

70. JOSEPH R. EATON[4] (GRACE[3], AARON[2], WM.[1])

Joseph Ross Eaton (b. 1904) married in Mar. of 1925 Mary Elizabeth Magee and had:
123. Joseph Magee Eaton b. 8 Jan. 1926.
124. Mary Elizabeth Eaton b. 27 Oct. 1927

73. GRACE L. EATON[4] (GRACE[3], AARON[2], WM.[1])

Grace Lee Eaton (b. 1910) married Nov. 19, 1930 Thomas Earl Seager and had:
125. Thomas Earl Seager b. 22 Sept. 1931.
126. Beatrice Grace Seager b. 27 June 1935.
127. Ruth Ann Seager
128. James Lee Seager b. 29 Mar. 1938.

77. CLARA T. DOUDNA[4] (ELIZABETH[3], EVAN[2], WM.[1])

Clara Thalia Doudna married James Wilson and had one daughter:
129. Elizabeth Wilson m. Nov. 21, 1939 Lt. Wiley Dixon a graduate of Annapolis, stationed in the Phillipine Islands. They have a daughter: Margaret P. Dixon.

94. HENRY C. PLUMLY[5] ELMER[4], JACOB[3], JONA[2], *WM.[1])

Henry Curtis Plumly married Jane Jackson and resides in Texas. They have two sons:
130. Curtis Plumly, Jr.
131. Jackson Plumly.

96. EDWARD C. PLUMLY[5] (ELMER[4], JACOB[3] JONA[2]., WM.[1])

Edward Cedric Plumly married Helen Hebert and had one son:
132. Edward Plumly, Jr. b. 1937.

107. CARL W. SIMPSON[5] (CORA[4], JACOB[3], JONA[2], WILLIAM[1])

Carl Wm. Simpson (b. 1905) married June 17, 1934 Lois M. Hill of Sioux Falls, S. D. and had issue:
132. Rollin William Simpson b. 28 Sept. 1938.
133. Barbara Sue Simpson b. 21 Jan. 1941.

108. SUSAN SIMPSON[5] (CORA[4], JACOB[3], JONA[2]., WM.[1])

Susan Simpson (b. 1907) married Sept. 12, 1929 Clifford Roberts at Sioux Falls, S. D., and had these children:
134. Richard Stuart Roberts b. 18 Aug. 1930.
135. Lou Ella Roberts b. 16 Mar. 1932.

136. Edwin Arthur Roberts b. 30 Jan. 1934.
137. Eugene Clifford Roberts b. 2 May 1935.
138. James William Roberts b. 13 June 1936.
139. Lenore E. Roberts b. 14 Sept. 1938.
140. Lawrence Elmer Roberts b. 27 Sept. 1941.

109. ROBERT J. SIMPSON[5] (CORA[4], JACOB[3], JONA[2], WM.[1])

Robert Jacob Simpson (b. 1908) married July 13, 1929 Lillian M. Borgandale and had issue:
141. Robert Jacob Simpson b. 8 Feb. 1930.
142. Cora Ann Simpson b. 9 July 1931.
143. Charles Stuart Simpson b. 14 Nov. 1932.
144. Helen Marie Simpson b. 7 Aug. 1934.
145. William Arden Simpson b. 14 Aug. 1935.

110. LOU SIMPSON[5] (CORA[4], JACOB[3], JONA[2]., WM.[1])

Lou Simpson married Sept. 12, 1934 Clyde Gardner. She died May 23, 1937. Their children were:
146. Ellen Lou Gardner b. 24 June 1935.
147. Dorothy Ann Gardner b. 19 May 1937.

113. MARGARET PLUMLY[5] (GUY[4], JACOB[3], JONA[2], WM.[1])

Laura Margaret Plumly (b. 1918) married Dec. 7, 1938 John Earl Halbirt a son of Earl and Bernice (Dorr) Halbirt of Athens County, Ohio, Margaret Plumly Halbirt is a graduate of Ohio University and member of Chi Omega fraternity. They have a daughter:
148. Donna Margaret Halbirt b. 13 Dec. 1939 at Beaumont, Texas.

The Name

Plumly is a local place name, receiving impetus as a surname from a township in the parish of Great Budworth in the county of Chester in England. The early use of the name seems to have originated as Henry Plomlegh (or Plomley) meaning: Henry who lives the meadow where the plum trees grow or Henry of the plum-tree meadows.

Plumly-Lineage Notes

The immigrant ancestor was Charles Plumly from Somersetshire in England to Bucks County, Pa. He married in England 12.11. 1665 Margery Page. They had five sons all of whom were born in England as follows:
1. William Plumly b. 10.7.1666, m. Elizabeth Thompson.
2. James Plumly b. 6.22.1668, m. Mary Budd.
3. Charles Plumly b. 12.9.1674, d. 1708 in Rose Budd.
4. John Plumly b. 7.8.1677, d. 1732, m. 1708 Mary Bainbridge, dau. of John and Sarah.
5. George Plumly 1680-1754, m. Sarah _____, no issue.
    Charles and Margery (Page) Plumly came from England in 1682 and settled at Middletown in lower Bucks County. He died in 1683 and the following year she married Henry Paxon.

Stackhouse Lineage Notes

1. Thomas Stackhouse 2nd. m. 1.1.1711 Mrs. Ann (?) From Yorkshire in Eng. to Mayos of Falls M. M. Middletown, Bucks Co. Pa. 1682. Colonial Assembly 1711-1715, d. 4.26.1744.

2. Isaac Stackhouse m. 10.29.1743 Mary Harding b. 7.5.1720 at Middletown. b. 6.17.1720 d. 1.17.1791 d. 3.4.1782. daughter of Thomas Harding, Jr. and Mary Comley eldest daughter of Henry Comley and Agnes (Heaton) Comly

3. Thomas Stackhouse m. 5.8.1771 Hannah White b. 7.29.1744

4. Ann Stackhouse m. William Plumly b. 3.18.1789 See Text.

References

Bucks County History
Bucks County Court Records
Belmont County Court Records
Washington County Court Records
Athens County Court Records
U. S. Census Records
Family Records